GNU Emacs

D0931949

Hewlett-Packard Press Series

GNU Emacs:

UNIX® Text Editing and Programming

Michael A. Schoonover
John S. Bowie
William R. Arnold

♠ Addison-Wesley Publishing Company, Inc.

Reading, Massachusetts   Menlo Park, California   New York
Don Mills, Ontario   Wokingham, England   Amsterdam   Bonn
Paris   Milan   Madrid   Sydney   Singapore   Tokyo   Seoul
Taipei   Mexico City   San Juan

Many of the designations used by manufacturers and sellers to distinguish their products are claimed as trademarks. Where those designations appear in this book and Addison-Wesley was aware of a trademark claim, the designations have been printed in initial capital letters.

The programs and applications presented in this book have been included for their instructional value. They have been tested with care, but are not guaranteed for any particular purpose. The publisher does not offer any warrantees or representations, nor does it accept any liabilities with respect to the programs or applications.

The publisher offers discounts on this book when ordered in quanity for special sales. For more information please contact:

Corporate & Professional Publishing Group
Addison-Wesley Publishing Company
One Jacob Way
Reading, Massachusetts 01867

Library of Congress Cataloging-in-Publication Data

Schoonover, Michael A.
GNU Emacs : Unix text editing and programming / Michael A.
Schoonover, John S. Bowie, William R. Arnold.
p.   cm.
Includes bibliographical references and index.
ISBN 0-201-56345-2 (pbk. : alk. paper)
1. Text editors (Computer programs) 2. GNU Emacs. 3. UNIX
(Computer file) I. Bowie, John., 1955– . II. Arnold, WIlliam R.
(William Robert), 1933–   . III. Title.
QA76.76.T49S36   1992   91-22336
652.5' 51--dc20   CIP

Copyright © 1992 by Addison-Wesley Publishing Company, Inc.

All rights reserved. No part of this publication may be reproduced, stored in a retrieval system, or transmitted, in any form or by any means, electronic, mechanical, photocopying, recording, or otherwise, without the prior written permission of the publisher. Printed in the United States of America. Published simultaneously in Canada.

ISBN: 0-201-56345-2

1 2 3 4 5 6 7 8 9 10   MW   9594939291
First printing, November 1991

For Jeanne, Judy, and Janie

Contents

Preface

GNU Emacs is a powerful, integrated computing environment for UNIX™ that lets you perform a wide range of editing, programming, and file management tasks. If you have never used Emacs, this book will gently but rapidly introduce you to its most serviceable features. If you are a casual Emacs user, we will attempt to show you ways to edit and manage your files more efficiently. And for experienced users, we have included advanced techniques and reference information to help you unlock the power and flexibility of the environment. Always our emphasis is on practical information, on the commands and features we have found in our own experience to be the most useful and powerful.

What Is GNU Emacs?

The name, Emacs, is an acronym derived from "Editor MACroS." A **macro** is a command that reduces a multi-step process to just a few keystrokes. Emacs uses the Control key and other keys to define a set of one, two, or three keystroke macros (commands) that execute all of its functions. The original set of macros from which Emacs evolved was developed by Richard Stallman and Guy Steele at MIT. Stallman later went on to form the Free Software Foundation, an organization that develops and distributes Emacs and other free software products.

"GNU"—pronounced "G-Nu"—is a self-referencing acronym derived from the phrase, "GNU's Not UNIX." GNU is the Free Software Foundation's name for a complete set of UNIX-compatible programs, of which Emacs is a part. When completed, GNU will replace many of the standard components of the UNIX operating system.

While many UNIX users regard GNU Emacs as an excellent alternative to the **vi** editor, true Emacs aficionados understand that Emacs is not merely an editor, but a complete *environment* for performing many common computing tasks. Some of the tasks you can perform in the Emacs environment include:

- **Text editing.** Emacs provides unrivaled text-editing power. You can edit multiple documents simultaneously, use specialized editing modes designed specifically for your editing task, create your own powerful keyboard macros, and spell-check your document, to name just a few capabilities.

- **Software development.** Emacs provides several programming language modes, including C, FORTRAN, and Lisp (Pascal mode, while not included with GNU Emacs, is available from other sources; see Appendix A). Emacs provides a complete environment for editing, formatting, and compiling source code.

- **File management.** Emacs provides facilities for manipulating files and directories on your UNIX system.

- **Outlining.** Emacs lets you create and edit outlines, using Emacs' special outline mode.

- **Electronic mail processing.** The Emacs mail handler lets you compose, send, and receive electronic mail (e-mail) messages.

- **Environment customization.** Emacs itself is open to customization and extension to suit your individual preferences and needs. You can replace one command key-sequence with another, and develop and integrate your own commands.

About This Book

This book is designed to be a practical companion to Emacs, with examples, tutorials, reference information, and advice for new and experienced users alike. Some of its key features include:

- **Graduated instructions.** New users will quickly learn the basics by working through the "Quick Tour" in Chapter 1, which introduces the key Emacs features and commands. Subsequent chapters build upon this foundation by introducing more efficient and advanced editing techniques.

- **Extensive tutorials and examples.** Every important feature is thoroughly explained, then demonstrated with an example or short tutorial that you can try on your own Emacs system.

- **Comprehensive Emacs reference.** Advanced users will appreciate the command and function reference in Appendix D, as well as the summary of commands and concepts provided at the end of each chapter.

- **vi-to-Emacs migration guide.** For **vi** users who want to move to Emacs, Appendix C lists Emacs equivalents for most **vi** editor commands.

- **Language-specific programming chapters.** Individual chapters are provided for programming with C, FORTRAN, Lisp, and Pascal, including advanced instructions for customizing indentation and commenting styles.

- **Customization instructions.** Advanced Emacs users will find helpful advice for customizing and extending Emacs, with a supporting introduction to Emacs-Lisp in Appendix B.

Because Emacs is such an extensive and versatile system, you should read this book selectively, focusing on the material that relates to your immediate needs.

Part 1, "Text Editing in Emacs," helps you build the basic skills you will need regardless of how you intend to use Emacs. It also describes more efficient and advanced editing techniques for those who need them. This part of the book, along with the reference information in Appendix D, may be all you need to read if you are interested solely in proficient text editing.

Chapters in this section include:

- **Chapter 1: A Quick Tour of Emacs.** This chapter briefly surveys all aspects of the Emacs environment. Here you will learn to use some common editing commands and be introduced to the online help facility, the electronic mail handler, and the file management facility.

- **Chapter 2: Basic Editing Commands.** This chapter teaches you how to load and save files, insert and delete text, move around your documents, cut and paste regions of text, and perform keyword searches. The features described here are prerequisites to using the more advanced capabilities described in the later chapters.

- **Chapter 3: More Efficient Editing.** This chapter describes more efficient ways to edit your documents, including performing operations multiple times, editing words, sentences, paragraphs and pages, using abbreviations and macros, and working with multiple windows.

- **Chapter 4: Advanced Editing.** This chapter describes advanced text-editing features, such as changing Emacs' default behavior, searching for regular expressions, and editing outlines, as well as advanced file, buffer, and window operations.

Part 2, "Programming in Emacs," describes how to use Emacs as a software development environment. Read Chapter 5 to get an overview of features that are common to all programming languages. Then read Chapter 6 (C), Chapter 7 (FORTRAN), Chapter 8 (Lisp), or Appendix A (Pascal) depending upon which programming language you are using. Chapters in this section include:

- **Chapter 5: Program Development in Emacs.** This chapter describes features that are common to all Emacs programming language modes, such as moving around your program, indenting and commenting programs, using tag tables to edit across multiple files, keeping track of source-code changes with ChangeLogs, and compiling programs.

- **Chapter 6: Editing in C Mode.** This chapter describes features that are particular to editing C programs, such as moving among and marking C functions, indenting and commenting C programs, working with sexps and lists, and customizing C indentation and commenting styles.

- **Chapter 7: Editing in FORTRAN Mode.** This chapter describes features that are particular to editing FORTRAN programs, such as moving among and marking subprograms, indenting and commenting FORTRAN programs, labeling lines, using keyword abbreviations, working with sexps and lists, and customizing FORTRAN indentation and commenting styles.

- **Chapter 8: Editing in Lisp Modes.** This chapter describes features that are particular to editing Lisp programs, such as moving among defuns, sexps, and lists, marking text, transposing sexps, killing sexps, indenting and commenting Lisp programs, evaluating Lisp code, and customizing Lisp indentation and commenting styles.

Part 3, "Additional Emacs Features," describes various supporting Emacs features such as the online help facility, electronic mail facility, file and buffer management facilities, and spelling checker. Scan these chapters for the features that interest you. Chapters in this section include:

- **Chapter 9: Getting Online Help.** This chapter describes how to get online help for Emacs commands, functions, and variables, and how to run the Emacs online tutorial.

- **Chapter 10: Using Emacs for Electronic Mail.** This chapter describes how to use the Emacs electronic mail facility, RMAIL, to read and send e-mail messages.

- **Chapter 11: Managing Files and Buffers.** This chapter describes how to use the Dired facility to manage your files, and the Buffer-Menu facility to manage your buffers.

- **Chapter 12: Miscellaneous Emacs Features.** This chapter summarizes the remaining features of Emacs, including the spelling checker, the auto-save feature, and the UNIX shell mode. Specialized modes for editing TeX, Troff and pictures are also discussed.

Part 4, "Customizing and Administering Emacs," describes how to customize, extend, install, configure, and maintain the Emacs environment. Chapters in this section include:

- **Chapter 13: Customizing the Emacs Environment.** This chapter describes several ways to customize Emacs to suit your needs and preferences. You will learn how to edit the `.emacs` start-up file, use variables to change Emacs's behavior, and change command key bindings.

- **Chapter 14: Administering Emacs.** This chapter provides UNIX system administrators with advice on installing and maintaining Emacs.

Finally, four appendices provide additional details on specialized Emacs topics:

- **Appendix A: Editing in Pascal Mode.** This appendix describes how to use a non-standard Pascal mode for editing Pascal programs in Emacs.

- **Appendix B: Emacs-Lisp Programming.** This appendix provides a brief introduction to Emacs-Lisp programming. It is intended for experienced Lisp programmers who want to write Emacs-Lisp functions to modify or extend the Emacs environment.

- **Appendix C: Switching from `vi` to Emacs.** This appendix helps `vi` users make the transition to Emacs by listing the Emacs equivalents for many common `vi` commands.

- **Appendix D: Emacs Command Reference.** This appendix provides a comprehensive quick reference to Emacs commands, functions, and variables.

A Word About Versions

This book describes the features of version 18.57 of industry-standard GNU Emacs as provided by the Free Software Foundation. You may be using a different version—or even a different implementation—of Emacs than ours.

During the past several years, programmers have modified, customized, extended, ported, and adapted Emacs until many implementations exist today (gnumacs, GNU Emacs, x11macs, gnuvo, and MicroEmacs, for example). Even if you are using version 18.57 of GNU Emacs, it's possible that someone has customized your Emacs to work differently than standard Emacs, has added specialized extensions, or has removed functionality that was deemed unnecessary. As a result, some of the commands we describe may be invoked by different key sequences on your system or may work differently. If your system behaves differently than this book describes, you should consult your UNIX system administrator about modifications made to your system.

Versions of Emacs have also been developed that run on the MS-DOS operating system on PCs (for example, MG, MicroEmacs, and Freemacs), and on other specialized hardware and operating systems. These implementations of Emacs are not discussed in this book, but most attempt to emulate many of the features and commands of GNU Emacs.

Don't be discouraged by these possible differences. If you have a recent version of Emacs, it will probably behave in much the same way as we describe. And the online help system, if kept up-to-date, may clarify any differences you discover.

Key Naming Conventions

Finally, before using Emacs, you should understand the key naming conventions used in this book and in the Emacs online help system. Some of these may be confusing if you have never used Emacs; if so, periodically refer back to this section as you gain experience working through the first few chapters.

Table 1.1 describes the default operation of commonly used Emacs keys.

Table Preface.1. Key Naming Conventions

Key	Name	Function
Return or Enter	**RET**	Inserts a newline character to move the cursor down a line and to the left margin. The Emacs command C-m does the same thing.
Rubout or Backspace	**DEL**	Moves back one space, removing the previous character. See note following this table.
Newline	**LFD**	Inserts a newline character. The physical key, if present, can have several labels. If your keyboard has no such key, or you cannot find the newline key, use C-j.
Escape	**ESC**	Can perform the function of the Meta. If your keyboard has no Escape key, C-[will work.
Control	**C-**	Used in combination with another key to generate control characters.
Meta	**M-**	Meta key; see "Meta Commands" in Chapter 1.
Space bar	**SPC**	Inserts a space character; also used in commands.
Tab	**TAB**	Inserts a Tab character. If your keyboard has no Tab key, or you cannot find the key that tabs, use C-i.

Note: The Backspace key, instead of backing over and erasing the previous character, may invoke the Emacs online help facility. If this is the case on your system see Chapter 1, "Finding Your Online Help and DEL Keys."

Acknowledgements

We would like to thank the many people who have contributed their time and talents to this project.

We are indebted to Alan Apt, our editor at Addison-Wesley, who had the foresight to recognize the need for such a book as this. And to our reviewers—Darryl Okahata, David Wolpert, Eddie Williamson, Jim Bigelow, Peter Salus, and Adil Lotia—we owe several of the book's features, and have them to thank for its accuracy and thoroughness. We would also like to thank the administrative and production staff at Addison-Wesley—Shirley McGuire and Peggy McMahon—for taking care of all the little and not so little details.

At Hewlett-Packard, we have Michael Kolesar, Marl Godfrey, and Bob Silvey to thank for including us in the first crop of Hewlett-Packard Press books.

Last and most, we appreciate the patience and support of our families over the course of this long and occasionally arduous project.

Part 1
Text Editing in Emacs

This part of the book describes Emacs' commands and features for editing text.

If you use Emacs only for creating and editing documents, this part of the book provides everything you need to edit proficiently. However, other sections—such as the command reference in Appendix D and the additional features discussed in Part 3—may also interest you.

If you use Emacs to write programs, you should become acquainted with the commands in Part 1 before moving on to the programming chapters in Part 2. In particular, many of the features and concepts introduced in Chapters 1 through 3 are prerequisites for using the programming modes.

The following chapters are included in Part 1:

- Chapter 1: A Quick Tour of Emacs

- Chapter 2: Basic Editing Commands

- Chapter 3: More Efficient Editing

- Chapter 4: Advanced Editing

1
A Quick Tour of Emacs

This chapter provides an overview of Emacs' principal capabilities and features. By spending a few minutes reading this chapter and trying our examples on your Emacs system, you will gain a good understanding of the range of tasks you can perform with Emacs. You can then refer to other chapters in this book for detailed instructions on using the features that interest you.

Specific topics introduced in this chapter are:

- Starting Emacs

- Exiting Emacs

- Understanding the Emacs screen

- Typing text

- Typing commands

- Using a basic set of editing commands

- Getting online help

- Using Emacs to process electronic mail

- Using Emacs to manage files

- Changing Emacs' behavior with variables

In subsequent chapters, we assume you have acquired the basic skills introduced here, so make sure you are familiar with topics discussed in this chapter before proceeding.

Starting Emacs

To start Emacs, type the **emacs** command from your UNIX prompt and press **RET**:

```
emacs
```

Once Emacs has started, you can use Emacs commands to load in the files you want to edit (see Table 1.7). To load files when starting Emacs, type the file names you want to load after the **emacs** command. For example, to start Emacs with the file **sample.txt**, run:

```
emacs sample.txt
```

You can also use a wildcard file specification. For example, to edit all files in the current directory whose names end with **.c**, run:

```
emacs *.c
```

Emacs also has command line options that control how Emacs starts. These are covered in detail in Chapter 4, "Advanced Editing."

What If Emacs Does Not Start?

If Emacs does not start, note any error messages that remain on the screen. If you have no idea what they mean, do not take any action that would remove the messages. Show the messages to the UNIX system administrator for your group.

Table 1.1 lists some possible circumstances that could prevent Emacs from starting. Beyond these common problems, ask your system administrator to help you set up your system to run Emacs. Refer to Chapter 14, "Administering Emacs," for additional information.

Table 1.1. Some Reasons Emacs May Not Start

Problem	Solution
You get a message like `emacs: not found` or `emacs: command not found`	On some systems, the command to start Emacs may go by a different name. For example, Emacs commonly goes by the names `xemacs`, and `x11macs`. Check with your system administrator to determine which version you should use. Another possible cause may be that your PATH environment variable does not include the directory where the Emacs program resides. If this is the case, you could start Emacs by typing the entire directory path. For example, if `emacs` is stored in `/usr/local/bin`, you could start Emacs like this: `/usr/local/bin/emacs` See "Where Does Emacs Reside?" in Chapter 14 if you need help locating the Emacs program. To avoid typing the path, edit your login initialization file (`.profile` for Bourne and Korn shell users, `.login` for C shell users) so that the PATH variable includes the path to the Emacs program file.

The screen is garbled	The TERM variable may be incorrectly set. Check with your system administrator for the correct setting, then execute:
	
	`TERM = value`
	`export TERM`
	`tset`

You get a message similar to `Can't open display`	You are not running X windows and the DISPLAY environment variable is set, or you do not have permission to open a window on the display.

Exiting Emacs

You can exit Emacs in either of the following ways:

- Temporarily suspend Emacs and return to your UNIX command prompt (shell).
- Permanently end your Emacs session.

Suspending Your Emacs Session

If using the C or Korn shell, you can temporarily suspend your Emacs session, return to your UNIX command prompt (shell) and execute UNIX commands, then resume your Emacs session:

1. Type **C-z**. Emacs is suspended and your UNIX prompt returns.

2. To resume your Emacs session:

   - If using the C shell, type: **%emacs**
   - If using the Korn shell, type: **fg %emacs**

If you started Emacs with a command other than **emacs**, substitute that command in place of **emacs** in these commands.

Suspending Emacs may not work with shells other than the C shell and Korn shell, or on versions of UNIX that do not support job control. On such systems, try typing **exit RET** to return to Emacs. To use Emacs most effectively, we recommend that you use the Korn shell.

Ending Your Emacs Session

Emacs provides two ways to exit: one that prompts you to save your work and one that doesn't. To save your work and end your Emacs session:

1. Type: **C-x C-c**

2. Before exiting, Emacs asks whether you want to save each buffer that has been modified. Type **y** to save the buffer or **n** to discard your changes. If you answer **n**, Emacs will ask once again whether you really want to exit and abandon your modified buffers. Answer **yes** to exit, or **no** to remain in Emacs.

Because Emacs considers the ***scratch*** buffer to be a temporary scratch pad, Emacs will not ask whether you want to save it before exiting, and its contents will be discarded. If ***scratch*** contains text you want to save, run the **C-x C-w** command, which lets you rename the buffer and then writes its contents to a file.

To end your Emacs session without saving your work:

Type: **C-u C-x C-c**

Emacs exits immediately; it does not prompt you to save your modified buffers.

Understanding the Emacs Screen

The Emacs screen should appear a few moments after you run the **emacs** command. You will probably see some initialization messages, and you may see an error message or two. The system may start up and work well despite getting a few error messages during the initialization process. If you run Emacs from an X11 window, you can resize, move, iconify, and otherwise manipulate the window according to features provided by the X11 windowing subsystem.

Figure 1.1 shows a typical Emacs screen. It consists of the following functional areas:

- the **workspace,** in which you compose and edit text

- the **cursor,** which points to the current position in the workspace

- the **mode line,** which provides a variety of status information

- the **echo area,** which displays messages and prompts

- **softkey labels** (not shown), a nonstandard feature which may appear on your system

These parts of the Emacs screen are described in more detail in the following sections. Your screen may differ somewhat, but should include these same basic components.

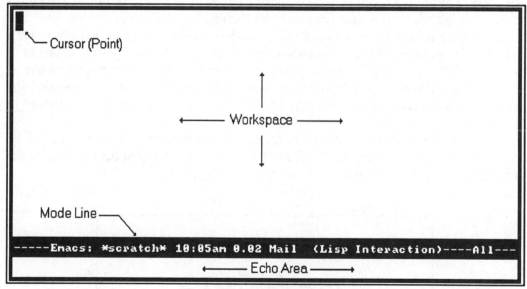

Figure 1.1. The Emacs Screen

The Workspace

To understand the workspace, you must first know a little bit about buffers. In Emacs, all editing takes place in buffers. A **buffer** is a temporary holding place for a file's text. When you edit a file, you actually edit a buffer, which you can then save back to the file. The **workspace** is a viewport into a buffer; you can see all or part of a buffer's contents through the workspace. Any text you type into a buffer appears in the workspace.

The workspace's width and height can vary from system to system. But a typical workspace is anywhere from 80 to 100 characters wide and 20 to 40 lines long.

When you first start Emacs, the workspace may contain copyright information. This information will clear when you type text or run any Emacs command.

Emacs lets you split the workspace into multiple **windows,** each corresponding to a different buffer that you are editing. You can even have two windows into the same buffer; for example, you could edit the top part of a buffer in one window and the bottom part of the buffer in another window. We will show you how to do this in Chapter 3.

The Cursor (Point)

The **cursor** shows where typed characters will appear in the workspace. There is only one cursor on the Emacs screen at any one time. You can move the cursor among windows. The window containing the cursor is called the **selected window;** the buffer in the selected window is called the **current buffer.**

In Emacs terminology, you may hear the term **point** used synonymously with cursor. For example, Emacs has commands to move point and get the location of point. Usually, you can consider point and cursor to be interchangeable terms. However, point is not precisely the same thing as the cursor. Point is the location for inserting characters into the buffer, and the cursor is the visible indicator of point in the buffer.

Point lies immediately to the left of the cursor and immediately to the right of the character preceding the cursor. You can think of point as lying at the left edge of the cursor, between the two characters, as shown in Figure 1.2.

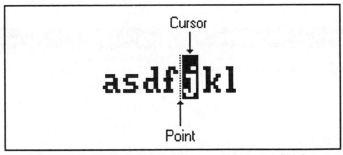

Figure 1.2. Relationship Between Cursor and Point

The Mode Line

The **mode line** provides information about a buffer, including the buffer's name, whether it has been modified, and the cursor's line position relative to the total number of lines in the buffer. In addition, the mode line can display system information such as date and time, system loading, and mail status. Figure 1.3 shows a typical mode line.

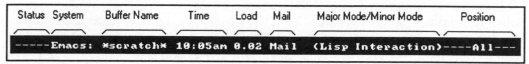

Figure 1.3. The Mode Line

Understanding what the mode line tells you can be invaluable to using Emacs effectively. Following are descriptions of each of the parts labeled in Figure 1.3.

Status The status field provides information about the current buffer. It can have the values shown in Table 1.2.

Table 1.2. Status Field Values

Value	Meaning
-----	Indicates the buffer contents have not changed since the last save.
--**-	Indicates the buffer contents have been changed since the last save.
--%%-	Indicates a read-only buffer.

System This field indicates which system is being used. Under most conditions, the system is **Emacs:**. However, Emacs includes some built-in subsystems that might change this. For example, the Emacs electronic mail handler, RMAIL, may set this field to **Emacs:RMAIL**.

Buffer Name Each buffer has a buffer name. When you load a file into a buffer for editing, Emacs usually gives the buffer the same name as the file. For example, if you edit the file **~/memos/report10**, Emacs would name the buffer **report10** (the ~ symbol represents your home directory). Some editing commands require you to specify a buffer name on which to operate.

Some Emacs commands create buffers for purposes other than editing text. Online help commands, for example, create buffers for the purpose of displaying help information. The names of such buffers are enclosed in asterisks to differentiate them from text-editing buffers. Online help buffers, for instance, are named **Help**.

In the sample mode line in Figure 1.3, the selected window contains a buffer named **scratch**. This special buffer is created every time you start Emacs. If you invoke Emacs without specifying a file, this is the buffer name you would see in the mode line. As the name implies, this buffer is usually used as a scratch pad area; you wouldn't normally edit in this buffer. It is also specially suited to evaluating Emacs Lisp expressions (see Chapter 8, "Editing in Lisp Modes" for details).

Time and Load   Time and load information is displayed only if it has been enabled (as described in Chapter 4, "Advanced Editing"). The time is displayed in am/pm format. The load field (not available on all systems) indicates the average number of processes running on the system recently. The higher the number, the higher the system load. Some versions of Emacs may display an additional field indicating the ratio of disk activity to CPU activity for all users. On version 18.56, load information will probably not be displayed.

Mail   If you have electronic mail messages that you have not yet read, the word **Mail** is printed after the time and load information.

Major Mode   Each buffer has an associated major mode that defines the editing capabilities and commands that are available for the buffer. A major mode is tailored to perform a specific kind of editing. For example, the **scratch** buffer uses Lisp Interaction mode, which has specialized commands for evaluating Emacs-Lisp expressions (Emacs-Lisp is a dialect of the Lisp programming language). Table 1.3 summarizes some useful major modes available in Emacs.

Table 1.3. Major Modes

Major Mode	Description
Fundamental	The most basic mode available in Emacs. You can use this mode for simple text editing. Default mode for buffers whose file name suffixes Emacs does not recognize.
Text	The complete mode for text editing. If you have serious text editing to do, use this mode rather than Fundamental mode. This mode is not the default mode for any buffers.
Dired	The mode used with the directory editor (file browser) named Dired. See Chapter 11.

Table 1.3, con't.

Major Mode	Description
C	The mode for editing C programs. Default mode for buffers whose names end in `.c`. See Chapter 6.
FORTRAN	The mode for editing FORTRAN programs. Default mode for buffers whose names end in `.f`. See Chapter 7.
Lisp Interaction	The mode for evaluating Emacs-Lisp expressions interactively. The results are placed in the buffer. Default mode for buffers whose names end in `.l`. See Chapter 8.
Emacs-Lisp	The mode for editing, compiling, and debugging Emacs-Lisp functions. Default mode for buffers whose names end in `.el`. See Appendix B.
Rmail	The mode used for processing electronic mail. See Chapter 10.

Emacs determines which mode to use by looking at the file name associated with the buffer. For example, if the name ends in `.c`, Emacs uses C mode; if the name ends in `.el`, Emacs uses Emacs-Lisp mode. Files whose suffixes Emacs does not recognize (e.g., `foo.asc`, `foo.txt`, `sample`) are assigned the default mode—usually Fundamental mode. (To change the default mode, see Chapter 4.)

Minor Mode   In addition to major modes, each buffer can have one or more associated minor modes. A minor mode augments or modifies the behavior of a major mode. For example, if Ovwrt minor mode is enabled, any text you type overwrites the existing text in the buffer. A minor mode, if enabled, is listed after the major mode. For example, Text mode with Ovwrt mode enabled would display **(Text Ovwrt)** in the mode line. Minor modes are discussed as appropriate in later chapters.

Position   As mentioned before, the workspace window is actually a viewport into a buffer. The position field tells what part of the buffer you are viewing. Values that may appear in this field and their meanings are listed in Table 1.4.

Table 1.4. Position Field Values

Value	Meaning
All	The entire buffer's contents are visible.

Table 1.4, con't.

Value	Meaning
Top	The first line in the buffer is the first line displayed in the window.
Bot	The last line in the buffer is displayed in the window.
xx%	A percent indicating your relative position in the buffer. For example, a value of 50% indicates you are halfway through the buffer.

The Echo Area

Emacs uses the **echo area** for two purposes:

- **Displaying status messages.** For example, after you save a file, Emacs displays a message, such as **Wrote /user/janie/report**, in the echo area.

- **Prompting you for arguments to commands.** For example, when you load a file, Emacs displays the prompt **Find file:** in the echo area. The cursor sits in the echo area until you type a response and press **RET**. The actual retrieval of arguments from the echo area is performed in a special buffer called the **minibuffer**. In this book, the terms "echo area" and "minibuffer" are often used synonymously.

Softkeys (Nonstandard)

On some systems, softkey labels may appear at the bottom of the screen, as shown in Figure 1.4. If present, they show the names of Emacs commands that you can execute by pressing the associated softkeys (f1 through f8) on your keyboard. Use of these keys is optional; they are merely a convenience for people who like to use them.

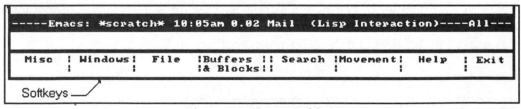

Figure 1.4. Emacs Softkeys

Typing Text

To insert text into the selected window, simply type it. Any printable characters—that is, the visible ASCII characters—will appear immediately. Characters are placed at the current cursor position. As you type, the cursor (and any text following it) moves to the right.

If you type past the right edge of the window, Emacs continues the line onto the next line *without breaking it* (this is the default behavior; to change it, see "Filling Text" in Chapter 3). To show that the two lines are actually one, Emacs places a backslash (\) in the right-most character on the line, as shown in Figure 1.5.

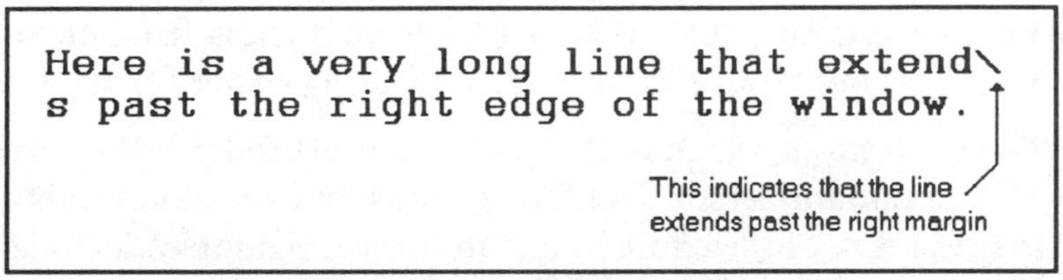

Figure 1.5. Long Lines in Emacs

You can create new lines by pressing **RET** (the Return or Enter key). To back up and delete a character, use the **DEL** (Rubout or Backspace) key. (On some systems, the Backspace key invokes the online help system. See "Finding Your Online Help and DEL Keys" later in this chapter for more information.)

If your cursor movement and delete keys don't work as expected, you may need to edit your Emacs configuration file (usually **.emacs**), as described in Chapter 13. Ask your UNIX system administrator to help you. You may, however, use the basic commands listed at the end of this chapter to move the cursor and delete text.

Typing Commands

All editing tasks are performed via commands. Each Emacs command has a name, and can be executed by typing **M-x** *name* **RET**, where **M** stands for a special "Meta" key that Emacs uses. For example, the command to move the cursor to the beginning of the line is named **beginning-of-line** and can be executed by typing **M-x beginning-of-line RET**.

Because typing command names requires considerable effort—as in the previous example, which requires no fewer than 19 keystrokes to move to the beginning of a line—Emacs has defined shorthand forms for frequently used commands. Thus, instead of typing the long **M-x** command to move to the beginning of a line, we can type **C-a** (hold down the Control key while pressing **a**).

The following sections describe how to execute these two main classes of commands: those executed with the Control key, and those executed with the Meta key.

Control Key Commands

To keep things short and simple, Emacs and this book use the notation C- for control characters. For example, to execute the C-d (Control-d) command, type d while holding down the Control key. Although you press two keys in this example, Emacs interprets this as a single key.

Emacs uses four main types of Control key commands:

- **Single-key commands,** such as C-k (delete characters from cursor to end of line), C-a (move cursor to start of line), and C-s (search for text).

- **Extended commands,** which start with C-x and are followed by another control sequence or command letter. Think of C-x as an extension prefix that signals Emacs that the rest of the command is to follow. Examples include C-x C-s (save buffer to a file), C-x C-f (visit a file), and C-x b (switch to another buffer). For example, to use the C-x C-f command, press x while holding down Control; then press f while holding down Control.

- **Three-key commands,** which start with C-x 4, such as C-x 4 b (switch to a buffer in another window; create the other window if necessary).

- **Custom commands,** which start with C-c. Like C-x, C-c is a command prefix that signals more will follow. Custom commands are tailored to a particular mode. For example, in Outline mode (described in Chapter 4, "Advanced Editing"), C-c C-n means to move to the next visible heading in the outline, and in FORTRAN mode, C-c C-n moves to the next statement.

Most UNIX systems have Control key commands that kill or suspend programs (for example, C-c, C-z, and C-d). To avoid conflicts, these UNIX Control commands are temporarily disabled while you run Emacs.

Meta Commands

Commands that start with the Meta key are known as **Meta commands.** The notation used for Meta commands is M-, where M represents the Meta key.

The Meta key is assigned differently on different computers. Four possible assignments for the Meta key are:

- **A key labeled "Meta."** If your keyboard has a key labeled Meta, you can execute Meta commands by holding down the Meta key and pressing the command key. For example, M-v, which scrolls to the previous screen, is executed by holding down the Meta key while typing **v**. To execute the **C-M-v** command, hold down both the Control and Meta keys and press **v**.

- **A key with a label other than Meta that Emacs has reassigned as the Meta key.** On our system, for example, the key labeled "Extend char" is the Meta key. Ask your system administrator for the Meta key on your keyboard. As in the previous case, you execute commands by holding down the key assigned as the Meta key while typing the command key.

- **The ESC key.** When no physical Meta key has been defined, you can execute Meta commands by typing key sequences that begin with **ESC** (the Escape key). To execute **M-v** in this case, you press **ESC**, then type **v**. You do *not* hold down **ESC** while typing **v**. To enter **C-M-v**, you would press **ESC**, then hold down Control while typing **v**. This technique also works on keyboards that have a dedicated physical Meta key.

- **The C-[sequence.** If your keyboard has neither a physical Meta key nor a physical **ESC** key, type **C-[** for the Meta key.

As you can see from the **C-M-v** examples above, sometimes both the Control and Meta keys are used to specify a command.

M-x commands are a special type of Meta command known as **named command extended**. Each of these commands contains a special, named Emacs function, preceded by **M-x**. For example, the **M-x goto-line** command is used to go to a specific line number in a buffer. To run this command, you type **M-x** followed by the string **goto-line** and **RET**. Emacs will then prompt you to enter the line number you want to go to.

Commands and the Echo Area

Commands that require several keystrokes (as in **M-x goto-line**) appear in the echo area as you type them. Emacs does this so you keep track of what you have typed. Imagine trying to type **M-x eval-current-buffer** without being able to see the characters as you type them! Emacs displays shorter commands in the echo area also, but because they execute almost immediately, you may not notice them before they disappear.

Aborting Commands

Any command—except those that execute immediately—can be aborted with **C-g**. For example, if you press **M-x** and type **goto-line**, you could abort this command by pressing **C-g** before you press **RET**. If a command prompts for additional information, you can abort it by typing **C-g** in response to the prompt.

Using a Basic Set of Editing Commands

Tables 1.5 through 1.7 contain basic text editing commands for moving the cursor, deleting text, and working with files. We suggest that you type in a page or two of text and experiment with these commands to get the "feel" of using Emacs. Remember that you can insert text in the selected window simply by typing it.

We have provided detailed instructions for executing each of the following commands, to help you learn to use the variety of command types available in Emacs. All of these commands will be described in more detail in subsequent chapters; you should focus here on simply familiarizing yourself with the different ways Emacs commands are executed.

We have also suggested a mnemonic association for each command, when possible, to help you remember the command.

Table 1.5. Cursor Movement Commands

To Do This...	Use Command...	Mnemonic	Instructions
Move back one character	C–b	C-back	Hold down Control, type **b**
Move forward one character	C–f	C-forward	Hold down Control, type **f**
Move to previous line	C–p	C-previous	Hold down Control, type **p**
Move to next line	C–n	C-next	Hold down Control, type **n**
Move to start of line	C–a	Think of **a** as start of alphabet	Hold down Control, type **a**
Move to end of line	C–e	C-end	Hold down Control, type **e**

Table 1.5, con't.

To Do This...	Use Command...	Mnemonic	Instructions
Move to beginning of buffer	`M-<`	Think of as jumping backward (<) to top of buffer	Hold down Meta (or press ESC), type <
Move to end of buffer	`M->`	Think of as jumping forward (>) to end of buffer	Hold down Meta (or press ESC), type >
Scroll forward one screenful of lines	`C-v`	v points down a page	Hold down Control, type **v**
Scroll backward one screenful of lines	`M-v`	Opposite of C-v	Hold down Meta (or press ESC), type **v**
Go to a specific line number	`M-x goto-line`	None	Hold down Meta (or press ESC), type **x**, then type `goto-line` and **RET**. Answer prompt for line number.

Table 1.6. Text Deletion Commands

To Do This...	Use Command...	Mnemonic	Instructions
Delete character under cursor	`C-d`	C-delete	Hold down Control, type **d**

Table 1.6. Text Deletion Commands

To Do This...	Use Command...	Mnemonic	Instructions
Delete character before cursor	DEL (Rubout or Backspace)	None	Press DEL (may need to edit Emacs configuration file to make this work)
Delete to end of line or delete blank line	C-k	C-kill	Hold down Control, type **k**
Delete non-blank line	C-a C-k C-k	None; this is actually three commands: **C-a** moves to start of line; two **C-k**'s kill text to end of line, then line itself	Hold down Control, type **a**; hold down Control, type **k**; hold down Control, type **k**
Undo a deletion	C-x u	C-extended, undelete	Hold down Control, type **x**; type **u**

Table 1.7. File Commands

To Do This...	Use Command...	Mnemonic	Instructions
Rename the buffer and write its contents to a file of that name	C-x C-w	C-extended, C-write	Hold down Control, type **x**; hold down Control, type **w**

Table 1.7, con't.

To Do This...	Use Command...	Mnemonic	Instructions
Save the buffer to a file of the same name	C-x C-s	C-extended, C-save	Hold down Control, type **x**; hold down Control, type **s**
Load a file into a buffer (visit the file)	C-x C-f	C-extended, C-find	Hold down Control, type **x**; hold down Control, type **f**

Getting Online Help

Emacs includes an extensive online help system that contains information on commands, modes, and an array of other useful topics. We will introduce only the basic help commands here; for complete information, refer to Chapter 9, "Getting Online Help."

Finding Your Online Help and DEL Keys

To access the online help system, you are supposed to type **C-h**. However, on many systems, the **DEL** key (Rubout or Backspace) accesses the online help system also, instead of backing over and deleting the previous character as you would expect. Why does this happen? Because the default Emacs command for invoking the help system, **C-h**, sends the same ASCII control code as the Backspace key. This means that, to Emacs, pressing Backspace has the same effect as typing **C-h**, and is interpreted as a request for help.

Emacs system administrators have devised various creative solutions to address this problem. A few common ones include:

1. **Swap the DEL and C-h keys.** If this has been done on your system, pressing **DEL** (Backspace or Rubout) will display the help system and typing **C-h** will back over and delete the previous character. This also means that, in this book and in the online help system, when told to press the **DEL** key you must type **C-h** and vice versa.

2. **Use C–h and Backspace to access help and the Delete key for DEL.** Many keyboards have a separate "Delete" key in addition to a Backspace or Rubout key. On such systems, the "Delete" key is used to back over and delete the previous character, and Backspace and **C–h** access the help system.

3. **Define a new help command, and use Backspace for DEL.** If your system uses this strategy, Backspace will behave as expected, but **C–h** will not access the help system (it will probably act like Backspace). Some other key is used for help; for example, on our system, **C–8** accesses the help system.

If this is a problem on your system, ask your system administrator which keys to use for help and **DEL**, or look in your `.emacs` file for clues (see Chapter 13). In the meantime, you can still use **C–b** followed by **C–d** to move backward and delete a character, and the **M–x help-for-help** command to access help.

Getting Help on Commands

To get a brief description of a command, type **C–h c**, or, if you haven't found your help key, type **M–x describe-key-briefly.** (Tip: rather than type the entire command, type **M–x**, then the first few letters, then press **TAB**. Emacs will complete as much of the command as is unique. Type a few more letters and press **TAB** again to complete the next portion of the command. Repeat until the command is complete, then press **RET**.)

Emacs prompts:

```
Describe key briefly:
```

Type the command you would like help with. For example, typing **C–b** at the prompt displays the following line in the minibuffer:

```
C-b runs the command backward-char
```

For a more complete description of the command, you can type either **C–h k** or **M–x describe-key.** Emacs then prompts:

```
Describe key:
```

Again, type the command you want to see. If you type **C–b**, Emacs creates a separate help window and displays the following message:

```
backward-char:
backward-char(n)
Move point left ARG characters (right if ARG negative).
On attempt to pass beginning or end of buffer, stop and signal error.
```

To remove the help window, type **C-x 1**.

Running the Online Tutorial

To run an online tutorial, type **C-h t** or **M-x help-with-tutorial**. If your system has the online tutorial, this command creates a buffer named **TUTORIAL** in Fundamental mode. You can learn basic Emacs editing commands by following the directions in the tutorial.

To exit the tutorial, type **C-x k RET**.

Other Online Information Sources

Emacs comes with several files that contain information about Emacs and the Free Software Foundation. These files were stored in the **/usr/local/emacs/etc** directory on our system; if you can't find this directory on your system, see Chapter 14, "Finding the Other Emacs Files."

Particularly useful is the **FAQ** ("Frequently Asked Questions") file, which contains over one hundred valuable tips on all aspects of Emacs. You can print this file, or view it in Emacs by running the **C-x C-f** command and typing the complete path for the **FAQ** file when prompted for a file name. Use the commands in Table 1.5 to move around the file (**C-v** and **M-v** are particularly useful).

For more current information, consult the UNIX News (Notes) groups that have been started to discuss Emacs. If you are not currently reading News, ask your system administrator to set you up as a News user. Browse through the groups that end in **.emacs**, such as **comp.emacs** and **gnu.emacs**. You can read about existing features and enhancements of Emacs, as well as other information that you might find useful. You can also post questions to the group and receive answers from experienced Emacs users.

Using Emacs to Process Electronic Mail

Emacs' electronic mail facility, RMAIL, lets you read, reply to, compose, and send e-mail messages without leaving the Emacs environment. However, because RMAIL is incompatible with other UNIX mail handlers such as **mailx** and **elm**, you should give careful consideration to your mail-handling options before trying RMAIL. At the very least, you should try RMAIL only after you have emptied your UNIX mailbox by reading, saving, or deleting all messages you have received to date. Otherwise, you will be forced to process all outstanding messages with RMAIL before you can revert back to another UNIX mail handler.

Use of RMAIL is discussed in detail in Chapter 10. At this point, we would just like you to be aware that it is available should you want to consider using it.

Using Emacs to Manage Files

Emacs' Dired facility, or "directory editor," lets you perform many common file management tasks—such as copying, deleting and renaming files—without leaving Emacs. To start Dired, run either the **C-x d** or **M-x dired** command. Emacs then prompts for the directory you want to "edit" with Dired:

```
Dired (directory): ~/█
```

Type the path name for the desired directory and press **RET**. Emacs then creates a Dired buffer and displays a long file listing in it, as shown in Figure 1.6.

```
█ total 5302
  drwxr-xr-x    5 michael  users      3072 Apr  4 20:18 .
  drwxr-xr-x   31 michael  users      3072 Mar 27 13:09 ..
  -rw-r--r--    1 michael  users       385 Feb 19 22:42 Abbrevs
  -rw-r--r--    1 michael  users       697 Feb 27 18:49 Apropos
  -rw-r--r--    1 michael  users      7540 Feb 27 18:50 Bindings
  -rwxr--r--    1 michael  users       193 Apr 15  1990 ChangeLog
  -rw-r--r--    1 michael  users       139 Feb 27 18:54 Cover
  drwxr-xr-x    2 michael  users        64 Apr  7 15:47 Examples
  -rw-r--r--    1 michael  users       348 Feb 27 18:58 Function
--%%-Dired: emacs           8:47pm 0.01 Mail  (Dired)----Top--------
Reading directory /user/michael/emacs/...done
```

Figure 1.6. File Listing in the Dired Buffer

You can then move around the buffer with standard cursor-movement commands (see those listed in Table 1.5), and manipulate the files in the directory with special Dired commands.

For example, to copy a file, move the cursor to the file you want to copy and type **c**. Emacs then prompts for the name you want to give the new copy; type it and press **RET**.

As another example, you can visit a file (load it into Emacs) by moving the cursor to the desired file and typing **e** or **f**. This is convenient for retrieving several files from the same directory into Emacs, particularly if you can't remember the exact names of the files.

To delete a file, move the cursor to the file and type **d** to mark it for deletion, then type **x** to actually delete it.

For more information on using Dired to manage your files, see Chapter 11.

Changing Emacs' Behavior with Variables

Emacs is an extremely flexible environment. If you don't like the way Emacs performs a particular operation, you can usually change its behavior by setting the value of a **variable**. An Emacs variable has a name, and can accept either a string value, a numeric value, or the special values **t** and **nil**.

For example, the variable named *mode-line-inverse-video* determines how the mode line is displayed. When the value is **t** (the default), the mode line is displayed in inverse video. If you would rather not have the mode line displayed in inverse video, you can change the value of *mode-line-inverse-video* to **nil**.

Variable values are assigned with the **M-x set-variable** command, which prompts for the name of a variable. When entering a string value, be sure to enclose it in double quotes. When entering **nil** or **t** or a numeric value, do *not* use quotes.

Continuing with the previous example, you could change the way your mode line is displayed like this:

```
M-x set variable RET                              ← Run the command
Set variable: mode-line-inverse-video RET         ← Type the variable name
Set mode-line-inverse-video to value: nil RET     ← Type the value
```

For more information about variables, see "Using Variables to Change Emacs' Behavior" in Chapter 13.

Summary

Table 1.8 summarizes the important points in this chapter.

Table 1.8. Chapter 1 Summary

Topic	Summary
Starting Emacs	Type: • **emacs** to start with an empty buffer • **emacs** *file1 file2* to load file(s) into Emacs when you start

Table 1.8, con't.

Topic	Summary

Exiting Emacs	• `C-x C-c` ends Emacs session; prompts you to save buffers
	• `C-u C-x C-c` ends Emacs without prompting to save buffers
	• `C-z` suspends Emacs session and returns you to UNIX
	  • C shell: `%emacs` returns you to Emacs
	  • Korn shell: `fg %emacs` returns you to Emacs

Parts of the Emacs Screen	• **workspace**: area in which you create and edit documents • **cursor**: points to the current position in the workspace • **mode line**: provides a variety of status information • **echo area (minibuffer)**: displays messages, prompts for command arguments • **softkey labels**: may appear on some systems
Buffers	• All editing takes place in **buffers** • Multiple buffers may be edited at once • The buffer name is usually the same as the file name • The `*scratch*` buffer is a scratch pad for temporary notes
Modes	• Emacs contains several major modes • A **major mode** is a set of commands designed for a specific type of editing (text, C programs, etc.) • The mode associated with a buffer is displayed on the mode line • **Minor modes** modify the behavior of a major mode
Control Key Commands	• **Single key commands**: hold down Control and press key (`C-k`) • **Extended commands**: `C-x`, followed by another command sequence (`C-x C-c`) • **Three-key commands**: `C-x`, followed by **4**, followed by another character (`C-x 4 b`) • **Custom commands**: `C-c`, followed by another command sequence (`C-c C-n`)

Table 1.8, con't.

Topic	Summary
Meta Key Commands	• Hold down Meta and press command key, or press **ESC** and then press command key • **Named command extended**: **M-x**, followed by a command string (**M-x goto-line**)
Aborting Commands	• Press **C-g**
Getting Online Help	• Access online help: **C-h** or **M-x help-for-help** • The **DEL** and **C-h** keys are swapped on some systems • Display brief help on a command: **C-h c** or **M-x describe-key-briefly** • Display complete help on a command: **C-h k** or **M-x describe-key** • Run the online tutorial: **C-h t** or **M-x help-with-tutorial** • Exit online tutorial: **C-x k RET**
Using Electronic Mail	• Emacs' e-mail facility is called RMAIL and is incompatible with other UNIX mail facilities • Empty your current UNIX mailbox before trying RMAIL
Managing Files	• Start the directory editor, Dired: **C-x d** or **M-x dired** • Copy current file: **c** • Visit (load) current file: **e** or **f** • Delete current file: **d**, then **x**
Variables	• Set value of a variable: **M-x set-variable**

2
Basic Editing Commands

This chapter describes a minimal set of Emacs commands that provide basic text editing capabilities. With these commands, you should be able to edit any file in any major mode, though perhaps not as efficiently as possible. Specifically, this chapter describes:

- Visiting a file

- Saving a buffer

- Listing buffers

- Switching to a different buffer

- Killing a buffer

- Setting the mode for a buffer

- Moving the cursor

- Using line numbers

- Deleting text

- Undoing mistakes

- Using regions

- Searching for text

- Searching and replacing text

- Overwriting text

We highly recommend that you become proficient with the commands in this chapter. Experiment with them on "dummy" files until you can use them comfortably, then proceed to the next chapter, which describes how to use Emacs more efficiently.

Visiting a File

In Emacs terminology, **visiting** (or **finding**) a file means loading a file into a buffer. To edit a file, you visit the file, edit the text in a buffer, and save the buffer back into the file. Changes made to the buffer are not made to the disk file until you **save** the buffer.

To visit a file, use the **C-x C-f** command, which prompts for the file's name. Emacs assumes you want to visit a file from the same directory as the current buffer's file. Emacs automatically supplies part of the file's path name in the prompt area. For example, if you start up Emacs from your home directory, then run **C-x C-f** to visit your first file, Emacs displays a prompt in the minibuffer, as shown in Figure 2.1.

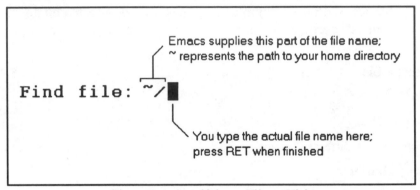

Figure 2.1. Specifying a File to Visit

If the file you want to edit resides in a different directory, you can edit the path name in the echo area. For example, to visit **/tmp/sample**, use **DEL** to back up over the **~/** and type the correct path name:

```
Find file: /tmp/sample RET
```

If the file is found, Emacs displays the file's contents in the new buffer on the screen. Emacs names the new buffer the same name as the file, minus the directory path. Thus, the buffer name for **/tmp/sample** is **sample**. The buffer's name appears in the mode line.

What happens when you visit a file that has the same name as a buffer already in use? Emacs appends **<2>** to the new buffer's name. Thus, if you visit **~/report** and **~/projects/report**, Emacs names the first buffer **report** and the second **report<2>**. Similarly, **<3>** would be used for the next buffer of the same name, and so on.

In addition to visiting existing files, the **C-x C-f** command creates new files. If you specify a file that doesn't exist, Emacs creates a new, empty buffer in which you can begin typing new text. When you are done creating the text, you can save it to the new file, just as you would an existing file.

Saving a Buffer

When you are finished modifying a buffer's contents, you can save it—that is, write it to a file—using the **C-x C-s** command. Emacs displays the message

> **Wrote** *filename*

where *filename* is the name of the buffer's file. If the buffer's contents have not changed since the last time it was saved, Emacs displays the message:

> **(No changes need to be written)**

Occasionally, you may need to save a buffer to a file other than the visited file. For example, you might visit a template file, fill in the blanks, and save it to a file other than the template file. To do this, execute the **C-x C-w** command, which prompts for the name of the file to save, as shown in Figure 2.2.

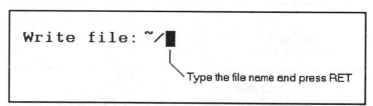

Figure 2.2. Saving to a Different File Name

This command assumes you want to save the file in the same directory as the visited file. If this is not the case, you can type a different path name.

This command also has the side effect of renaming the buffer to the name of the saved file. For example, if you visit the file **~/templates/address**, edit the buffer, then save it as **~/addresses/caroline**, Emacs renames the buffer to **caroline**. Subsequent saves with the **C-x C-s** command will save the buffer to **~/addresses/caroline**.

Listing Buffers

If you edit several buffers at once, you may lose track of them. To list the names of all resident buffers, use the **C-x C-b** command. Emacs displays the list in separate window, leaving the cursor in your current window. Executing **C—x 1** removes the window that contains the list of buffers. (We will describe more window management techniques in Chapter 4, "Advanced Editing.")

A sample buffer listing is shown below.

```
MR Buffer        Size  Mode               File
-- ------        ----  ----               ----
 *   main         294  Text               /user/caroline/main
   % sample       592  Fundamental        ~/sample
     *scratch*    167  Lisp Interaction
     *Buffer List*  0  Buffer Menu
```

The fields in this sample are described in Table 2.1.

Table 2.1. Buffer Listing Information

Field	Meaning
MR	**%** beneath the **R** indicates a read-only buffer; type **C—x C—q** to toggle read-only status ***** beneath the **M** indicates buffer has been modified since the last save **.** preceding either of the above indicates this buffer is the current buffer
Buffer	The name of the buffer. ***Buffer List*** is the name of the buffer containing the buffer listing. ***scratch*** is the scratch pad buffer. **main** and **sample** are text-editing buffers.
Size	The size of the buffer, in characters.
Mode	The mode used with each buffer. ***Buffer List*** has its own Buffer Menu mode. The text buffer, **sample**, uses Fundamental mode, the basic text-editing mode, while **main** uses Text mode, a more full-featured text-editing mode. ***scratch*** uses Lisp Interaction mode.
File	The file name associated with each buffer, if any.

Switching to a Different Buffer

You can visit multiple buffers, but only one can be the current buffer in which you are actively editing. To switch current buffers, use **C—x b**, which prompts for the name of the new buffer and provides a possible default, as shown in Figure 2.3. If no buffer exists by the name you specify, Emacs creates a new, empty buffer.

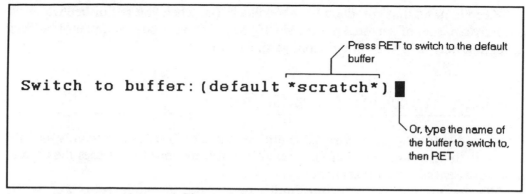

Figure 2.3. Switching Buffers

The previous current buffer is typically used as the default buffer. For example, if you edit in buffer **foo**, then switch to buffer **bar**, Emacs will assume you want to switch back to buffer **foo** if you type **C-x b** again:

```
Switch to buffer: (default foo)  ▮
```

You can also specify the buffer name in the command, as in **C-x b foo RET**, if you prefer.

If you are unsure of buffer names, you can press the **TAB** key at the prompt to display a listing of all buffers in use.

Killing a Buffer

When you are finished with a buffer—that is, when you have made all necessary edits and have saved the buffer—you may find it useful to remove, or "kill," the buffer with **C-x k**. Killing a buffer removes the buffer and its associated resources. Emacs prompts for the name of the buffer to kill, using the current buffer as a default. For example, if the current buffer is named **sample**, Emacs prompts:

```
Kill buffer (default sample)  ▮
```

To kill the default buffer, just press **RET**. Otherwise, enter the name of the buffer you want to kill. If the buffer has been modified since it was last saved, Emacs prompts:

```
Buffer sample modified; kill anyway? (yes or no)  ▮
```

You must type **yes** or **no** (in full) to respond to this prompt.

Keep in mind that you don't have to kill a buffer when you're finished with it; it is purely a matter of personal preference. If you have a very large number of buffers, though, it may help keep things from getting cluttered.

Setting the Mode for a Buffer

As we said before, a buffer's mode determines the set of Emacs commands that are available to operate on the buffer. Therefore, ensuring your buffer uses the correct mode is essential for editing efficiency.

The easiest way to set your buffer to the proper mode is to assign the corresponding file name the proper suffix. When Emacs visits a file whose suffix it recognizes, it automatically sets the buffer to the mode appropriate to the file's contents. Table 2.2 lists suffixes that Emacs recognizes and their corresponding modes.

Table 2.2. File Suffixes and Default Modes

File Name Suffix	Default Mode	Mode Name
`.c` or `.h`	C	c-mode
`.p`	Pascal	pascal-mode
`.f`	FORTRAN	fortran-mode
`.l`	Lisp	lisp-mode
`.el`	Emacs-Lisp	emacs-lisp-mode
—	Text	text-mode

If Emacs cannot ascribe a mode based on a buffer's suffix, it uses Fundamental mode by default. Fundamental mode contains a core set of commands for editing and manipulating buffers and files. Fundamental mode commands are applicable in all other modes as well.

The other primary mode for editing text files is Text mode. Emacs does not recognize a particular file name extension for Text mode, although you can customize Emacs to associate an extension with Text mode (see Chapter 13, "Customizing the Emacs Environment"). Text mode is the recommended mode for editing human language text.

To change the mode of a buffer, type an **M-x** *modename* command, where *modename* is selected from those listed in Table 2.2. For example, to enable Text mode in a buffer, use the **M-x text-mode** command.

Moving the Cursor

Table 2.3 lists commands for moving the cursor in the selected window, including some you may be familiar with from the last chapter. As the cursor moves, point moves to the corresponding location in the buffer. If a command takes the cursor past the top or bottom of the selected window, Emacs scrolls the window appropriately. For example, if you are in the middle of a buffer and execute **M-<**, Emacs moves the first line of the buffer to the top of the window.

Table 2.3. Cursor Movement Commands

Move the Cursor...	Command
Forward one character	C-f
Backward one character	C-b
Forward one word	M-f
Backward one word	M-b
Down one line (next line)	C-n
Up one line (previous line)	C-p
To the end of the current line	C-e
To the beginning of the current line	C-a
To the end of sentence	M-e
To the beginning of sentence	M-a
To beginning of paragraph	M-[

Table 2.3, con't.

Move the Cursor...	Command
To end of paragraph	`M-]`
Forward one page	`C-x ]`
Backward one page	`C-x [`
To the end of the buffer	`M->`
To the beginning of the buffer	`M-<`
To a particular line	`M-x goto-line` Answer the prompt with the number of line to go to and press **RET**.
To the first nonblank character	`M-m`
To a particular character position	`M-x goto-char` Answer the prompt with the number of the character to go to and press **RET**.

Using Arrow Keys

If your keyboard has arrow keys, you can use them to move the cursor if your version of Emacs supports this. If arrow keys are supported, some other keys, such as a Home and Shift-Home, may also be bound to Emacs cursor movement capabilities. The only way to know for sure is to experiment.

Using a Mouse

As with arrow keys, mouse support is not a standard part of Emacs. However, it is often supported in various vendors' implementations. For example, on our system, the cursor can be moved by clicking the left mouse button while the mouse pointer is in an Emacs window.

Using Line Numbers

Table 2.4 summarizes commands for going to a specific line number in a buffer and getting line number information. (The first line in a buffer is line 1.)

Table 2.4. Line Number Commands

Operation	Command and Comments
Go to line	`M-x goto-line` Emacs prompts for a line number; type it and press RET. If you enter a line greater than the total lines in the buffer, Emacs goes to the last line.
Show current line number	`M-x what-line` Emacs displays the line number containing the cursor.

Deleting Text

Table 2.5 lists the basic commands for deleting text from a buffer. Unlike **vi**, Emacs lets you backspace over a line ending, thereby deleting it and joining two lines. There are, of course, more powerful ways to delete text. For example, Emacs allows you to delete blocks (regions) of text; this is discussed later under "Moving a Region of Text."

Table 2.5. Text Deletion Commands

Operation	Command and Comments
Delete previous character	DEL If the cursor is positioned at the start of a line, this joins the current line with the one above it.

Table 2.5, con't.

Operation	Command and Comments
Delete current character	C-d If the cursor is positioned at the end of a line, this joins the current line with the one below it.
Delete to end of line	C-k Deletes (kills) all characters from the cursor to the end of the line, as shown in Figure 2.4. If the cursor is positioned at the end of a line, this joins the current line with the one below it.

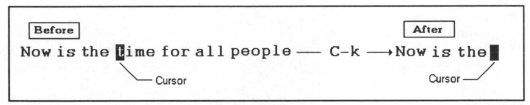

Figure 2.4. Deleting to End of Line

Note that one quick way to delete a line entirely is to go to the start of the line with **C-a**, then issue two **C-k** commands. For example, suppose the cursor is over the letter **t** in the second line of the following text:

```
Line one
Line ▮wo
Line three
```

If you run **C-a**, the cursor moves to the start of the line:

```
Line one
▮ine two
Line three
```

Now if you type **C-k**, all characters to the end of the line are removed, but the line remains:

```
Line one
▮
Line three
```

The second line is now blank, containing only a newline character. To delete the line, run **C–k** again; the cursor will now be on the first character in the new second line:

```
Line one
Line three
```

Undoing Mistakes

As you edit, you will probably run some unwanted commands—for example, executing **C–k** to kill to the end of line when you really mean to use **C–d** to delete a single character. Emacs does an excellent job of recovering from such errors. The **C–x u** command reverses the effects of the last editing command (it also goes by the alternate form **C–_**).

As an example, suppose you are editing the line shown in Figure 2.5.

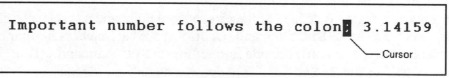

Figure 2.5. A Line of Text

If you wanted to delete the semicolon and type a colon in its place, you would run the **C–d** command, then type a colon. Suppose that you accidentally type **C–k** rendering the line as shown in Figure 2.6.

If you couldn't remember what the number was, you could retrieve the deleted text by typing **C–x u**, restoring the line to its original state, as shown in Figure 2.7.

Figure 2.6. Same Line with a Different Error

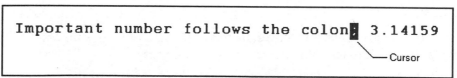

Figure 2.7. A Restored Line of Text

You can use **C-x u** repeatedly to undo multiple mistakes. For example, suppose you are working in a buffer and notice that it has been modified (it has --**-- in the status field of the mode line), but you don't remember making any changes since the last save. To be safe, you could run **C-x u** until the --**-- changes to -----, indicating that the buffer is back to the state it was in when you last saved it. Be aware, however, that versions of Emacs prior to 18.57 limit undoing to deletions of approximately 8,000 characters or less.

Using Regions

Many Emacs commands operate on **regions** of text. For example, commands are provided to kill (delete) a region, indent the lines in a region, check for spelling errors in a region, and sort all the lines in a region. In other editors, regions are often referred to as **blocks**. Unlike line-oriented editors, such as **vi**, Emacs regions don't have to enclose whole lines, but can contain any area of text (the middle of one line to the middle of the next, for example).

In Emacs, a region is defined as the text between point and a special placeholder known as **mark**. The **C-SPC** command (Control-space bar) anchors the mark at the location of point. (**C-@** is an alternate form of the **C-SPC** command.) Thus, here is the typical way to use **C-SPC** or **C-@** to define a region:

1. Move the cursor to the character that you want to be at the start of the region.

2. Type **C-SPC** (or **C-@**) to anchor the mark.

3. Move the cursor to the character that you want to be at the end of the region.

It doesn't matter whether you move the cursor backward or forward from the mark; either way will establish a region that sits between the two.

As an example, suppose you want to put a region around the third and fourth lines of the following stanza:

```
I felt it by a mountain stream,
Drifting off into a dream,
Toes dipped in the icy flow,
Numbed within a minute or so,
Touching runoff from glacial snow.
```

To do this:

1. Move the cursor to the **T** in **Toes**, then type **C-SPC** or **C-@**. Emacs responds by displaying the message **Mark set** in the echo area.

2. Move the cursor down to the **T** in **Touching**. Why there? Because you want the region to include the entire previous line. If, instead, you moved the cursor to the

end of the fourth line, point would fall before the newline at the end as shown in Figure 2.8.

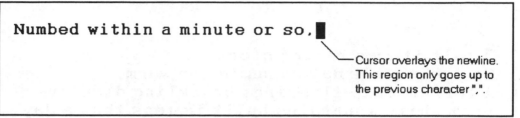

Figure 2.8. Defining a Region

Once you've defined a region, you can run a command that operates on the region. For example, if you defined the region described above, you could kill (delete) the region with the **C-w** command (more on this in a later section, "Moving a Region of Text").

Emacs can actually keep track of up to 16 marks, but only one mark is the **active mark** at a given time. And the **region** between the active mark and point is known as the **current region**. (Using multiple marks is discussed in Chapter 4.)

Seeing the Bounds of a Region

Some editors highlight the text of a region or block. Standard Emacs does not do this. Therefore, you must remember where a region starts and ends. However, Emacs includes a command that shows you the start and end of a region. **C-x C-x** exchanges point and mark. For example, suppose you set the mark on the first **I** in the following stanza, then move the cursor to the **F** in the last line, as shown Figure 2.9.

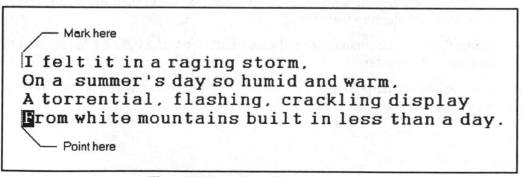

Figure 2.9. Location of Point and Mark

If you now run the **C-x C-x** command, mark and point are swapped, as shown in Figure 2.10.

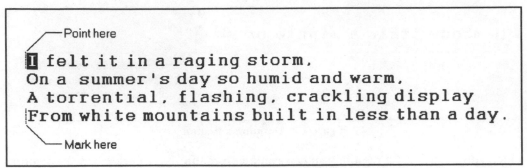

Figure 2.10. Location of Point and Mark Reversed

This command is even more useful if the mark is somewhere off the edge of the window. When you execute **C-x C-x**, the screen scrolls to the line containing the old mark and places the cursor there. Thus, if you had a region that was larger than the window, you could use **C-x C-x** to see its bounds.

Moving a Region of Text

You can use regions to move blocks of text. This operation is called "kill and yank" in Emacs; other editors call it "cut and paste" or "yank and put" (**vi**). The procedure is:

1. Define the region that you want to move (as described in the previous section).

2. Kill the region with **C-w**. The text is not destroyed completely, but is moved into an invisible, temporary holding place called the **kill ring**.

3. Determine where you want to move the deleted block; then move the cursor immediately following that location.

4. Using the **C-y** command, **yank** the text back from the kill ring to the desired location in the buffer.

An example should help clarify. To fix the following limerick, you would have to move two lines as shown in Figure 2.11.

There once was a variable named Foo,
Its friend was named bar,
And both would go far,
That was used in an example or two,
They made it in this book, too.
Move 2 lines down here.

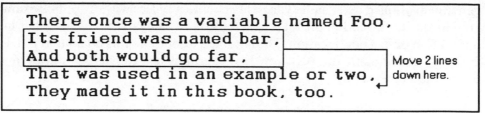

Figure 2.11. Original Limerick That Needs Editing

Following the procedure outlined above, you would:

1. Define the region:

   a. Move the cursor to the `I` in `Its friend....`

   b. Run `C-SPC` to set the mark.

   c. Move the cursor to the `T` in `That was....`

2. Kill the region using `C-w`. The text now looks like Figure 2.12.

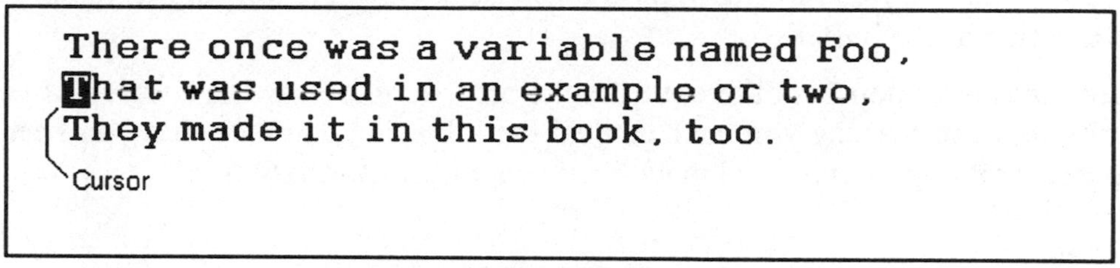

There once was a variable named Foo,
That was used in an example or two,
They made it in this book, too.
Cursor

Figure 2.12. Limerick with Region Removed

3. Since you want to move the couplet immediately before the last line, move the cursor to the `T` in `They made....`

4. Now yank the killed lines back with the `C-y` command; the cursor remains at the same character, as shown in Figure 2.13.

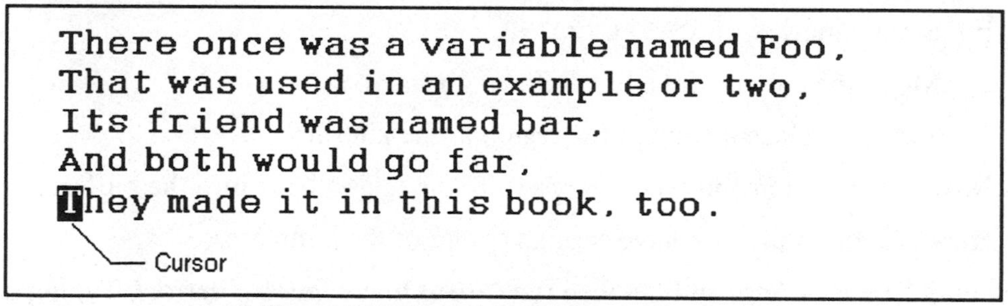

There once was a variable named Foo,
That was used in an example or two,
Its friend was named bar,
And both would go far,
They made it in this book, too.
Cursor

Figure 2.13. Limerick with Region Moved

In general, any killed text can be yanked back into a buffer with **C-y**. For example, if you kill text to the end of the line (with **C-k**), you can yank it back—either in the same location or in a new location. The notable exception to this is text that is deleted with the **C-d** command and **DEL** key. However, this text can still be retrieved with **C-x u** (undo command).

Copying a Region of Text

The procedure for copying a region is very similar to that used for moving a region. The main difference is that instead of using **C-w** to kill the region, you use the **M-w** command to **copy** the region into the kill ring. The procedure is:

1. Define the region you want to copy.

2. Type **M-w** to copy the region into the kill ring.

3. Determine where you want to move the deleted block; then move the cursor immediately following that location.

4. Using the **C-y** command, yank the text back from the kill ring to the desired location in the buffer.

Notice that only step 2 is different from the procedure for moving a region of text.

As an example, say you have created the following template that you need to make several copies of and fill in with name/address information:

```
Name:
Street:
City:                          State:        Zip:
Phone:
```

One way to do this would be:

1. Define the region:

   a. Move the cursor to the **N** in **Name:**.

   b. Set the mark with **C-SPC** or **C-@**.

   c. Move the cursor to the line following **Phone:**.

2. Type **M-w** to place a copy of the region in the kill ring.

3. Move down a line and type **C-y** to yank the region back into the buffer.

4. Repeat step 3 until you have enough copies of the template.

You only type **M-w** once and can then run **C-y** as many times as desired. Typing **C-y** does not remove the yanked region from the kill ring; it only copies the region from the kill ring. The same is true if the kill ring contains text deleted with **C-w**.

Searching for Text

Emacs has exceptional capabilities for searching for strings (for more advanced search techniques than discussed here, see Chapter 4). Emacs performs an **incremental search**—that is, it moves the cursor to matching text *as you type the search string*. The advantage of this method is that you immediately see matching text as you type the search string. Table 2.6 summarizes the search commands.

Table 2.6. Search Commands

Operation	Command and Comments
Search forward	`C-s` Emacs prompts for a search string: `I-search:` ▮ As you type the search string, the cursor moves to the next occurrence of text that matches the string.
Search backward (reverse search)	`C-r` Same as `C-s`, but searches backward.
Regular expression search	`C-M-s` Searches forward for a regular expression. This type of search is very powerful, allowing you to search for generalized text patterns (see Chapter 4, "Advanced Editing" for more information).

By default, the search is not case sensitive. Thus, the search string `foobar` matches `foobar`, `FOOBAR`, and `FooBar`. You can make searches case-sensitive (see Chapter 4, "Advanced Editing").

As you type a search string, the cursor moves forward (or backward, in the case of `C-r`) to the next text that matches the search string. If you eventually type a character that does not match any text in the buffer, Emacs displays the message `Failing I-search:` in the echo area. In this event, you can either terminate the search using one of the methods described in Table 2.7, or you can back up using **DEL** and retype part of the search string.

Figure 2.14 shows how an incremental search works on the line `Peter Piper picked a peck of pickled peppers.` In this example, you use the `C-s` command to search for the string `pickl`. Note how the cursor moves as each character of the search string is typed.

Search String	Effect on Cursor
I–search: <u>p</u>	**P**eter Piper picked a peck of pickled peppers.
I–search: <u>pi</u>	Peter P**i**per picked a peck of pickled peppers.
I–search: <u>pic</u>	Peter Piper pi**c**ked a peck of pickled peppers.
I–search: <u>pick</u>	Peter Piper pic**k**ed a peck of pickled peppers.
I–search: <u>pickl</u>	Peter Piper picked a peck of pickl**l**ed peppers.

Figure 2.14. Incremental Search

Stopping the Search

Once you've found the search string in the text, you need to terminate the search command. Emacs provides three different ways to do this, as shown in Table 2.7.

Table 2.7. Ways to Terminate a Search

If you want to...	Do this...
Leave the cursor at the end of the matching text.	Press **ESC**.
Go back to where the search started.	Type **C-g**.
Execute a command at the current cursor location.	Run the command—for example, **C-a** would move the cursor to the start of the line that contains the matching text.

Figure 2.15 shows the effects of each of these methods on the cursor position.

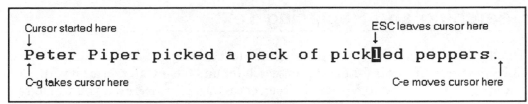

Figure 2.15. Terminating a Search

Editing the Search String with DEL

You can use **DEL** to backup in a search string. It basically undoes the effect of typing the previous character in the search string. This is useful if you make a mistake when typing the search string—you can simply back up to correct the typo. In the example of Figure 2.15, if you pressed **DEL** when the cursor is sitting on the **l** in **pickl**, the search string changes to **pick** and the cursor backs up to its previous location (in the **k** of **pick**). Perhaps the best way to see how this works is to experiment.

Reusing a Search String

Emacs keeps track of the last search string used. If you issue successive search commands, without any other intervening commands, Emacs reuses the last search string. Figure 2.16 shows the effect of issuing another **C-s** command when the search string is **pick**.

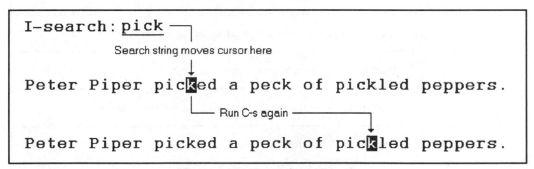

Figure 2.16. Repeating a Search

Similarly, if you type **C-r** at this point, the cursor moves back to the start of the word **pickled**. This is because the **C-r** command uses the same search string that is used by **C-s**. If you type **C-r** again, the cursor moves back to the start of the word **picked**.

Searching and Replacing Text

The **M-%** command allows you to search for text and replace it with alternate text. This command prompts for the text to search for and the text to replace it with. For example, if you wanted to replace all occurrences of **Mr.** with **Mrs.**, you would run **M-%** and respond to the prompts in the minibuffer as follows:

```
Query replace: █                          ← The search string prompt
Query replace: Mr. RET                     ← Type Mr. and press RET
Query replace Mr. with: █                  ← Replacement string prompt
Query replace Mr. with: Mrs. RET           ← Type Mrs. and press RET
```

Emacs then begins searching from the cursor location to the end of the file. For each string of text that matches the search string, Emacs moves the cursor to the string and displays this prompt:

```
Query replacing Mr. with Mrs.: █
```

Valid responses to this prompt are shown in Table 2.8.

Table 2.8. Responses to the String-Replace Prompt

Response	Effect
SPC	Replace this string and go on to the next one.
DEL	Skip on to the next string without replacing the current one.
,	Replace this string and do not move on.
!	Replace all the remaining matches without further interaction.
^	Back up to the position of the previous matching string.
ESC	Exit the query-replacement operation.

As with searching operations, letter case is not important in search-and-replace operations. However, Emacs will preserve the case of letters that are replaced. If, for example, you search and replace **dog** with **cat** in the following text:

```
Doggedly, he pursued the dog through the streets.
```

The text then becomes:

```
Catgedly, he pursued the cat through the streets.
```

Note that the letter case of **Doggedly** was preserved in **Catgedly**.

    To become proficient and learn how to adapt the procedure, you should practice using replacement operations in some sample text so you can see how the replacement occurs. Doing this can help you avoid getting incorrect replacements in an important text file.

Overwriting Text

Whether you use Fundamental or Text mode for editing text, Emacs typically invokes these modes in an insert (or normal) minor mode. To insert text, just type it.

    At times, you may want to work in overwrite (type-over) mode, where typed text overwrites the existing characters. To get into the overwrite minor mode, execute **M-x overwrite-mode**. The mode line displays **Ovwrt** to indicate the new mode. Some experimenting will show how it works.

    To get out of overwrite mode and get back into normal (insert) mode, type **M-x normal-mode**, or type **M-x overwrite-mode** again.

Summary

Table 2.9 summarizes the main points in this chapter.

Table 2.9. Chapter 2 Summary

Topic	Summary
File commands	• Visit a file: **C-x C-f** • Save buffer to file: **C-x C-s** • Save buffer to different file: **C-x C-w**
Buffer commands	• List buffers: **C-x C-b** • Switch current buffer: **C-x b** • Kill a buffer: **C-x k** • Change buffer's mode: **M-x** *modename*

Table 2.9, con't.

Topic	Summary
Cursor movement commands	Forward one: • character: `C-f` • word: `M-f` • line: `C-n` • sentence: `M-e` • paragraph: `M-]` • page: `C-x ]` Backward one: • character: `C-b` • word: `M-b` • line: `C-p` • sentence: `M-a` • paragraph: `M-[` • page: `C-x [` To end of: • line: `C-e` • buffer: `M->` To beginning of: • line: `C-a` • buffer: `M-<` Go to: • character position: `M-x goto-char` • line number: `M-x goto-line`
Line number commands	• Go to line number: `M-x goto-line` • Show line number: `M-x what-line`

Table 2.9, con't.

Topic	Summary
Delete text commands	Delete: • previous character: `DEL` • current character: `C-d` • to end of line: `C-k` • current line: `C-a  C-k  C-k`
Undo command	• Undo deletion: `C-x  u` or `C-_`
Region commands	• Set mark: `C-SPC` or `C-@` • Show region (exchange point and mark): `C-x  C-x` • Delete region: `C-w` • Move region: `C-w`; move cursor to new location; `C-y` • Copy region: `M-w`; move cursor to new location; `C-y`
Incremental search commands	Start search: • forward: `C-s`; enter search string; type `C-s` again to search for next occurrence • backward: `C-r`; enter search string; type `C-r` again to search for next occurrence • for regular expression: `C-M-s` Stop search: • leave cursor at location of search string: `ESC` • go back to where search was started from: `C-g` • execute command at location of search string: type command Search and replace: `M-%` or `M-x query-replace`; replace string by: • `SPC`: replace this string and look for next • `DEL`: skip this string and look for next • `,` : replace this string and stop searching • `!`: replace all further strings without interaction • `^`: back up to previously matched string • `ESC`: exit search-and-replace

Table 2.9, con't.

Topic	Summary
Overwrite minor mode	• Enable overwrite mode: `M-x overwrite-mode` • Return to normal (insert) mode: `M-x normal-mode`

3
More Efficient Editing

This chapter discusses more efficient editing techniques than were described in Chapter 2. For example, this chapter shows you how to kill an entire sentence, rather than deleting it one character at a time. Specifically, this chapter describes:

- Running a command multiple times
- Modifying command behavior with arguments
- Inserting control characters into a buffer
- Working with words, sentences, and paragraphs
- Working with pages
- Working with blank lines
- Getting cursor, line, and page information
- Transposing text
- Filling text
- Indenting text
- Changing letter case
- Searching and replacing text
- Narrowing a buffer
- Moving the cursor to previous marks (the mark ring)
- Using the kill ring
- Completing long command names
- Completing file names
- Using abbreviations (text expansions)
- Using macros for repeated editing tasks

- Scrolling windows

- Working with multiple windows

- Printing a buffer

- Listing a directory

You do not need to know all the commands in this chapter before reading Chapter 4, but you should at least understand how to use numeric arguments as described in the next two sections.

Running a Command Multiple Times

Often it is useful to run a command multiple times. For example, to move down 20 lines in a buffer, you would want to run **C-n** 20 times. An easy way to do this is to use a **numeric argument** as a repeat count. Some commands, however, do not interpret numeric arguments as repeat counts; instead, the numeric argument alters the way the command works (see the next section).

For commands that interpret numeric arguments as a repeat count, specifying no numeric argument is usually the same as specifying a numeric argument of 1. Thus, **C-n** by itself is the same as specifying a numeric argument of 1 to **C-n**. However, this is not always the case. For example, the **C-k** command normally kills text to the end of a line. If given a numeric argument of 1, **C-k** kills the entire line! So, in some instances, using a numeric argument as a repeat count may also alter the command's behavior.

One of the best examples of using numeric arguments is going to a specific line number in a file. One way to do this is to run the **M-x goto-line** command, which prompts for a line number. A faster way is to run **M-<** to go to the first line of a buffer, then run **C-n** with a numeric argument specifying the line you want to go to. (Actually, this takes you to the line *after* the one you want to go to, because it moves down n lines from the first line, finally resting at line $n + 1$.)

Negative arguments are often meaningful to commands. For example, if you specify an argument of -10 to the **C-n** command, it moves backward 10 lines, which has the same effect as running **C-p** with an argument of 10.

There are two ways to specify numeric arguments to a command: with the **C-u** command or with the Meta key.

Specifying Numeric Arguments with C-u

The **C-u** command lets you type a number followed by a command. For example, to run **C-n** 10 times, you would run **C-u 10 C-n**; here is what you could see in the echo area:

```
C-u 1 0 C-n
```

Emacs separates each digit you type by a space. The number is considered finished when you type a command. To specify a negative number, type a minus sign before the first digit. For example, to move backward 10 characters, you could run **C-f** minus 10 times, which is the same as running **C-b** 10 times:

```
C-u - 1 0 C-f
```

Specifying Numeric Arguments with the Meta Key

On systems that have a functional Meta key, an easy way to specify numeric arguments is to type digits while holding down the Meta key. As with the **C-u** command, Emacs considers a number finished when you type a command. So, to run the **C-n** command 15 times, you would type **M-1 M-5 C-n**. The command is displayed in the echo area as:

```
M-1 M-5 C-n
```

To specify negative numbers this way, type **M--** (Meta-minus) before the digits.

Modifying Command Behavior with Arguments

As mentioned above, some commands do not interpret a numeric argument as a repeat count. For example, the **M-x goto-line** command normally prompts for the line number you want to go to. If run with a numeric argument, it goes to that line *without* prompting. Thus, the following command moves the cursor to line 256 in the buffer:

```
C-u 2 5 6 M-x goto-line
```

Some commands only check to see if a numeric argument was specified and don't care about the value. For such commands, it is sufficient to type **C-u** immediately followed by the command, without specifying a numeric value. For example, the **C-x C-b** command displays information about all buffers currently visited by Emacs:

```
MR Buffer          Size  Mode              File
-- ------          ----  ----              ----
.* main            294   Text              /user/caroline/main
   *scratch*       167   Lisp Interaction
   *Buffer List*   0     Buffer Menu
```

If run as **C-u C-x C-b**, it displays this information only for the nonsystem buffers (buffers whose names are not enclosed by asterisks):

```
MR Buffer        Size  Mode          File
-- ------        ----  ----          ----
.* main          294   Text          /user/caroline/main
```

Inserting Control Characters into a Buffer

If you do not know what control characters are and don't care, you can probably skip this section. Otherwise, read on.

To insert nonprinting characters (e.g., control characters) into a buffer, use the **C-q** command ("q" stands for "quote the following character"). For example, to insert **C-l** into a buffer (to cause a formfeed in a printout), type **C-q C-l**. Emacs then displays **^L** in the window at the current cursor location.

An alternative method is to insert an octal code; this is done by pressing **C-q** followed by three octal digits. This method is typically used for character codes greater than 127. For example, to insert the character code 255 (octal 377) in a buffer, you would type **C-q 3 7 7**, which is displayed in the echo area as you type it. Then, Emacs inserts **\377** into the window at the cursor location.

Note that moving the cursor over such control characters causes the cursor to jump over the entire control-character sequence, as shown in Figure 3.1.

```
Insert █^L to get a newpage.        Cursor starts before ^L

Insert █L to get a newpage.         C-f moves to the ^

Insert ^L█to get a newpage.         C-f skips L
```

Figure 3.1. Skipping Over Control Characters

Working with Words, Sentences, and Paragraphs

One of the most time-saving features of Emacs is its ability to operate on entire words, sentences, and paragraphs. For example, there are commands to "kill the next word," "move to the end of the sentence," and "place the cursor at the start of a paragraph and mark at the end" (forming a region around the paragraph).

Typically, you would use these commands in Text mode, which is the best mode for editing such human-language constructs. To enable Text mode in a buffer, use the **M-x text-mode** command.

Words

Table 3.1 lists the commands for working with words. An easy way to remember these commands is that they mirror similar commands for working with characters. For example, **C-f** moves forward one character, and **M-f** moves forward one word; **C-d** deletes a character and **M-d** kills a word.

Table 3.1. Commands That Operate on Words

Operation	Command and Comments
Move forward one word	**M-f** Moves the cursor to the start of the next word.
Move backward one word	**M-b** Moves to the start of the current or previous word.
Delete to the end of a word	**M-d** Deletes all characters from the current cursor position to the end of the word.
Delete backward to the beginning of a word	**M-DEL** Deletes all characters from the current cursor position to the beginning of the word.
Mark the end of the next word	**M-@** Sets a mark at the character following the current word.
Transpose two words	**M-t** If the cursor lies on the first character of the word, transposes the current word and the following word. If the cursor lies between two words, transposes the current word and the preceding word.

Sentences

Emacs assumes a sentence ends with a period (.), question mark (?), or exclamation point (!) followed by a line end or two spaces. As well, a sentence begins or ends wherever a paragraph begins or ends.

Table 3.2 lists commands for working with sentences. You can include an argument to make the command operate multiple times. A negative argument reverses the action of a command. For example, `C-u -2 M-a` moves the cursor *forward* to the beginning of the second sentence, rather than backward as it normally does. Using minus one (-1) as an argument causes `M-k` to delete back to the beginning of a sentence. Otherwise, an argument provides a repeat count.

A variable named *sentence-end* determines the recognition of a sentence by matching the last few characters and the following white space. See Chapter 13, "Customizing the Emacs Environment," for more information about variables.

Table 3.2. Commands That Operate on Sentences

Operation	Command and Comments
Move backward to the beginning of the sentence	`M-a` Moves the cursor backward to the first character of the current sentence.
Move forward to the end of the sentence	`M-e` Moves the cursor forward to the character following the end of the current sentence.
Delete to the end of the sentence	`M-k` Deletes all characters from the cursor to the end of the sentence, including ending punctuation.
Delete backward to the beginning of the sentence	`C-x DEL` Deletes all characters from the current cursor position to the beginning of the sentence.

Paragraphs

In Text mode, blank lines and formatting commands delimit paragraphs. In programming modes (discussed in Chapters 5 through 8), only blank lines delimit paragraphs. An indented line also begins a new paragraph. If a fill prefix is in effect (as described in the "Filling Text" section later in this chapter), paragraphs are delimited by lines that do not begin with the fill prefix.

Table 3.3 contains commands that let you perform operations on paragraphs. You can use numeric arguments similarly to the ways discussed in the last section.

Table 3.3. Commands That Operate on Paragraphs

Operation	Command and Comments
Move backward to the beginning of the paragraph	**M-[** When the cursor is in paragraph text, moves the cursor backward to the start of the current paragraph; when cursor is at the start of paragraph, moves the cursor backward to start of previous paragraph.
Move forward to the end of the paragraph	**M-]** Same as **M-[**, but moves the cursor forward.
Mark a region around the paragraph	**M-h** When the cursor is in paragraph text, moves the cursor to the start of the current paragraph and marks it as a region; if the cursor is in a space between paragraphs, marks the next paragraph as a region.

Working with Pages

A page is not necessarily a certain number of lines. A page is typically defined by the location of the ASCII formfeed character, Control-L (**^L**). Note that the **^L** must be placed at the start of a line to be interpreted as a page break. Emacs treats a page-separator character like any other character. You can insert it with **C-q C-l** and delete it with **DEL**. By inserting the character, you can paginate a file. Table 3.4 contains commands that let you perform operations on pages.

Table 3.4. Commands That Operate on Pages

Operation	Command and Comments
Move backward to top of page	`C-x [` Moves the cursor backward to the previous `^L` page break.
Move forward to top of next page	`C-x ]` Moves the cursor forward to the next `^L` page break.
Mark a region around the page	`C-x C-p` Marks a region around the current page, or around the next page when the cursor is between pages. The region includes the page delimiter. You can include an argument to specify the page to mark relative to the current page: 1 means the next page, 0 means this page, −1 means the previous page.

Count number of lines in this page	`C-x l`
	
	Displays the number of lines in the current page. For example,
	
	`Page has 82 (10+73) lines`
	
	Values enclosed in `()` show the location of the cursor. In this example, the cursor is on line 10 of the page. The sum is off by one when point is not at the beginning of a line.

Working with Blank Lines

Emacs provides two useful commands for creating and deleting blank lines in a file, summarized in Table 3.5.

Table 3.5. Commands That Operate on Blank Lines

Operation	Command and Comments
Open a blank line above the current line	`C-o` Inserts a newline at the cursor. When used at the start of a line, this has the effect of opening a line above the current line. When used within a line, it has the effect of breaking the line at the cursor position, while leaving the cursor on the same line, as shown in Figure 3.2.
Delete blank lines	`C-x C-o` This command deletes blank lines, but works differently, depending on the context of surrounding lines: • If the cursor is on a blank line surrounded by blank lines, `C-x C-o` deletes all but one blank line, thus compressing several blank lines into one. • If the cursor is on a blank line surrounded by nonblank lines, `C-x C-o` deletes the blank line. • If the cursor is on a nonblank line, followed by one or more blank lines, `C-x C-o` removes the following blank lines.

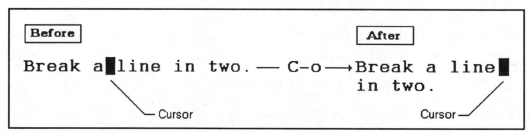

Figure 3.2. Behavior of C-o in Middle of a Line

Getting Cursor, Line, and Page Information

Emacs provides several useful commands for getting cursor position, line number and page number information, as summarized in Table 3.6. All these commands display their information in the echo area.

Table 3.6. Commands That Display Cursor, Line, and Page Information

Operation	Command and Comments
Display line number containing point	`M-x what-line` Displays the number of the line containing the cursor.
Display location, column and ASCII code of cursor character	`C-x =` Displays the following information (see Figure 3.3): • Location of the character in the buffer, including relative location expressed as a percent. • Column containing cursor (column 0 is left-most) • ASCII code for character including octal value.
Display number of lines in the current region	`M-=` Displays the number of lines in the current region.
Display the current page number	`M-x what-page` Displays the page number containing the cursor. If buffer has no `^L` characters, the page number is 1.

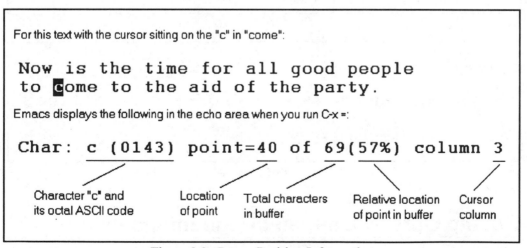

Figure 3.3. Cursor Position Information

Transposing Text

Table 3.7 lists commands that **transpose** (reverse the position of) characters, words, and lines. Often you use these commands to fix typing mistakes. For example, if you misspell `clear` as `clera`, you could move the cursor over the `a` and run `C-t`, which transposes (swaps) the two characters around point. (Remember that point actually lies immediately between the cursor's character and the previous character.)

Table 3.7. Commands That Transpose Text

Operation	Command and Comments
Transpose characters	`C-t` Transposes the two characters on either side of point: swaps the character under the cursor with the character immediately preceding the cursor.
Transpose words	`M-t` Transposes two words. How it works depends on the cursor's location (see Figure 3.4): • If the cursor is between two words, `M-t` swaps them. • If the cursor is on the first letter of a word, `M-t` swaps that word with the previous word. • If the cursor falls on a letter other than the first letter of a word, `M-t` swaps the word with the next word.
Transpose lines	`C-x C-t` Swaps the line containing the cursor with the previous line. If the cursor is on line 1, swaps it with the second line.

```
I got my mixed█talk up. ── M-t ──→ I got my talk mixed█up.
I got my mixed █alk up. ── M-t ──→ I got my talk mixed█up.
I got my mixed t█lk up. ── M-t ──→ I got my mixed up talk█
```

Figure 3.4. Transposing Words with M-t

Filling Text

Emacs supports commands for **filling** text. Filling means reformatting the text so that lines do not extend past a predefined **fill column**. Emacs filling commands use 70 as the default fill column. Figure 3.5 shows the relationship between the fill column and filled text.

```
Tom Smith awoke to the grinding sound of the
garbage truck crushing his neighbor's garbage.
Realizing that he'd forgotten to set out his
own garbage, he jumped out of bed, and raced
outside.
                                          Fill Column
```

Figure 3.5. Relationship Between Fill Column and Line Wrapping

If you wish, you can automate text filling by enabling Auto-Fill minor mode. In addition, you can specify that a **fill prefix**—a sequence of characters—be placed at the start of each line when text is filled. Before using these features, you should understand the commands described in Table 3.8.

Table 3.8. Commands That Fill Text

Operation	Command and Comments
Fill the current paragraph	`M-q` Fills the text in the paragraph containing the cursor. To right-justify text, include a numeric prefix.
Fill each paragraph in current region	`M-g` Fills text in all paragraphs in the current region. To right-justify text, include a numeric prefix.
Set the fill column	`C-x f` Without an argument, sets the fill column to the column containing the cursor. With an argument, sets the values as specified. The default value is 70.

Using the Fill Prefix

Occasionally, you may want all filled lines to begin with a particular string. For example, when responding to electronic mail messages, people often use prefix strings to indicate who said what in a series of messages—for example:

```
fred> Let's have a surprise birthday party for
fred> Karen who is turning 40 this Thursday.

pat> Maybe you shouldn't have included
pat> Karen on the distribution list for
pat> this mail message.

karen> It's OK.  It's not my birthday anyway,
karen> and even if it was, I wouldn't be 40!
```

The above text has three fill prefixes: `fred>`, `pat>`, and `karen>`.

Commands that fill text ignore the fill prefix. It is as if the fill prefix has zero length. The default fill prefix is `nil` (none). If you change the fill prefix, it applies only to the current buffer.

The `C-x .` (period) command sets the fill prefix. When you run this command, any text from the start of the line to the cursor is used as the fill prefix. A good way to use this command is to move the cursor to a blank line, type the fill prefix, then run the `C-x .` command. For example, to set the fill prefix to `:-)`, you would use the `C-x .` command as shown in Figure 3.6. Emacs then displays the message:

```
fill-prefix: ":-)"
```

Thereafter, filling commands will insert the fill prefix at the start of each filled line.

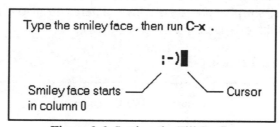

Figure 3.6. Setting the Fill Prefix

Enabling Auto-Fill Minor Mode

If you would like filling to occur automatically as you type text past the fill column, enable Auto-Fill minor mode with **M-x auto-fill-mode**. The mode line will be updated accordingly. For example, if you run **M-x auto-fill-mode** while in Text mode, the mode line shows **(Text Fill)**. To turn off Auto-Fill mode, run **M-x auto-fill-mode** again.

When Auto-Fill mode is on, it is possible to override auto-filling. Auto-filling normally occurs when you type **SPC** or **RET** when the cursor is past the fill column. To get around this, use **C-q SPC** or **C-q LFD**, respectively. **C-o** will also insert a newline without auto-filling.

If you like Auto-Fill mode and want to have it on all the time, you can customize your system to do this, as described in Chapter 13, "Customizing the Emacs Environment."

Indenting Text

Emacs provides powerful commands for indenting text. For example, programming major modes, such as C and FORTRAN modes, have special commands for indenting program lines in a style appropriate for the programming language. Indentation commands are also quite useful in Fundamental and Text modes; for example, there are commands to indent an entire region of lines. Using indentation commands in programming modes is discussed in Chapter 5, "Program Development in Emacs." This section discusses how to use indentation commands in Fundamental and Text modes.

Table 3.9 summarizes indentation commands and how they work in Fundamental and Text modes. These commands insert actual tabs, spaces, or a combination of both to indent lines. Occasionally, you may want to ensure that Emacs inserts a tab character; to do this, simply type **C-q TAB**. There are also ways to ensure that Emacs inserts only tabs or spaces (discussed below).

Table 3.9. Commands That Indent Text

Operation	Command and Comments
Center line	**M-s** Indents the current line so that it is centered between the left margin (column 0) and the current fill column. Can be used with numeric arguments to center multiple lines.

Table 3.9, con't.

Operation	Command and Comments
Indent to next tab stop	**TAB** or **M-i** (programming modes) In Fundamental and Text modes, **TAB** causes Emacs to insert spaces or tabs to the next **tab stop**. By default, tab stops are set to every 8th column, out to column 120. Like a typewriter, Emacs allows you to set tab stops (described in the next section, "Setting Tab Stops"). Note that in programming modes, **TAB** does not work as described here. To get the same functionality in those modes, use **M-i** instead.

Indent lines to same level	**C-M-**
	
	Given a numeric argument, **C-M-** indents all lines in a region to the specified level. For example, given the following lines:
	
	`    Line one.`
	`              Line two.`
	`          Line three.`
	
	`C-u 4 C-M-\\` indents all lines to column 4:
	
	`        Line one.`
	`        Line two.`
	`        Line three.`
	`    ↑`
	`    Column 4`

Table 3.9, con't.

Operation	Command and Comments

Indent lines rigidly	`C-x TAB`
	
	Given a numeric argument, `C-x TAB` indents all lines in a region sideways (rigidly) by the specified amount. For example, given the lines:
	
	`    Line one.`
	`        Line two.`
	`            Line three.`
	`↑ ↑    ↑      ↑`
	`0 2    6      10 (column #)`
	
	`C-u 4 C-x TAB` indents all lines by 4 columns:
	
	`        Line one.`
	`            Line two.`
	`                Line three.`
	`↑ ↑    ↑    ↑      ↑`
	`0 2    6    10    14 (column #)`
	
	Note that negative arguments can be specified to this command, moving lines to the left. For example, `C-u -4 C-x TAB` would move the above lines back to their original positions.

Merge indented lines	`M-^` Merge a line with the previous line, removing indentation from the current line.

Split lines and indent	`C-M-o`
	
	Insert a newline at the cursor position and indent the remainder of the line to the cursor column.
	
	`    Split this line█and indent it.`
	
	becomes:
	
	`    Split this line█`
	`                    and indent it.`

Setting Tab Stops

As mentioned above, Emacs sets tab stops to every 8th column by default. To change tab stops, use the **M-x edit-tab-stops** command. If you run this command, Emacs creates a buffer named ***Tab Stops*** in Text mode with Overwrite and Auto-Fill minor modes enabled, as shown in Figure 3.7.

　　The colons on the first line represent tab stops. To change tab stops, simply type in colons where you want tab stops to appear. To install the changes into Emacs for the remainder of the editing session, type **C-c C-c**.

Figure 3.7. Setting Tab Stops

Converting Tabs to Spaces

To minimize the amount of characters in a buffer, Emacs uses both tabs and spaces to do indentation. For example, if you use **C-M-** to indent lines 12 spaces, Emacs actually inserts a tab followed by 4 spaces. Sometimes, this may be undesirable—for example, if you're editing files for a text formatting language that doesn't know how to treat tabs. Table 3.10 shows two commands to help you correct this problem.

Table 3.10. Commands That Convert Tabs to Spaces and Vice Versa

Operation	Command and Comments
Convert all tabs to spaces	**M-x untabify** In the current region, expands all tabs into spaces, preserving the indentation. (This is similar to using the UNIX **expand** filter on a file.)
Convert all spaces to tabs	**M-x tabify** In the current region, converts spaces to tabs, wherever possible, preserving indentation.

CHAPTER 3

Using Auto-Indent Mode

You can have a variation of Text mode called Indented Text mode by executing **M-x indented-text-mode**. You may want to use this mode when editing text in which most lines are indented. In this mode:

- All lines are automatically indented from the right margin.

- **TAB** indents lines relative to the automatic indentation.

- The auto filling feature and a **LFD** will indent the lines they create according to the previous line.

Changing Letter Case

The commands in Table 3.11 change the letter case of words and regions.

Table 3.11. Commands That Change Letter Case

Operation	Command and Comments
Convert a word to uppercase	**M-u** Converts to uppercase all characters from the cursor to the end of the word.
Convert a word to lowercase	**M-l** Converts to lowercase all characters from the cursor to the end of the word.
Capitalize a word	**M-c** Capitalizes the current word, leaving the character at the cursor uppercase and the following characters lowercase.
Convert a region to uppercase	**C-x C-u** Like **M-u**, but works on the current region.
Convert a region to lowercase	**C-x C-l** Like **M-l**, but works on the current region.

Searching and Replacing Text

In addition to incremental searches, Emacs can perform:

- Nonincremental searches

- Word searches (which match words, regardless of whether they occur at the start, middle, or end of a line)

- Noninteractive search-and-replace operations (which do a search-and-replace without verifying if it's OK first)

Nonincremental Searches

Emacs has two commands for doing nonincremental searches (shown in Table 3.12). These commands prompt for a search string and don't begin searching until you press **RET** to terminate the search string. If successful, these commands move the cursor to the matching text; otherwise, Emacs displays an error message.

Table 3.12. Commands for Nonincremental Searching

Operation	Command and Comments
Search forward	`C-s ESC` Performs a nonincremental search forward from the cursor. `C-s` invokes the incremental search command, displaying `I-search:` in the echo area. But when you press **ESC**, the prompt changes to `Search:`. You can then type the search string and press **RET**.
Search backward	`C-r ESC` Same as `C-s ESC`, but searches backward from the cursor.

Word Searches

A **word search** is a nonincremental search for a string delimited by blanks, tabs, newlines, or punctuation. Compare this with an incremental search, which finds **any** occurrence of the search string, regardless of whether it occurs within another word. For example, suppose you want to find the next occurrence of **King** in this text:

```
They carried the Viking, kicking and screaming, to the King.
```

If you used **C-s**, it would find **king** in **Viking** and **kicking** before finding the word you really want. If you used a word search instead, **King** would be the first word found. This is a contrived example; nevertheless, in larger blocks of text, such problems often arise. Table 3.13 summarizes the word searching commands.

Table 3.13. Commands for Word Searches

Operation	Command and Comments
Search forward	**C-s ESC C-w** Searches for word forward from the cursor. Prompts with: **Word search:** ▉ Type the word and press **RET**.
Search backward	**C-r ESC C-w** Same, but searches backward from the cursor.

Unconditional Search-and-Replace

The **M-%** command described in the previous chapter searches and replaces text, prompting you at each occurrence for whether you really want to replace it. To bypass this prompting, use the **M-x replace-string** command, which prompts for a search string and a string to replace it with. You should use this command only if you are absolutely confident you are replacing the correct text.

Narrowing a Buffer

Sometimes you may want to restrict, or **narrow**, your viewing and editing to a portion of the entire buffer. For example, you may want to perform a search-and-replace operation on a specific section of the buffer only.

To narrow your buffer to a particular region, first define or move to the desired region, then type **C-x n**. All text before and after the region disappears; it is still in the buffer, but it cannot be viewed or edited in any way. To indicate narrowing is in effect, the word **Narrow** appears in the mode line.

To turn off narrowing (**widen** the buffer), type **C-x w**.

Moving the Cursor to Previous Marks (the Mark Ring)

Occasionally, you may want to move the cursor back to the location of the current mark or to a previous mark. Emacs keeps track of previous mark locations in a construct called the **mark ring**. Each mark command (C-SPC or C-@) inserts the mark location into the mark ring. Each buffer has its own mark ring that holds the last 16 mark locations. If you run more than 16 mark commands, the oldest mark location is deleted to make room for the newest one. (You can change the size of the mark ring via the variable *mark-ring-max*. See Chapter 13, "Customizing the Emacs Environment," for more information about variables.)

To go to the previous mark location, run the mark command with a numeric argument (C-u C-SPC or C-u C-@). Executing this command repeatedly takes you further and further back in the mark ring until you eventually come back to the start. The best way to learn how to use this command is to experiment: Try setting mark in several different locations in a buffer; then run C-u C-SPC several times to see what happens.

Using the Kill Ring

With the exception of individually deleted characters, killed text is placed in a **kill ring**. This is the mechanism used to move and copy regions of text, as described in the previous chapter. Understanding how the kill ring works can improve your productivity and effectiveness with kill and yank commands.

Emacs has one kill ring for all buffers. Thus, you can kill or save text from one buffer and yank it into another.

You can think of the kill ring as a set of buckets into which you place killed text. Each kill command places text into the "most-recent bucket." In Emacs terminology, these buckets are known as **blocks**. When you yank text with C-y, Emacs pulls back text from the most recent block.

Emacs keeps track of the order of the blocks, assigning a number to each one. Thus, the most recent block is block 1; the second most recent block is block 2; and so on. If given a numeric argument, C-y yanks the numbered block from the kill ring. For example, C-u 2 C-y yanks the second most recent block from the kill ring. (See "Stepping Through the Kill Ring," later in this section, for details on an easier method of retrieving blocks from the kill ring.)

How Text Is Placed in the Kill Ring

As long as you run successive kill commands, without other intervening commands, Emacs continues to place the text in the most recent block. This enables you to run multiple deletion commands and retrieve the killed text with a single yank command. Commands that delete forward from point append the killed text to the most recent block. Commands that delete backward from point insert the text before the previously killed text. This allows Emacs to preserve the order of deleted text.

Table 3.14 illustrates the above concepts. Notice that the three consecutive deletion commands insert the killed text into the block in the correct order. Thus, running C-y brings the text back correctly. Note, also, that C-y does not destroy the contents of the block; they are merely copied from the block into the buffer.

Table 3.14. Effect of C-y on Most Recent Block

Step	Text in Buffer	Command	Effect on Most Recent Block
1.	Line one. ■ine two. Line three. Line four.	C-k C-k	Line two.
2.	Line one. ■ine three. Line four.	M-d	Line two. Line
3.	Line one. ■three Line four.	M-DEL	one. Line two. Line
4.	Line ■three. Line four.	C-y	one. Line two. Line
5.	Line one. Line two. Line■three. Line four.		one. Line two. Line

Running a nondeletion command tells Emacs to place the next killed text in a new block in the kill ring. This new block becomes the most recent block, while the other blocks are shifted appropriately: The previous block 1 becomes block 2, block 2 becomes block 3, and so on. Running C-y in step 4 of the above example does just that. If you now issued a **C-k** command, Emacs places "three." in the most recent block and shifts the old contents to block 2.

The kill ring has a limit. On our system, there can be at most 30 blocks in the kill ring. (This can be changed—see Chapter 13, "Customizing the Emacs Environment.") Eventually, the kill ring becomes full. When this happens, the oldest block's contents are removed, making room for the latest yanked text.

Stepping Through the Kill Ring

An easier way of yanking older blocks in the kill ring is to step through them and visually inspect their contents. To do this, run **C-y**; then run **M-y**, which replaces the most recently yanked text with the previous block in the kill ring. So, for example, you could yank the next-to-last block in the kill ring by running **C-y M-y**.

Each successive **M-y** command displays the next previous block in the kill ring. Eventually, when you reach the maximum length of the kill ring, **M-y** cycles back to the most recent block. Thus, you can "step through" all the blocks in the kill ring with **M-y**.

As with the **C-y** command, **M-y** does not destroy the contents of blocks in the kill ring; it merely retrieves them. Also, **M-y** has no effect on which block is the most recent. If you run several **M-y** commands, **C-y** still retrieves the most recent block.

Completing Long Command Names

When you run **M-x** commands, Emacs has a string-completion feature. After typing **M-x** you can type a partial command name and press **TAB**. If the portion of the command name you type uniquely identifies the command, Emacs will finish it for you. For example, if you type **M-x goto-l TAB**, Emacs displays **M-x goto-line** in the echo area. To run the command, press **RET**.

If the typed portion does not uniquely identify the command, Emacs completes the command only as far as it is unique. For example, if you type **M-x wha TAB**, Emacs completes the command up to the point where multiple matches are possible, and displays the partially completed command in the echo area:

```
M-x what-█
```

In addition, Emacs may display a list of possible completions in another window (on some systems, you must press **TAB** a second time to see this):

```
Possible completions are:
what-cursor-position            what-line
what-page
```

If you wanted to run the **what-page** command, you could type **p** and press **TAB**; Emacs completes the command name in the echo area:

```
M-x what-page█
```

Press **RET** to run the command. Emacs then kills the window containing the possible completions (see "Editing Your Responses in the Minibuffer" in Chapter 4).

Completing File Names

Like the command name completion feature, Emacs provides a similar file name completion capability. This is used with commands that prompt for a file name. For example, **C-x C-f** (visit a file) prompts for a file in the echo area with:

```
Find file: ~/█
```

The tilde (~) is a shorthand for the path name of your home directory. Now suppose you have three files in your home directory named **foo**, **forms**, and **fortran**. If you typed **f** and **TAB**, Emacs would complete as much of the file name for you as possible—in this case "fo":

```
Find file: ~/fo█
```

In addition, Emacs displays a list of possible completions in another window (on some systems, you must press **TAB** again to see this):

```
Possible completions are:
foo                        forms
fortran
```

To visit the file **fortran**, you could type **rt** to distinguish it from the **forms** file; then press **TAB**. Emacs completes the rest of the file name for you:

```
Find file: ~/fortran█
```

To visit this file, press **RET**. Emacs then removes the list of possible completions.

Completion also works with directories. If you have a complete path name for a directory, pressing **SPC** causes Emacs to display a list of files in the directory. For example, to list all the files in your home directory, press **SPC** at the prompt:

```
Visit file: ~/█
```

All the files are displayed in another window, as with the **TAB** command. Once you select a file, the possible selections disappear.

Using Abbreviations (Text Expansions)

To Emacs, an **abbreviation** is text that expands to longer text as you type it. For example, you can define the abbreviation **stc** for the text "Society for Technical Communication". Thereafter, when you type the letters **stc** followed by any nonword character (for example, punctuation or **SPC** or **RET**), Emacs expands it to "Society for Technical Communication". Notice that in addition to conserving keystrokes, abbreviations help reduce typos inherent in repeatedly typing long strings.

Enabling Abbreviations

Most commands for creating, modifying, and using abbreviations work only in Abbrev minor mode. Some commands, such as **M-/**, which retypes long words, work even when Abbrev minor mode is disabled. To enable Abbrev mode, run **M-x abbrev-mode**. To turn off Abbrev mode, run **M-x abbrev-mode** again, or run it with a negative argument (**C-u - M-x abbrev-mode**).

Any abbreviations defined during Abbrev mode are remembered for the duration of the editing session, but can be used only when Abbrev mode is enabled. Later in this section we will describe commands to save frequently used abbreviations in files, which can then be read back for use later.

Some modes—for example, FORTRAN mode—have their own built-in abbreviations. Such **mode-specific abbreviations** can only be accessed when Abbrev minor mode is enabled.

Defining Abbreviations

There are two main types of abbreviations, global and mode-specific. **Global abbreviations** apply to all modes, while **mode-specific abbreviations** can be used only in the mode in which they are defined. For example, if you define a global abbreviation in Text mode, you can use that abbreviation in any other mode. However, if you define a mode-specific abbreviation, you can use it only in buffers that use Text mode. Table 3.15 summarizes the different commands for setting abbreviations.

Table 3.15. Defining Abbreviations

Operation	Command and Comments

Create *global* abbrev for word(s) before cursor	`C-x +`
	
	With the cursor positioned at the end of a word, this command prompts for the abbreviation string that you want to expand to the word. The abbreviation is made *global*. For example, if the cursor follows the word `subroutine`, and you run `C-x +`, Emacs prompts with:
	
	    `Global abbrev for "subroutine":`
	
	To create an abbreviation named `;sub`, you would type that string and press **RET**. Thereafter, whenever you type `;sub` followed by **SPC**, **RET**, or punctuation, Emacs inserts the expansion text "subroutine". Since the abbreviation is global, it will work in any buffer that has enabled Abbrev minor mode.
	
	You will often want to create an abbreviation for multiple words. To do this, specify a numeric argument for the number of words preceding the cursor. For example, if the words "United States of America" precede the cursor, you can define an abbreviation for them with `C-u 4 C-x +`.

Create *mode-specific* abbrev for word(s) before cursor	`C-x C-a` Same as `C-x +`, but creates a *mode-specific* abbreviation. This abbreviation is expanded only in buffers that use the same mode and that have enabled Abbrev minor mode.

Table 3.15, con't.

Operation	Command and Comments

Assign expansion text to *global* abbrev before cursor	`C-x -`
	
	Unlike `C-x +`, `C-x -` expects the text before the cursor to be the abbreviation string; it prompts for the expansion text. It then assigns the text before the cursor as a global abbreviation for the expansion text you typed. For example, if the cursor follows the letters `usa`, you can define the expansion text by running `C-x -`. Emacs prompts:
	
	    `Global expansion for "usa":`
	
	To make `usa` expand to "United States of America", type this string and press **RET**. Thereafter, the abbreviation can be used in all buffers that have enabled Abbrev minor mode.

Assign expansion text to *mode-specific* abbrev before cursor	`C-x C-h` Same as `C-x -`, but creates a mode-specific abbreviation. This abbreviation is expanded only in buffers that use the same mode and that have enabled Abbrev minor mode.

If you try to redefine an existing abbreviation, Emacs asks you to verify before replacing it. For example, if you attempted to redefine the `usa` abbreviation defined by the `C-x -` command in Table 3.15, Emacs would prompt with:

    `usa expands to "United States of America"; redefine (y or n)`

Letter Case in Abbreviations

Another interesting feature of abbreviations is that Emacs uses the same letter case in expansion text as used in the abbreviation string. For example, if you define `func` to expand to "function", then type `FUNC` as the abbreviation, Emacs expands it to "FUNCTION". Similarly, if only the first letter of the abbreviation is uppercase, Emacs expands the text the same way. For example, `Func` expands to "Function".

Expanding Abbreviations

As mentioned above, the normal way to expand an abbreviation is to type it, followed by **SPC**, **RET**, **TAB**, or any punctuation. This allows you to conveniently type along as you normally would, without having to run special commands to insert the expansion text. Normally, this is sufficient for most abbreviations, but there are occasions when it is not. For example, what if you want to expand an abbreviation when Abbrev mode is not enabled? Or what if you want to expand an abbreviation *within* a larger word (for example, expand `func` to "functional" after the prefix **dys**, making the word "dysfunctional")? Table 3.16 describes commands for doing such actions with abbreviations.

Table 3.16. Expanding Abbreviations

Operation	Command and Comments
Separate prefix text from abbrev	**M-'** (Meta-apostrophe) Expands abbreviations after a prefix. For example, suppose you define the abbreviation `fm` to expand to "formation". This abbreviation could also be used after prefixes such as `in` (information) and `mal` (malformation). However, if you type `infm` and press **SPC**, Emacs cannot expand the word to "information" because it thinks the abbreviation is `infm`, which is not defined. To override this behavior, use the **M-'** command to separate the prefix from the abbreviation. Using the above example, you would: 1. Type `in`. 2. Run **M-'**. Emacs then displays `in-`. 3. Type `fm`. Emacs displays `in-fm`. 4. Press **SPC**. Emacs expands the abbreviation and removes the hyphen.
Expand abbrev before cursor (when not in Abbrev mode)	**C-x '** (C-x apostrophe) Expands an abbreviation when Abbrev minor mode is not enabled. Running this command at the end of an abbreviation acts just as if you typed a **SPC**, **TAB**, **RET**, or punctuation in Abbrev mode.

Table 3.16, con't.

Operation	Command and Comments
Undo the last abbrev expansion	**M-x unexpand-abbrev** Undoes the last abbreviation expansion, leaving the character that caused the expansion. **C-x u** (undo) also works, but removes the character that caused the expansion.
Expand abbrevs in current region	**M-x expand-region-abbrevs** Expands abbreviations in the current region. For each abbreviation in the region, Emacs moves the cursor to the end of the abbreviation text and prompts in the minibuffer with: **Expand this? (y or n)** If you type **y**, Emacs expands the abbreviation; otherwise, it leaves the abbreviation text unexpanded.

Listing Abbreviations

For each abbreviation defined, Emacs stores the following information:

1. The abbreviation text

2. The expansion text

3. How many times the abbreviation has been expanded

You can view this information using **M-x list-abbrevs**, which displays all mode-specific and global abbreviations defined in the current editing session. It displays this information in a buffer named ***Abbrevs*** that uses a special Edit-Abbrevs mode. Figure 3.8 shows how the window for this buffer looks on our system.

In this particular example, the mode-specific abbreviations are listed for C, Text, Lisp, and Fundamental modes. Because abbreviations are not yet defined for these modes, the lines following each heading are blank. Notice, however, that the mode line indicates that only the top part of the buffer is displayed. To see if there are any abbreviations defined, run **C-x 4 b *Abbrevs* RET** or **C-x o** to move the cursor into the ***Abbrevs*** window and scroll through it, looking for defined abbreviations.

```
(o-mode-abbrev-table)

(text-mode-abbrev-table)

(lisp-mode-abbrev-table)

(fundamental-mode-abbrev-table)

-----Emacs: *Abbrevs*      9:39pm 0.01 Mail (Edit-Abbrevs Fill)----Top---
```

Figure 3.8. Listing Abbreviations

On our system, scrolling to the bottom of the buffer revealed the global definitions shown in Figure 3.9. This indicates that:

1. There are three global abbreviations: **usa**, **fm**, and **func**.

2. They expand to "United States of America", "formation", and "function", respectively.

3. The abbreviation **usa** has been used 4 times; **fm** has been used 5 times; and **func**, 3 times.

```
(lisp-mode-abbrev-table)

(fundamental-mode-abbrev-table)

(global-abbrev-table)
"usa"        4       "United States of America"
"fm"         5       "formation"
"func"       3       "function"

-----Emacs: *Abbrevs*      9:39pm 0.01 Mail (Edit-Abbrevs Fill)----Bot---
```

Figure 3.9. Global Abbreviations Listing

This information is useful to see exactly how abbreviations are defined, as well as to determine how often abbreviations are used. If an abbreviation is seldom used, you can delete it (as described below).

Modifying Abbreviations

In most cases, it is easiest to modify an abbreviation by redefining it. For example, suppose you had defined **fm** to expand to "formation", but now you want it to expand to "information" instead. To do this, you could simply use one of the commands to define the abbreviation again.

In some cases, though, this method may not be sufficient—for example, if you wanted to delete an abbreviation altogether. For such modifications, Emacs provides the **M-x edit-abbrevs** command. This command displays abbreviations in exactly the same format as the **M-x list-abbrevs** command. The difference is that you can edit the abbreviation information and save it with the **C-c C-c** command. Thereafter, the changes you made to the abbreviations stay in effect till the end of the editing session or until changed again.

An example should help clarify. Suppose when you run **M-x edit-abbrevs**, it lists the global abbreviations shown in Figure 3.9 above. If you were to kill the line containing the definition for **func**, then run **C-c C-c** to save the changes, the string **func** would no longer expand to "function". Similarly, you could modify the abbreviation text—changing "formation" to "information" for example.

Removing All Abbreviations

Occasionally, you might want to purge all abbreviations defined in the editing session. Use the **M-x kill-all-abbrevs** command to do this.

Saving Abbreviations for Later Use

If you have a set of abbreviations that you use often, it is useful to save these abbreviations for use in a later Emacs session. Table 3.17 summarizes Emacs commands for doing this.

Table 3.17. Saving and Retrieving Abbreviations

Operation	Command and Comments
Write abbrevs to file	**M-x write-abbrev-file** Writes all currently defined abbreviations into a file that can be read later. Prompts you with: **Write abbrev file:** ▮ Specify the name of the file in which you want to save definitions.

Table 3.17, con't.

Operation	Command and Comments

Read abbrevs from file	`M-x read-abbrev-file`
	
	Reads back an abbreviation file created by `M-x write-abbrev-file`. Prompts with:
	
	`Read abbrev file: ▮`

Define abbrevs from buffer	`M-x define-abbrevs` Causes Emacs to define abbreviations from the contents of the current buffer. The abbreviation definitions must be of the same format as that displayed by an `*Abbrevs*` buffer.
Retrieve abbrevs into buffer	`M-x insert-abbrevs` Inserts abbreviation definition information into current buffer. You can edit the abbreviations, then: 1. Install the definitions into the current editing session with `M-x define-abbrevs`. 2. Save it to a file that can be read and installed later using `M-x read-abbrev-file`.

Retyping Long Words with Dynamic Abbreviation Expansion

If you find yourself typing long words repeatedly, the **M-/** command allows you to retype such words without actually defining an abbreviation. This is known as **dynamic abbreviation expansion.**

To use this command:

1. You must have already completely typed the word you want to retype.

2. When you want to retype the word, you must type the first few letters that uniquely match the word you already typed in step 1.

3. Then issue the **M-/** command. This command looks backward from the cursor to the previous word whose first characters match those typed in step 2.

For example, suppose you are writing a report that frequently uses the word "antidisestablishmentarianism." To use dynamic abbreviation expansion, you would go ahead and type the full word the first time you use it. Then, the next time you need to type it, you could type the uniquely identifying letters `antidis`, then run **M-/**, and Emacs would expand it to the full word (assuming that there were no intervening words that matched `antidis`). Figure 3.10 shows how **M-/** works.

```
        1. You must type the whole
           word the first time.
   ─────────────────────────────────
Antidisestablishmentarianism is an extremely long
word to type. To use dynamic abbreviation expansion
to retype this word, first type letters that uniquely
match the word--for example antidis
                                   ───────
                    2. Now type the
                       unique letters.

   ...word--for example antidisestablishmentarianism
                                                    ──
                             3. Now run M-/ and Emacs
                                expands the rest of it.
```

Figure 3.10. Dynamically Expanding Words

If you typed only **a** before running **M-/** in this example, Emacs would expand **a** to "abbreviation" because, looking backward from the cursor, that is the next word that matches **a**. Therefore, it is important to type text that uniquely identifies the start of the word you want to expand. In the example above, **an** would have been enough to uniquely identify "antidisestablishmentarianism".

Using Macros for Repeated Editing Tasks

Emacs lets you define and use keyboard macros. A **macro** is similar to the abbreviations discussed in the last section, but instead of defining a short cut for a word or phrase, macros define short cuts for command sequences. If you need to repeat an editing task that requires running several commands, you can define a macro to run the commands with just a few keystrokes.

Why Use a Macro?

Macros are useful whenever you have to do repetitious editing tasks. In general, if you find yourself running a sequence of commands over and over again, it may be more efficient to define a macro for the commands.

A prime example is the task of converting text from one format or style to another. For instance, suppose you want to convert lists of textual items from this format:

```
This  chapter  covers  these  topics:   using  numeric  arguments;
inserting control characters into a buffer; working with words,
sentences, and paragraphs; working with pages...
```

Into this format:

```
This chapter covers these topics:

* Using numeric arguments
* Inserting control characters into a buffer
* Working with words, sentences, and paragraphs
* Working with pages...
```

To do this, you would have to repeatedly perform the following editing tasks, each of which involves one or more Emacs commands:

1. Find the start of the next list item.

2. Put the list item on a new line.

3. Put "*" in front of the line.

4. Capitalize the first word.

5. Go to the end of the list item and delete the semicolon.

If you defined a macro to do these tasks, you could then run the macro (just like any other Emacs command) for each list item. Imagine the time and effort it could save if there were several list items to convert.

Defining Macros

Once you've identified a sequence of commands to make into a macro, you can define the macro as follows:

1. Run C–x (to begin the macro definition.

2. Run the sequence of commands.

3. Run C–x) to end the macro definition.

You can now run the macro using C–x e, which runs the last macro defined. If you specify a numeric argument, Emacs runs the macro the specified number of times; for example, C–u 4 C–x e runs the macro 4 times. A numeric argument of 0—C–u 0 C–x e—will run the macro as many times as possible.

You can also run the macro immediately after ending it by specifying a numeric argument to the **C-x)** command; for example, **C-u 100 C-x)** ends the macro definition, then runs the macro 100 times.

If you wish to add additional commands to the end of the current macro, run **C-u C-x (**, type the additional commands, then run **C-x)** to end the macro. The effect is the same as if you had run the macro, followed by the additional commands.

After defining a macro, you should consider naming the macro, as described next.

To Name or Not to Name

Naming a macro allows you to run that macro with **M-x**, just as if it were any Emacs command. For example, if you named a macro **ace**, you could run it with **M-x ace**. Since you can use **C-x e** to run the last macro defined, why should you name a macro? There are two main reasons:

1. **You use multiple macros.** Naming a macro allows you to distinguish it from other macros. If you define a new macro without giving a name to the previous one, you lose the capability to run the previous one!

2. **You want to save a macro for use in a later editing session.** When you quit Emacs, macro definitions are lost unless you explicitly save them for later retrieval.

Basically, the only macros that don't need naming are "disposable" ones that you define, run several times in succession, then discard.

Naming and Running a Macro

To name the last macro defined, run **M-x name-last-kbd-macro**, which prompts:

> **Name for last kbd macro:** █   ← Type the name, then press RET

Keep macro names short and meaningful. For instance, in the example above, you might name the macro **list** or **lc** (for list convert).

To run the macro, use **M-x** followed by the macro name—for example, **M-x list RET** or **M-x lc RET**. (You could also use **C-x e** to run the macro until you define a new one, at which point you must refer to the macro by its name.) You can specify a repeat count to named macros (the same as with **C-x e**).

Saving Macros

To understand the process of saving and retrieving macros, it helps to know a little about how Emacs keeps track of macros. If you would rather not learn this, you can skip down to the steps below for saving a macro.

Internally, Emacs encodes macros in Emacs-Lisp code, which is the computer programming language in which much of Emacs is written. In other words, when you define a macro, Emacs generates some Emacs-Lisp code that tells Emacs what to do when you run the macro. For example, Figure 3.11 shows the Emacs-Lisp code for a macro named `list` on our system.

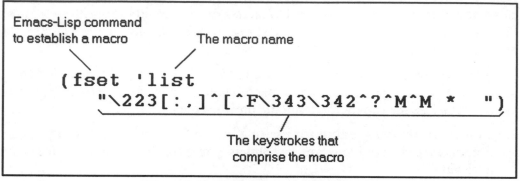

Figure 3.11. Emacs-Lisp Code for Macro

Therefore, saving macros involves saving the Emacs-Lisp code to a file, which you then "load" into the Emacs environment in a later editing session. Doing this requires the following steps:

1. **Decide what file to store the macro definitions in.** Often, users store macros in their Emacs start-up file (`.emacs`), which Emacs reads each time you start it. Macros saved this way are installed whenever you start Emacs. (For details on using a start-up file, see Chapter 13, "Customizing the Emacs Environment.")

   Another useful strategy is to store the macros in the directory in which they are most frequently used. In this case, you must explicitly load the macros for them to take effect. This allows you to have custom macros for different project directories.

2. **Visit the file.** For example, to store the macros in your `.emacs` start-up file, run `C-x C-f ~/.emacs RET`.

3. **Run `M-x insert-kbd-macro` to insert the macro definition into the buffer.** Emacs then prompts for the name of the macro you want to insert. For instance, to insert the macro named `list`, respond to the prompt as follows:

```
Insert kbd macro (name): list RET
```

If run with the **C-u** prefix (**C-u M-x insert-kbd-macro**), this command also inserts code for any custom key bindings you may have defined for the macro. (Setting key bindings is described in Chapter 13, "Customizing the Emacs Environment.")

Note: Make sure you insert the definition code in a place that makes sense. For example, don't insert the definition in the middle of another definition or within other Emacs-Lisp code.

4. **Save the file.** Later, you can load and "install" the macros. If you saved the definitions in your **.emacs** file, they are automatically installed when you start your next editing session.

Retrieving Saved Macros

If you saved macro definitions in your **.emacs** start-up file, they are automatically loaded and installed whenever you start Emacs. If you saved them in some other file, you must explicitly load them using **M-x load-file**, which prompts for the file name. For example, if you saved your macro definitions in a file named **~/convertMacros**, you would respond to the prompt as follows:

```
Load file: ~/convertMacros RET
```

This command, which is described in more detail in Chapter 8, "Editing in Lisp Modes," reads and evaluates a file containing Emacs-Lisp code, installing the code into the current editing session. It does *not* create a buffer for the file.

Including a Query in a Macro Definition

The **C-x q** command lets you include a query feature in your macro definition. This works as follows:

1. Define a macro as described above.

2. At points in the definition where you want a query to occur, type **C-x q**. Nothing occurs at this point, but later, when you use the macro, the **C-x q** causes the macro to query you for a character that determines how to continue.

In response to a macro query, you can use the commands shown in Table 3.18.

Table 3.18. Query Commands

Command	Action
SPC	Continue executing the macro.
DEL	Skip the rest of this macro and start again at the beginning of the macro at the next place where the macro is valid.
C-d	Skip the rest of this macro and cancel further use (repetition) of the macro.
C-l	Redraw the screen and ask for a character to specify continued operation of the macro.
C-r	Enter a recursive editing level in which you can perform editing that is not part of the macro. Execute C-M-c to exit any recursive editing.

Note: Using a prefix argument alters the behavior of C-x q. If you provide a prefix argument during the definition of a macro, you enter a recursive editing level in which typed text or commands do not become part of the macro. If you do this while using a macro, you enter a recursive editing level in which typed text or commands are not part of any operations performed by the macro. In either case, execute C-M-c to end the recursive editing.

An Example of Using Macros

Suppose you receive a file containing a report written in a text-formatting language that encodes chapter, section, and subsection headings as follows:

<chap>*Chapter Title*

<sec>*Section Title*

<subsec>*Subsection Title*

Unfortunately, you don't have the text processor that reads the files and converts the headings into appropriate fonts. In fact, all you have is a "dumb" printer that can only do typewriter fonts. But you would still like to be able to print the file and be able to differentiate headings for chapter, section, and subsection titles. One way to do this would be:

1. If a line starts with **<chap>**, strip off the prefix, make the line all uppercase, and center the line.

2. If a line starts with **<sec>**, strip off the prefix and make the line all uppercase.

3. If a line starts with **<subsec>**, strip off the prefix and underline the line.

That is, given the text:

```
<chap>A Quick Tour of Emacs

<sec>Starting Emacs

<sec>The Mode Line

<subsec>Status

<subsec>System

<subsec>Buffer Name

<sec>The Echo Area
```

You want to change it to:

```
                    A QUICK TOUR OF EMACS

STARTING EMACS

THE MODE LINE

Status

System

Buffer Name

THE ECHO AREA
```

Table 3.19 contains the sequence of commands for defining a macro named **chap** to convert the next **<chap>** line as described above. The macros for **<sec>** and **<subsec>** lines are left as an exercise.

Table 3.19. Procedure for Defining the chap Macro

Command	Action
`C-x (`	Begin the definition.
`C-s <chap> ESC`	Search for "<chap>".
`C-x q`	Ask if it's OK to continue. Do this to ensure that you don't accidentally do the macro on an inappropriate line.
`C-u 6 DEL`	Backspace over the "<chap>" string.
`C-SPC`	Set the mark at the start of the chapter title.
`C-e`	Move the cursor to the end of the line, thus defining a region around the title.
`C-x C-u`	Change the title to all uppercase.
`M-s`	Center the line.
`C-x )`	End the macro definition.
`M-x name-last-kbd-macro RET chap RET`	Name the macro "chap".

You could now run this macro with either **C-x e** or **M-x chap**. If you run it again and it finds another line that matches **<chap>**, the **C-x q** command causes Emacs to display the message:

```
Proceed with macro? (Space, DEL, C-d, C-r or C-l)
```

As described previously under "Including a Query in a Macro Definition," you could type **SPC** to continue with the macro, or **DEL** to stop. The query feature, in this case, provides a nice safety net against accidentally changing the wrong text.

If you wanted to save the **chap** macro so that it is automatically installed the next time you start Emacs, do the following:

1. Run **C-x C-f ~/.emacs RET** to visit your start-up file.

2. Run **M->** to go to the end of the file.

3. Run **M-x insert-kbd-macro RET chap RET** to insert the code for the macro definition at the end of your start-up file.

4. Run **C-x C-s** to save the changes.

Scrolling Windows

Emacs provides several commands for scrolling text within a window. Commands for vertical scrolling (top to bottom) let you view the various parts of a large buffer. Commands for horizontal scrolling (left or right) are particularly useful for viewing programs that contain lines longer than the visible width of the screen.

When you scroll a window horizontally, lines of text are truncated. A **$** appears in the line to indicate the truncation. The **$** appears in the first column when the text is truncated to the left, and in the last column when the text is truncated to the right.

All scrolling commands accept numeric arguments. Try experimenting with negative, zero, and positive arguments to better understand the behavior.

Table 3.20 describes Emacs commands for scrolling text.

Table 3.20. Commands for Scrolling

Operation	Command and Comments
Scroll to next screen	**C-v** Moves the bottom two lines to the top of the window, bringing enough additional lines of text to fill the window. This lets you read the contents of a buffer a windowful at a time.
Scroll to previous screen	**M-v** Same as above, but the lines move down to reveal the previous text.
Scroll the screen left	**C-x <** The window scrolls to the left one screen-width less 2 columns. If a numeric argument is included, the screen moves left the specified number of columns. For example, **C-u 10 C-x <** scrolls the window 10 columns.

Table 3.20, con't.

Operation	Command and Comments
Scroll the screen right	`C-x >` Same as above, but the window scrolls to the right.
Redisplay all windows	`C-l` Clears the screen and redraws all windows, scrolling the current window so the cursor is centered. With a numeric argument, `C-l` does not redraw the screen, but instead scrolls the current window the number of lines specified by the argument and in the implied direction of the argument: **0** scrolls the window until the line containing the cursor is the top line; **5** scrolls the window until the cursor is 5 lines from the top; **−7** scrolls the window until the cursor is 7 lines from the bottom.

Working with Multiple Windows

Table 3.21 summarizes commands that split windows horizontally and vertically, and that delete windows. Splitting a window creates two new windows from the current window. Each window operates on the same buffer, and the cursor is initially in the same location in each window. However, you can move the cursor to different locations in each window, thus allowing you to edit separate parts of the same buffer simultaneously!

Note that deleting a window does not affect the buffer's contents; it merely removes the window from the Emacs screen. Additional commands for manipulating windows are covered in Chapter 4, "Advanced Editing."

Table 3.21. Commands for Manipulating Windows

Operation	Command and Comments
Split window vertically	`C-x 2` Divides the current window into duplicate top and bottom windows. The dividing "line" is a horizontal mode line. You can edit different parts of the buffer in each window. A numeric argument is interpreted as the height of the top window. For example, if the current window contains 10 lines, then `C-u 7 C-x 2` would replace the current window with a seven-line and a three-line window for the same buffer.
Split window horizontally	`C-x 5` Divides the current window into duplicate left and right windows. A vertical boundary is placed between the two windows. A numeric argument specifies the width of the first window; this is analogous to numeric arguments with `C-x 2`.
Delete current window	`C-x 0` Deletes the window containing the cursor. This is useful for removing a split window created by either `C-x 2` or `C-x 5`.
Delete all other windows	`C-x 1` Deletes all windows other than the window containing the cursor. This is useful for cleaning up an Emacs screen that has become cluttered with windows.
Move the cursor to another window	`C-x o` Moves the cursor to another window. Experiment with this command to see how it works.

Printing a Buffer

Besides escaping to a UNIX shell and executing the `lp` command, you can print text by executing Emacs commands.

Table 3.22 describes the Emacs printing commands. By default, Emacs uses the UNIX command `lpr` for printing. You can specify additional options to these commands via the *lpr-switches* variable. For more information, see Table D.55 in Appendix D.

Table 3.22. Commands for Printing Buffer Text

Operation	Command and Comments
Print with page headings	`M-x print-buffer` Sends the contents of the current buffer to the UNIX command `lpr -p`, which includes page headings that contain the file name and page number.
Print without page headings	`M-x lpr-buffer` Sends the contents of the current buffer to the UNIX `lpr` command without the `-p` option, which eliminates page headings.
Print region with page headings	`M-x print-region` Works like the `M-x print-buffer` command, but prints the current region.
Print region without page headings	`M-x lpr-region` Works like `M-x lpr-buffer`, but prints the current region.

Listing a Directory

Commands that let you manipulate, edit, and view files ask you to specify a file name. When you cannot remember the names of your files, you can list the files in a directory with the command, `C-x C-d` *dir_or_pattern*.

The *dir_or_pattern* means you can specify a directory path or a pattern. A pattern includes special wildcard characters (for example, `*` and `?`) according to the conventions for your UNIX system. If you do not include a directory specification, the command prompts you to enter one.

The listing appears in a buffer named `*Directory*` that uses Fundamental mode. This means you get a listing and no additional commands for manipulating the files. If you want to get a listing and be able to edit (manipulate) the files, use the Dired facility, which is described in Chapter 11. To get a long listing of files (a verbose listing), run `C-u C-x C-d` *dir_or_pattern*.

You can alter the `ls` command used to list files, as described in Chapter 13, "Customizing the Emacs Environment." For example, you could tell Emacs to use the `-t` option to list files in order of last modification rather than by file name.

Summary

Table 3.23 summarizes the main points in this chapter.

Table 3.23. Chapter 3 Summary

Topic	Summary
Specifying numeric arguments	• `C-u` *n command* (*n* is the numeric argument) • `M-`*d1* [`M-`*d2*...] command (*d1*, *d2*, etc., are digits of the numeric argument
Inserting control characters	• `C-q` `C-x` (`C-x` is the control character to be inserted) • `C-q` *octal_number*
Manipulating words	• Move forward one word: `M-f` • Move backward one word: `M-b` • Delete to end of word: `M-d` • Delete to beginning of word: `M-DEL` • Mark end of next word: `M-@` • Transpose two words: `M-t`
Manipulating sentences	• Move backward to beginning of sentence: `M-a` • Move forward to end of sentence: `M-e` • Delete to end of sentence: `M-k` • Delete to beginning of sentence: `C-x DEL`
Manipulating paragraphs	• Move backward to beginning of paragraph: `M-[` • Move forward to end of paragraph: `M-]` • Mark a region around paragraph: `M-h`

Table 3.23, con't.

Topic	Summary
Manipulating pages	• Move backward to top of page: `C-x [` • Move forward to top of next page: `C-x ]` • Mark a region around this page: `C-x C-p` • Count number of lines in this page: `C-x l`
Manipulating blank lines	• Split line or open a blank line above current line: `C-o` • Delete blank lines: `C-x C-o`
Displaying cursor, line and page info	• Display line number containing point: `M-x what-line` • Display information about character under cursor: `C-x =` • Display number of lines in current region: `M-=` • Display current page number: `M-x what-page`
Transposing text	• Transpose characters: `C-t` • Transpose words: `M-t` • Transpose lines: `C-x C-t`
Filling (formatting) text	• Fill current paragraph: `M-q` • Fill current region: `M-g` • Set the fill column: `C-x f` • Set the fill prefix: `C-x .` • Enable Auto-fill minor mode: `M-x auto-fill-mode`
Indenting text	• Center a line: `M-s` • Indent to next tab stop: `TAB` or `M-i` • Move to first nonblank character: `M-m` • Indent lines to same level: `C-M-\` • Indent lines rigidly: `C-x TAB` • Merge indented lines: `C-^` • Split lines and indent: `C-M-o` • Set Indented Text mode: `M-x indented-text-mode`

Table 3.23, con't.

Topic	Summary
Set tab stops	• Set tab stops: `M-x edit-tab-stops`, set tab stops, then type `C-c C-c`
Tab/space conversion	• Convert all tabs to spaces: `M-x untabify` • Convert spaces to tabs where possible: `M-x tabify`
Changing letter case	• Convert word to uppercase: `M-u` • Convert word to lowercase: `M-l` • Capitalize a word: `M-c` • Convert region to uppercase: `C-x C-u` • Convert region to lowercase: `C-x C-l`
Nonincremental search	• Search forward: `C-s ESC` • Search backward: `C-r ESC`
Word search	• Search forward: `C-s ESC C-w` • Search backward: `C-r ESC C-w`
Unconditional search-and-replace	• Do not prompt before replacement: `M-x replace-string`
Narrowing the buffer	• Restrict (narrow) view to current region: `C-x n` • Restore (widen) view to entire buffer: `C-x w`
Moving through the mark ring	• Move to next/previous mark: `C-u C-SPC` or `C-u C-@`
Using the kill ring	• Step through and view contents of kill ring: `C-y`, then `M-y`
Completing long command and file names	• Type uniquely-identifying portion of command or file name, then press `TAB`

Table 3.23, con't.

Topic	Summary
Using abbreviations	• Enable/disable Abbrev mode: `M-x abbrev-mode` • Create global abbreviation for words before cursor: `C-x +` • Create local abbreviation for words before cursor: `C-x C-a` • Assign expansion text to global abbreviation before cursor: `C-x -` • Assign expansion text to local abbreviation before cursor: `C-x C-h` • Separate prefix text from abbreviation: `M-'` • Expand abbreviation before cursor (when not in Abbrev mode): `C-x '` • Undo the last abbreviation expansion: `M-x unexpand-abbrev` • Expand abbreviations in current region: `M-x expand-region-abbrevs` • List abbreviations: `M-x list-abbrevs` • Edit abbreviations: `M-x edit-abbrevs`, edit, then `C-c C-c` to save • Kill all abbreviations: `M-x kill-all-abbrevs` • Write abbreviations to a file: `M-x write-abbrev-file` • Read abbreviations from a file: `M-x read-abbrev-file` • Define abbreviations from a buffer: `M-x define-abbrevs` • Retrieve abbreviations into buffer: `M-x insert-abbrevs` • Dynamic abbreviation expansion: `M-/`

Table 3.23, con't.

Topic	Summary
Using macros	• Define a macro: 　• `C-x (` 　• Type commands 　• `C-x )` • Run last macro definition: `C-x e` • Add more commands to end of macro definition: 　• `C-u C-x (` 　• Type additional commands 　• `C-x )` • Name last macro definition: `M-x name-last-kbd-macro` • Run named macro: `M-x macro_name` • Save macros: 　• Visit file you will store macros in: `C-x C-f` *filename* 　• Run `M-x insert-kbd-macro` 　• Save the file • Retrieve saved macros: `M-x load-file` • Including queries during macro execution: `C-x q`
Scrolling text	• Scroll to next screen: `C-v` • Scroll to previous screen: `M-v` • Scroll screen left: `C-x <` • Scroll screen right: `C-x >` • Redisplay all windows: `C-l`
Manipulating windows	• Split window vertically: `C-x 2` • Split window horizontally: `C-x 5` • Delete current window: `C-x 0` • Delete all other windows: `C-x 1` • Move the cursor to another window: `C-x o`

Table 3.23, con't.

Topic	Summary
Printing a buffer	• Print buffer with page headings: `M-x print-buffer` • Print buffer without page headings: `M-x lpr-buffer` • Print region with page headings: `M-x print-region` • Print region without page headings: `M-x lpr-region`
Listing a directory	• `C-x C-d` *dir-or-pattern*

4
Advanced Editing

This chapter describes "advanced" Emacs features: capabilities that are more specialized and less frequently used.

Read this chapter selectively. The topics are presented in no particular order and are independent. However, you should understand the concepts presented in the previous chapters before attempting to read any of these sections.

This chapter covers the following topics:

- Changing Emacs' behavior with commands

- Changing Emacs' behavior with command-line arguments

- Searching for regular expressions (regexps)

- Searching and replacing regexps

- Editing outlines

- Manipulating buffers

- Advanced file operations

- Managing auto-saving

- Managing Emacs backup files

- Reverting a buffer to its original contents

- Preventing simultaneous editing

- Advanced window operations

- Editing your responses in the minibuffer

- Sorting text

- Using rectangles

- Using registers

Changing Emacs' Behavior with Commands

This section describes Emacs commands that let you customize Emacs' behavior. For information on changing Emacs' behavior with variables, see Chapter 13.

Changing the Goal Column for C-p and C-n Commands

By default, the **C-p** and **C-n** commands attempt to keep the cursor in the same column when moving from line to line. This behavior can be overridden with the *track-eol* variable (as described in Table 13.1 in Chapter 13, "Customizing the Emacs Environment"); it can also be changed by setting a **goal column**. If you set a goal column, Emacs attempts to keep the cursor in that column when moving from line to line with **C-p** and **C-n**.

To set the goal column, use the **C-x C-n** command, which sets the goal column to the current cursor column. To cancel the goal column and return to the default behavior, run **C-x C-n** with a numeric argument (**C-u C-x C-n**).

Displaying Date and Time in the Mode Line

As mentioned in Chapter 2, Emacs can display date, time, and system load information in the mode line. To enable this feature, run the **M-x display-time** command. To turn it off, run **M-x display-time** again.

Changing Emacs' Behavior with Command-Line Arguments

Command-line arguments are options to the **emacs** command that change some aspect of Emacs' behavior. For example, the following command line starts an Emacs session, retrieves the file named **report.txt** into a buffer, and moves the cursor to line 20:

```
emacs +20 report.txt
```

Command-line arguments are not required to use Emacs productively, but they can save a few steps in some tasks, and occasionally offer features that are not available by other means. Perhaps the most common reason for using arguments is to alter some aspect of the default Emacs behavior for one session only.

You may use as many arguments as you wish. Emacs processes arguments in the order you type them; some arguments must be listed before others. The arguments in

Table 4.1 must appear in the command line before the arguments in Table 4.2. In addition, if you use more than one argument from Table 4.1, they must be typed in the order they appear in the table. If they are not typed in the order shown, Emacs ignores them.

Table 4.1. Command-Line Arguments That Must Appear in a Specific Order

Argument	Description
`-t` *device*	Run Emacs in another window (X window systems) or on another terminal. For example, suppose you have two X windows on your display. You move to the window you want to run Emacs in and type the `tty` command to find out the *device* file for the window; `/dev/ttyp2` is returned. To run Emacs in the `ttyp2` window, you would execute the following command from *the other* window: `emacs -t /dev/ttyp2`

`-d` *display*	Run Emacs on another computer on the network, but route Emacs input and output to an X window on your display.
	
	Suppose you don't have Emacs installed on your computer, but you have an account on another computer that does have Emacs installed. If your *display* is named `xyz:0.0`, you could run Emacs on the other computer, and display Emacs on your display with:
	
	`emacs -d xyz:0.0`
	
	To find out the name of your *display*, type:
	
	`echo $DISPLAY`

Table 4.1, con't.

Argument	Description
`-batch`	Run Emacs in Batch mode. Usually, you will use this argument in conjunction with the `-l` or `-f` arguments, which load and run a Lisp program or function that operates on a file. Emacs sends all messages that would normally be displayed in the minibuffer to standard out (usually the screen); otherwise, Emacs runs invisibly. Files edited during the batch session are not saved unless you include commands to save them. The `.emacs` file is **not** read before the session is run. Batch processing can be interrupted with standard UNIX interrupt commands, such as `C-c`. See the example following Table 4.2.
`-q` or `-no-init-file`	Do not read the Emacs start-up file, `~/.emacs`, when you start this session.
`-u` *user* or `-user` *user*	Read another *user*'s `~/.emacs` file instead of loading your own. The file is assumed to be in the user's home directory. For example, to read the `.emacs` file for the user named `mary`, type: `emacs -u mary`

Table 4.2 contains arguments that can be used anywhere in the command line, provided they follow any arguments you include from Table 4.1.

Table 4.2. Command-Line Arguments That Can Appear in Any Order

Argument	Description
file	Visit *file*. For example: `emacs report.txt`

Table 4.2, con't.

Argument	Description
+*linenum* *file*	Visit *file* and move to the line numbered *linenum*. For example, to visit the file `report.txt` and move to line 20, type: `emacs +20 report.txt`
`-1` *file* or `-load` *file*	Load and execute the Lisp file named *file*. For example: `emacs -1 custom.el`
`-f` *function* or `-funcall` *function*	Call the Lisp function named *function* with no arguments. For example, the following command line starts Emacs, visits the file `report.txt`, and enables Abbrev minor mode for its buffer: `emacs report.txt -f abbrev-mode`
`-i` *file* or `-insert` *file*	Insert the contents of *file* into the buffer (same as executing `M-x insert-buffer`). For example, this command line starts Emacs, visits the file `report.txt` and moves the cursor to line 40, and inserts the contents of the file `may.data`: `emacs +40 report.txt -1 may.data`
`-kill`	When you start Emacs with this option, Emacs will **not** ask whether you want to save each modified file when you exit.

The following example demonstrates the power of command-line arguments. Suppose you have created a UNIX shell script that, among other things, needs to find all occurrences of the string `foo` in the file named `report.txt`, and replace them with the string `bar`. The following command, included in the shell script, would accomplish this:

```
emacs -batch report.txt -1 editfile.el -f save-buffer
```

This command performs the following sequence of operations:

1. Start Emacs in Batch mode (`-batch`).

2. Visit the file **report.txt**.

3. Load and run the Emacs-Lisp file **editfile.el** (**-l editfile.el**). This file contains the function:

```
(replace-string "foo" "bar" nil)
```

which, when evaluated, replaces all occurrences of the string **foo** with the string **bar** in the current buffer.

4. Save the buffer back to a file by evaluating the function **save-buffer** (**-f save-buffer**).

Notice that the *file* argument in this example (**report.txt**) is the second argument in the command line. You may be familiar with UNIX commands that require file specifications to be placed at the end of the command line, *after* all other arguments. Emacs does not have this requirement. In fact, if we had placed **report.txt** at the end of the command line, as in

```
emacs -batch -l editfile.el -f save-buffer report.txt
```

no editing would have occurred, because the **-l** and **-f** arguments would be executed before the file **report.txt** was visited. Remember, each argument performs some action, and the actions are performed in the order specified on the command line.

Searching for Regular Expressions (Regexps)

In addition to word-searching commands, Emacs provides commands that search for textual patterns. For example, you could search for the next word containing all uppercase letters, or the next line in which the first nonblank character is an asterisk, or the next line that does not contain the word "the." Such a textual pattern is defined using a **regular expression** (or **regexp** for short). Table 4.3 summarizes the Emacs commands that search for regular expressions.

Table 4.3. Commands That Search for Regular Expressions

Operation	Command and Comments
Incrementally search forward for regexp	`C-M-s` Prompts for a regexp and performs an incremental forward search for it, similar to the `C-s` command. If it finds the regexp, it positions the cursor at the first letter. The next time you invoke `C-M-s`, you can retrieve the last regexp you used by pressing `C-s` or `C-r`, which retrieve the forward and backward regexp, respectively.
Incrementally search backward for regexp	`M-x isearch-backward-regexp` Like `C-M-s`, but searches backward.
Nonincrementally search forward for regexp	`M-x re-search-forward` Like `C-M-s` but does not perform an incremental search. That is, it doesn't search as you type the regexp; it waits until you press RET at the prompt before searching. Another way to invoke this command is by running `C-M-s`, then pressing ESC.
Nonincrementally search backward for regexp	`M-x re-search-backward` Like `M-x re-search-forward`, but searches backward.

Emacs regexps are almost identical to UNIX regexps, such as those used by **vi**, **sed**, and **grep**. If you are familiar with UNIX regexps, you can skip the next section.

Constructing Regexps

To search for a text pattern, you must construct a regexp that matches it. A regexp consists of ordinary and special characters. **Ordinary characters** match only themselves. For example, the letters of the alphabet are ordinary characters. Searching for a regular expression that contains only ordinary characters is essentially the same as a normal incremental search. For example, the following search commands have the same effect:

```
C-s foobar        ← Incremental word search for "foobar"
C-M-s foobar      ← Incremental regexp search for "foobar"
```

Note that, by default, Emacs regular expressions are not case-sensitive: Lowercase letters match uppercase letters. To make search operations case-sensitive, set the variable *case-fold-search* to `nil`. To toggle back to case-insensitive searches, set *case-fold-search* to `t`.

Unlike ordinary characters, **special characters** do not match themselves; instead, they specify some general characteristic of a text pattern. For example, "." is a special character that matches any single character. Thus, the command **C-M-s** `...-....` searches for a string of at least three characters, followed by a hyphen, followed by at least four more characters. This particular regexp would match any of the following:

```
555-1212
fgh-klmn
444-22-3
```

In general, regexps do not match across line endings. Thus, the following text patterns would *not* match the above regexp:

```
12-3456                           Only two characters precede the hyphen


         foo-                     The pattern wraps across a line
bars                              ending
↑                 ↑
column 0          end of line
```

In Emacs regexps, the special characters are . (period), ^ (carat), $ (dollar sign), * (asterisk), + (plus sign), ? (question mark), [(opening bracket),] (closing bracket), and \ (backslash). Table 4.4 summarizes the meaning of these special characters in regexps.

Table 4.4. Special Characters in Regexps

To Match This	Use	Description
Any character	.	Matches any single character but the newline.

Table 4.4, con't.

To Match This	Use	Description
Start of line	^	When used at the start of a regexp, it matches the beginning of a line. For example, the regexp ^TAB matches a tab at the start of a line. When used *within* a regexp, it matches itself (i.e., it becomes an ordinary character). For example, the regexp .^ matches any character followed by ^.
End of line	$	When used at the end of a regexp, it matches the end of a line. For example, ^$ matches an empty line. When used *within* a regexp, it matches the dollar sign.
Zero or more occurrences of character	*	Matches zero or more occurrences of the previous ordinary character or group. (Groups are described later in this section.) For instance, run-*time matches runtime and run-time, as well as run---time.
One or more occurrences of character	+	Like * but matches *one or more* occurrences of the preceding ordinary character or group. For example, 00+ matches two or more consecutive zeros.
Zero or one occurrences of character	?	Matches zero or one occurrences of the preceding ordinary character or group. For example, run-?time matches only runtime and run-time.

Table 4.4, con't.

To Match This	Use	Description
Range of characters	[...]	The open bracket [indicates the start of a character range delimited by a closing bracket]. Such character ranges match any character that appears within the brackets. For example, [abc] matches a single occurrence of the letter a, b, or c. As another example, to find any occurrence of the letter c followed by ie or ei, you could use the regexp: c[ie][ie]. Note, however, that this would also match cii and cee. To specify ranges of characters within [...], use the hyphen (–) between a starting and ending character. For example, to match any digit from 0 to 9, use [0-9], which is much more convenient than the alternative [0123456789]. Multiple ranges are also allowed. For example, the following range matches any letter or digit or underscore: [A-Za-z0-9_]. Only one of either A-Z or a-z is necessary if searching is case-insensitive (the default).
Anything *but* a range of characters	[^ ...]	Sometimes you might want to *not* match a particular range of characters—for example, find the next word within a line that does not contain a, e, i, o, or u. To not match a range, include ^ as the first character in the range. To match a word without the vowels described above, you could use " +[^aeiou]+ +". Note that this definition of a word would not work with words at the start or end of a line unless those words had spaces on both sides.

Table 4.4, con't.

To Match This	Use	Description
A special character	\	Escapes special characters, including itself, so they don't have special meaning. For example, `^\$.*\$$` matches a line that starts and ends with the dollar sign. The backslash also introduces additional special constructs, described next.

Using the Special Character \

The backslash character (\) introduces additional special characters that let you build more powerful or more succinct regexps. For example, assuming that all words are composed of letters only, you could use the characters in Table 4.4 to construct the following regexps to search for the start and end of a word, respectively:

`[^a-z][a-z]+` ← Search for start of word: a non-letter (e.g., space) followed by one or more letters (e.g., a word)

`[a-z]+[^a-z]` ← Search for end of word: one or more letters followed by non-letter

Thus, to search for the next word that ends with **ing**, you could use the regexp `[^a-z][a-z]+ing[^a-z]`, which is somewhat long and inaccurate (words may contain characters other than letters). To be more succinct and precise, you could use the backslash escape **\b**, which is a shorthand for the start or end of a word. The regexp then becomes **\b.+ing\b**.

Table 4.5 summarizes all the special character escapes.

Table 4.5. Special Character Escapes (\)

To Match This	Use	Description
A tab character	\t	Matches an ASCII tab character.
A newline character	\n	Matches a newline character.
A backslash	\\	Use two backslashes in a row to match a single backslash.

Table 4.5, con't.

To Match This	Use	Description
Start or end of a word	`\b`	Matches an empty string at the start or end of a word. (See the example above.)
Next string *not* in a word	`\B`	Matches an empty string that is not at the start or end of a word.
Start of a word	`\<`	Matches an empty string at the start of a word. For example, `\<anti` matches the next occurrence the string `anti` at the start of a word.
End of a word	`\>`	Like `\<` but matches the *end* of a word. For example, `'s\>` matches any occurrence of an apostrophe followed by the letter *s* at the end of a word. If you have trouble with such contractions, this would be a good way to find all of them in a file and correct them.
Start of buffer	`\``	Matches the empty string at the start of the buffer. This is useful for determining whether a string occurs in the first line of the buffer. For example, `` \`[\t ]*;+ `` matches the first line if it contains a Lisp comment preceded by optional whitespace.
End of buffer	`\'`	Matches the empty string at the end of the buffer. This is useful for determining whether the buffer ends with a search string. For example, `THE END\'` matches the last line in the file if it ends with **THE END**.
Any word character	`\w`	Matches any character that would be considered part of a word. For example, to look up any word containing the Latin root `semi`, use `\<\w*semi\w*\>`.
Any *non*-word character	`\W`	Matches any character that would *not* be part of a word.

Table 4.5. Special Character Escapes (\)

To Match This	Use	Description

Multiple patterns	\		Allows you to search for multiple patterns with a single C-M-s command by separating each pattern with \ |. For example, to search for ing, ed, or s at the end of a word, you could use ing\>|ed\>|s\>. The first text matching any one of these sub-regexps will be found first; to find subsequent text that matches, use C-s again. For instance, here is how C-M-s followed by two C-s commands worked on the following text:
			
			 `Matching strings popped up.`
			 `         ↑         ↑        ↑`
			 `       C-M-s    C-s      C-s`
			 `        (1)     (2)      (3)`
			
			 This special character escape is also useful in parenthetical groupings (see the next section).

A group of characters	\ (. . . \ )	The characters appearing between \ (and \ ) constitute a group of characters that must be matched as shown. For example, \ (DoBe\) + matches DoBe, DoBeDoBe, and so on. For details, see the following section.

Table 4.5, con't.

To Match This	Use	Description
A syntactic class	\s*c*	Matches a single character of a syntactic class denoted by character *c*. Useful values for *c* and their meanings are as follows: **Value** — **Syntactic Class** BLANK — Whitespace w — Words – — Symbol names . — Punctuation (— Open balanced expression) — Close balanced expression " — String delimiters < — Comment start > — Comment end For instance, to match the next character that would be considered punctuation, use "\s.". And to match the next character that would be considered whitespace, use "\s ".
A character *not* in a syntactic class	\S*c*	Like \s*c* but matches the first character that does *not* have the syntactic class denoted by *c*. For example, "\S " matches the first character that is not whitespace.

Defining Groups with \(and \)

Thus far the regexps we've worked with have dealt only with single characters that can be repeated and combined in strings. The **\(** and **\)** special character escapes create **groups** of characters that can be repeated zero or more times with the *****, **+**, and **?** operators. For example, **\(to\)+** matches **to**, **toto**, **tototo**, and so on. Groups are often used to enclose multiple patterns. For example, suppose you wanted to find any of the following words ending in **ing**:

```
flying
driving
swimming
running
sailing
```

Using groups, you could specify the regexp as:

```
\(fly\|driv\|swimm\|runn\|sail\)ing
```

As another example, suppose you are working on a word puzzle and need to find a word starting with **e** that you know ends in the root **graph** or **gram**. If you had a comprehensive word list in the buffer, you could search for such a word using the regular expression:

```
\<e\w*\(graph\|gram\)\>
```

Let's dissect this regexp:

- The **\<e** tells Emacs to search for a word beginning with the letter **e**.

- The **\w*** says that the initial **e** is followed by zero or more word letters.

- The group **\(graph\|gram\)** indicates that these letters are followed by either **graph** or **gram**.

- **\>** says that this group is at the end of the word.

This regexp matches the words **epigraph** and **epigram**, but does not match the words **epigrammatical** or **anagram**.

Referencing Prior Groups in a Regexp

Another useful feature of groups is that once they are defined in a regexp, they can be reused later in the same regexp without having to be retyped. This is accomplished by the *****n*** escape, which substitutes prior grouping *n* into the current location in the regexp.

For example, suppose you want to find all occurrences of double words in a buffer (for example, **the the** or **to to**). With group references, it is fairly easy to do this. The regexp **\(\<\w+\>\)\Sw+\1** will match a double word, including double words that break over line endings. The first grouping, **\(\<\w+\>\)**, matches any word. The **\Sw+** says that the word must be followed by one or more non-word characters. And the ending **\1** says to substitute whatever pattern was matched by the first group, and match it. Let's look at how this regexp works on the following line:

```
Paris in the the spring!
```

Upon entry to this line, the first group matches **Paris**. The regexp expands to **\<Paris\>\Sw+\<Paris\>**, which would match **Paris Paris**, but which does *not* match `Paris in`. So Emacs moves to the next word, causing the regexp to expand to `\<in\>\Sw+\<in\>`, which also does not match. Emacs then moves to `the`, making the regexp expand to `\<the\>\Sw+\<the\>`, which successfully matches `the the`! Note that this would also work across line endings because the `\Sw+` would match the newline between `the` on the end of a line and `the` at the start of the next.

As another example, the following regexp finds all occurrences of words that contain three or more consecutive consonants:

```
\<\w*\([b-df-hj-np-tv-xz]\)\1\1+\w*\>
```

The group defines the set of consonants—all letters except the vowels. The `\1\1+` portion matches two or more occurrences of a letter that matches the group and that immediately follows the group.

Searching and Replacing Regexps

Emacs commands for searching and replacing regexps are summarized in Table 4.6.

Table 4.6. Regexp Search-and-Replace Commands

Operation	Command and Comments
Search-and-replace with verification	**M-x query-replace-regexp** Prompts for a regexp to replace and a string to replace it with. Before replacing a string, it prompts for verification. This is similar to **M-%** (query-replace on strings), except that it searches for regexps. Note that the replacement string can reference a group in the search regexp (see discussion following table).
Search-and-replace without verification	**M-x replace-regexp** Like **M-x query-replace-regexp** *but does not perform verification!* Use this command only if you are very confident with regexps. Consider the effect of **M-x replace-regexp** `\<\w+\>` **RET foo RET**: It replaces every word in the buffer with `foo`! To undo this command, you would have to run **C-x u** (undo) *for every word in the buffer.* And remember, there is a system-determined limit to the number of undo commands!

Referencing regexp groups is especially useful in search-and-replace operations. For example, suppose you want to put a leading dollar sign on all words containing only uppercase letters—changing **FLAME** to **$FLAME**, for instance. The first thing you must do is ensure that the search is case-sensitive; do this by setting the Emacs variable *case-fold-search* to **nil**. Next, invoke **M-x query-replace-regexp** and specify a search string that will match any uppercase word:

```
M-x query-replace-regexp RET                                    ← Invoke it
Query replace regexp: \<\([A-Z]+\)\> RET                        ← Type regexp with
                                                                  group
Query replace regexp \<\([A-Z]+\)\> with: $\1 RET              ← Substitute with $
                                                                  followed by the
                                                                  matched group
```

When you define the regexp, the regexp that matches an uppercase word, namely **[A-Z]+**, must appear within a group, **\([A-Z]+\)**. Then, when you type the replacement string, you can reference that group. In this instance, **$\1** means replace the group with **$** immediately followed by the group.

As another example, to search-and-replace all consonants that occur three or more times in a row with only two in a row:

```
M-x query-replace-regexp RET
Query replace regexp: \([b-df-hj-np-tv-xz]\)\1\1+ RET
Query replace regexp \([b-df-hj-np-tv-xz]\)\1\1+ with: \1\1 RET
```

Finally, suppose you want to change all lines of the form

```
Name: Firstname Lastname
```

to

```
Name: Lastname,Firstname
```

You could do this as follows:

```
M-x query-replace-regexp RET
Query replace regexp: \(Name: \)\([a-z]+\) \([a-z]+\) RET
Query replace regexp \(Name: \)\([a-z]+\) \([a-z]+\) with: \1\3,\2
```

Editing Outlines

Emacs provides Outline mode for creating and editing outlines. This mode is similar to Text mode but is modified to handle the special needs of outline editing. For example, there are commands that move to the next or previous outline heading at the same level, and commands that narrow (make invisible) all lines under a heading. To enable this mode, use `M-x outline-mode`.

What Is an Outline?

Figure 4.1 shows the classic form of an outline, to which most people are accustomed.

```
I. Introduction
   A. What is Soil?
      1. Soil Components
         a. Sand
         b. Clay
         c. Silt
      2. The Soil Classification Triangle
      3. Nutrients
         a. Nitrogen (N)
         b. Phosphorous (P)
         c. Potassium (K)
         d. Trace Elements
   B. What is Compost?
   C. Composting Methods
      1. Anaerobic (Slow)
      2. Aerobic (Fast)
      3. Costs and Benefits of Each
```

Figure 4.1. Classic Outline

In Outline mode, each heading's number is replaced with a string of asterisks denoting the **level** relative to other subjects. Figure 4.2 shows how the above outline segment looks in Outline mode.

For a line to be interpreted as a heading, the first asterisk must appear in column 0. There cannot be spaces between asterisks. Each heading can be followed by additional text or blank lines. Figure 4.3 shows part of the above outline, filled in with descriptive text.

In Emacs terminology, a line beginning with an asterisk is called a **heading**, the text following a heading is called the **body**, and together they are called an **entry**.

```
* Introduction
** What Is Soil?
*** Soil Components
**** Sand
**** Clay
**** Silt
*** The Soil Classification Triangle
*** Nutrients
**** Nitrogen (N)
**** Phosphorous (P)
**** Potassium (K)
**** Trace Elements
** What Is Compost?
** Composting Methods
*** Anaerobic (Slow)
*** Aerobic (Fast)
*** Costs and Benefits of Each
```

Figure 4.2. Emacs Outline

```
* Introduction

** What Is Soil?
*** Soil Components
    Describe the components of soil, heavy vs light soils,
    loam, peat, etc.

**** Sand
    Tiny rock particles.

**** Clay
    Extremely tiny rock particles.

**** Silt
    Decomposed organic matter.

*** The Soil Classification Triangle
    Soils are often classified using a triangle, with 100%
    sand, 100% clay, and 100% silt at each point.

*** Nutrients
    Explain the N-P-K numbers found on fertilizer packaging.
```

Figure 4.3. Emacs Outline with Text

Moving Among Headings

Emacs provides several commands for moving among headings at the same or different levels. Table 4.7 summarizes these commands.

Table 4.7. Commands for Moving Among Headings

Operation	Command and Comments
Next heading	`C-c C-n` Moves to the next heading at any level.
Previous heading	`C-c C-p` Moves to the previous heading at any level.
Next heading at same level	`C-c C-f` Moves to the next heading at the same level as the current heading.
Previous heading at same level	`C-c C-b` Moves to the previous heading at the same level as the current entry.
Next higher level	`C-c C-u` Moves to a heading at the next higher level—that is, a heading that encompasses all headings at the current entry's level. Note that there is not a corresponding command for going "down" a level, but one is not needed because `C-c C-n` does the same thing conceptually. That is, if you are at a level 2 entry (**), then `C-c C-n` takes you to the next lower subhead (***) if it exists.

These commands can also be given a numeric argument. For example, `C-u 5 C-c C-n` means move forward five headings. Figure 4.4 shows the effect of various outline motion commands on a sample outline.

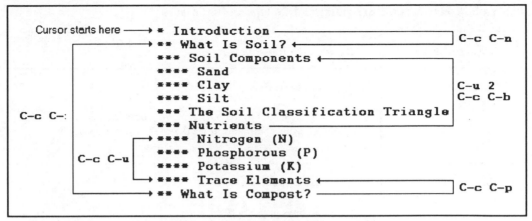

Figure 4.4. Outline Motion Commands

Hiding and Showing Lines

When an outline gets filled in with descriptive text, its structure often becomes less visible. To make the structure visible, Outline mode provides commands for **hiding** (**collapsing**) entries—that is, making a heading's body and/or subentries invisible. Outline mode also provides commands for showing hidden entries.

Emacs denotes **hidden lines** (also known as **invisible lines**) by placing an ellipsis (**. . .**) at the end of the heading line. Figure 4.5 shows the effect of hiding the body of a heading with the **C-c C-h** command.

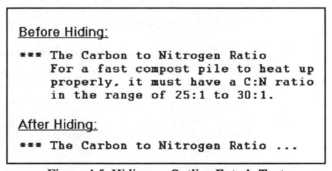

Figure 4.5. Hiding an Outline Entry's Text

The invisible text is not lost. To bring it back, use the **C-c C-s** command. Table 4.8 summarizes the commands for collapsing and expanding entries.

Table 4.8. Commands for Expanding and Collapsing Outlines

Operation	Command and Comments
Hide all body lines	`M-x hide-body` Hides all body lines in the buffer, leaving only the headings visible. Use this command to see the overall structure of an outline.
Show all body lines	`M-x show-all` Shows all lines in the buffer.
Hide all lines under heading	`C-c C-h` Hides the body and all entries of the current heading.
Show all lines under heading	`C-c C-s` Shows the body and all subentries of the current heading.
Hide bodies of entry and subheadings	`M-x hide-leaves` Hides the body of the current heading and its subheadings, used to see the complete structure of the current entry.
Show all subheadings	`M-x show-branches` Shows all subheadings of the current heading. Typically used after `C-c C-h`.
Show immediate subheadings	`C-c C-i` Shows only the *next* level of subheadings. Use this to see the next level of headings under the current heading.
Hide entry's body	`M-x hide-entry` Hides the body of the current heading.
Show entry's body	`M-x show-entry` Shows the body of the current heading.

Note: It is unwise to execute editing commands while the cursor is positioned over the "**...**" of a hidden entry, because you cannot see the effects of the editing command! Of course, you can use **C-x u** to undo such "invisible" editing commands. Before doing so, you should make the entry visible with the **M-x show-entry** command.

Changing the Heading Prefix

For most users, the asterisk prefix is acceptable and need not be changed. However, there are cases where it might not be acceptable—for example, if you want to use Outline mode to edit files for a text-formatting language that uses a different nomenclature for headings.

The heading prefix is determined by the Emacs variable *outline-regexp*, which defines a regular expression that constitutes a heading. Emacs assumes that the pattern always starts in column zero. The default value of *outline-regexp* is **[*^L]+**, which matches one or more asterisks.

Emacs determines the level of a heading *from the length of the matched pattern*. The shorter the heading pattern length, the "higher" its level; the longer its length, the "lower" the level. Thus, ***** is a higher level than ******, which is a higher level than *******, and so on.

Suppose you want to change *outline-regexp* so that it matches headings in an text-formatting language that defines headings as shown in Figure 4.6.

```
<chapter n>        Like * in Outline Mode

<s1>               Like **

<s2>               Like ***

<s3>               Like ****
```

Figure 6.6. Changing the Outline
Heading Prefix

To match the above heading tags, you could set the value of *outline-regexp* to **"<s[1234]>\\|<chapter [0-9]>"**. (The double backslash, ****, is necessary to get the **\|** escape in the string.) However Outline mode motion, hiding, and showing commands would *not* work as expected. This is because **<chapter [0-9]>** has a *longer* length than the **<s[1234]>**, and thus, has a lower level.

To make such a scheme work, you have to do something to the tags to make each successive level longer than the previous one. For example, the tags above could be rewritten as shown in Figure 4.7.

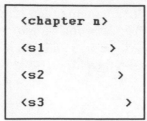

**Figure 4.7. Setting the
Prefix**

Then set *outline-regexp* to `"<chapter [0-9]>\\|<s[1234] +>"`. You *must*
enclose the regexp in double quotes when responding to the `Set variable:`
prompt.

Manipulating Buffers

In the previous chapters, we've examined several commands that manipulate buffers.
Table 4.9 describes more commands for managing buffers and manipulating their
contents, and provides additional details for commands you are already familiar with.

Table 4.9. Commands for Managing Buffers and Buffer Contents

Operation	Command and Comments
Reset modification status	`M-~` Makes Emacs ignore the fact that the current buffer may have been modified. Removes the `*` in the mode line, and displays the message: `Modification-flag cleared`. This can prevent the buffer from being saved to a file, since Emacs will not save buffers that have not been modified.
Select another buffer	`C-x b` Changes the current buffer. Emacs prompts you to enter the buffer name to switch to. Enter the desired name and press `RET`. If the buffer does not exist, Emacs creates an empty buffer. The default directory for this new buffer is inherited from the previous current buffer.

Table 4.9, con't.

Operation	Command and Comments
Select another buffer in another window	`C-x 4 b` Like `C-x b`, but selects (or creates) a specified buffer in another window.
List all buffers	`C-x C-b` Splits the screen into two windows and displays a list of all buffers in the new window, leaving the cursor in the current window. With a numeric argument (`C-u C-x C-b`), displays only the buffers that have an associated file. If you move the cursor into the buffer menu window, you can use all the Buffer-Menu commands (as described in Chapter 11, "Managing Files and Buffers"). Type `C-x 1` to remove the window containing the listing.
Kill a buffer	`C-x k` Prompts you to enter a buffer name to kill (remove). Accept the default (kill the current buffer), or enter a name and press **RET**.
Kill selected buffers	`M-x kill-some-buffers` Lets you kill buffers one at a time. Emacs prompts you to confirm each kill by typing **y**.
Toggle buffer read-only status	`C-x C-q` Make a read-only buffer writable, or vice versa. The command toggles the value of the variable named *buffer-read-only*.
Rename buffer	`M-x rename-buffer` Emacs prompts you for a new buffer name. The name of the file associated with the buffer remains unchanged.
View buffer	`M-x view-buffer` Displays the specified buffer in View mode, which provides commands for scrolling only; you cannot edit the buffer's contents.

Table 4.9, con't.

Operation	Command and Comments
Insert buffer contents	`M-x insert-buffer` Inserts the contents of the specified buffer into the current buffer, at the location of the cursor.
Move region to another buffer	`M-x copy-to-buffer` Remove a buffer's contents and copy a region from the current buffer.
Append region to another buffer	`C-x a` or `M-x append-to-buffer` Appends a copy of the current region of the current buffer to another buffer. Emacs prompts for the buffer to append the text to. The current buffer is unchanged.
Prepend region to another buffer	`M-x prepend-to-buffer` Inserts a region at the start of the specified buffer; the current buffer is unchanged.

Advanced File Operations

The preceding chapters have introduced basic ways to retrieve and save files. The following sections provide additional commands for manipulating files.

Creating, Retrieving (Visiting), and Inserting Files

Emacs provides several commands for creating, retrieving (visiting) and inserting files into a buffer. Table 4.10 summarizes these commands. For completeness, all file retrieval commands are listed, including those mentioned in the preceding chapters.

All commands in Table 4.10 prompt you to specify the name of the file you want to create, visit, or insert. If you specify a directory instead of a file (perhaps accidentally), Emacs runs the Dired facility (see Chapter 11, "Managing Files and Buffers"). You can eliminate this behavior by setting the *find-file-run-dired* variable to `nil`.

Table 4.10. Commands for Creating, Visiting, and Inserting Files

Operation	Command and Comments
Visit (find) a file	`C-x C-f` Loads a file into a buffer and sets the buffer's mode appropriately. Prompts for a name; type a specification as desired and press RET. The buffer receives the same name as the file.
Visit (find) a file in another window	`C-x 4 C-f` Like `C-x C-f`, but displays the buffer in another window. Creates a new window if only one window currently exists.
Create a new file	`C-x C-f` When you enter the name of a nonexistent file at the `C-x C-f` prompt, Emacs creates a new, empty buffer and displays the message `(New File)` in the minibuffer. However, the file is not actually created until you save the buffer with one of the commands listed in the next section.
Replace buffer with another file	`C-x C-v` Works essentially like `C-x C-f`, but lets you replace existing buffer contents with the contents of a new file.
Insert file into current buffer	`M-x insert-file` Insert the contents of the specified file at the cursor position.

Saving and Writing Files

Table 4.11 lists commands that save or write buffers to files. *Saving* a file stores it in a file of the same name as the buffer; *writing* a file gives you the opportunity to enter a file name different from the buffer name.

Emacs will not save a buffer that has not been modified since the last save or write. Instead, Emacs reports the following message in the echo area:

```
(No changes need to be written)
```

So, to *prevent* a buffer from being saved (an action that would write over the previous version of the file), you can change the modification status with the **M-~** command (see Table 4.9). This makes the file appear unmodified, so Emacs will not save it.

Another way to prevent Emacs from replacing the original file with the modified file is to associate a new file name to the buffer. Once this is done, all subsequent saves will be sent to the new file name, leaving the original intact. This can be done with the **C-c C-w** command (see Table 4.11) or **M-x set-visited-filename** (see Table 4.12).

If a backup file exists, you can restore the file to the state of the last backup with **M-x revert-buffer** (see "Reverting a Buffer to Its Original Contents" later in this chapter).

Before a file is saved or written, Emacs may report that the buffer contains no newline at the end, and will offer to add one. Type **y** to add a newline, **n** otherwise. To automatically add a newline to each file that doesn't end in one, set the variable *require-final-newline* to a non-**nil** value (e.g., **t**).

Table 4.11. Commands for Saving and Writing Files

Operation	Command and Comments
Save current buffer to a file	**C-x C-s** Immediately saves the buffer contents to a file of the same name. Emacs prompts for a file name only if the buffer does not yet have an associated file. With a numeric argument (**C-u C-x C-s**), saves all buffers without verification.
Save selected buffers to file(s)	**C-x s** Emacs asks you to confirm saving each modified buffer to its associated file. This is the same function that is performed when you exit Emacs. With a numeric argument (**C-u C-x s**), saves all buffers without verification.
Write buffer to specified file	**C-x C-w** When you begin working in a new buffer and the buffer does not yet have an associated file, executing this command lets you specify a file and save the buffer's contents to it. Also, use this command to save the buffer to a file name different than the buffer name. After the file is written, this command renames the buffer to the new file name you specified.

Changing a Buffer's Associated File and Directory

Each buffer has a file name and a default directory associated with it. Table 4.12 describes commands that display or change the file or directory associated with a buffer.

Table 4.12. Commands for Changing a Buffer's File and Directory

Operation	Command and Comments
Display current buffer's default directory	**M-x pwd** Display the name of the default directory for the current buffer. Each buffer has an associated directory where files will be retrieved and stored. This default directory is stored as the value of the variable *default-directory*.
Change current buffer's default directory	**M-x cd** Prompts for a new default directory for the current buffer. All subsequent file retrievals will use this new directory.
Change buffer's associated file	**M-x set-visited-filename** Change the file name to which a buffer's contents will be saved. This command provides an easy way to change the name of the file before saving it with **C-x C-s**. For example, you might want to change the file name to preserve the original file as a backup copy, and save all new modifications to a file under a different name. Of course, it would be easier to use the **C-x C-w** command to write the buffer to a different file (the same effect).

Managing Auto-Saving

To prevent you from losing large amounts of work in the event of a power failure or system crash, Emacs automatically saves (auto-saves) your buffers to disk at intervals based on the number of keystrokes you have typed. Emacs displays the message

```
Auto-saving...
```

to notify you that buffers are being saved.

The designers of Emacs recognize that you may not want the buffer you are editing to be auto-saved to the original file. For example, you might load an empty form template into Emacs to fill out, but you would not want your completed form to overwrite (via an auto-save) the original template file.

To avoid this problem, Emacs auto-saves your buffers into special "auto-save" files. Auto-save files have the same name as the original file, preceded and followed by #. Thus, a file named `report` would be auto-saved in a file named `#report#`. Special buffers, such as those used for mail, help, and so on, are auto-saved only upon your request, and are saved in files named by attaching #% to the beginning and # to the end of the buffer name (e.g., `#%*mail*#`).

To force Emacs to auto-save a buffer, type `M-x do-auto-save`.

Enabling/Disabling Auto-Saving

Auto-saving is used for all visited buffers by default, but you can toggle it on and off for individual buffers with the `M-x auto-save-mode` command. Alternatively, you can type `M-x auto-save-mode` with a positive numeric argument to turn on auto-saving, or with a zero or negative argument to turn it off.

The variables listed in Table 4.13 are used to control auto-saving.

Table 4.13. Variables to Control Auto-Saving

Behavior	Variable and Comments
Enable/disable autosaving	*auto-save-default* Default: `t` If `t` (default), auto-saving is enabled for each visited file. If `nil`, auto-saving is disabled.
Auto-save buffer to original file name	*auto-save-visited-file-name* Default: `nil` If non-`nil` (e.g., `t`), Emacs auto-saves the buffer to its associated file, instead of creating a separate, auto-save file. If `nil`, this variable has no effect.

Table 4.13, con't.

Behavior	Variable and Comments
Prevent deletion of auto-save file	*delete-auto-save-files* Default: t If t (default), delete the auto-save file when the buffer is saved or written to its file. If nil, the auto-save file is not deleted.
Specify interval between auto-saves	*auto-save-interval* Default: 300 Sets the number of characters that must be typed before buffers are auto-saved.

Managing Emacs Backup Files

Emacs, by default, creates a **backup** copy of each file the *first* time you save it. Subsequent saves during the same editing session do not create additional backup copies. However, if you kill the buffer and visit the file again during the same editing session, Emacs makes a new backup just before the first save.

Selecting a Backup Strategy

Emacs creates either a single backup file or a series of numbered backup files for each file you edit, depending on the value of the variable *version-control*. *version-control* can be set uniquely for each buffer, so you may choose to back up some buffers using a single file, and others using multiple numbered files. Table 4.14 shows the possible values *version-control* can have, and the effect of each.

Table 4.14. Effect of the Version-Control Variable

Value	Behavior
t	Emacs creates numbered backup files.

Table 4.14, con't.

Value	Behavior
nil (default)	Emacs creates a single backup file, unless a file already has existing numbered backup files.
never	Emacs creates a single backup file, regardless of whether a file has existing numbered backup files.

Backup File Naming Conventions

Backup files are named according to the following conventions:

- Single backup files are named the same as the original file, but with an appended ~ (tilde). For example, the backup file for **report** would be named **report~**.

- Multiple backup files are named the same as the original file, but with an appended **.~n~**, where *n* is the sequence number of the file. For example, **report.~1~** is the first backup file created for **report**, **report.~2~** is the second backup file created, and so on.

- If UNIX file permissions prevent Emacs from creating the backup file using the conventions above, it creates a single backup file named **%backup%~** in your home directory containing the most recent backup.

Controlling the Method of Creating Backup Files

Emacs can create a backup file by renaming the original file to the new backup file name, or by copying the original file to the new backup file. The method used is determined by three variables, shown in Table 4.15.

Table 4.15. Variables to Control Method of Backup File Creation

Behavior	Variable and Comments
Create backup file by copying	*backup-by-copying* Default: nil If nil, the backup file is created by renaming the original; if non-nil (e.g., t), it is created by copying the original.

Table 4.15, con't.

Behavior	Variable and Comments
Create backup file by copying if file has multiple names	*backup-by-copying-when-linked* Default: `nil` If • *backup-by-copying* is `nil` (that is, renaming is usually done), and • the file has multiple names, and • *backup-by-copying-when-linked* is non-`nil` (e.g., `t`), then Emacs creates the backup file by copying. Files that do not have multiple names are still backed up by renaming. If the value of *backup-by-copying-when-linked* is `nil`, it has no effect.
Create backup file by copying when renaming changes owner or group	*backup-by-copying-when-mismatch* Default: `nil` If • *backup-by-copying* is `nil` (that is, renaming is usually done), and • *backup-by-copying-when-mismatch* is non-`nil` (e.g., `t`), • creating the backup by renaming would change the file's owner or group, then Emacs creates the backup file by copying. If the value of *backup-by-copying-when-mismatch* is `nil`, it has no effect.

Renaming is usually used to create the backup file. Creating the backup file by copying may be desirable under the following circumstances:

1. **When a file has multiple names.** UNIX allows you to assign multiple names to (link) a file. If a file has multiple names and renaming is used to create the backup file, all of the other names linked to the file will now be linked to the backup file. Usually, this is not desirable; you would prefer that all names continue to refer to the most current version. The backup file, of course, contains the old version.

   When creating the backup file by copying, however, the other names for the file remain linked to the current version of the file (the one that you just saved). Thus, setting the variable *backup-by-copying-when-linked* to non-`nil` is a good idea.

2. **When you do not want the file's owner and group to change.** When you create a backup file by renaming, the owner of the file is changed to the person who last edited it, and the group is changed to the default setting for the operating system. Usually, this is desirable behavior, because the owner field shows who last edited the file. However, if you do not want the file's owner or group to change, set the variable *backup-by-copying-when-mismatch* to non-`nil`.

Controlling the Deletion of Backup Files

If you wish, Emacs will automatically delete backup files to conserve disk space. The variables listed in Table 4.16 control how Emacs deletes backup files.

Table 4.16. Variables to Control Backup File Deletion

Behavior	Variable and Comments
Number of low-numbered backup files to keep	*kept-old-versions* Default: 2 Sets the number of low-numbered (oldest) backup files to retain.
Number of high-numbered backup files to keep	*kept-new-versions* Default: 2 Sets the number of high-numbered (newest) backup files to retain.
Delete backup files with or without asking	*trim-versions-without-asking* Default: `nil` If `nil`, deletes backup files without asking for confirmation; if non-`nil` (e.g., `t`), asks you to confirm the deletion first.

For example, suppose you have the following backup files:

```
report.~1~        report.~4~
report.~2~        report.~5~
report.~3~        report.~6~
```

You edit the report file again, and you have just saved it for the first time during this session. Emacs creates the new backup file before saving the modified file, leaving the following backup files in your directory:

```
report.~1~      report.~4~      report.~7~
report.~2~      report.~5~
report.~3~      report.~6~
```

Emacs now examines the values of the *kept-old-versions* and *kept-new-versions* variables; assume they are both set to **2** (the default). Assuming *trim-versions-without-asking* is `nil`, Emacs would ask you whether it should proceed with the deletion. If you confirm the action, all files except the two oldest and two newest would be deleted, leaving:

```
report.~1~      report.~7~
report.~2~
report.~6~
```

If *kept-old-versions* was **0**, and *kept-new-versions* was **5**, the following files would be retained:

```
report.~3~      report.~6~
report.~4~      report.~7~
report.~5~
```

Turning Off Automatic File Backup

To prevent Emacs from making automatic backup copies, set the value of the variable *make-backup-files* to `nil`.

Reverting a Buffer to Its Original Contents

You may occasionally make changes to a buffer and then decide to discard them. When this happens, you can **revert** (restore) the buffer to its original contents (i.e., re-read the file from the disk) by running the **M-x revert-buffer** command. When prompted for confirmation, type **yes**. Emacs discards the current contents of the buffer and re-reads the file into the buffer. Note that this will *not* be the original file contents that existed at the start of your editing session *if* you have since saved or written the buffer to the file. To restore the original file, you must retrieve the backup file (see the previous section).

When a buffer has been auto-saved since it was last saved (see "Setting Up Auto-Save Mode" earlier in this chapter), **M-x   revert-buffer** asks if you would rather read the auto-saved file (which is more current) instead of the visited (original) file. Type **y** if you want to retrieve the auto-save file, **n** if you don't.

Preventing Simultaneous Editing

You should try to avoid **simultaneous editing**, a situation where two users visit the same file at the same time, make changes, and save the file. The user who saves the file last overwrites the changes made by the user who saves it first.

Emacs marks as **locked** all buffers that have been modified but not yet saved. When you save a buffer, the lock is removed. When you attempt to edit a file that another user has locked, Emacs sends a message asking how to proceed. You can respond in one of three ways:

- Type **s** to "steal" the lock from the other person who is editing the file.

- Type **p** to proceed with your editing session.

- Type **q** to quit editing this buffer immediately. All of your modifications to this point are discarded.

Emacs cannot detect an attempt to edit a locked file on all UNIX systems, so the message above may not appear. But it will always warn you when you attempt to overwrite a file that has been modified since it was lasted saved. Emacs will ask:

```
Disk file has changed since visited or saved. Save anyway? (yes or no)
```

Unless you have a good reason for doing otherwise, cancel by typing **no**.

In summary, to avoid overwriting another user's revisions to a file:

- **Heed warning messages.** Emacs, when possible, sends a warning message when you begin making changes to a file that another user is editing, and again warns when you are about to save a file and overwrite another user's revisions.

- **Customize the ask-user-about-lock function.** This function sets how Emacs responds to simultaneous editing, and produces the message described earlier in this section. See Appendix B, "Emacs-Lisp Programming," for more information about creating your own functions.

- **Avoid editing files that have multiple file names (linked files).** Emacs cannot detect simultaneous editing when two users edit the same file with different file names.

- **Contact the other editor.** When warned about simultaneous editing, type **C-u C-x C-d** to list the directory and find out who is editing the file. The last person to write the file will be listed as the file's owner. Contact that person to prevent further simultaneous editing. Perhaps you can both write the file to different names and use the UNIX **diff** command to determine what has changed.

Advanced Window Operations

In addition to the window management commands described in the previous chapter, Emacs provides the advanced commands for working in other windows besides the current window (Table 4.17) and changing window size (Table 4.18).

Working in Other Windows

Each of the commands in Table 4.17 will create a second window if only one window currently exists.

Table 4.17. Commands for Working in Another Window

Operation	Command and Comments
Select buffer in another window	**C-x 4 b** Prompts for a buffer name, and makes the other window current.
Find file in another window	**C-x 4 f** Prompts for the file to find, loads the file into a buffer in the other window.
Run Dired in another window	**C-x 4 d** Prompts for the directory for Dired, and starts Dired in the other window, showing the specified directory. See Chapter 11 for more information on Dired.

Table 4.17, con't.

Operation	Command and Comments
Compose mail in another window	`C-x 4 m` Provides another window with appropriate buffer and mode for composing and sending a mail message. (More on mail in Chapter 10, "Using Emacs for Electronic Mail.")
Scroll another window	`C-M-v` Scrolls the text in the other window.

Changing Window Size

The `C-x ^` command changes a window's height; the `C-x }` command changes window width. Table 4.18 summarizes the different variations of these commands.

Table 4.18. Commands That Change Window Size

Operation	Command and Comments
Increase window height	`C-x ^` Increases the window height by one line each time you execute the command.
Reduce window height	`C-u -n C-x ^` Decreases the window height by *n* lines.
Increase window width	`C-x }` Increases the window width by one column.
Reduce window width	`C-u -n C-x }` Decreases the window height by *n* columns. `C-x {` may work also.

Editing Your Responses in the Minibuffer

Many Emacs commands prompt you to complete a command in the minibuffer. For example, commands that retrieve and write files often ask you to enter a file specification in the minibuffer. **M-x** commands, also, prompt you to supply a function name in the minibuffer.

Since the minibuffer is an editing buffer, you can use normal editing commands when entering your responses to Emacs prompts. For example, to move the cursor to the beginning or end of your response, use **C-a** or **C-e**, respectively. You can even insert (yank) text killed in another buffer into the minibuffer.

However, editing in the minibuffer is unique in the following ways:

1. Because **RET** exits the minibuffer, you must use **C-o** or **C-q LFD** to include a linefeed in a response.

2. You can use **C-x o** to switch to an editing buffer from the minibuffer.

3. You cannot split the minibuffer screen, but you can make it taller with **C-x ^**.

4. When you execute a command from the minibuffer that provides help in another window, that window scrolls if you type **C-M-v** from the minibuffer. This scrolling lasts until you exit the minibuffer, and can help you during response completion (see "Letting Emacs Complete Your Responses" later in this section).

Specifying a file name in the Emacs minibuffer works like it does when you specify a file name in UNIX with one exception: UNIX does not allow typing two slashes in a row, for example, **/users//sue**. Emacs does allow you to type two slashes, which means to ignore everything that precedes the second slash. For example, **/etc/emacs//stuff/myfile** specifies the **/stuff/myfile** directory, and **~/misc/foo//~/reports/january** specifies the **~/reports/january** directory. This is useful when you don't want to backspace over a long default file name prompt.

Using Emacs' Command History

Each command that uses the minibuffer is saved in a history list, together with any responses that you enter. Table 4.20 describes commands for manipulating this command history list.

Table 4.20. Commands for Manipulating the Command History List

Operation	Command and Comments
Re-execute previous minibuffer command	`C-x ESC` With no argument, recalls the last command executed in the minibuffer; press **RET** to execute it. You can use a numeric argument to repeat earlier commands.
Display previous command	`M-p` After executing `C-x ESC`, moves to the previously recorded command. Pressing **RET** re-executes the command.
Display next command	`M-n` After executing `C-x ESC` and one or more `M-p` commands, moves to the next (more recent) command. Pressing **RET** re-executes the command.
Display command history	`M-x list-command-history` Display the entire command history, showing commands that `C-x ESC` can re-execute, most recent commands first.

Exiting the Minibuffer

You can exit the minibuffer in two ways:

1. Type **C-g** to cancel the command you are editing.

2. Complete your response to the current command and press **RET**.

Letting Emacs Complete Your Responses

The minibuffer can save you from typing long responses by completing a buffer, file, function, command, or variable name as soon as you type a few, uniquely identifying characters. When you have typed enough of your response for Emacs to identify it, you can press **RET** and let Emacs complete it.

For example, suppose you want to insert a file into a buffer. You could type:

```
M-x insert-f RET
```

Emacs completes the specification of the command for you (**M-x insert-file**), and prompts you to provide a file name. If you had executed:

```
M-x inser RET
```

Emacs would not be able to complete the specification because several command names begin with **inser**. However, you can display a list of possible completions by pressing **TAB**. Table 4.21 lists all keys you can use to perform completion.

Table 4.21. Completion Keys

Key	Description
RET	Attempts to complete your entire response and execute the command, based on what you have typed. RET works differently depending on the command: • **Strict completion:** Executes the command only when the response completes to a valid response for the command. For example, when killing a buffer, valid responses are the set of existing buffers. • **Cautious completion:** Executes the command only when you have already typed the complete response; that is, the response does not need completion. If the response is not complete, RET completes it but does not execute the command. Pressing **RET** a second time executes the completed command. This is used for commands that must read existing files, such as **M-x insert-file**. • **Permissive completion:** Executes the command with whatever you have typed; no completion occurs. This is used when any response is valid, as when creating a new file with the **C-x C-f**.
SPC	Attempts to complete only the current word you are typing. You can then type more characters, and press SPC to attempt to complete the next word.
TAB	Attempts to complete your entire response, but does not attempt to execute the command. Emacs will complete as much of the specification as it can. If you have not yet uniquely identified the complete response, Emacs displays a list of possible completions in another window.

Case is typically significant: **Junk** is not equivalent to **junk**.

If you attempt completion on file names, some file extensions that are reserved by Emacs are ignored, for example, **.o** and **.dvi**.

Displaying Completion Alternatives

All completion commands will display a list of completion alternatives when your current entry does not uniquely specify a valid response. You can scroll the list if necessary by executing **C-M-v** in the minibuffer to see undisplayed alternatives. You can also type **?** at any time to display a list of valid alternatives that match your current entry.

The variables listed in Table 4.22 control completion behavior.

Table 4.22. Variables That Control Response Completion

Behavior	Variable and Comments
Turn on/off display of alternatives	*completion-auto-help* Default: **t** If **t**, displays a list of completion alternatives for the current response. If **nil**, display is turned off.
Ignore this list of file name extensions	*completion-ignored-extensions* Default: a list of file name extension strings (use **C-h v** to see) Contains a list of strings that will not be allowed as extensions when completing file names.

Sorting Text

Emacs has commands for sorting lines, paragraphs, and pages within regions. Sorting is done in accordance with the ASCII character set, unless you do a numeric sort (described later in this section). Some important features to note about the ASCII sequence are:

- The space character comes before all other visible characters.

- Digits (**0** through **9**) come before letters.

- Uppercase letters (**A** through **Z**) come before lowercase letters (**a** through **z**).

Table 4.23 summarizes commands for sorting text. These commands operate on all lines in the current region (between mark and point). Examples of using these commands follow the table.

Table 4.23. Commands for Sorting Text

Operation	Command and Comments
Sort by comparing entire lines	`M-x sort-lines` The simplest form of sort. Lines are compared character by character from the start of each line. If run with a numeric argument (`C-u M-x sort-lines`), the sort is performed in descending order.
Sort by a field in each line	`M-x sort-fields` Sorts on a particular field within the line, specified by a numeric argument. For example, `C-u 2 M-x sort-fields` sorts on field two in each line in the region. A **field** is defined as a string of text surrounded by whitespace (any number of blanks, tabs, or newlines). If you do not specify a numeric argument, the sort uses field 1. If a negative argument is specified for the field, the sort is done in descending order.
Sort by numeric fields	`M-x sort-numeric-fields` Like `M-x sort-fields`, but expects the specified field to contain a numeric value. In a regular field sort, 10 would come before 2 because 1 precedes 2 in the ASCII sequence. With a *numeric* sort, 2 comes before 10 because the number 2 is less than 10. If a negative argument is specified, Emacs sorts in descending order.

Table 4.23, con't.

Operation	Command and Comments
Sort on columns	`M-x sort-columns` Sorts lines according to the data in selected columns. You select the columns by setting mark at the first column of the first line, and then moving the cursor to the last column and last line. **Note:** *This command does not work if the lines contain tab characters!* If you try to use the command on lines that contain tabs, Emacs displays a message telling you to remove the tabs with `M-x untabify`.
Sort by entire paragraph	`M-x sort-paragraphs` Compares entire paragraphs with each other and sorts them. With a numeric argument, the sort is performed in descending order.
Sort by entire page contents	`M-x sort-pages` If a region contains pages, this command compares entire pages' text and sorts them. With a numeric argument, it sorts in descending order.

Example of Sorting Entire Lines

The `M-x sort-lines` command is useful for sorting lists of words. For example, suppose the current buffer contains this list of words:

```
mark
region
911 emergency number
 ed out                    ← This line starts with a space
currents
current buffer
Auto-Fill mode
Wankel rotary engine
```

If you define a region including the first and last line, `M-x sort-lines` rearranges (sorts) the words as follows:

```
 ed out
911 emergency number
Auto-Fill mode
Wankel rotary engine
current buffer
currents
mark
region
```

Some important points to note about the sorted text are:

1. The line that starts with a space comes before all other lines.

2. The next line starts with a digit.

3. Lines starting with uppercase letters come before those starting with lowercase letters.

If you run **C-u M-x sort-lines** on the same region, the lines are reversed (sorted in descending order):

```
region
mark
currents
current buffer
Wankel rotary engine
Auto-Fill mode
911 emergency number
 ed out
```

Example of Sorting by Fields

As mentioned above, a field is defined as a string of text delimited by whitespace. Below is an example line containing six fields (shown underlined):

NAME	(Last,	First,	MI)	EMPNO.	SALES
1	2	3	4	5	6

Sorting by fields is often used on lines of tabular data—that is, text arranged in columns. For example, suppose the current buffer contains the following lines that list salespeople, their sales region, and total sales:

```
SALESPERSON                             REGION        SALES ($)
Foo B. Johnson                          East          30458.02
Ned G. Feenburger                       West           9246.58
Gertha H. Fenson                        East          15667.22
Sitka T. Spruce                         West          32768.00
Hoonrah Z. Specklemeyer                 Midwest       21867.33
Keldish O. Almex                        South         38489.85
```

To sort these lines by sales region, create a region around the lines (not including the header line), then sort on field 4 using the command C-u **4 M-x sort-fields**. The lines are sorted in the following order:

```
Foo B. Johnson                          East          30458.02
Gertha H. Fenson                        East          15667.22
Hoonrah Z. Specklemeyer                 Midwest       21867.33
Keldish O. Almex                        South         38489.85
Ned G. Feenburger                       West           9246.58
Sitka T. Spruce                         West          32768.00
```

Fields 1 through 3 are occupied by the first name, middle initial, and last name of each salesperson, respectively; field 4 contains the sales region. *Note that this example assumes that each salesperson always has a middle initial.* What would happen if a salesperson didn't have a middle initial? On that particular line, the first name and last name would be fields 1 and 2, but *the sales region would become field 3.* Keep in mind that this command will probably give desired results only if all lines have the same number of fields.

Example of a Numeric Field Sort

Suppose in the example above, you want to sort lines by total sales, from highest to lowest. You might try using C-u **-5 M-x sort-fields**, which would sort on the sales field in each line in reverse alphabetical order. However, this puts **Ned** at the top of the sales list because his sales field starts with a **9**, which is alphabetically greater than the next line, which starts with **3**!

```
Ned G. Feenburger                       West           9246.58
Keldish O. Almex                        South         38489.85
Sitka T. Spruce                         West          32768.00
Foo B. Johnson                          East          30458.02
Hoonrah Z. Specklemeyer                 Midwest       21867.33
Gertha H. Fenson                        East          15667.22
```

To sort lines on numeric fields, you should use **`M-x sort-numeric-fields`** instead of **`M-x sort-fields`**. Running **`C-u -5 M-x sort-numeric-fields`** on the above lines produces the correct ordering:

```
Keldish O. Almex              South        38489.85
Sitka T. Spruce               West         32768.00
Foo B. Johnson                East         30458.02
Hoonrah Z. Specklemeyer       Midwest      21867.33
Gertha H. Fenson              East         15667.22
Ned G. Feenburger             West          9246.58
```

Example of Sorting Columns

Occasionally, you may want to sort on specific columns that do not constitute a field—that is, columns of text that are not delimited by whitespace. To do this, use mark and the cursor to define a rectangle around the columns you want to sort; then run **`M-x sort-columns`**. For example, Figure 4.8 shows how to sort a list of names and social security numbers by the middle two digits of the social security number.

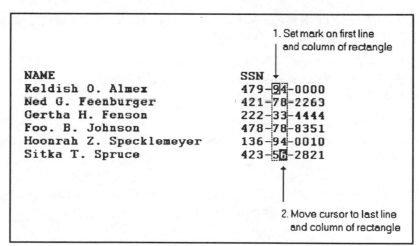

Figure 4.8. Defining the Column Rectangle

Figure 4.9 shows how the lines would look after running **`M-x sort-columns`**.

```
NAME                              SSN
Gertha H. Fenson                  222-33-4444
Sitka T. Spruce                   423-56-2821
Foo. B. Johnson                   478-78-8351
Ned G. Feenburger                 421-78-2263
Hoonrah Z. Specklemeyer           136-94-0010
Keldish O. Almex                  479-94-0000
```

Figure 4.9. Lines Are Sorted by Columns

Example of Sorting Paragraphs

M-x sort-paragraphs compares and sorts entire paragraphs. For example, this is useful when creating a glossary in which each term is followed immediately by a paragraph describing it. Typically, you might add terms in an unsorted order as you create the glossary, then "kill and yank" the entries into sorted order when you're finished. Doing this manually with yank and kill commands could be quite tedious. The **M-x sort-paragraphs** command could alleviate such drudgery.

For example, suppose you have the following unsorted glossary entries in a buffer:

```
mark
Defines the start of a region of text that is delimited on the
other end by the cursor (point).

cursor
Highlights the character that immediately follows point in the
current buffer.

mode
Determines what commands and capabilities can be used when editing
a buffer that uses the mode.
```

To sort these paragraphs, define a region around all lines, then run **M-x sort-paragraphs**, which sorts the lines as follows:

```
cursor
Highlights the character that immediately follows point in the
current buffer.

mark
Defines the start of a region of text that is delimited on the
other end by the cursor (point).

mode
Determines what commands and capabilities can be used when editing
a buffer that uses the mode.
```

Imagine the time such a feature could save you if you had several paragraphs to sort! It has saved these authors *lots* of time.

Using Rectangles

A rectangle is a special case of a region that is defined by a marked area lying between a specified pair of columns and a specified range of lines. Rectangles can be killed, yanked, and otherwise processed like text. They can also be placed in a register (see "Using Registers" later in this chapter).

Defining a Rectangle

To define a rectangle, follow these steps:

1. Move the cursor to the column and line where you want to place the upper-left corner rectangle and set a mark (for example, 10th column, 5th row).

2. Move the cursor down and to the right to where you want to place the lower-right corner of the rectangle. (for example, 60th column, 15th row).

Manipulating Rectangles

After you have defined a rectangle, you can use the commands in Table 4.24 to manipulate it.

Table 4.24. Commands That Operate on Rectangles

Operation	Command and Comments
Clear rectangle	`M-x clear-rectangle` Clears a rectangle, replacing its contents with spaces.
Delete rectangle	`M-x delete-rectangle` Deletes all text in the rectangle and moves the remaining text to the left edge of the rectangle.

Table 4.24, con't.

Operation	Command and Comments
Kill rectangle	`M-x kill-rectangle` Like `M-x delete-rectangle`, but saves the contents of the rectangle in a special location. You can yank this rectangle back into a buffer. Only the most recently killed rectangle is saved.
Yank rectangle	`M-x yank-rectangle` Yanks the last rectangle killed with `M-x kill-rectangle`, inserting the upper-left character at the cursor.
Open rectangle	`M-x open-rectangle` Inserts blank spaces, filling the area of the rectangle and pushing the previous contents of the rectangle to the right.

Using Registers

A **register** is a named storage location that can contain text, a position, or a rectangle. A register holds its contents until you store something else in it. Anything you save in a register can be copied into a buffer, once or many times. Any single character can be used to name a register; for example, a through z work well.

Using Registers to Mark Positions in a Buffer

You can save your current buffer location (a **position**) in a register, and then jump to that saved position later. Table 4.25 describes the commands that do this.

Table 4.25. Commands to Save/Retrieve Buffer Positions

Operation	Command and Comments
Save current cursor position	`C-x / r` Saves the current cursor position in a register named r. The command is very handy for marking a sequence of positions (for example, **a**, **b**, ..., **m**) in a large buffer.

Table 4.25, con't.

Operation	Command and Comments
Jump to position in register	`C-x j` *r* Jumps to the position saved in register *r*, placing the cursor just after the position. The command does not alter the contents of the register.

Using Registers to Save and Retrieve Text

Killing and yanking text works well for spontaneous cut-and-paste operations, but when you want to repeatedly insert a block of text at various locations in a buffer, it is easier to put the text in a register. The text can be inserted as often as you like. Using a set of registers, each containing a different chunk of text, can streamline routine editing operations. Table 4.26 lists the commands for manipulating text in registers.

Table 4.26. Commands to Manipulate Text in Registers

Operation	Command and Comments
Copy current region to register	`C-x x` *r* Copies the current region into register *r*. You must have first created the region, which can be any amount of text from a character to the entire buffer. Using a numeric argument (`C-u C-x x` *r*) deletes the region as well as copies it.
Retrieve text from register	`C-x g` *r* Inserts the text in register *r* into the current buffer, beginning at the current cursor location. The command leaves the point at the beginning of the insertion and sets a mark at the end. If you use a numeric argument (`C-u C-x g` *r*), the command reverses the locations of the point and mark.

Table 4.26. Commands to Manipulate Text in Registers

Operation	Command and Comments
Copy rectangle to register	`C-x r r` Copies a rectangle to a register *r*. Using a numeric argument deletes the rectangle after copying it. See the previous section, "Using Rectangles" for more information.
Retrieve rectangle from register	`C-x g r` Inserts the rectangle stored in register *r*. The upper-left character is placed at the current cursor position. See the previous section, "Using Rectangles" for more information.

Summary

Table 4.27 summarizes the main points in this chapter.

Table 4.27. Chapter 4 Summary

Topic	Summary
Changing Emacs' behavior with commands	• Set goal column to current cursor column: `C-x C-n` • Toggle date/time display: `M-x display-time`

Table 4.27, con't.

Topic	Summary
Changing Emacs' Behavior with command-line arguments	Order-Sensitive Arguments: • Run Emacs in another X window or terminal: `-t` *device* • Run Emacs remotely: `-d` *display* • Run Emacs in Batch mode: `-batch` • Do not read *.emacs* start-up file: `-q` or `-no-init-file` • Read another user's start-up file: `-u` *user* or `-user` *user* Order-Insensitive Arguments: • Visit file: *file* • Visit file and move to line number: `+`*linenum* • Load and execute Lisp file: `-l` *file* or `-load` *file* • Call Lisp function: `-f` *function* or `-funcall` *function* • Insert file into buffer: `-i` *file* or `-insert` *file* • Exit Emacs without prompting for saves: `-kill`
Regexp search commands	• Incrementally search forward for regexp: `C-M-s` • Retrieve last forward-search regexp: `C-s` • Incrementally search backward for regexp: `M-x` `isearch-backward-regexp` • Retrieve last backward-search regexp: `C-r` • Nonincrementally search forward for regexp: `M-x` `re-search-forward` • Nonincrementally search backward for regexp: `M-x` `re-search-backward`

Table 4.27, con't.

Topic	Summary
Regexp special characters	• Match single character except newline: **.** • Match start of line: **^** • Match end of line: **$** • Match zero or more occurrences of character or group: ***** • Match one or more occurrences of character or group: **+** • Match zero or one occurrence of character or group: **?** • Match range of characters: **[. . .]** • Match anything *but* a range of characters: **[^ . . .]** • Escape special characters: **** • Match start or end of a word: **\b** • Match next character *not* in a word: **\B** • Match start of a word: **\<** • Match end of a word: **\>** • Match start of buffer: **\ `** • Match end of buffer: **\ '** • Match any word character: **\w** • Match any *non*-word character: **\W** • Match multiple patterns: **\ |** • Match a syntactic class: **\s***c. c* can be: 　　• BLANK for whitespace 　　• **w** for words 　　• **–** for symbol names 　　• **.** for punctuation 　　• **(** for opening of balanced expressions 　　• **)** for closing of balanced expressions 　　• **"** for string delimiters 　　• **<** for comment start 　　• **>** for comment end • Match any character *not* in a syntactic class: **\S***c* • Match group: **\ (. . . \)** • Substitute prior group *n* into regexp: *****n*

Table 4.27, con't.

Topic	Summary
Regexp search-and-replace	• Search-and-replace with verification: `M-x query-replace-regexp` • Search-and-replace without verification: `M-x replace-regexp`
Editing outlines	Move to: • Next heading: `C-c C-n` • Previous heading: `C-c C-p` • Next heading at same level: `C-c C-f` • Previous heading at same level: `C-c C-b` • Next higher level: `C-c C-u` Collapsing and Expanding: • Hide all body lines: `M-x hide-body` • Show all body lines: `M-x show-body` • Hide all lines under heading: `C-c C-h` • Show all lines under heading: `C-c C s` • Hide body of current heading and its subheadings: `M-x hide-leaves` • Show all subheadings of current heading: `M-x show-branches` • Show next level of subheadings: `C-c C-i` • Hide current heading's body: `M-x hide-entry` • Show current heading's body: `M-x show-entry` Variable: • Define regexp for heading prefix: *outline-regexp*

Table 4.27, con't.

Topic	Summary
Buffer manipulation	• Change buffer's mode: `M-x` *modename* • Reset buffer's modification status: `M-~` • Select another buffer: `C-x b` • Select another buffer in another window: `C-x 4 b` • List all buffers: `C-x C-b` • Kill a buffer: `C-x k` • Kill selected buffers: `M-x kill-some-buffers` • Toggle buffer's read-only status: `C-x C-q` • Rename buffer: `M-x rename-buffer` • View buffer: `M-x view-buffer` • Insert buffer contents: `M-x insert-buffer` • Move region to another buffer: `M-x copy-to-buffer` • Append region to another buffer: `C-x a` or `M-x append-to-buffer` • Prepend region to another buffer: `M-x prepend-to-buffer`
File Operations	Creating, Retrieving and Visiting: • Visit (find) file: `C-x C-f` • Visit (find) file in another window: `C-x 4 C-f` • Create a new file: `C-x C-f`; specify new file name • Replace buffer with another file: `C-x C-v` • Insert file into current buffer: `C-x i` Saving and Writing: • Save current buffer: `C-x C-s` • Save selected buffer(s): `C-x s` • Write buffer to specified file: `C-x C-w` Change Buffer's File and Directory: • Display current default directory: `M-x pwd` • Change default directory: `M-x cd` • Change associated file: `M-x set-visited-filename`

Table 4.27, con't.

Topic	Summary
Auto-Save mode	Auto-Save File Names: • Visited files: *#filename#* • Other buffers: *#%*buffername*#* Commands: • Toggle auto-save mode: `M-x auto-save-mode` • Perform auto-save: `M-x do-auto-save` Variables: • Enable/disable auto-saving: *auto-save-default* • Auto-save to original file: *auto-save-visited-file-name* • Prevent deletion of auto-save files: *delete-auto-save-files* • Specify autosave interval: *auto-save-interval*
Backup files	Backup File Names: • Single backup files: *filename~* • Numbered backup files: *filename.~1~*, *filename.~2~*, etc. Variables: • Create numbered backup files: *version-control* = `t` • Create single backup file: *version-control* = `never` • Create single backup file unless numbered backup files exist: *version-control* = `nil` • Create backup file by copying original: *backup-by-copying* • Create backup file by copying if original has multiple names: *backup-by-copying-when-linked* • Create backup file by copying when renaming would change owner or group: *backup-by-copying-when-mismatch* • Number of low-numbered backup files to keep: *kept-old-versions* • Number of high-numbered backup files to keep: *kept-new-versions* • Delete backup files without confirmation: *trim-versions-without-asking*
Reverting a buffer	• Discard changes and reread disk file: `M-x revert-buffer`

Table 4.27, con't.

Topic	Summary
Preventing simultaneous editing	• Emacs may send a message when editing a file that is already "locked" by another user, and will always send a message when you attempt to save a file that has been changed since you last saved your buffer (presumably by another user who revised the file). • Emacs cannot detect simultaneous editing of files having multiple names (linked files).
Advanced window operations	Working in Other Windows: • Select buffer in another window: `C-x 4 b` • Visit (find) file in another window: `C-x 4 f` • Run Dired in another window: `C-x 4 d` • Compose mail in another window: `C-x 4 m` • Scroll another window: `C-M-v` Resizing Windows: • Increase height one line: `C-x ^` • Decrease height n lines: `C-u -n C-x ^` • Increase width: `C-x }` • Decrease width n lines: `C-u -n C-x }` (or `C-x {`)

Table 4.27, con't.

Topic	Summary
Editing responses in the minibuffer	Minibuffer Editing Commands: • Editing commands work in the minibuffer (e.g., `C-a`, `C-e`). • Increase height of minibuffer: `C-x ^` • Scroll help window from minibuffer: `C-M-v` Command History Commands: • Re-execute previous minibuffer command: `C-x ESC` • Display previous command: `M-p` • Display next command: `M-n` • Display command history: `M-x list-command-history` Response Completion: • Attempt to complete response and execute command: `RET` • Attempt to complete current word: `SPC` • Attempt to complete response, but don't execute command: `TAB` • Display list of alternatives for response: `?` Response Completion Variables: • Turn on/off display of alternatives: *completion-auto-help* • Ignore some file name extensions: *completion-ignored-extensions*
Sorting text	• Sort by comparing entire lines: `M-x sort-lines` • Sort by a field in each line: `M-x sort-fields` • Sort by numeric fields: `M-x sort-numeric-fields` • Sort on columns: `M-x sort-columns` • Sort by entire paragraph: `M-x sort-paragraphs` • Sort by entire page: `M-x sort-pages`

Table 4.27, con't.

Topic	Summary
Rectangles	• Replace rectangle text with spaces: **M-x clear-rectangle** • Delete rectangle: **M-x delete-rectangle** • Kill rectangle: **M-x kill-rectangle** • Yank rectangle: **M-x yank-rectangle** • Fill rectangle with spaces and push contents to right: **M-x open-rectangle**
Registers	• Save cursor position in register r: **C-x /** r • Jump to cursor position in register r: **C-x j** r • Copy current region to register r: **C-x x** r • Retrieve text from register r: **C-x g** r • Copy rectangle to register r: **C-x r** r • Retrieve rectangle from register r: **C-x g** r

Part 2
Programming in Emacs

This part of the book describes Emacs' commands and features for writing programs in C, FORTRAN, and Lisp. Make sure you are familiar with the primary text-editing commands discussed in Part 1 before reading the programming chapters in Part 2.

Chapter 5 discusses Emacs features that are common to all programming languages. After becoming familiar with the commands in Chapter 5, skip to the chapter for the programming language you use. There you will find language-specific instructions for moving among and marking subprograms, working with sexps and lists, and controlling indentation and commenting styles.

In addition, Pascal programmers will want to read Appendix A, which describes a nonstandard but widely available Pascal programming mode for Emacs (Emacs itself does not include a Pascal Mode). Lisp programmers may also be interested in the summary of the Emacs-Lisp programming language provided in Appendix B.

The following chapters are included in Part 2:

- Chapter 5: Program Development in Emacs

- Chapter 6: Editing in C Mode

- Chapter 7: Editing in FORTRAN Mode

- Chapter 8: Editing in Lisp Modes

5
Program Development in Emacs

Emacs has modes for editing C, FORTRAN, and Lisp programs. Each mode is sensitive to the syntax of the language for which it was designed, with commands for indenting source appropriately, adding comments, and many other common program development tasks. Emacs supports the following features that are useful to programmers:

- **Parenthesis matching,** which displays matching parentheses as you type them. This feature also works with braces {} and brackets [], depending on the language mode. These programming modes also include commands to force balanced parentheses, braces, and brackets.

- **Tag tables,** which allow you to easily find definitions of functions across multiple source files, or to do search-and-replace operations across multiple files. This is useful if you work on projects involving more than one source file.

- **Selective display of program lines,** wherein only the function definition lines are displayed in the source file. This provides a useful summary or overview of the source in a file.

- **Online manual entries,** which you can use to get documentation on system commands and routines without having to leave Emacs.

- **ChangeLog files,** which allow you to document changes to source files in a given directory. This is useful if you wish to keep a chronological record of changes made to source files in your project.

- **Compilation using the UNIX make facility,** which Emacs hooks into. If a compile results in syntax errors, you can use Emacs commands to go directly to the lines containing errors, without leaving the Emacs environment.

Together, these capabilities make Emacs a productivity-enhancing program development environment that is so versatile and powerful that you can probably do all of your program development from within Emacs.

This chapter covers the following topics:

- Supported editing modes
- Using Fundamental and Text mode commands in programming modes
- Moving by function
- Marking functions
- Indenting programs
- Commenting programs
- Matching parentheses, braces, and brackets
- Forcing balanced parentheses
- Selectively displaying program lines
- Getting documentation on system commands and routines
- Editing across multiple files with tag tables
- Keeping track of changes to source with a ChangeLog
- Compiling programs
- Sexp commands (advanced usage)

Supported Editing Modes

Emacs supports modes for editing C, FORTRAN, Lisp, and other languages. You may also be able to find "unsupported" modes developed by individuals outside the Free Software Foundation. This book describes the C, FORTRAN, and Lisp modes provided as part of the standard Emacs offering, as well as an unsupported Pascal mode (described in Appendix A, "Editing in Pascal Mode").

If you need to develop your own mode, you can get help on doing so from Chapter 13, "Customizing the Emacs Environment." If you need more help than is provided in that chapter, refer to the Free Software Foundation's *Emacs Lisp Reference Manual*, an excellent book on the subject.

If Emacs does not provide a needed mode, and you don't want to develop a custom mode, you may be able to use an existing mode for a language that has a similar syntax; for example, C++ programs can be edited in C mode fairly easily.

Determining the Mode from the File Name

Usually, Emacs can determine what mode to use for a source file by looking at the file name's suffix. Table 5.1 shows which mode Emacs uses for various file name suffixes.

Table 5.1. Programming Mode Selection

If the suffix is...	For example...	Emacs uses this mode...
.c	xprint.c	C
.f	numcrunch.f	FORTRAN
.el	newmode.el	Emacs-Lisp
.l or .lisp	lists.l	Lisp

If Emacs cannot determine the mode from the file name suffix, it defaults to Fundamental mode. There are two other ways to specify the file mode, described next.

Specifying the Mode within the Source File

To override the default mode, make the first nonblank line in the file contain a mode specification of the form:

    -*-mode_name-*-

where *mode_name* is the name of the mode to use. This is useful when you develop programs on a system in which the file name suffixes don't correspond to the default file name suffixes used by Emacs. For example, suppose FORTRAN file names end with a .f77 suffix on your system. Emacs would not recognize this suffix and so would default to Fundamental mode. To override this behavior, make the first line in the file a comment line containing the file mode specification, like this:

    c   -*-fortran-*-

Explicitly Setting the Editing Mode

If you don't want to include the mode specification in the source file, you can change the mode after visiting the file in Emacs. Table 5.2 shows the commands for enabling each programming mode.

Table 5.2. Commands That Set Programming Modes

To enable this mode...	Use this command...
C	`M-x c-mode`
FORTRAN	`M-x fortran-mode`
Emacs-Lisp	`M-x emacs-lisp-mode`
Lisp	`M-x lisp-mode`

Using Fundamental and Text Mode Commands in Programming Modes

The usual Fundamental and Text mode motion commands also apply in programming modes. For example, **C-f** and **C-b** move forward and backward one character, **C-v** and **M-v** scroll to the next and previous screen, and **M-f** and **M-b** move to the next and previous word. Likewise, Text mode commands for killing, deleting, and marking can be used in programming modes.

However, since some natural language text constructs don't exist in programming languages, the corresponding Text commands act differently in programming modes. For example, C, FORTRAN, and Lisp modes don't have a "paragraph" construct. In the C and Lisp modes, a "paragraph" is instead defined as any code delineated by blank lines; in FORTRAN, every line or block of comments is a paragraph.

A similar situation occurs with sentences. Actual sentences may be found within comments or strings. In such cases, **M-e** and **M-a** move to the end or beginning of the sentence as usual. Outside of comments or strings, **M-e** and **M-a** usually move to the next or previous blank line.

The best way to see how Fundamental and Text mode commands work in various programming modes is to experiment. If you make any mistakes, you can almost always undo them with the **C-x u** command.

Each mode has its own unique editing commands. But some commands are common to all programming modes, although they may act somewhat differently for each language. The remaining sections in this chapter introduce these common commands. For more details, see the appropriate language mode chapter.

Moving by Function

In all programming modes, the **C‑M‑a** command moves to the start of the current function, and the **C‑M‑e** command moves the end of the current or next function. What constitutes a "function" is defined uniquely for each language, as shown in Table 5.3.

Table 5.3. What Is a Function?

In Mode...	C-M-a and C-M-e Move to the Start or End of...
C	function
FORTRAN	program, subroutine, function, or block data subprogram
Lisp	defun

Marking Functions

In addition to the Text mode commands for marking text, all programming modes support the **C‑M‑h** command, which puts a marked region around the current function. This command is useful when you want to perform operations on an entire function—say, to delete it, or cut and paste it in a different location. Again, this function behaves somewhat differently in each language mode (See Table 5.4).

Table 5.4. Behavior of the C-M-h Command

Mode	Behavior
C	Puts the region around the current function, including the function's parameter declarations, name, and type (if present).
FORTRAN	Puts the region around the current subprogram—that is, around the main program unit, subroutine subprogram, function subprogram, or block data subprogram.
Any Lisp mode	Puts the region around the current defun.

Indenting Programs

Programming modes provide commands for indenting program lines in a readable and aesthetically pleasing manner. Such commands are quite useful to organizations that wish to maintain stylistic conventions among all programmers. If all programmers on a project use the same Emacs indenting commands, source files will have a similar look. Such standardization can help improve productivity because everyone quickly learns to read the "standard" style.

Emacs lets you modify the indentation styles; if you don't like the default, you can change it. These modifications are discussed in the individual language mode chapters.

Line indentation depends on how the indentation style is defined within each programming mode. Figure 5.1 shows a source file created using default indentation of the C mode.

```c
#include <stdio.h>

main(argc, argv)
     int    argc;
     char   *argv[];
{
  if (bogus())
    {
      printf("This is a bogus program.\n");
      exit(1);
    }
}

int bogus()
{
  return 1;
}
```

Figure 5.1. Default C Program Indentation

Some indentation commands work differently in different modes. But the commands in Table 5.5 work similarly in all programming modes. They can indent single or multiple source lines.

Table 5.5. Common Indentation Commands

Operation	Command and Comments
Indent Line	**TAB** Indents the current line appropriately.
Finish line and open a new line	**C-j** or **LFD** Finishes the current line and opens a line below with proper indentation; equivalent to **RET** followed by **TAB**.
Indent all lines within a region	**C-M-** Appropriately re-indents all lines in the current region. For example, **C-M-h** followed by **C-M-** re-indents all lines within the current function.
Insert tab into source file	**C-q TAB** Inserts an actual tab character into the source file. This provides a way to override default indentation.

Commenting Programs

Emacs provides several powerful commands for commenting program source. The basic command to add a comment is **M-;**. Each mode inserts comments using the appropriate syntax for the language, as shown in Table 5.6.

Table 5.6. How Commenting Works in Each Language Mode

Mode	How **M-;** Works
C	Appends a comment of the form **/* */** to the current line.
FORTRAN	Opens a comment line above the current line with a **c** in column 1.
Lisp	If the current line is empty, opens a comment line of the form **; ; ;** in the first column. If the current line contains lisp code, appends a comment that starts with **;** to the end of the current line.

In all cases, Emacs puts the comment in a column it thinks is appropriate. Which column is used depends on the language mode and the type of comment within that mode. In addition, Emacs places the cursor at an appropriate location within the comment delimiters; you can simply start typing the comment without having to move the cursor to the correct location within the comment.

The **M-;** command can also be used to align existing comments. This is useful for lining-up comments in a source file to make it more readable. **M-;** can also be used simply to move to the text within a comment.

Table 5.7 summarizes the commands used for creating and manipulating comments. Each language mode has additional commenting commands and customization capabilities. For details, see the appropriate language mode chapter.

Table 5.7. Commands for Commenting Programs

Operation	Command and Comments
Create or align comment	**M-;** Creates a new comment or aligns an existing one.
Set comment column	**C-x ;** Sets the **comment column** at which **M-;** places new comments.
Delete comment on line	**C-u - C-x ;** This is **C-x ;** with a negative argument, and deletes the comment on the current line.
Continue comment	**C-M-j** or **M-LFD** Continue the current line on to the next line.

There are three ways to do multi-line comments:

- Use the **M-;** command on each line.

- Use the **C-M-j** command to continue a comment on to the next line.

- Use **M-x auto-fill** to enable auto-filling while in the language mode. This causes comment lines to automatically wrap to the next line when the cursor moves past the fill column.

As with most other Emacs features, commenting commands can be customized to your particular needs. Except for setting the comment column (with `C-x   ;`), comment customization depends largely on the language mode used. For details on comment customization, see the appropriate language mode chapter.

Matching Parentheses, Braces, and Brackets

As you edit program source, you may notice that whenever you type expressions involving parentheses, Emacs shows matching parentheses by moving the cursor. For example, if you type the following line,

```
if ( a < b )...
```

the cursor jumps back to the opening **(** momentarily after you type the closing **)** ; then it positions the cursor after the closing **)** . This **parentheses matching** is done automatically in all language modes and can help you catch typos (that would cause syntax errors) before you compile. In languages that involve lots of parentheses nesting, such as Lisp, such a capability is invaluable.

Emacs may also match braces **{ }** and brackets **[ ]**, depending on whether these characters are syntactically important in the language. For example, in C mode, Emacs shows matching braces around a compound statement if the opening and closing brace occur on the same visual page:

```
if ( a > b )
  {                          ← The opening brace.
    tmp = a;
    a = b;
    b = tmp;
  }                          ← When you type the closing brace, the cursor jumps
                               back momentarily to the opening brace.
```

If you incorrectly match parentheses, braces, or brackets, Emacs displays an error message. For instance, if you type **(}**, Emacs displays the message **Mismatched parentheses**.

You can turn off automatic matching by setting the Emacs variable *blink-matching-paren* to **nil**. Its default value is **t**, which enables the feature. By default, Emacs searches backward up to 4000 characters to find a matching element. You can increase or decrease this amount by setting the value of the variable *blink-matching-paren-distance*. For details on setting variables, see Chapter 13, "Customizing the Emacs Environment."

Forcing Balanced Parentheses

The **M-** **(** command causes Emacs to insert a pair of balanced parentheses at the current cursor position. This is especially useful in Lisp modes but is also useful whenever you type expressions containing nested pairs of parentheses. Incidentally, this and the matching parentheses feature are supported in Fundamental mode, too.

Selectively Displaying Program Lines

When a source file becomes large, you may want to see the general structure of the file *without* having to see all of the code contained in it. For example, you might want to see only the lines containing function or procedure definitions, but not the code contained within them. Assuming that the lines within a function are indented further than the functions definition line, you can use the **C-x** **$** command to do this.

C-x **$** hides lines that have an indentation level greater than its numeric argument. Emacs denotes hidden lines with an ellipsis (**...**).

For example, suppose you have written the C program shown in Figure 5.1, earlier in this chapter. The lines of code within each function are indented at least 2 columns. Therefore, to see only the function definition lines, run **C-u** **2** **C-x** **$**. Figure 5.2 shows how the screen would look.

```
#include <stdio.h>

main(argc, argv)
int     argc;
char    *argv[];
{...
}


int bogus()
{...
}
```

Figure 5.2. Sample C Program with Hidden Lines

To make the hidden lines visible again, use **C-x** **$** without a numeric argument.

When viewing a file with hidden lines, you can still move up and down through the file with the usual Text mode motion commands, such as **C-p** and **C-n**. However, you shouldn't attempt to edit a file in this state as you cannot see some of the lines.

Getting Documentation on System Commands and Routines

Using the **M-x manual-entry** command, you can view **man-pages**—online UNIX reference pages displayed by the **man** command—within an Emacs window. If your system does not have the **man** command or if the man-page files are not stored on your system, the **M-x manual-entry** command won't work.

This command prompts for the name of a UNIX command or routine. For example, to get information on **fopen**, you would use **M-x manual-entry** as follows:

```
M-x manual-entry RET                        ← Invoke the command
Manual entry (topic): fopen RET             ← Type the name of the entry
```

Emacs then displays a message such as **"looking for formatted manual entry"**. If the entry is found, Emacs displays it in a separate window that you can scroll through. If Emacs cannot find the entry, it displays the following message in another window:

```
No manual entry for entry.
```

When searching for *entry*, Emacs searches *all* of the following UNIX references sections, in the order shown:

Section 1	User Commands
Section 1M	System Administration Commands
Section 2	System Calls
Section 3	Subroutines and Subroutine Libraries
Section 4	File Formats
Section 5	Miscellaneous
Section 6	Games
Section 7	Device Special Files
Section 9	Glossary

If a matching entry is found in more than one section, Emacs displays all matching entries, one after another in the display window. For example, **chown** exists both as a user command and a system call. If you run **M-x manual-entry RET chown RET**, Emacs displays the text for **chown**(1) and **chown**(2).

Within a manual-entry window, you can use the usual search commands to find text. To make searching straightforward, Emacs strips all embedded formatting codes, if any, from the text.

Editing Across Multiple Files with Tag Tables

When working on a project involving several source files, it can be tedious to switch
back and forth among source files and downright difficult to do search-and-replace
operations across multiple files. For example, suppose you're working on a project
that involves these files:

tio.c	Contains low-level terminal I/O routines for cursor positioning, text highlighting, etc.
inout.c	Contains high-level I/O routines that call routines in the **tio.c** file to do things like display strings, read strings, etc.
inout.h	Contains type definitions for **inout.c**.
menu.c	Contains routines that display programmer-defined menus for reading selections from users. It calls routines from **tio.c** and **inout.c**.
menu.h	Contains type definitions for **menu.c**.
main.c	Main program that calls routines from **tio.c**, **inout.c**, and **menu.c**. Also has some routines of its own.

Figure 5.3 shows the relationship among these files. Trying to keep track of where
each routine is defined and how it is used can be tedious in a situation like this. And
what if you wanted to search and replace on a string that occurred in each file? Emacs
tag tables provide an easy solution to such problems.

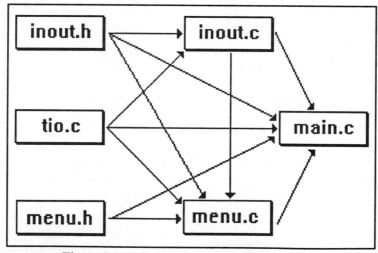

Figure 5.3. Relationship among Program Files

What Is a Tag?

What constitutes a **tag** depends on the programming language. Table 5.8 shows how a tag is defined for each of the supported programming modes.

Table 5.8. Definition of Tag for Each Language Mode

Language Mode	A Tag is...
C	Any function. (Typedefs can also be considered tags, as determined by the **etags** command, described below.)
FORTRAN	Any functions or subroutine.
Lisp	Any function defined with **defun**, any variable defined with **defvar** or **defconst**, and generally, the first argument of any expression that starts with **(def** in column zero.

Setting Up Tag Tables

Before using tag commands on a set of files, you must first build a tag table for the set of files. This is done with the **etags** command, which builds a tag table containing the names of all component files and the location (line number) of routines defined within each. **etags** places the tag table in a file named **TAGS**.

   etags is an executable program. You can run **etags** from the UNIX command line, or from within Emacs using the **M-!** command or in a ***Shell*** window. The syntax of **etags** is:

```
etags file1 file2...
```

For example, to create a **TAGS** file for the example source files described previously, use **etags** as follows from the operating system command line:

```
etags main.c menu.h menu.c inout.h inout.c tio.c
```

If you were to use the **M-!** command to run **etags**, Emacs would prompt you for the command (as **Shell command:**), and you would type it exactly as above.

   Note that the order in which the files are specified is significant because it determines the order in which Emacs searches through the files for a tag.

Selecting the Tag Table

Before using tag commands, you must select a tag table. If you try to use a tag command without selecting a tag table, Emacs will prompt for the name of a tag table file. You can also explicitly select a tag table with the **M-x visit-tags-table** command, which prompts for a **TAGS** file containing a tag table. For example, if the above **TAGS** file was created in your home directory, Emacs would prompt:

```
Visit tags table: (default TAGS) ~/█    ← Press RET to accept default or
                                           type tag file name and press RET.
```

The **M-x visit-tags-table** command sets the variable *tags-file-name* to the path name of the **TAGS** file. Thus, you could also select the **TAGS** file by setting this variable with **M-x set-variable**.

Finding Tags

To find a tag, use the **M-.** command, which prompts for tag name. If it finds the tag, Emacs visits the file containing the tag and positions the cursor at the start of the line containing the tag's definition. The mode line is updated to show the file containing the tag. For example, if you search for **get_menu_selection**, it might display something similar to Figure 5.4, indicating the tag was found in the file **menu.c**.

```
        .
        .
        .
char    get_menu_selection(title, size, items, descrs, selectors)
/*
 * Input a valid menu selection from the user; display the item
 * description string. The [RETURN] key causes the currently
 * highlighted menu item to be selected. The [SPACE] key highlights
 * the next menu item to the right; the [BACKSPACE] key highlights
 * the next left menu item. Menu items can also be selected directly
 * by entering the letter.
/*      .
        .
        .
-----Emacs: menu.c       10:05am 0.02 Mail  ( C)---- 8% ---------------


  Misc  | Windows| File  |Buffers || Search |Movement| Help | Exit
        |        |       |& Blocks||        |        |      |
```

Figure 5.4. Sample Display

If you specify a substring to **M-.** (say, `get` instead of `get_menu_selection`), **M-.** finds the first tag that matches the substring. For instance, if you have the tags `get_menu_selection`, `get_type`, and `forgetmenot`, **M-.** will find whichever one is first. In such cases, it is useful to find the *next* occurrence. The **C-u M-.** command does this; it is simply the **M-.** command with a numeric argument. **C-u M-.** finds the next occurrence, regardless of what argument is used.

Each file that **M-.** visits is loaded into a buffer. However, Emacs does *not* create a separate window for the buffer. To get a separate window, use the **C-x 4 .** command. Table 5.9 summarizes the commands used to find tags.

Table 5.9. Commands That Find Tags

Operation	Command and Comments
Find tag	`M-.` Prompts for a tag and finds the first occurrence.
Find tag in another window	`C-x 4 .` Prompts for a tag and finds the first occurrence. Displays the tag in another window. Creates a new window if necessary.
Find next occurrence of tag	`C-u M-.` or `M-,` Finds the next occurrence of the last search tag.

Searching and Replacing Text

When editing multiple files with a tag table, you can also search for and replace text *other than tags*, across all files defined in the current tag table. Table 5.10 summarizes these commands.

Table 5.10. Tag Table Search-and-Replace Commands

Operation	Command and Comments
Search for regular expression	`M-x tags-search` Prompts for a regular expression to search for in all the files in the current tag table.

Table 5.10, con't.

Operation	Command and Comments
Query-replace	`M-x tags-query-replace` Prompts for a search string (not a regular expression) and a replacement string; then calls the query-replace function on all files in the current tag table.
Repeat last search command	`M-,` Repeat the last search or replace command. This is useful for finding the next occurrence of a regular expression without having to retype the regular expression each time.

The `M-,` command is useful when used with the `M-x tags-query-replace` command, which sometimes terminates prematurely upon encountering unrecognized characters.

Visiting Files

Emacs keeps track of which tag table file it last visited. The `M-x next-file` command makes Emacs visit the next file in the current tag table. When given an argument (as `C-u M-x next-file`), this command visits the first file in the tag table.

Listing Tags in a File

Emacs can also list all the tags defined with a particular file. Table 5.11 summarizes the commands that do this.

Table 5.11. Commands That List the Tags in a File

Operation	Command and Comments
List all tags in file	`M-x list-tags` Prompts for the name of a file (contained in the current tag table), and creates a window listing all the names of tags defined within the file.

Table 5.11, con't.

Operation	Command and Comments
Search for tags matching regular expression	`M-x tags-apropos` Prompts for a regular expression: `Tag apropos (regexp): ` ▮ Searches for all the tags that match the regular expression and displays them in another window.

Keeping Track of Changes to Source with a ChangeLog

The `M-x add-change-log-entry` command allows you to document changes made to source files in a given directory. It records changes into a file named, by default, `ChangeLog`. Changes are made in reverse chronological order; that is, more recent changes appear before older changes in the file. Emacs assumes there is one `ChangeLog` file per directory; therefore, it records changes for *all* the source files in the directory.

For the first entry you add to `ChangeLog` on a given day, Emacs includes a header giving the date and your name. Then Emacs opens a line, starting with a tab and asterisk, on which you describe the change. For example, running `M-x add-change-log-entry` on April 15 added an entry to the `ChangeLog` file that looks like Figure 5.5.

There are no restrictions on the format of the description other than each line must start with a tab. However, you should use a consistent format, such as the one shown here, which identifies the file and name of the routine in which the change was made.

Note, also, that the `ChangeLog` buffer uses Auto-Indent minor mode, meaning that any text you type past the fill column is automatically wrapped and indented on the next line. This frees you from having to type TAB on each line. An additional feature of Auto-Indent mode is that the fill commands will automatically fill paragraphs indented to the appropriate level (one tab space).

To describe additional changes under a single date-name entry, run `M-x add-change-log-entry` again. This opens another change line starting with tab and asterisk. For example, once we finished the description of the change on April 15, we added another one by invoking `M-x add-change-log-entry` again (as shown in Figure 5.6).

```
Sun Apr 15 22:56:24 1990 Michael Schoonover (michael)


        * █              ← Type description of the change here


Tue Mar 13 10:30:31 1990  Michael Schoonover (michael)


        * xprint.c (initialize):
        Recognize options -D, -B, -A:
                -B <cmd>   Run command <cmd> before
                           printing
                -A <cmd>   Run command <cmd> after
                           printing
                -D <dir>   Start running in directory
                           <dir>
        Working directory path length increased from 50
        to 255


        * whatsits.c (display_lines):
        Bug fixed when output lines are longer than
        screen width. This was causing messy output on
        some systems. Lines longer than screen width are
        now truncated before display.
```

Figure 5.5. Sample ChangeLog

```
Sun Apr 15 22:56:24 1990  Michael Schoonover (michael)


        * █              ← Emacs waits for entry of the next description
            .
            .
            .
        * xtaxes.c (deductions):
        Added code to find additional legal itemized
        deductions, just in time for filing for 1989.
```

Figure 5.7. Next Entry in ChangeLog

You can save the changes, just as you save any other buffer. For example, **C-x C-s** saves the **ChangeLog** file.

Compiling Programs

You can compile programs from Emacs using the **M-x compile** command. Emacs assumes you want to compile source files via the UNIX **make** command, which requires a **Makefile** to be present. When you run **M-x compile**, Emacs prompts with:

```
Compile command: make -k ▮
```

To compile using this **make** command, just press **RET**. To compile using some other UNIX command, simply edit the command line and press **RET**. (The default compile command is stored in the variable *compile-command*.) Thereafter, **M-x compile** will use the previous compile command as the default.

The compile doesn't actually work on files that are currently in the buffer. Instead, it runs **make**, which looks for files that you saved from Emacs. Therefore, if any changes have been made to a file that is currently loaded, Emacs will ask whether you want to save it before starting the compile.

To perform the compilation, Emacs spawns the compile command in a subshell, and all output from the compile goes to a buffer named ***compilation***. The compile command is run in the same directory as the buffer from which it was invoked. For example, if you run **M-x compile** from a buffer that contains the file **/users/emacs/prog.p**, then the compile command is run in the directory **/users/emacs**.

Compilation Status and Aborting

If a window doesn't already exist for the ***compilation*** buffer, Emacs automatically creates one. The status line of the ***compilation*** buffer's window indicates the status of the compilation: When the compilation is in progress, **run** is displayed; when the compilation is finished, **exit** is displayed.

Occasionally, it may be necessary to abort a compilation process—for example, if you compiled the incorrect file. To kill a compilation already in progress, use the **M-x kill-compiler** command. This causes the status line to display **signal**.

Correcting Syntax Errors

If errors occur from a **make** compilation, you can use the **C-x `** command to move to the line in the source file containing the next error. It displays two buffers simultaneously: the ***compilation*** buffer, and the buffer containing the compilation error. Emacs automatically moves the cursor to the start of the line on which the error occurred.

If multiple files were compiled, Emacs visits all files that generated error messages. Then it moves to the line containing first error in the first file. When all the errors in a buffer have been viewed, **C-x `** switches to the first line containing an error in the next buffer; and so on, until all files containing errors have been viewed.

You need not wait for the compilation to finish before viewing the next error with the **C-x `** command. You can begin correcting syntax errors before the compilation is finished.

Suppose you've written the program shown in the **prog.c** buffer in Figure 5.8, and the **Makefile** shown in Figure 5.7, both of which reside in the same directory. The program contains two syntax errors:

• The first assignment includes a colon.

• The program is missing a closing brace.

```
prog:prog.c
    cc prog.c
    mv a.out prog
```

Figure 5.7. Makefile for Compiling the Program

Figure 5.8 also shows the ***compilation*** buffer produced by running the **M-x compile** command with the default **make -k** argument.

```
#include <stdio.h>
main()
{
  int i,j,k;

  i :- 10;
  j - i * 10;
  k = j - 10;
-----Emacs: prog.c                       ( C)---- All-----------------
cd /users/michael/emacs
make -k
        cc prog.c
"prog.c", line 7: redeclaration of i
"prog.c", line 7: syntax error
"prog.c", line 12: syntax error
*Error code 1

Compilation finished at Mon Apr 30 15:22:18
-----Emacs: *compilation*               (Compilation: exit)---All--
```

Figure 5.8. prog.c Program and *compilation* Buffer

At this point, if you run the **C-x `** command, the Emacs window changes, placing the cursor at line 7 in the **prog.c** buffer (see Figure 5.9). Notice also that the ***compilation*** buffer moves to the top of the screen and only the lines containing error messages are displayed.

```
"prog.c", line 7: redeclaration of i
"prog.c", line 7: syntax error
"prog.c", line 12: syntax error
-----Emacs: *compilation*              (Compilation: exit)---22%--
#include <stdio.h>
main()
{
  int i,j,k;

  i := 10;      ◄———— The cursor moves to the start of this line
  j = i * 10;
  k = j - 10;




-----Emacs: prog.c                     ( C)---- All----------------
C-x `         ◄———— The command is displayed in the minibuffer
```

Figure 5.9. Using C-x ' to Find Errors

Run **C-x `** again, and the cursor stays on the same line because the next error, according to the error listing in **\*compilation\*** is also on line 7. To get the error on line 12, repeat the **C-x `** command.

Clearly, this command is extremely useful. It doesn't take long to get proficient with compilation commands, and you can greatly improve your programming productivity with them.

Re-Viewing Errors

When you have viewed all errors in all files, **C-x `** displays the message **no more errors** in the minibuffer. To go back to the start to view the errors again, run **C-u C-x `** (that is, **C-x `** with a numeric argument).

Sexp Commands (Advanced Usage)

Each mode also provides a set of commands for moving over and among **sexps**, a Lisp term for expressions. These commands are especially useful when writing Lisp programs, but can be useful in other languages as well.

What Are Sexps?

Like functions, sexps are defined uniquely for each language mode via the mode's syntax table (described in Chapter 13, "Customizing the Emacs Environment"). Although sexp definitions differ in each language, all have the following characteristics in common:

- An sexp can usually be any symbol, numeric constant, or string constant. For example, **foo**, **+**, and **"This is a string."** are all valid sexps.

- An sexp can be anything contained within balanced parentheses **()**, braces **{}**, or brackets **[]**. Thus, the following are all valid sexps:

  - **In C:**

    ```
    {
      i++;
      str[i] = *s++;
    }
    ```

  - **In FORTRAN:**

    ```
      (1x,/
    $     1h ,i5,/
    $     1h ,f10.2/
    $     )
    ```

  - **In Lisp:**

    ```
    (defun dummy (line)
     "This is a dummy lisp defun that
      doesn't do anything."
     (interactive "")
    )
    ```

- What actually constitutes an sexp depends on where the cursor is located. For instance, in the examples above, the cursor is on or immediately preceding the first character of each sexp. In each example, the sexp actually contains several sexps.

- In languages that have comments within balanced delimiters—for example, **/* */** in C—comments are not sexps. In languages that have unbalanced comment delimiters—for example, end-of-line (**!**) comments in FORTRAN—such comments may be interpreted as sexps when moving backward over them.

The Commands

Table 5.12 summarizes commands for moving about and manipulating sexps. It also summarizes commands for navigating and reformatting **lists**—groups of nested parentheses, braces, and brackets. These commands are invoked with the Control and Meta keys simultaneously.

Table 5.12. Sexp and List Commands

Operation	Command and Comments
	Sexp Commands
Forward sexp	`C-M-f` If the cursor is within an sexp, move it to the end; otherwise, move the cursor to the end of the next sexp.
Backward sexp	`C-M-b` Same as `C-M-f` but moves backward instead.
Kill sexp	`C-M-k` Kills from point to the end of the sexp.
Transpose sexps	`C-M-t` Transposes (swaps) expressions on either side of the cursor.
Mark after sexp	`C-M-@` Places the mark after the following sexp, leaving the cursor as is.

Table 5.12, con't.

Operation	Command and Comments
	List Commands
Up list	`C-M-u` Moves backward to the next highest level in the list structure in which the cursor currently resides.
Down list	`C-M-d` Moves forward to the next nested level in the list structure in which the cursor currently resides.
Forward list	`C-M-n` If within a list, moves to the end of the list; otherwise, moves to the end of the next list.
Backward list	`C-M-p` Same as `C-M-n`, but moves backward instead.
Indent list	`C-M-q` Properly indents all lines within a list.
Shift list	`C-u TAB` Rigidly shifts a list so that its first line is properly indented with respect to the previous lines.

Summary

Table 5.13 summarizes the important points in this chapter.

Table 5.13. Chapter 5 Summary

Topic	Summary
Mode selection	1. Default mode determined by file name suffix: • `.c` selects C mode • `.f` selects FORTRAN mode • `.el` selects Emacs-Lisp mode • `.l` or `.lisp` selects Lisp mode 2. Determined by first nonblank line in source file (overrides default): *-*-mode_name-*-* 3. After Emacs visits file, change mode with: • `M-x c-mode` • `M-x fortran-mode` • `M-x emacs-lisp-mode` • `M-x lisp-mode`
Basic cursor movement	Same as in Fundamental mode.
Commands that operate on functions	A function is: • A function in C mode • A main program, subroutine, function, or block data subprogram in FORTRAN • A defun in Lisp modes Commands: • Move to the start of a function: `C-M-a` • Move to the end of a function: `C-M-e` • Put a region around the current function: `C-M-h`

Table 5.13, con't.

Topic	Summary

Indentation commands	• Indentation styles are unique to each mode, and customizable.
	• Indentation commands common to all programming modes:
	  • Indent the current line appropriately: `TAB`
	  • Finish the current line and starts a new line, indented appropriately: `C-j`
	  • Re-indent all lines in the current region: `C-M-\`

Inserting tabs into file	Use `C-q` `TAB`

Commentin g programs	• Commenting styles are unique to each mode, and customizable.
	• Comments are aligned at a column defined by the *comment-column* variable.
	• Commenting commands:
	  • Add comment to current line: `M-;` (If a comment exists on the current line, aligns the comment and places the cursor at the start of the comment.)
	  • Set *comment-column* to cursor's column: `C-x ;`
	  • Delete comment on current line or region: `C-u - C-x ;`
	  • Finish current comment and continue onto next line: `C-M-j`
	• If Auto-Fill minor mode is enabled, comments automatically wrap to next line when you type comment text past fill margin.

Parentheses matching	• Emacs automatically matches parentheses as you type them. • Matching also works on braces { } and brackets [ ], if syntactically significant for mode. • Turn off parenthesis matching, set variable *blink-matching-paren* to `nil`. • Insert a pair of balanced parentheses at the cursor position: `M-(`
Hiding lines	Hides lines that are indented more than *n* columns: `C-u` *n* `C-x $`

Table 5.13, con't.

Topic	Summary
Display man page	Display man-page for *name*: `M-x manual-entry RET` *name* `RET`
Tag tables for editing across multiple files	• Create tag table for a set of source files: `etags` *source_file1 source_file2* ... Tag table is stored in a file named `TAGS` in current directory and contains pointers to all tags defined in the source files. • Tags are: • Functions and (optionally) typedefs in C • Functions or subroutines in FORTRAN • Any expression that starts with `(def` in column 0 in Lisp • Select a `TAGS` file: `M-x visit-tags-table` • Commands that operate on selected `TAGS` file: • Find a tag in the source files: `M-.` • Find a tag and display it in another window: `C-x 4 .` • Find the next occurrence of last search tag: `C-u M-.` • Find a regular expression in the source files: `M-x tags-search` • Search-and-replace regular expression: `M-x tags-query-replace` • Repeat last search command: `M-,` • List all tags within a file: `M-x list-tags` • Search for tags matching regular expression: `M-x tags-apropos`
Using Changelogs to record changes	• Document changes made to a source file: `M-x add-change-log-entry` • Changes are time-stamped and added in reverse-chronological order in a file named `ChangeLog` in the current directory.

Table 5.13, con't.

Topic	Summary
Compiling programs	• Compile a program (`make -k` by default): `M-x compile` • Abort compilation: `M-x kill-compiler` • Emacs understands the error output produced by `make`: • Go to next line containing compilation error: `C-x '` • Go back to first compilation error: `C-u C-x '`
Operating on sexps and lists	• Sexp is an expression containing balanced parentheses, or braces `{ }` and brackets `[ ]` (in some languages). • Sexp and list commands: • Move forward over sexp: `C-M-f` • Move backward over sexp: `C-M-b` • Move up and backward in list: `C-M-u` • Move down and forward in list: `C-M-d` • Move forward over list: `C-M-n` • Move backward over list: `C-M-p` • Kill to end of sexp: `C-M-k` • Transpose sexps around cursor: `C-M-t` • Place mark after sexp: `C-M-@` • Re-indent lines within list: `C-M-q` • Shift list: `C-u TAB`

6
Editing in C Mode

Emacs provides a C mode for editing C source files that adhere to the Kernighan and Ritchie standard or the ANSI standard. This chapter describes the following C mode features:

- Invoking C mode
- Assumptions about C source
- Moving among functions
- Marking functions
- Indenting programs
- Commenting programs
- Working with sexps and lists (advanced usage)
- Customizing indentation (advanced usage)
- Customizing commenting (advanced usage)

For general information on programming language modes, including many C mode features, see Chapter 5, "Program Development in Emacs."

Invoking C Mode

Emacs uses C mode for files whose names end in `.c`. If your system uses a different naming convention for C source files, you can enter C mode in either of two ways:

• After loading a C source file, invoke C mode with the **M-x c-mode** command.

• Make sure the first nonblank line of your source file is a comment that includes the string −*−c−*−, as in:

    `/* -*-c-*- */`

Assumptions About C Source

In C mode, Emacs assumes that an open brace ({) at the beginning of a line marks the start of a function body. If you need an open brace at the start of a line that is not the beginning brace for a function body, escape it with a backslash (\\).

For example, suppose you have defined a string that extends across multiple lines, and the string breaks such that the { is the first character on the line. You would escape it with a backslash on the second line, as follows:

```
#include <stdio.h>
main()
{
   char *longstring = "This is a string that contains a brace,\
\{, on the second line.";

   printf("longstring = %s\n", longstring);
}
↑
column 0
```

If you typed this example in a C buffer, you would notice that Emacs would match the last closing brace with the opening brace after **main()**, not the opening brace within the string constant. If the opening brace in the string were not escaped, Emacs would incorrectly match the closing brace with the one in the string.

Note that the sequence \\{ within the string would be interpreted as { by the C preprocessor; thus, the backslash does not interfere with the string's value.

Moving Among Functions

In addition to the usual Fundamental and Text mode cursor motion commands, you can use function motion commands, described in Table 6.1.

Table 6.1. C Mode Function Motion Commands

Operation	Command and Comments
Move to start of function or previous function	**C-M-a** If the cursor is inside a function body, this command moves to the start (opening brace) of the function body. If the cursor is already at the start or between functions, then this command moves to the start of the previous function.
Move to end of function or next function	**C-M-e** If the cursor is inside a function body, this command moves to the line following the end of the function body (the line following the closing brace). If the cursor is at the end or between functions, this command moves to the end of the next function.

Marking Functions

Often, it is useful to perform editing operations on entire C functions. For example, you might want to delete a function from a buffer, or yank it into the kill ring to be pulled into another buffer. **C-M-h** can be used for this purpose. When used within a function, **C-M-h** places mark at the end of the function and moves the cursor to the first character in the function. When used between functions, it does the same thing for the *next* function.

As an example, suppose you wanted to delete a function from the buffer. You would run **C-M-h** followed by **C-w**. Emacs removes the function from the buffer, placing it in the kill ring.

Indenting Programs

The usual programming mode indentation commands are available in C mode, as described in Table 6.2. These commands produce indentation appropriately for the current indentation style, as defined by C mode indentation variables. The rest of this section summarizes how to use default indentation style. For details on customizing the indentation style, refer to "Customizing Indentation" later in this chapter.

Table 6.2. C Mode Indentation Commands

Operation	Command and Comments
Indent current line	**TAB** By default, the **TAB** command indents the current line appropriately for the current indentation style. To alter this behavior, see "Altering the Behavior of TAB" later in this chapter.
Finish line and indent next	**C-j** or **LFD** Finishes current line and starts a new line indented according to the current indentation style. This is a nice shorthand for the **RET TAB** sequence.
Indent all lines in region	**C-M-** Re-indents all lines in the current region appropriately for the current indentation style. For example, to re-indent all the lines in the current function, use **C-M-h** to put a region around the function; then use **C-M-** to indent all the lines. To re-indent all lines in the current buffer, use **C-x h** to put a region around the entire buffer, then use **C-M-**.

Automatically Indenting Braces

As you type opening and closing braces { }, Emacs will automatically insert newlines around the brace and indent it appropriately for the current style, provided that the variable *c-auto-newline* is non-**nil**. For example, suppose *c-auto-newline* is set to **t** on your system and you type the following text *without* typing **TAB** or **LFD**:

```
struct XYZ{
```

As soon as you type the opening brace, Emacs places it on the next line, indented two spaces, and moves the cursor to the following line, ready for you to type the next line indented appropriately:

```
struct XYZ
   {
   
```

   ← Emacs wraps the brace to the next line
   ← and places the cursor at the correct column.

To disable this behavior, set *c-auto-indent* to `nil`. Emacs will still indent braces automatically for you, but will not insert the newlines before and after the brace.

For details on making changes to variables "permanent," see Chapter 13, "Customizing the Emacs Environment."

Indenting Function Argument Declarations

Emacs can accommodate two indentation styles with ANSI C argument declarations:

- All arguments on the same line as the function name:

```
main (int argc, char *argv[])
```

- Arguments on separate lines, one per line:

```
main (int argc,
      char *argv[])
```

With the first style, there is really no indentation involved; you simply type the arguments all on the same line. In the second style, you use **TAB** or **LFD** (**C–j**) to indent each argument to line up with the one on the previous line:

```
main (int argc,                      ← Press RET to finish this line.
      char *argv[])                  ← Press TAB to indent the next line
{      ↑                               (or simply press LFD or C-j).
↑          column that lines up with argument on previous line
column 0
```

If you declare function arguments the non-ANSI C way (after a function's parameter list), Emacs indents them 5 spaces. For example, the following declaration of the **main** function was created using **TAB** on the lines that declare **argc** and **argv**:

```
main(argc, argv)
      int argc;                      ← Type the line, then press TAB.
      char *argv[];                  ← (Same on this line)
{      ↑
↑          column 5
column 0
```

Note that Emacs does *not* automatically indent argument declarations as you type them. To get this indentation, you must use **TAB** or **LFD**. In other words, C mode does not force you to indent argument declarations. For example, if you don't want the argument declarations indented at all, you would simply type them *without* pressing **TAB** or **LFD**:

```
main(argc, argv)
int argc;                        ← Press RET at the end of each line
char *argv[];                    ← if you don't want indentation.
{
↑
column 0
```

Indenting Function Bodies

C mode assumes that the opening and closing brace of every function (including **main**) start in column 0. Statements within the function body are indented 2 columns. Shown below is a program illustrating this indentation:

```
void foo(char * str)
{
  printf("%s\n", str);
}

main (int argc,
      char *argv[])
{
  foo("Good-bye blue monday.");
} ↑
↑ column 2
column 0
```

Various C mode commands require that the opening and closing brace of a function body be in column 0 (for example, **C-M-a** and **C-M-e**); therefore, you should not indent them to a different column. C mode attempts to enforce putting the braces in column 0. For example, if you space in to column 2, type **{**, and press **RET**, then Emacs automatically puts the **{** back in column 0. You don't have to use **TAB** to indent the **{** properly.

In contrast, you must explicitly use **LFD** or **TAB** to indent lines within the function body:

```
void foo(char * str)
{
  printf("%s\n", str);           ← This line indented with LFD.
}

main (int argc,
      char *argv[])
{
  foo("Good-bye blue monday.\n");  ← This line indented with LFD.
}
```

Indenting Continued Statements

A continued statement is any statement that contains a substatement—for example, the body of a **for**, **while**, or **if** statement. By default, Emacs indents the substatement 2 spaces. You must use **LFD** or **TAB** to indent the substatement—for example:

```
for (i = 0; i < 10; i++)        ← Type the continued statement and press LFD.
  a[i] = 10 - i;                ← Type the substatement.

└┘
   2 spaces
```

Indenting Compound Statements

A compound statement is a block of statements enclosed within an opening and closing brace (**{** ... **}**). When used as a substatement (for example, as the body of a **while** loop or **if** statement), the opening and closing brace are indented just as continued statements. Unlike continued statements, however, Emacs automatically indents the opening and closing brace; you need not use **TAB** to indent them properly.

```
if (a[i] > a[i+1])              ← You type the if clause and press RET.
  {                             ← You type the { and Emacs indents it 2 spaces
                                  more than the previous line.
    ...
  }                             ← Likewise, Emacs indents the } appropriately.

└┘
    2 spaces
```

Note that you could also simply type **LFD** at the end of the expression above, and Emacs would place the cursor appropriately for the opening brace on the next line.

Emacs also lets you put the opening brace at the end of the line containing the introductory **if**, **while**, etc. However, Emacs indents differently for this style:

```
if (a[i] > a[i+1]) {            ← You type the { here instead.
  ...
}                               ← The closing brace is not indented.

└
   0 spaces
```

Within the body of a compound statement, Emacs indents statements 2 spaces from the opening and closing brace. You must use **LFD** or **TAB** to indent simple statements within the body—for example:

```
if (a[i] > a[i+1])          ← Type the line and press RET.
  {                         ← Type the { and Emacs indents it.
    tmpint = a[i];          ← Type TAB and the line, or
    a[i] = a[i+1];          ← vice versa (or simply type LFD
    a[i+1] = tmpint;        ← to get RET TAB).
  }                         ← Type the } and Emacs indents it.
```

⊔⊔ 2 spaces

This also holds true for compound statements in which the opening brace appears at the end of the line introducing the statement:

```
if (a[i] > a[i+1]) {        ← Type the opening brace at the end of the line.
  tmpint = a[i];            ← Type TAB and the line,
  a[i] = a[i+1];            ← or vice versa (or type LFD
  a[i+1] = tmpint;          ← at the end of each line).
}                           ← Type the closing brace and Emacs indents it.
```

⊔⊔ 2 spaces

The only exceptions to this are `case` and `default` statements (which appear within the body of a `switch` statement) and `label` statements (which appear within the body of any compound statement).

Indenting case, default, and label Statements

By default, Emacs indents `case`, `default`, and `label` statements in the same column as the compound statement in which they occur. Also, Emacs automatically indents these statements when you type the terminating colon; you don't have to use **TAB** to indent such lines. The following code illustrates this:

```
switch (ch)
  {                              ← The start of the compound statement.
  case 'q':                      ← You type :, Emacs indents case.
    save_files();                ← You must use LFD
    quit_prog();                 ← or TAB to indent
    break;                       ← these lines.
  case 's':
    save_files();
    break;
  case 'i':
    insert_file();
    break;
  default:                       ← When you type :, Emacs indents default.
```

```
        error_message("bad command");
        break;
    }
  ↑
```

The **case** statements and **default** statement are indented at the same level
as the enclosing braces.

In this style, a **case** or **default** statement is always on a line by itself, followed by
the statements that are executed for that case. Following a **case** or **default**
statement with another statement on the same line is allowed, but Emacs will produce
"ugly" indentation, such as shown below. Therefore, it is better to keep a **case** or
default statement on a line by itself.

```
switch (ch)
  {
  case 'q': save_files();                    ← save_files does not
    quit_prog();                               line up with quit_prog.
    break;
  case 's': save_files();                    ← The same is true
    break;                                     for these
  case 'i': insert_file();                   ← case statements.
    break;
  default:  error_message("bad command");    ← Same for default.
    break;
  }
```

A **label** is indented as follows:

```
{
        . . .
      if (meltdown)
        goto Oops;
        . . .
Oops:                              ← When you type the :, Emacs indents the label
}
↑
```

The label is indented at the same level as the enclosing braces

Indenting Extra-Long Lines

Occasionally a statement may be so long that it must span two or more lines. A
typical example is a function call that has so many parameters that it exceeds the fill
column, and wraps around to the next line. On such lines, you can use **LFD** or **TAB**
to indent them in an aesthetically pleasing manner, as shown in the following
example:

```
printf("SYS: %s\nNODE: %s\nMACH: %s\n",    ← Press RET here.
        un.sysname,                        ← Press TAB to align these lines
        un.nodename,                       ← with the opening parenthesis
        un.machine);                       ← to the parameter list.
```

Again, instead of typing **RET** and **TAB** on each line, you could simply use **LFD**, which would move to the next line, leaving the cursor at the proper indentation level.

Altering the Behavior of TAB

Usually, when you want to insert a tab character in C mode, you type **C-q TAB**. You might do this to align variable names in a group of declaration statements—for example:

```
int     foo;
char    *bar;
float   x,y,z;
        ↑
        You use C-q TAB to get the variable names lined up.
```

This default behavior is controlled by the *c-tab-always-indent* variable, which is normally **t**. This means that the **TAB** command should *always* indent the current line, regardless of where the cursor is located on the line. If *c-tab-always-indent* is set to **nil**, **TAB** indents the current line *only if the cursor is at the start of the line or within whitespace preceding a statement.* Otherwise, **TAB** inserts an actual tab character!

For example, given the following line and cursor location, Emacs inserts a tab if *c-tab-always-indent* is **nil**:

```
int█
  ↑
  Pressing TAB here will insert a tab character; rather than re-indenting the line.
```

In contrast, with the cursor positioned as follows, Emacs would *indent* the line:

```
█   while (1)
↑
Pressing TAB here indents the line appropriately.
```

Commenting Programs

The primary command for adding comments to program lines is **M-;**, which works in all programming modes. New comments are placed at the current comment column, and the cursor is placed inside the comment delimiters, waiting for you to type the comment text, as shown in Figure 6.1.

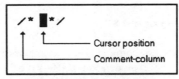

Figure 6.1. C Comments

The current comment column is stored in the Emacs variable *comment-column*, which can be changed either directly (with **M-x set-variable**), or by using various comment alignment commands.

Table 6.3 summarizes all the C mode commenting commands.

Table 6.3. C Mode Commenting Commands

Operation	Command and Comments
Add or align comment	**M-;** If the current line does not contain a comment, **M-;** creates a new comment, as described above. If the line already contains a comment, **M-;** aligns the comment at *comment-column* and places the cursor at the start of the comment text. This usage is helpful when you wish to edit comment text.
Set comment column at cursor	**C-x ;** Sets the *comment-column* variable to the column in which the cursor resides.
Set comment column same as previous comment	**C-u C-x ;** This is simply **C-x ;** with a non-negative numeric argument. It sets *comment-column* to the column in which the comment "above" begins. This is useful for aligning a new comment with existing comments above it.
Kill comment on line	**C-u - C-x ;** This is **C-x ;** with a negative numeric argument. It deletes the comment on the current line.

Table 6.3, con't.

Operation	Command and Comments
Add or align comment on next line	`C-M-j` or `M-LFD` Inserts new comment on next line or aligns comment on next line; if Auto-Fill mode is on, `C-M-j` is called automatically when the cursor advances past the fill column.

Working with Sexps and Lists (Advanced Usage)

This section describes commands for working with sexps (or expressions) and lists in C mode. Specifically, the following areas are covered:

- An overview of sexps and lists in C mode
- Moving in and among sexps and lists
- Putting regions around sexps
- Transposing sexps around point
- Killing sexps

What Are Sexps and Lists in C Mode?

Emacs C mode provides commands for navigating through and manipulating balanced expressions containing parentheses `()`, braces `{}`, and brackets `[]`—that is, sexps and lists. To use these commands effectively, you must know what constitutes an sexp or list in C mode.

A **list** is any balanced grouping of parentheses, braces, or brackets. Thus, the following are all valid lists:

- Parenthetical Expressions:

    ```
    (idx < max)
    (left + text_width[i]*font_width)
    ```

- Parameter Lists:

    ```
    (int argc, char *argv[])
    (int *first, int *second)
    ```

- Compound Statements and Function Bodies:

```
{
  int swapvar;
  swapvar = *first;
  *first = *second;
  *second = swapvar;
}
```

- Array Indexes:

```
[]
[MAXX, MAXY]
```

An **sexp** (or "expression" in C terminology) is a symbol, number, or list. Thus, the following are all valid sexps:

- Each of these symbols:

```
swapvar
int
"Here are the arguments:"
'\n'
*first
```

- Each of these numbers:

```
-100
3.14159
6.02E23
```

- This list:

```
(int argc, char *argv[])
```

- This list:

```
(left + text_width[i]*font_width)
```

- This list:

```
{
  int swapvar;

  swapvar = *first;
  *first = *second;
  *second = swapvar;
}
```

Notice that an sexp can actually contain other sexps, which in turn can contain more sexps. For example, the sexp (left + text_width[i]*font_width) contains these sexps:

```
left            A symbol
text_width      A symbol
[i]             A list
font_width      A symbol
```

And the embedded list [i] contains the sexp i.

The fact that lists and sexps can contain nested lists and sexps is important because it affects the way the list and sexp motion commands work. Specifically, what constitutes a list or sexp depends on where the cursor is located.

Moving Among Sexps and Lists

Table 6.4 summarizes the most useful commands for navigating in and among sexps and lists in C mode. The best way to learn how to use these commands is to experiment with them.

Table 6.4. C Mode Sexp and List Motion Commands

Operation	Command and Comments
Forward over sexp	C-M-f Move forward over the current or next sexp, where sexp is defined to be any symbol, number, string constant, or list.
Backward over sexp	C-M-b Move backward over the current or previous sexp.

Table 6.4. C Mode Sexp and List Motion Commands

Operation	Command and Comments
Forward over list	`C-M-n` Move over next list.
Backward over list	`C-M-p` Move backward over the previous list.
Up a list	`C-M-u` Move backward into the next higher list in a nested list.
Down a list	`C-M-d` Move forward into the next lower list in a nested list.

Marking Sexps

To place a region around an sexp, use the `C-M-@` command, which places mark at the end of the sexp and moves the cursor to the start of the sexp. As an example of `C-M-@`, Figure 6.2 shows how a region is placed around the entire compound statement following the `for`.

```
                                          ┌─ Cursor is here
for (i = i; i < argc; i++)█
{
    printf( "Arg %d: %s\n", i, argv[i] );
    act_on( argv[i] );
}[]
     └─ Mark is placed down here because the compound
        statement following the for statement is a single sexp
```

Figure 6.2. Sample Code with Marked Region

Now if you executed `C-w` (kill region), the code would look like Figure 6.3.

```
for (i = 1; i < argc; i++)█
```
                                                        ┌─ Cursor is still here,
                                                        │ but the compound
                                                        │ statement is gone

Figure 6.3. Code with Region (Sexp) Killed

Transposing Sexps Around Point

The **C-M-t** command transposes sexps around point. For example, in the following **if** statement, **max** and **num** are in the incorrect order in the expression:

```
if (max > num) max = num;
      ↑
     cursor
```

Using the **C-M-t** command, you can switch **max** and **num** around the greater-than operator (**>**). When the command is finished, the cursor is placed after the expression following the **>**:

```
if (num > max) max = num;
          ↑
         cursor
```

If you specify a positive argument to this command, it is used as a repeat count. Interestingly, this has the effect of shifting an sexp forward past other sexps. For example, suppose the cursor is positioned as follows:

```
one█two three four five six
```

If you run **C-u 5 C-M-t**, Emacs shifts the sexp **one** forward to the end of the line, making it look like this:

```
two three four five six one█
```

To see why this works this way, look what happens if you instead run five **C-M-t** commands on the example line:

```
one█two three four five six          0. The initial line.
two one█three four five six          1. Run C-M-t first time.
two three one█four five six          2. Run C-M-t second time.
two three four one█five six          3. Third time.
two three four five one█six          4. Fourth time.
two three four five six one█         5. You get the idea...
```

A negative argument has the same effect, but works backward instead. So, for example, running C-u -5 C-M-t on the last line above would return the line to its original state.

Killing Sexps

The C-M-k command kills forward to end of the current or next sexp. It is equivalent in effect to running C-M-@ to mark the end of the next sexp; then executing C-w to kill the marked region. For example, suppose you incorrectly declare the **main** function's **argc** argument to be an array:

```
void main(int argc[], char *argv[])
```

To remove the unnecessary [ ] sexp following **argc**, first move the cursor as shown below:

```
void main(int argc[], char *argv[])
                  ↑
               cursor
```

Then execute C-M-k, and the [ ] will be removed:

```
void main(int argc, char *argv[])
                  ↑
               cursor
```

Customizing Indentation (Advanced Usage)

The default indentation style produces programs that are aesthetically pleasing and consistent in style. However, there may be occasions where you need to alter the default style. This is done through C mode indentation variables.

Table 6.5 summarizes the variables used to modify the indentation style. By setting these variables in your .emacs start-up file (as described in Chapter 13, "Customizing the Emacs Environment"), you can make the changes occur whenever you start up Emacs. Following Table 6.5 are examples of how to modify indentation styles using these variables.

Note that changing these variables does *not* cause the current indentation of your program to change. To make the current indentation conform to the style defined by the current variable settings, you must re-issue indentation commands. For example, to re-indent all the lines in the current buffer, use C-x h to place a region around the buffer; then run C-M-\.

Table 6.5. C Mode Indentation Variables

Variable	Default Value and Purpose
c-argdecl-indent	Default: 5 Sets distance to indent argument declarations from column 0.
c-indent-level	Default: 2 Sets distance to indent statements in a compound statement (`{ . . . }` block).
c-label-offset	Default: −2 Added to *c-indent-level* to determine the indentation of `case`, `default`, and `label` statements. This default value of -2 is what causes these statements to line up with the left brace of the compound statement in which they appear.

Table 6.5, con't.

Variable	Default Value and Purpose
| *c-continued-statement-offset* | Default: 2 <br><br> Sets distance to indent a substatement that follows an `if`, `while`, `do`, `for`, etc. This applies to simple statements: <br><br> ```
if (error)
  exit_prog();
``` <br><br> └┘ c-continued-statement-offset = 2 <br><br> It also applies to compound statements in which the opening brace starts the first line: <br><br> ```
if (error)
  {
    clean_up();
    exit_prog();
  }
``` <br><br> └┘ c-continued-statement-offset = 2 <br><br> For compound statements in which the opening brace occurs at the end of the introducing statement, this variable does not determine indentation of the closing brace; the variable *c-brace-imaginary-offset* is used instead. |

Table 6.5, con't.

Variable	Default Value and Purpose

c-brace-imaginary-offset	Default: 0
	
	Used with compound statements in which the opening brace occurs at the end of the previous line. Emacs uses this value to determine how far to indent the closing brace. With its default value of 0, the closing brace is indented at the same level as the introducing statement:
	
	<pre>for (i=1; i<argc; i++) {
	  printf("%s: ", argv[i]);
	  act_on_it(argv[i]);
	}</pre>
	↑
	c-brace-imaginary-offset = 0, don't indent the brace
	
	Emacs determines the indent level of statements within the braces by adding *c-indent-level* to *c-brace-imaginary-offset*. In general, you should set *c-brace-imaginary-offset* to a non-zero value if *c-indent-level* is 0. Otherwise, you will get indentation like this:
	
	<pre>for (i=1; i<argc; i++) {
	printf("%s: ", argv[i]);
	act_on_it(argv[i]);
	}</pre>

Table 6.5, con't.

Variable	Default Value and Purpose

c-continued-brace-offset	Default: **0**
	
	Extra indentation given to the opening and closing brace of compound statement that comprises a continued statement. By specifying the negative value of *c-continued-statement-offset*, the opening and closing brace can line up with the introductory statement, producing the following style:
	
	``
	while (not_dead)
	{
	  work();
	  worry();
	  consume();
	  pay_taxes();
	}
	``
	→| c-continued-statement-offset = 2
	|← c-continued-brace-offset = -2
	
	This variable does not affect the style in which the opening brace is left on the previous line; that is controlled solely by *c-brace-imaginary-offset*.

c-brace-offset	Default: **0**
	
	Extra indentation given to lines that start with an opening brace. As mentioned in "Indenting Function Bodies," above, Emacs puts the opening brace of function bodies in column 0. You can change this column with this variable, but it is not recommended since it will violate the C mode assumption of having the opening brace of functions in column 0. However, suppose you change it to value 2; Emacs would produce this style of indentation:
	
	``
	void foo(str)
	    char *str;
	  {
	    printf("%s\n", str);
	  }
	``
	c-brace-offset = 2

Setting Indentation of Arguments

You can use *c-argdecl-indent* variable to change the indentation used in older style, non-ANSI C function declarations:

```
void swap(one, two)
      int *one;
      int *two;
      ↑
↑        c-argdecl-indent
column 0
```

For example, setting *c-argdecl-indent* to **0** (zero), produces argument indentation as follows:

```
void swap(one, two)
int *one;
int *two;
↑
column 0
```

Setting Indentation of Continued Statements

The *c-continued-statement-offset* variable controls the indentation of continued statements—statements that follow an introducing statement such as an **if**, **struct**, **while**, **for**, etc. It affects simple continued statements:

```
if ( ch == EOF )
  finished = TRUE;

└┘
  └── c-continued-statement-offset
```

It also affects compound statements in which the opening brace of the compound statement starts the line:

```
if ( argc > 6 )
  {
    fprintf(stderr, "usage: emacstoc [-lpp n] [-chap n] file\n");
    exit(1);
  }

└┘
  └── c-continued-statement-offset
```

When *c-continued-statement-offset* is changed to 4, the indentation produced for the above statements looks like this:

```
if ( ch == EOF )
    finished = TRUE;

if ( argc > 6 )
    {
        fprintf(stderr, "usage: etoc [-lpp n] [-chap n] file\n");
        exit(1);
    }
```

    c-continued-statement-offset = 4

Note that *c-continued-statement-offset* does *not* affect compound statements in which the opening brace is at the end of the line containing the introductory statement:

```
if ( argc > 6 ) {
    fprintf(stderr, "usage: emacstoc [-lpp n] [-chap n] file\n");
    exit(1);
}
```

In other words, changing this variable would have no effect on this style of continued compound statement.

Changing Compound Statement Indentation

There are basically two kinds of compound statement styles: those in which the opening brace starts a new line, and those in which the opening brace is at the end of the line containing the introducing statement. Emacs supports both styles, as shown in Table 6.6.

Table 6.6. Compound Statement Indentation Styles

Opening Brace Starts Line	Opening Brace at End of Line

<pre>if (finished)
    {
        printf("Done\n");
        cleanup();
        exit(0);
    }</pre>
	<pre>if (finished) {
	    printf("Done\n");
	    cleanup();
	    exit(0);
	}</pre>

Within these styles, you can vary indentation. For example, you could modify these styles to look like Table 6.7.

Table 6.7. Modified Compound Statement Indentation Styles

Opening Brace Starts Line	Opening Brace at End of Line
``
if (finished)
{
  printf("Done\n");
  cleanup();
  exit(0);
}
↑
``` The braces are aligned with the introducing statement. | ```
if (finished) {
    printf("Done\n");
    cleanup();
    exit(0);
}
↑
``` The brace is indented 2 spaces instead of being aligned with the introducing statement. |

For both styles, the *c-indent-level* variable controls how far statements are indented within the { } block. For example, by changing *c-indent-level* to 4, the two default styles would change as shown in Table 6.8.

Table 6.8. Compound Statement Indentation Styles with c-indent-level of 4

Opening Brace Starts Line	Opening Brace at End of Line
``
if (finished)
   {
      printf("Done\n");
      cleanup();
      exit(0);
   }
``` └──┘ └─ c-indent-level = 4 | ```
if (finished) {
      printf("Done\n");
      cleanup();
      exit(0);
}
``` └──┘ └─ c-indent-level = 4 |

For each style, a different set of variables controls the placement of the braces. Table 6.9 lists these variables and describes how they affect the indentation level for the braces.

Table 6.9. Variables That Control Compound Statement Styles

Opening Brace Starts Line	Opening Brace at End of Line
c-continued-statement-offset *c-continued-brace-offset* *c-brace-imaginary-offset* *c-brace-offset* These variables are added together to determine how far the opening brace is indented relative to the previous line. When using default values, the sum of these variables is 2; therefore, the braces are indented 2 spaces.	*c-brace-imaginary-offset* This is added to the indentation level of the previous line to determine the placement of the closing brace. By default, this variable's value is zero; therefore, the closing brace is not indented relative to the start of the opening line.

If you use the style where the opening brace starts the line, you would normally use defaults of zero for *c-brace-imaginary-offset* and *c-brace-offset*. Thus, control over this style is provided primarily by the *c-continued-statement-offset* and *c-continued-brace-offset* variables. Table 6.10 shows a fairly common style achieved through these variables.

Table 6.10. Modified Style for Opening Brace on Starting Line

Variable	Value	Indentation Produced
c-continued-statement-offset	2	

c-continued-brace-offset	-2	`if (a[i] > a[i+1])`
		`{`
		`    tmpint = a[i];`
		`    a[i] = a[i+1];`
		`    a[i+1] = tmpint;`
		`}`

c-brace-imaginary-offset	0	
c-brace-offset	0	
c-indent-level	2	

Setting Indentation of case, default, and label Statements

The *c-label-offset* variable controls indentation of **case** and **default** statements within a **switch** statement. It also controls the indentation of labels. The indentation level is determined by adding *c-label-offset* to *c-indent-level*. Table 6.11 shows the default indentation for a switch statement, compared to the indentation produced when *c-label-offset* is 0.

Table 6.11. Case Statement Indentation Styles with c-indent-level of 4

c-label-offset = -2	c-label-offset = 0

<pre>   switch (choice)
     {
    case QUIT:
      quit_prog();
      break;
    case SAVE:
      save_files();
      break;
    default:
 	
    unknown_opt(choice);
      break;
     }</pre>
	<pre> switch (choice)
	     {
	        case QUIT:
	        quit_prog();
	        break;
	        case SAVE:
	        save_files();
	        break;
	        default:
	        unknown_opt(choice);
	        break;
	     }</pre>

If you feel that setting *c-label-offset* to 0 makes the `switch` statement less readable, you could achieve a more aesthetically pleasing style by setting *c-indent-level* to 4 and *c-label-offset* to -2:

```
    switch (choice)
     {
        case QUIT:
          quit_prog();
          break;
        case SAVE:
          save_files();
          break;
        default:
          unknown_option(choice);
          break;
     }

    └──┘
       └─ c-indent-level = 4

      └┘
       └─ c-label-offset = -2
```

Changing *c-indent-level* will affect all compound statements—for example:

```
if (gossip)
  {
      this();
      that();
  }
else
  {
      other();
      thing();
  }
```

|___|
  |___ c-indent-level = 4

Setting Indentation of Function Bodies

Although it is not recommended, you can change the indentation of the opening and closing brace of a function body (as well as any line containing an opening or closing brace) with the *c-brace-offset* variable. For example, setting *c-brace-offset* to 2 produced the following indentation:

```
void swap(one,  two)
    int *one;
    int *two;
  {
    int tmpVar;

    tmpVar = *one;
    *one = *two;
    *two = tmpVar;
  }
```

|_|
 |_ c-brace-offset = 2
↑
column 0

However, such indentation is not recommended as it violates the C mode requirement that the opening and closing brace of a function appear in column 0. Commands that operate on entire functions (**C-M-a**, **C-M-e**, and **C-M-h**) are not useful with such indentation.

An Example: Using Kernighan and Ritchie Indentation Style

This section shows how to set the variables described above to get the indentation style used by Kernighan and Ritchie in their book *The C Programming Language*. Shown below is a program created using this style. (The program reads characters from standard input and outputs the corresponding Morse code to standard output.)

```c
#include <stdio.h>
#include <string.h>
#define MAXLINE 79

char        *convertToMorse();

main()
{
    char        outLine[MAXLINE + 1];  /* holds line to display */
    char        *tmpCode;              /* holds Morse code for inChar */
    char        *padding = "    ";     /* displayed between Morse codes */
    int         inChar;                /* character read from stdin */

    while ((inChar = getchar()) != EOF) {
        tmpCode = convertToMorse(inChar);
        if (strlen(tmpCode) + strlen(outLine) + strlen(padding) >
MAXLINE) {
            puts(outLine);             /* output string and start over */
            outLine[0] = '\0';
        }
        strcat(outLine, tmpCode);      /* append code to outLine */
        strcat(outLine, padding);      /* append padding after code */
    }
    if (strlen(outLine) > 0)           /* output any leftover codes */
        puts(outLine);
}

char *convertToMorse(ch)               /* converts ASCII to Morse */
int     ch;
{
    static char *code;

    ch = tolower(ch);                  /* convert uppercase to lowercase */
    switch (ch) {
    case '\n': case '\t': case ' ':    /* whitespace */
        code = "***";
        break;
    case 'a':
        code = ". _";
        break;
    case 'b':
        code = "_ . . .";
        break;
```

```
              ↓                           Code for letters, numbers, and punctuation omitted.
      case '-':
          code = "_ . . . . _";
          break;
      case '(': case ')':
          code = "_ . _ _ . _";
          break;
      default:                                      /* unknown character */
          code = "???";
          break;
      }
      return code;
  }
```

Listed below are various characteristics of the Kernighan and Ritchie indentation style, and how they are achieved through indentation variables:

- **Function arguments are not indented:**

```
      char *convertToMorse(ch)                      /* converts ASCII to Morse */
      int      ch;
      ↑
      column 0
```

To get this indentation, set *c-argdecl-indent* to **0** (zero).

- **Continued statements are indented five columns:**

```
      if (strlen(outLine) > 0)             /* output any leftover codes */
          puts(outLine);

      └─────┘
            └─ 5 columns
```

To get this indentation, set *c-continued-statement-offset* to **5**.

- **The opening brace of a compound statement is on the same line as the introducing statement, and the closing brace is aligned with the start of the introducing statement:**

```
                                                                opening brace
                                                                      ↓
      if (strlen(tmpCode) + strlen(outLine) + strlen(padding) > MAXLINE) {
          puts(outLine);                    /* output string and start over */
          outLine[0] = '\0';
      }
      ↑
      closing brace
```

To do this, set *c-brace-imaginary-offset* to **0** (zero), the default. In addition, make sure that *c-auto-newline* is `nil` so that Emacs doesn't automatically put the opening brace on a new line! *c-continued-brace-offset* should also be set to **0** so as to avoid giving the closing brace any further indentation.

- **Statements within a { ... } compound statement block are indented five spaces:**

```
while ((inChar = getchar()) != EOF) {
     tmpCode = convertToMorse(inChar);
     if (strlen(tmpCode) + strlen(outLine) + strlen(padding) > MAXLINE)
{
          puts(outLine);                 /* output string and start over */
          outLine[0] = '\0';
     }
     strcat(outLine, tmpCode);           /* append code to outLine */
     strcat(outLine, padding);           /* append padding after code */
}
```

```
          └──┘
            └ 5 columns
     └────┘
         └ 5 columns
```

To do this, set *c-indent-level* to **5**.

- **In the body of a `switch` statement, `case` and `default` statements are aligned flush with the opening `switch` statement:**

```
switch (ch) {
case '\n': case '\t': case ' ':      /* whitespace */
     code = "***";
     break;
case 'a':
     code = ". _";
     break;
case 'b':
     code = "_ . . .";
     break;
               ↓              Code for letters, numbers, and punctuation omitted.
case '-':
     code = "_ . . . . _";
     break;
case '(': case ')':
     code = "_ . _ _ . _";
     break;
default:                          /* unknown character */
     code = "???";
     break;
}
↑
switch, case, default, and } all aligned
```

To get this indentation, set *c-label-offset* to −5. When this value is added to the value of *c-indent-level* (5), the indent level becomes zero.

Customizing Commenting (Advanced Usage)

Like indentation, the behavior of commenting is controlled through variables. You can view a variable's value with **C-h v** or **M-x describe-variable**; you can change its value with **M-x set-variable**.

Commenting variables are summarized in Table 6.12, which is followed by more detailed descriptions of how to customize commenting with these variables.

Table 6.12. C Mode Commenting Variables

Variable	Default Value and Purpose
comment-column	Default: **32** Column at which new comments are displayed or existing comments are aligned.
comment-start	Default: **"/*"** String to use to start a comment.
comment-end	Default: **" */"** String to use to end a comment.
comment-start-skip	Default: **"/*+ *"** Regular expression for Emacs to use when searching for the start of a comment.

Table 6.12, con't.

Variable	Default Value and Purpose

comment-multi-line	Default: `nil`
	
	 Affects how Emacs handles multi-line comments.
	
	 Multi-line comments are produced either with the `C-M-j` command, or by typing past the *fill-column* when Auto-Fill mode is enabled.
	
	 The default value `nil` produces multi-line comments of the form:
	
	 `/* The first line of a */`
	 `/* multi-line comment. */`
	
	 A non-`nil` value (say `t`) produces multi-line comments of the form:
	
	 `/* The first line of a`
	 `   multi-line comment. */`

Changing the Comment Column

The *comment-column* variable determines which column the next comment starts in. You would normally set this variable with the `C-x ;` or `C-u C-x ;` command (described in Table 6.3). For example, if you wanted to change *comment-column* to match the column used in comments on previous lines, you would use `C-u C-x ;`.

Each C mode buffer has a local copy of *comment-column*. However, you can make the variable **global**, forcing it to apply to all C buffers. To do this, execute **M-ESC** `(setq-default comment-column` *n*`)` **RET**, where *n* is the new comment-column to use in all buffers.

Changing Comment Delimiters

The *comment-start* and *comment-end* variables control the appearance of delimiters around comment text. Their default values produce a comment of the form:

```
/* comment text that you type */
↑↑↑                          ↑↑↑
comment-start                comment-end
```

Suppose you are revising source code for a new release, and you want to mark all comments that were added for the new release. You could do this by setting *comment-start* to include release information:

```
M-x set-variable RET
Set variable: comment-start RET
Set comment-start to value: "/* v1.21: " RET      ← Quotes are required
```

Then, if you issued a **M-;** command, it would create a comment that looked like this:

```
for (i = 0; i < 10; i++)    /* v1.21: █*/
  a[i] = 10 - i;                     ↑
                             The cursor is here, waiting for you to
                             type comment text.
```

Changing the Comment Search Pattern

The *comment-start-skip* variable contains a regular expression that C mode uses to find the start of a comment. Therefore, you should set this variable such that Emacs can find the start of comments as defined by *comment-start*. It should **never** match the null string, `""`. The value of this variable is `"/\\*+ *"`, which matches `/` followed by one or more asterisks, followed by zero or more spaces. For most users, this comment string is sufficient. You would probably only change this variable if you used a dialect of C that had different comment syntax (like C++).

Handling Multi-Line Comments

The *comment-multi-line* variable controls how **C-M-j** or auto-filling acts within a comment. Its default value is `nil`, causing the comment on the current line to be terminated with *comment-end*, and a new comment started on the next line. For example, it produces multi-line comments of this style:

```
/* This is the first line of the comment. */
/* And this is the second line. */
```

If it is not `nil`, then the comment on the current line is *not* terminated, and the comment is continued on the next line—for example:

```
/* This is the first line of the comment.
   And this is the second line. */
```

There is no clear advantage to either style. It's a matter of personal taste.

Summary

Table 6.13 summarizes the important points in this chapter.

Table 6.13. Chapter 6 Summary

Topic	Summary
Selecting C Mode	• Name your source file with a `.c` extension, or • Invoke C mode with the `M-x c-mode` command, or • Make sure the first nonblank line of your source file is a comment that includes the string `-*-c-*-`
Assumptions about C mode	Emacs assumes { in column zero is an opening brace of a function body.
Motion commands	• Move to opening brace of function containing cursor: `C-M-a` • Move to closing brace of function containing cursor: `C-M-e` • Move forward over sexp: `C-M-f` • Move backward over sexp: `C-M-b` • Move over next list: `C-M-n` • Move backward over list: `C-M-p` • Move to next higher list in nested list: `C-M-u` • Move to next lower list in nested list: `C-M-d`
Region commands	• Put region around function containing cursor: `C-M-h` • Put a mark after the next sexp: `C-M-@`
Transpose command	Transpose sexps around cursor: `C-M-t`
Kill command	Kill forward to end of current or next sexp: `C-M-k`

Table 6.13, con't.

Topic	Summary
Indentation	Commands: • Indent current line: **TAB** • Finish current line and open next line indented: **C-j** • Re-indent all lines in current region: **C-M-** Style Variables: • Distance to indent argument declarations from column 0: *c-argdecl-indent* • Distance to indent statements in compound statement: *c-indent-level* • Set indentation of **case**, **default**, and **label** relative to *c-indent-level*: *c-label-offset* • Distance to indent a substatement that follows an **if**, **while**, **do**, **for**, etc.: *c-continued-statement-offset* • Distance to indent closing brace of compound statements having opening brace at end of previous line: *c-brace-imaginary-offset* • Extra indentation given to opening and closing brace of compound statement that comprises a continued statement: *c-continued-brace-offset* • Extra indentation given to lines starting with opening brace: *c-brace-offset*

Table 6.13, con't.

Topic	Summary
Comments	Commands: • Create new comment on line containing no comment: `M-;` • Align existing comment on current line: `M-;` • Set *comment-column* to current cursor column: `C-x ;` • Set *comment-column* to *n*: `C-u n C-x ;` • Set *comment-column* same as previous comment: `C-u C-x ;` • Delete comment on current line or all in region: `C-u - C-x ;` • Insert new comment on next line or align next comment: `C-M-j` Style Variables: • Column where comments are created/aligned: *comment-column* • String to use as start of comment (`"/* "`): *comment-start* • String to use as end of comment (`" */"`): *comment-end* • Regular expression used when searching for start of a comment (`"/\\*+ *"`): *comment-start-skip* • Affects handling of multi-line comments: *comment-multi-line*

7
Editing in FORTRAN Mode

FORTRAN mode frees FORTRAN programmers from much of the drudgery of
ensuring that various syntactic elements (comments, labels, continuation characters)
appear in the correct columns. FORTRAN mode does all this for you automatically.
This chapter describes the following aspects of FORTRAN mode:

- Invoking FORTRAN mode

- Assumptions about FORTRAN source

- Moving among subprograms and statements

- Marking subprograms

- Indenting programs

- Labeling lines

- Commenting programs

- Using FORTRAN keyword abbreviations

- Working with sexps and lists (advanced usage)

- Customizing indentation (advanced usage)

- Customizing commenting (advanced usage)

For general information on programming modes, refer to Chapter 5, "Program
Development in Emacs."

Invoking FORTRAN Mode

FORTRAN mode is used, by default, for source files whose names end in `.f`. If your system uses a different convention for naming FORTRAN source files, you can enter FORTRAN mode in one of these ways:

- After loading your FORTRAN source file, invoke FORTRAN mode with the **M-x fortran-mode** command.

- Make sure the first nonblank line of your source file is a comment that includes the string **-*-fortran-*-**, as in:

      c -*-fortran-*-

Assumptions About FORTRAN Source

Listed below are assumptions that Emacs makes about FORTRAN program source. These assumptions are important because they affect how Emacs commands work.

- FORTRAN mode supports FORTRAN 77 syntax. Most of the elements of FORTRAN 90 will work correctly in FORTRAN mode. The main exception is free source forms, where columns are not significant. Such free-form coding violates the assumptions of Emacs' FORTRAN mode.

- When using abbreviations, FORTRAN mode expands FORTRAN keyword abbreviations to lowercase. Most compilers can handle this, but some do not.

- Emacs numbers columns starting at zero; FORTRAN numbers columns starting at 1. So, from Emacs standpoint:

  - comments start in column 0

  - labels appear in columns 1 through 4

  - continuation lines start in column 5

  - statements start in column 6

  - statements end in column 71

- Nested **do** loops should never share a **continue** statement. For example, certain FORTRAN mode commands would not work correctly with the following code:

      do 100 i=1,10
        do 100 j=1,10
          a(i,j) = i * j
  100   continue

Use this coding instead:

```
      do 110 i =1,10
        do 100 j=1,10
          a(i,j) = i * j
100       continue
110     continue
```

- By default, continuation lines have a **$** in column 5. To override this default, set the *fortran-continuation-char* variable. If you use a character other than that specified by *fortran-continuation-char*, indenting will get confused.

Moving Among Subprograms and Statements

Table 7.1 summarizes the FORTRAN mode motion commands. **C-c C-n** and **C-c C-p** are unique to FORTRAN mode. In these commands, the term "subprogram" refers to any subroutine, function, block data subprogram, or to the main program.

Table 7.1. FORTRAN Mode Motion Commands

Operation	Command and Comments
Move to start of subprogram	**C-M-a** Move to the start of the current or previous subprogram.
Move to end of subprogram	**C-M-e** Move to the end of the current or next subprogram.

Move to next statement	**C-c C-n**
	
	Moves to the start of the next statement, skipping any continuation lines and comments. For example, if the cursor is on the **integer** statement below, **C-c C-n** moves the cursor to the assignment statement **one = 1**:
	
	`      program footran`
	`      integer one,two,█      ← Cursor`
	`$        three, four`
	`c        Start main...`
	`      one = 1              ← C-c C-n moves here.`
	`      two = one + one`

Table 7.1, con't.

Operation	Command and Comments

Move to previous statement	`C-c C-p`
	
	Like `C-c C-n` but moves to the start of the previous statement. For example, `C-c C-p` moves the cursor from the assignment statement `one = 1` back to the `integer` statement:
	
	`    program footran`
	`    integer one,two,` ← C-c C-p moves here.
	`$       three, four`
	`c       Start main...`
	`    one = 1`███ ← Cursor
	`    two = one + one`

Marking Subprograms

In addition to the Fundamental and Text mode marking commands, FORTRAN provides the command **C-M-h** to mark subprograms. It places the cursor at the start of the current subroutine, function, block data subprogram, or main program, and places mark at the end. You can then use any command that operates on a region; for example, you could use **M-w** to copy the subprogram's text into the kill ring to be yanked into another buffer.

Indenting Programs

Table 7.2 summarizes the program indentation commands available in FORTRAN mode. These commands indent lines appropriately for the current indentation style, as defined by FORTRAN mode indentation variables. To change the indentation style, see "Customizing Indentation (Advanced Usage)" later in this chapter.

Table 7.2. FORTRAN Mode Indentation Commands

Operation	Command and Comments
Indent current line	**TAB** Indents the current line appropriately.

Table 7.2, con't.

Operation	Command and Comments
Make continuation line	`C-M-j` or `M-LFD` Finishes the current line and starts a continuation line on the next line.
Re-indent all lines in region	`C-M-\` Indent all lines in region appropriately. For example, you could use `C-M-h` to mark the current subprogram, then use `C-M-\`. The current subprogram will be re-indented.
Re-indent subprogram	`C-M-q` Indents all lines in current or next subprogram appropriately. This is equivalent in effect to running `C-M-h`, then `C-M-\`.

Making Continuation Lines

The `C-M-j` (or `M-LFD`) command creates an appropriately indented continuation line. It does this by breaking the current line at the cursor position and creating a continuation line with the *fortran-continuation-char*, usually $, in column 5. The text of the continued statement is then indented 5 columns from the continuation character. For example, Figure 7.1 shows a statement that was continued using `C-M-j`.

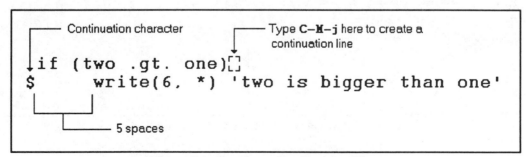

Figure 7.1. Creating a Continuation Line

Both the continuation character and the level of indentation can be changed, as described later in the section "Customizing Indentation (Advanced Usage)."

Visual Aids for Indentation

FORTRAN 77 is column-sensitive; that is, various constructs in the FORTRAN 77 language *must* appear in a particular column, and lines cannot extend past column 72. FORTRAN mode takes care of putting such constructs in the correct columns for you: Comments are placed in column 1, labels are placed in columns 2 through 5, and continuation lines are placed in column 6, and statements are placed in column 7.

Sometimes, though, you might want to type such constructs explicitly. To help you see where the columns are, FORTRAN mode provides the visual aids described in Table 7.3.

Table 7.3. FORTRAN Mode Visual Aids (Ruler and Split)

Operation	Command and Comments
Display ruler	`C-c C-r` Displays a "ruler" above the current source line, showing the columns of special significance to FORTRAN source programs. To make the ruler disappear, press any key or command.
Split window at column 72	`C-c C-w` Splits the FORTRAN window horizontally at column 72, thus making it easy to see when you are at the end of a standard FORTRAN source line. To get rid of the split window and return to one FORTRAN window, use `C-x 1`.

Figure 7.2 shows the format of the ruler created by the `C-c C-r` command. (The column markers shown in the ruler are Emacs column markers; standard FORTRAN column marking starts with column 1.) Columns 0 through 4, marked by `[ ]`, are used for FORTRAN labels; column 5, marked by `|` is used for the continuation character; columns 6 through 71, marked by `{...}` are used for FORTRAN statements.

```
0    4 6  10       20      30      40      50      60      70
[    ]!<   !    !    !    !    !    !    !    !    !    !    !    !>
```

Figure 7.2. Format of the FORTRAN Column Ruler

Labeling Lines

By default, labels less than 5 digits (e.g., 1, 12, 123, 1234) are placed in columns 1 through 4. If a label is 5 digits long (e.g., 12345), it is placed in columns 0 through 4. How labeling works depends on whether you are typing a new line or adding a label to an existing line:

- On new lines—lines that do not yet contain a FORTRAN statement—Emacs places any numbers you type into the label field (columns 1 through 4). If you type a five-digit label, the label starts in column 0, rather than column 1. When you begin typing a statement, Emacs automatically places the statement in the correct column; you don't have to bother moving over to the column.

- On existing statement lines—lines that contain FORTRAN statements—Emacs inserts a label in the label field, if you type the label while the cursor is positioned on or before the start of the statement.

This feature works intuitively and is best understood through experimentation.

Commenting Programs

By default, FORTRAN mode uses standard comments—i.e., comments beginning with a c in column 0. The text of standard comments is automatically indented to the same level as statements (controlled by the *fortran-comment-line-column* variable):

```
column 0
↓
c
c       these are standard comments
c       ↑
        fortran-comment-line-column
```

FORTRAN mode also supports nonstandard comments that begin with ! and follow a statement on the same line. (Check whether your FORTRAN dialect allows them.) These comments begin in the column specified by the *comment-column* variable:

```
10      format(I5)          ! this is a nonstandard comment
                            ↑
                            comment-column
```

To enable nonstandard comments, set the variable *comment-start* to " ! " (be sure to include the double quotes). For example, here is the sequence of commands for setting comment-start in the minibuffer:

```
M-x set-variable RET
Set variable: comment-start RET
Set comment-start to value: "!" RET
```

Table 7.4 shows the commands used to comment programs in FORTRAN mode.

Table 7.4. FORTRAN Mode Commenting Commands

Operation	Command and Comments
Create or align comment	**M-;** **In standard comment mode:** Open a comment line above the current line, or align an existing standard comment line. **In nonstandard comment mode:** If the current line is blank, insert a standard comment. Otherwise, insert a new nonstandard ! (end-of-line) comment at the current comment column, or align an existing ! comment.
Set comment column for nonstandard comments	**C-x ;** **Nonstandard Comments Only:** Sets the alignment column for nonstandard comments. Does not apply to standard comments, which are always aligned in column 0.
Comment-out all lines in region	**C-c ;** Inserts a c$$$ comment string in front of all lines in the current region. Lines already containing standard comments are converted to the form: c$$$c comment Using C-u C-c ; on a region converts reverts lines to their original form. You can change the comment prefix by changing the value of the variable *fortran-comment-region*.
Remove all comments from region	**C-u C-c ;** Really just the C-c ; command with a numeric argument, this command removes all comments in a region that were created with the C-c ; command. Lines that originally contained comments are returned to comment lines.

Using FORTRAN Keyword Abbreviations

To facilitate faster typing of FORTRAN programs, FORTRAN mode provides several abbreviations for commonly used keywords. To enable abbreviations, you must turn on Abbreviation minor mode with the **M-x abbrev-mode** command. All FORTRAN abbreviations start with a semicolon. For instance, the abbreviation for the **continue** statement is **; c**. To see a list of all FORTRAN abbreviations in Emacs, type **; ?** or **; C-h** while in FORTRAN Abbrev mode. Table 7.5 summarizes FORTRAN keyword abbreviations.

Table 7.5. FORTRAN Mode Keyword Abbreviations

Keyword	Abbrev.	Keyword	Abbrev.
byte	;b	implicit byte	;ib
character	;ch	implicit character	;ich
close	;cl	implicit complex	;ic
common	;cm	implicit integer	;ii
complex	;cx	implicit logical	;il
continue	;c	implicit real	;ir
dimension	;di	include	;inc
do while	;dw	integer	;in
double	;do	intrinsic	;intr
double complex	;dc	logical	;l
double precision	;dp	open	;op
else	;e	parameter	;pa
elseif	;el	print	;p
enddo	;ed	program	;pr
endif	;en	read	;r
entry	;ey	real	;re
equivalence	;eq	return	;rt
external	;ex	rewind	;rw
format	;f	stop	;s
function	;fu	subroutine	;su
goto	;g	type	;ty
implicit	;im	write	;w

Working with Sexps and Lists (Advanced Usage)

This section describes commands for working with sexps (or expressions) and lists in FORTRAN mode. Specifically, the following areas are covered:

• An overview of sexps and lists in FORTRAN mode

- Moving in and among sexps and lists
- Putting regions around sexps
- Killing sexps

What Are Sexps and Lists in FORTRAN Mode?

FORTRAN mode provides commands for moving within and among balanced parenthetical expressions (lists) and expressions (sexps). To use these commands effectively, you must know what expressions and lists are.

A **list** in FORTRAN is any balanced grouping of parentheses. Thus, the following are all valid lists:

- Parenthetical Expressions:

```
(idx .LT. max)
(left + text_width(i)*font_width)
```

- Parameter Lists:

```
(idx, arr)
```

- Array Subscripts:

```
(idx)
(xcoord, ycoord, zcoord)
```

An **sexp** (or "expression") is a symbol, number, or list. Thus, the following are all valid sexps:

- Each of these symbols:

```
'Enter the number: '
format
.LT.
int_var
```

- Each of these numbers:

```
6.02E23
-100
3.14159
```

- This list:

      ```
      (arr(idx1), arr(idx2), 0)
      ```

- This list:

      ```
      (left + text_width(i)*font_width)
      ```

- This list:

      ```
      (xcoord, ycoord, zcoord)
      ```

Notice that an sexp can actually contain other sexps, which in turn can contain more sexps. For example, the sexp `(arr(idx1), arr(idx2))` contains these sexps:

`arr`	A symbol
`(idx1)`	A list
`(idx2)`	A list
`0`	A number

And the embedded list `(idx1)` contains the sexp `idx1`, and the list `(idx2)` contains the sexp `idx2`.

The fact that lists and sexps can contain nested lists and sexps is important because it affects the way the list and sexp motion commands work. Specifically, what constitutes a list or sexp depends on where the cursor is located.

Moving Among Sexps and Lists

Table 7.6 summarizes the most useful commands for navigating in and among sexps and lists in FORTRAN mode. The best way to learn how to use these commands is to experiment with them.

Table 7.6. FORTRAN Mode List and Sexp Motion Commands

Operation	Command and Comments
Forward over sexp	`C-M-f` Move forward over the current or next sexp, where sexp is defined to be any symbol, number, string constant, or list.

Table 7.6, con't.

Operation	Command and Comments
Backward over sexp	`C-M-b` Move backward over the current or previous sexp.
Forward over list	`C-M-n` Move over next list.
Backward over list	`C-M-p` Move backward over the previous list.
Up a list	`C-M-u` Move backward into the next-higher list in a nested list.
Down a list	`C-M-d` Move forward into the next-lower list in a nested list.

Marking Sexps

The `C-M-@` command puts the mark at the end of the sexp following the cursor. As an example of using `C-M-@`, Figure 7.3 shows how the mark is placed after the `(num .GT. max)` expression:

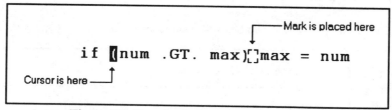

Figure 7.3. Sample Code with Marked Region

The `C-w` command kills the expression and places it in the kill ring (Figure 7.4).

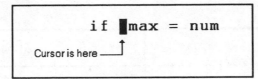

Figure 7.4. Sample Code with Region
(Sexp) Deleted

Killing Sexps

The **C-M-k** command kills to the end of the current or next sexp. It is equivalent in effect to running **C-M-@** to mark the next sexp, then running **C-w** to kill it, as we did in Figures 7.1 and 7.2.

Customizing Indentation (Advanced Usage)

FORTRAN indentation style is controlled by the variables listed in Table 7.7. Following the table are more detailed descriptions of how to use these variables.

Table 7.7. FORTRAN Mode Indentation Variables

Variable	Default Value and Purpose
fortran-minimum-statement-indent	Default: **6** Defines the column in which FORTRAN statements, other than continuation statements, start. If this variable is set to less than 6, Emacs indentation commands may not work properly.
fortran-do-indent	Default: **3** Defines how far to indent the body of a **do** statement.
fortran-if-indent	Default: **3** Defines how far to indent each level of an **if-then** or **if-then-else** statement.

Table 7.7, con't.

Variable	Default Value and Purpose
fortran-continuation-indent	Default: **5** Defines how far to indent continuation lines from the continuation character in column 5.
fortran-continuation-char	Default: **$** The continuation character to use in column 5.
fortran-check-all-num-for-matching-do	Default: `nil` Allows for optimization in indenting. If this variable is `nil`, Emacs assumes that the body of each **do** loop ends with a `continue` statement. If the above condition is **not** true in your programs, then set this to `t`.

Changing Indentation of Statements

The *fortran-minimum-statement-indent* variable controls the indentation of any FORTRAN statements that are not within **do** or **if** statements. Since FORTRAN statements must usually start in column 7, this variable defaults to Emacs' column 6. You could however, change it to a greater indentation level, although there would not be much advantage to this.

Changing Indentation of do Statements

The *fortran-do-indent* variable defines how far to indent the body of a **do** loop from the **do** statement; it defaults to 3:

```
        do 10 i = 1,10
           a(i) = i
10      continue
```

```
           └─┘
            └─ fortran-do-indent = 3
```

Changing Indentation of if Statements

The *fortran-if-indent* variable sets the indentation for each level of an **if** statement; it defaults to 3:

```
if (i .eq. j) then
   print *, "i equals j"
else
   print *, "i does not equal j"
end if
```

fortran-if-indent = 3

Changing Indentation of Continuation Lines

The *fortran-continuation-indent* variable defines how much to indent continuation lines from the continuation column; it defaults to 5:

```
100   format(1X,/
      $    1H ,I5,/
      $    1H ,F10.2/
      $    )
```

fortran-continuation-indent = 5

To change the continuation character, set the *fortran-continuation-char* variable.

Customizing Commenting (Advanced Usage)

Like indentation, commenting behavior is controlled through variables. You can view a variable's value with **C-h v** or **M-x describe-variable**; you can change its value with **M-x set-variable**. For details on how to make such changes "permanent," refer to Chapter 13, "Customizing the Emacs Environment." Different variables are used to customize standard and nonstandard comments.

Customizing Standard Comments

By default, standard comment line text is indented at the same level as statements (column 6). To change the default column, use *fortran-comment-line-column*. For example, if you changed *fortran-comment-line-column* to 2, comments would look like this:

```
column 0
↓
c   This comment text starts in column 2.
      ↑
    fortran-comment-line-column = 2
```

You can change this default customizing behavior via the *fortran-comment-indent-style* variable. Table 7.8 summarizes the different commenting styles you can obtain by changing *fortran-comment-indent-style*.

Table 7.8. Changing the Default Comment Style

Comment Style	fortran-comment-indent-style value
Indent comment text at column set by *fortran-comment-line-column* (default).	`fixed`
Indent comment text relative to statements. Comment text column is set by adding *fortran-comment-line-column* to statement column (column 6).	`relative`
Turn off automatic indenting of comment text; you must indent.	`nil`

For example, if you set *fortran-comment-indent-style* to **relative** and *fortran-comment-line-column* to –2, comments will be indented two columns less than statements (in column 5).

Customizing Nonstandard Comments

If nonstandard end-of-line (**!**) comments are enabled, they are placed in the column set by the *comment-column* variable. This variable is set with the commands in Table 7.9. These comments are customized similarly to those in other language modes.

Table 7.9. Setting the Comment Column for End-of-Line Comments

Operation	Command and Comments
Set comment column at cursor	`C-x ;` Sets *comment-column* to column containing the cursor.

Table 7.9, con't.

Operation	Command and Comments
Set comment column same as previous comment	`C-u C-x ;` Sets *comment-column* to the column in which the comment above begins. This is useful for aligning a new comment with existing comments above it.

Additional Customizations

Table 7.10 summarizes some additional variables you can set to change commenting style.

Table 7.10. Additional FORTRAN Mode Commenting Variables

Variable	Default Value and Purpose
comment-start	Default: `"c"` String to use to start a comment. Change to `"!"` to enable nonstandard comments.
fortran-comment-indent-char	Default: SPC The character that Emacs inserts before comment text on standard comment lines. For example, if you set this variable to #, a comment line would look like this: `c#####Comment text.`
fortran-comment-region	Default: c$$$ Comment string used when commenting-out a region.
fortran-comment-ruler	Default: See Figure 7.2. Changes the ruler text displayed by the ruler command, `C-c C-r`.

Summary

Table 7.11 summarizes the important points to remember in this chapter.

Table 7.11. Chapter 7 Summary

Topic	Summary
Selecting FORTRAN Mode	• Name your source file with a `.f` extension, or • Invoke FORTRAN mode with the `M-x fortran-mode` command, or • Make sure the first nonblank line of your source file is a comment that includes the string `-*-fortran-*-`

Assumptions about FORTRAN mode	• FORTRAN keyword abbreviations are expanded to lowercase.
	• Emacs numbers columns starting at zero, thus:
	   • comments start in column 0
	   • labels appear in columns 1 through 4
	   • continuation lines start in column 5
	   • statements start in column 6
	   • statements end in column 71
	• Nest **do** loops should never share a terminating `continue` statement.
	• By default, continuation lines have a `$` in column 5, as defined by the *fortran-continuation-char* variable.

Table 7.11, con't.

Topic	Summary
Motion commands	• "Subprogram" refers to any subroutine, function, or block data subprogram, or the main program. • Move to start of current or previous subprogram: `C-M-a` • Move to end of current or next subprogram: `C-M-e` • Move to the start of next statement: `C-c C-n` • Move to the start of the previous statement: `C-c C-p` • Move forward over sexp: `C-M-f` • Move backward over sexp: `C-M-b` • Move over next list: `C-M-n` • Move backward over list: `C-M-p` • Move to next-higher list in nested list: `C-M-u` • Move to next-lower list in nested list: `C-M-d`
Region commands	• Put region around subprogram containing cursor: `C-M-h` • Put a mark after the next sexp: `C-M-@`
Kill command	• Kill forward to end of current or next sexp: `C-M-k`
Visual aids for indentation	• Display a "ruler" above current line showing columns: `C-c C-r`. • Use the variable *fortran-comment-ruler* to define text of ruler. • Split window vertically at column 72: `C-c C-w` • Remove vertical window split: `C-x 1`
Abbreviations	• All keyword abbreviations start with `;` • Enable keyword abbreviations: `M-x abbrev-mode`. • List all abbreviations: `; ?` or `; C-h` (while in Abbrev mode)

Table 7.11, con't.

Topic	Summary
Indentation	Commands: • Indent current line: **TAB** • Finish current line and start a continuation line: **C–M–j** • Re-indent all lines in current region: **C–M–** • Re-indent all lines in current subprogram: **C–M–q** Style Variables: • Set starting column for statements (except continuation statements: *fortran-minimum-statement-indent* • Set indentation for **do** statement body: *fortran-do-indent* • Set indentation for each level of **if–then** or **if–then–else** statement: *fortran-if-indent* • Set indentation of continuation lines: *fortran-continuation-indent* • Optimize indenting: *fortran-check-all-num-for-matching-do*
Labels	• If you type a label on an empty line, Emacs automatically places it in columns 1 through 4. If label is longer than 4 characters, Emacs uses columns 0 through 5. • To get a label on a line containing a statement, place cursor on or before the start of the statement, then enter label.

Table 7.11, con't.

Topic	Summary
Comments	Comment Types: • Standard comments (default): start with **c** in column 0. • Nonstandard comments: end-of-line (!) comments (set *comment-start* variable to **"!"**). Create Comments: • Create standard comment: **M-;** (typed on empty line) • Create standard or nonstandard comment: **M-;** (type of comment created depends on value of *comment-start*) Set Comment Column for Nonstandard Comments: • Set *comment-column* to current cursor column: **C-x ;** • Set *comment-column* to *n*: **C-u** *n* **C-x ;** • Set *comment-column* same as previous comment: **C-u C-x ;** Other Commands: • Comment-out all lines in current region, placing **c$$$** before all lines: **C-c ;** • Remove **c$$$** comment prefix from all lines in current region: **C-u C-c ;** Style Variables: • Column where nonstandard comments are created/aligned: *comment-column* • String to use as start of comment (**"c"**): *comment-start* • Default column where standard comment line text is placed: *fortran-comment-line-column* • Set default region comment string (**c$$$**): *fortran-comment-region* • Set ruler text displayed by ruler command: *fortran-comment-ruler*.

8
Editing in Lisp Modes

This chapter describes how to edit Lisp programs in the various Lisp modes available in Emacs. Specifically, this chapter discusses the following topics:

- Lisp major modes
- Assumptions about Lisp source
- Moving among defuns
- Moving among sexps and lists
- Marking text
- Transposing sexps
- Killing sexps
- Indenting programs
- Commenting programs
- Evaluating Lisp code
- Customizing indentation (advanced usage)
- Customizing commenting (advanced usage)

A detailed discussion of programming in Emacs-Lisp is beyond the scope of this book. However, there is a brief introduction to this topic in Appendix B, "Emacs-Lisp Programming." For an excellent tutorial and reference on Emacs-Lisp programming, refer to the *GNU Emacs Lisp Reference Manual*, available from the Free Software Foundation.

Lisp Major Modes

Emacs provides several modes for editing Lisp programs. These modes have special commands for editing Lisp programs, as well as commands for evaluating (executing) the programs. *The commands for editing Lisp source files are exactly the same in all Lisp modes.* Where the modes differ is the way in which they allow you to evaluate Lisp code. Which Lisp mode to use depends on what dialect of Lisp you use and how you want to evaluate the Lisp code.

Table 8.1 summarizes the different Lisp modes and when to use them. For details on evaluating Lisp programs in each mode, see the section "Evaluating Lisp Code" later in this chapter.

Table 8.1. Description of Lisp Modes

To Do This	Use This Mode	Description
Develop Emacs-Lisp defuns and programs	Emacs-Lisp	Emacs-Lisp is a dialect of Lisp in which Emacs itself is written. In addition to the editing commands available in all Lisp modes, Emacs-Lisp mode has special features that are useful for developing Emacs-Lisp programs: Emacs-Lisp libraries, compilation, and debugging. (For details on these additional features, see Appendix B, "Emacs-Lisp Programming.") Emacs uses this mode, by default, for files whose names end with `.el`. To change a buffer's mode to Emacs Lisp mode, use `M-x emacs-lisp-mode`, or put the mode specification as a comment in the first nonblank line in the file—for example: `;;; -*-emacs-lisp-*-`

Table 8.1, con't.

To Do This	Use This Mode	Description
Evaluate Emacs-Lisp defuns interactively	Lisp Interaction	In this mode, `C-j` makes Emacs evaluate the expression immediately preceding the cursor, and places the result in the buffer after the cursor. This mode is useful for debugging and testing smaller pieces of larger Emacs-Lisp programs. Emacs uses this mode, by default, for the start-up `*scratch*` buffer. To change a buffer's mode to Lisp Interaction mode, use `M-x lisp-interaction-mode`.
Develop Lisp defuns and programs in other Lisp dialects	Lisp	In contrast to Emacs-Lisp mode, which has a built-in Lisp interpreter, this mode provides similar capabilities by passing Lisp defuns to an "external" Lisp interpreter for evaluation. Emacs uses this mode for files whose names end with `.l` or `.lisp`. To change a buffer's mode to Lisp mode, use `M-x lisp-mode`, or make the first line of the file a comment containing a mode specification line—for example: `;;; -*-lisp-*-`
Evaluate Lisp defuns interactively	Inferior Lisp	Like Lisp Interaction mode, this mode provides an interactive Lisp session, but with an "external" Lisp dialect. Emacs passes defuns to an external Lisp process for evaluation, and inserts the output into the buffer, like Lisp Interaction mode. To select this mode, use `M-x run-lisp`. This command creates a buffer named `*lisp*`.

Assumptions About Lisp Source

Emacs assumes that an open parenthesis, (, in the first column indicates the start of a defun. To ensure that editing commands work properly, never put an open parenthesis in the first column unless it is the start of a defun.

If an opening parenthesis must appear at the start of a line—for example, as part of a string that extends across multiple lines—then escape it with a backslash \ (or slash / in some Lisp dialects). For example, the following code would be acceptable:

```
(defun longstring ()
  "This very long string has an open parenthesis\
\( on the second line.")
↑
column 0
```

If you typed this example in a Lisp buffer, you would notice that parentheses matching would match the last parenthesis with the one immediately preceding the **defun** keyword. If the open parenthesis in the string hadn't been escaped, Emacs would incorrectly match that parenthesis with the ending one.

Moving Among Defuns

The usual function motion commands, summarized in Table 8.2, can be used to move among defuns.

Table 8.2. Lisp Modes Defun Cursor Motion Commands

Operation	Command and Comments
Move to start of current or previous defun	`C-M-a` If the cursor is inside the body of a defun, moves to the defun's opening parenthesis. If the cursor is already at the opening parenthesis or between defuns, moves to the opening parenthesis of the previous defun.
Move to end of current or next defun	`C-M-e` If the cursor is inside the body of a defun, moves to the defun's closing parenthesis. If the cursor is already at the closing parenthesis or between defuns, moves to the closing parenthesis of the next defun.

Moving Among Sexps and Lists

Sexp and list motion commands are especially useful in Lisp. For less experienced Lisp programmers, this section first describes what sexps and lists are. The remainder of the section describes commands that move the cursor in and among sexps and lists.

What Are Lists and Sexps in Lisp Modes?

A **list** is any balanced parenthetical grouping. Thus, the following are all valid lists:

```
()                                              ← Empty list
(x)                                             ← List containing the symbol x
(+ x 1)                                         ← List containing symbols: + x 1
(defun addone (x) "Add one to x." (+ x 1))      ← List containing various symbols
                                                  and two nested lists: (x) and
                                                  (+ x 1).
```

An **sexp** is a symbol, number, or list. Thus, the following are all valid sexps:

```
x                                               A symbol
1                                               A number
"Add one to x."                                 A string constant
(defun addone (x) "Add one to x." (+ x 1))      A parenthetical grouping (list)
```

Notice that the string "Add one to x." contains these nested sexps:

```
Add             A symbol
one             A symbol
to              A symbol
x               A symbol
.               A symbol
```

And the **addone** defun, shown above, contains these sexps:

```
defun           A symbol
addone          A symbol
(x)             A list
"Add one to x." A string constant
(+ x 1)         A list
```

The fact that lists and sexps can contain nested lists and sexps is important because it affects the way the list and sexp motion commands work. What constitutes a list or sexp depends on the cursor location.

For instance, the **C-M-f** command moves forward over the current or next sexp. Where this actually moves the cursor depends on where the cursor is to begin with. Figure 8.1 shows the effect of the **C-M-f** command for various cursor locations within the **addone** defun:

The last **C-M-f** command would generate the error message **Containing expression ends prematurely**. This is because at that cursor location, there is no valid sexp to move over: There is no symbol, no number, no string constant, nor is there a balanced list.

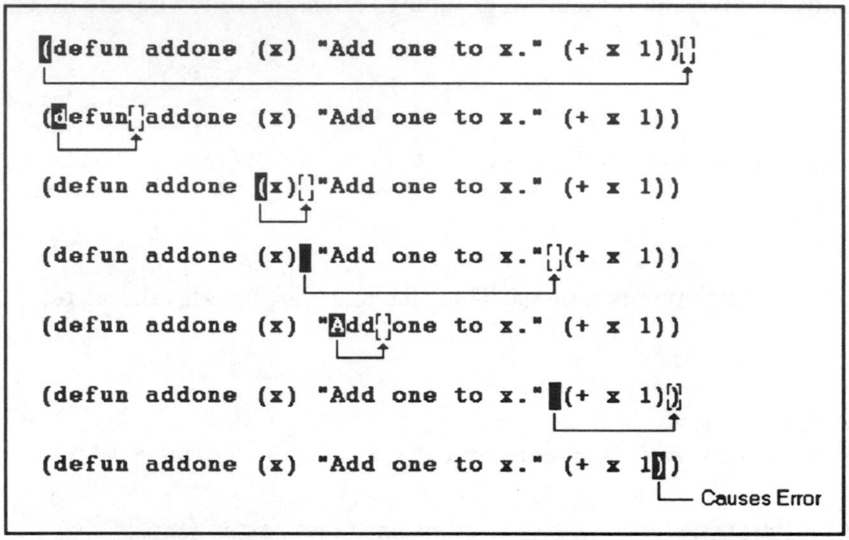

Figure 8.1. Effect of C-M-f at Various Cursor Locations

Context is also important with list motion commands. For example, **C-M-n** moves the cursor forward over the next list, which depends on the cursor's location. Figure 8.2 shows the effect of **C-M-n** for various cursor locations in the **addone** defun.

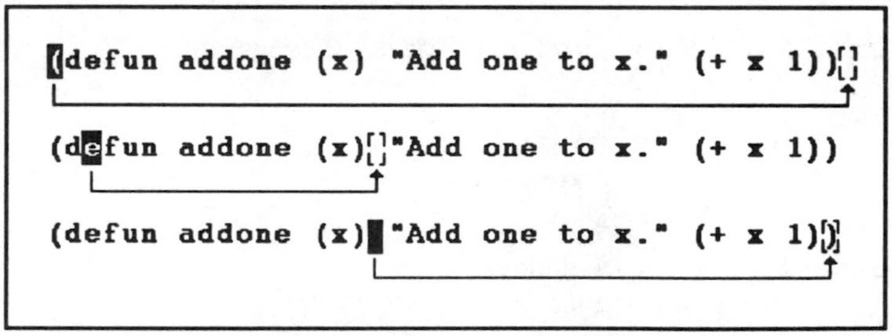

Figure 8.2 Effect of C-M-n at Various Cursor Locations

The **C-M-d** command moves forward into the next deeper level of nesting. Figure 8.3 shows the effect of **C-M-d** at various cursor positions within the **addone** defun.

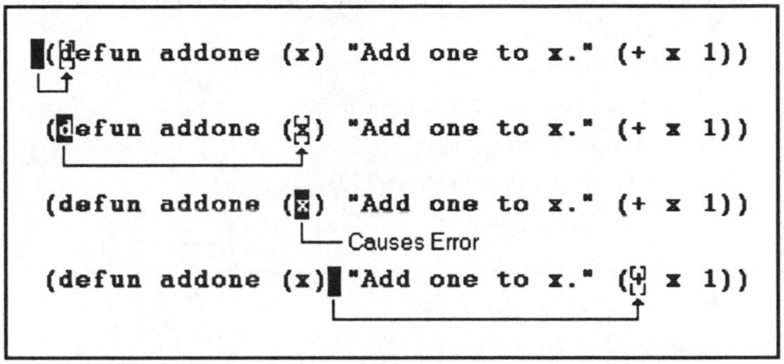

Figure 8.3. Effects of C-M-d at Various Cursor Locations

The third example causes an error because there is no nested list to move into.

List and Sexp Motion Commands

Table 8.3 summarizes the commands for navigating in and among sexps and lists.

Table 8.3. List and Sexp Motion Commands

Operation	Command and Comments
Forward over sexp	**C-M-f** Move forward over the current or next sexp, where sexp is defined to be any symbol, number, string constant, or list—for example: `(defun zed ())`
Backward over sexp	**C-M-b** Move backward over the current or previous sexp—for example: `(defun zed ())` (This command may not act as expected when backing up over comments.)

Table 8.3, con't.

Operation	Command and Comments
Forward over list	**C-M-n** Move over next list—for example: (one (two (three)))
Backward over list	**C-M-p** Move backward over the previous list—for example: (one (two (three)))
Up a list	**C-M-u** Move backward into the next higher list in a nested list—for example: 2nd (one (two (three))) 1st
Down a list	**C-M-d** Move forward into the next lower list in a nested list—for example: 2nd (one (two (three))) 1st

Marking Text

In addition to the usual Fundamental and Text mode marking commands, Lisp modes support commands for marking defuns and sexps, summarized in Table 8.4.

Table 8.4. Commands for Marking Defuns and Sexps

Operation	Command and Comments
Put region around defun	C-M-h Puts a region around the current defun and places the cursor at the start of the defun and mark at the end.
Put mark at end of sexp	C-M-@ Puts a mark after the next sexp.

For example in Figure 8.4, **C-M-@** places mark in the **addone** defun.

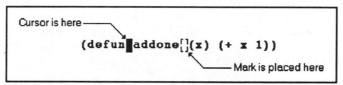

```
Cursor is here ──────┐
                     ↓
              (defun█addone[](x) (+ x 1))
                                   └──── Mark is placed here
```

Figure 8.4. Marking an Sexp

Now running **C-w** (kill-region) makes the line look like Figure 8.5

```
(defun█(x) (+ x 1))
       └──── Cursor and mark are both here
```

Figure 8.5. Sexp with Region Deleted

Transposing Sexps

C-M-t transposes sexps around the current cursor position. For example, in the following defun, the **(+ x 1)** and **(x)** sexps are in the incorrect order:

```
(defun addone (+ x 1) (x))
              ↑
              cursor
```

Using the **C-M-t** command, you can transpose the expressions. When the command is finished, the cursor is placed after the second sexp:

```
(defun addone (x) (+ x 1))
                        ↑
                      cursor
```

Different behavior can be obtained by specifying negative or positive arguments to this command. Experiment to see how this works.

Killing Sexps

The **C-M-k** command kills forward to the end of the current or next sexp. It is equivalent in effect to running **C-M-@** to mark the end of the next sexp; then executing **C-w** to kill the marked region. For example, when issued in the following line, **C-M-k** kills the extra pair of empty parentheses in the defun:

```
(defun addone () (x) (+ x 1))
                ↑
              cursor
                ↓
(defun addone (x) (+ x 1))
```

Indenting Programs

Lisp modes support all the program line indentation commands available in other programming modes. Table 8.5 summarizes these commands. Since the **TAB** key is used to perform special indenting functions, you must escape it with **C-q** if you want to insert an actual tab into the file—that is, **C-q TAB**.

Table 8.5. Lisp Modes Indentation Commands

Operation	Command and Comments
Indent current line	**TAB** Indents the current line in a manner consistent with the indentation used on previous lines in the defun.
Finish line and indent next	**C-j** or **LFD** Ends the current line and starts a new line with proper indentation.

Table 8.5, con't.

Operation	Command and Comments
Indent all lines in region	C–M–\ Re-indents all lines in the current region. For example, to re-indent all the lines in a defun, you could use C–M–h to mark the defun, then use C–M–\. This command re-indents lines that are out of alignment with other lines in the region.
Indent list contents	C–M–q Re-indents the contents of a list (see below).
Shift list to correct alignment	C–u TAB Shifts the entire contents of a list so that its first line is aligned properly (see below).

While the **TAB**, **C–j** and **C–M–** commands are straightforward and act similarly in all programming modes, **C–M–q** and **C–u TAB** require further explanation.

Indenting a List's Contents

To re-indent a list, place the cursor before the list and run **C–M–q**. For example, suppose you've written the defun shown in Figure 8.6.

```
      (defun pow (x y) "Compute x to y power."
     ▮(if (equal y 0)
       1
       (if equal y 1)
       x
       (* x (pow x (- y 1))
       )
       )
       )
       )
```
Cursor

Figure 8.6. Sample Defun

To make the list following the cursor more readable, use **C–M–q**, which produces the indentation shown in Figure 8.7.

```
(defun pow (x y) "Compute x to y power."
 ▌(if (equal y 0)
      1
    (if (equal y 1)
        x
      (* x (pow x (- y 1))
        )
      )
    )
  )
```

Figure 8.7. Defun Indented with C-M-q

Shifting a List to Correct Alignment

To use **C-u TAB**, move the cursor to the start of a list and type the command. Suppose the list beginning with (if (equal y 0) ... in the last example is not indented two columns as it should be, but starts in column 0, as shown in Figure 8.8.

```
        (defun pow (x y) "Compute x to y power."
        (if (equal y 0)
        )      1
Column 0 (if (equal y 1)
            x
        (* x (pow x (- y 1))
            )
        )
        )
```

Figure 8.8. Improperly Indented Defun

In Figure 8.9, the **C-u TAB** command has shifted all lines two columns to the right.

```
        (defun pow (x y) "Compute x to y power."
        )  (if (equal y 0)
Column 0 )     1
   Column 2  (if (equal y 1)
                x
            (* x (pow x (- y 1))
                )
            )
        )
```

Figure 8.9. Defun Indented Properly with C-u TAB

Commenting Programs

The usual programming mode commenting commands apply in Lisp modes. Specifically, there are commands for creating new comments, aligning existing comments, setting the comment column, killing comments, and creating multi-line comments.

Creating New Comments

If the current line does not contain a comment, **M-;** appends a comment to the line of the form:

```
                    ; comment text
                    ↑
                    comment column
```

Emacs places the semicolon at the current comment column (32 by default), and places the cursor after it, waiting for you to type the comment text. Shown below are some comments added with **M-;** to lines of a defun that computes x to the y power. Notice how the comments line up at the same comment column.

```
(defun pow (x y)
  "Compute X to the Y power, where Y is non-negative."

  (if (equal y 0)                   ; If y=0, return 1
      1
    (if (equal y 1)                 ; If y=1, return x
        x
      (* x (pow x (- y 1)))))))     ; Else return x * pow(x,y-1)
                                    ↑
                                    comment column
```

If the Lisp source line extends past the comment column, Emacs appends the comment one space after the end of the line. For example, adding a comment to the second line of the **pow** defun looks like this:

```
  "Compute X to the Y power, where Y is non-negative." ; Comment
                                                       ↑
                                                       The comment is appended one
                                                       space after the source line.
```

Typing Multi-Line Comments

There are two ways to get comments that continue for multiple lines. If auto-filling is enabled, and you type past the fill margin, Emacs automatically creates another comment line for you on the next line; you don't press **RET** at the end of each line:

```
; This is a very long comment
; that extends past the fill
; column.
↑                                                    ↑
The comment column                          The fill column
```

The other way to get multi-line comments is to use the **C-M-j** (or **M-LFD**) command, which is identical to typing **RET** followed by **M-;** .

If you use a different comment style, Emacs will attempt to copy the comment style on subsequent lines. Suppose you create a comment like the following:

```
;;; This comment starts in column 0.
↑
column 0
```

If you continue the line by typing past the fill column or by **C-M-j**, Emacs creates a continued comment in the same column, using the same number of semicolons:

```
;;; This comment starts in column 0.         ← Press C-M-j.
;;; █                                        ← Continued comment.
    ↑
    cursor
```

A similar situation would occur for comments that begin with two semicolons:

```
(defun sgml-show-short-form (s)
   ;; Show the short form of the tag.         ← Press C-M-j.
   ;; Supported tags are computer, var, term  ← Continued comment.
   (cond ((equal s "computer") (insert "'\'/'"))
         ((equal s "var")      (insert "%%%%"))
         ((equal s "term")     (insert "++++")))
   (backward-char 2))
```

Aligning Comments

If a line already contains a comment, the **M-;** command aligns it appropriately. If the comment is already aligned appropriately, then **M-;** simply moves to the start of the comment field, which can be useful if you want to edit the comment field.

Emacs aligns comments based on a common convention used by Lisp programmers:

- Comments that begin with a *single* semicolon are assumed to start at the comment column.

- Comments that start with *two* semicolons are indented as if they were lines of code.

- Comments that start with *three* or more semicolons left as is (usually in column 0).

The Lisp code below shows examples of all three types of comment alignment:

```
;;; The following function computes x to the y power recursively.
;;; Y must be a non-negative integer, but no such checks are made.
(defun pow (x y)
  ;; The following line is for Emacs-Lisp documentation:
  "Compute X to the Y power."
  ;; Begin the body of the function:
  (if (equal y 0)                      ; If y=0, return 1
      1
    (if (equal y 1)                    ; If y=1, return x
        x
      (* x (pow x (- y 1))))))))       ; Else, return x * pow(x,y-1)
```

Note that the **M-;** command does not create **;;;** or **;;** comments. **M-;** only aligns such comments. If you want such comments, you must type them explicitly.

Setting the Comment Column

You can determine the default comment column by looking at the value of the *comment-column* variable. You can change the comment column with the **C-x ;** command. To do this, first move the cursor to the column in which you want comments to start, then use **C-x ;**. Emacs displays the message **Comment column set to** *nnn*, where *nnn* is the cursor column.

If you specify an empty argument to this command (e.g., **C-u C-x ;**), Emacs sets the comment column to whatever comment column was used for the previous comment; then it aligns the comment on the current line to the new comment column. This is useful for aligning comments that are not at the usual comment column.

Killing Comments

To kill a comment on the current line, use **C-x ;** with a negative argument (**C-u - C-x ;**).

Moving Comments

To move a comment, first kill it with **C–u – C–x ;**. Then move to the end of the line on which you want to place the comment. Then yank it back into the buffer, using **C–y**. You can then use **M–;** to align it properly.

Evaluating Lisp Code

Emacs has a built-in interpreter for the Emacs-Lisp language. In fact, Emacs is written mainly in Emacs-Lisp. Emacs provides the Emacs-Lisp and Lisp Interaction modes for evaluating Emacs-Lisp code. Emacs-Lisp expressions can also be evaluated in the minibuffer in any mode.

Some programmers may want to use a Lisp dialect other than Emacs-Lisp. Emacs provides the Lisp and Inferior Lisp modes for evaluating such "external" Lisp programs. In these modes, Emacs doesn't actually evaluate such code; instead, it is passed to an external Lisp process for evaluation.

Evaluating Code in the Minibuffer

To evaluate Emacs-Lisp code in the minibuffer, use the **M–ESC** (or **ESC–ESC**) command. It prompts you for the expression to evaluate in the minibuffer:

    Eval: █   ← You type the Emacs-Lisp expression to evaluate.

It then displays the result of the evaluation in the minibuffer. For example, if you typed the expression **(+ 1 1)** to the **Eval:** prompt, as:

    Eval: (+ 1 1) RET

Emacs displays the result **2** in the minibuffer.

Note that **M–ESC** is normally a disabled command, which means that Emacs prompts you for verification before allowing you to execute it. If you enable the command, Emacs will discontinue prompting you for verification. For details on disabling and enabling commands, see Chapter 13, "Customizing the Emacs Environment."

Emacs-Lisp Mode

Emacs-Lisp mode is used for editing and running code written in Emacs-Lisp. You would use this mode to create any custom Emacs functions or modes. Emacs uses

Emacs-Lisp mode automatically for files whose names end with a `.el` suffix. You can also select Emacs-Lisp mode with the **M-x emacs-lisp-mode** command.

Emacs-Lisp mode provides commands for evaluating a single defun, all the code within a region, or an entire buffer. Any expressions evaluated in this mode are "installed" into Emacs for the duration of the Emacs session. For instance, if you evaluate a defun named **foo**, it can be called by other Emacs-Lisp functions or can be executed from the minibuffer using **M-ESC** (or **ESC-ESC**).

Table 8.6 summarizes the various commands for evaluating Lisp code. Note that code evaluated by these commands is installed *in the current Emacs session only.* To install code whenever you start up Emacs, you can put it in your `.emacs` start-up file, or you can load Emacs-Lisp files from your start-up file. For details, see Chapter 13, "Customizing the Emacs Environment."

Table 8.6. Summary of Emacs-Lisp Mode's Evaluation Commands

Operation	Command and Comments
Evaluate preceding expression	`C-x C-e` Evaluates the Emacs-Lisp expression preceding the cursor and displays the result in the minibuffer.
Evaluate expression	`C-M-x` This command is essentially the same as `C-x C-e`, except that it evaluates the expression that *contains* the cursor or that immediately follows the cursor.
Evaluate code in region	`M-x eval-region` Evaluates all the Emacs-Lisp code in the current region.
Evaluate all code in buffer	`M-x eval-current-buffer` Evaluates all Emacs-Lisp code in the buffer. This command is useful for installing all changes from an Emacs-Lisp buffer into Emacs for the duration of the session.

As an example of how **C-x C-e** evaluation works, suppose you've written the following and positioned the cursor after the ending parenthesis:

```
(defun foo (x) (concat "foo" x))█
```

If you type **C-x C-e**, the message **foo** is displayed in the minibuffer. Now, if you type **M-ESC** (or **ESC-ESC**) to evaluate an expression in the minibuffer, and type:

```
Eval: (foo "bar")
```

The message **foobar** is displayed in the minibuffer, indicating that Emacs evaluated the defun **foo** that you defined above.

When given a numeric argument, the **C-M-x** and **C-x C-e** commands insert the resulting value of the evaluation into the buffer at the location of the cursor.

Lisp Interaction Mode

Lisp Interaction mode is useful for building up and testing a new function in pieces. This mode is identical to Emacs-Lisp mode, except that it has an additional command, **LFD** (or **C-j**). The **LFD** command evaluates the Lisp expression preceding the cursor and inserts the resulting value into the buffer. This is why the mode is called Lisp Interaction mode: it shows the interaction between you and the Lisp interpreter in the same buffer.

Shown below is the output resulting in a Lisp Interaction buffer. Underscored lines were typed in; all others Emacs inserted.

```
(+ 1 2 3) C-j
6
(defun foo (x) (concat "foo" x)) C-j
foo
(foo "bar") C-j
"foobar"
```

Thus, Lisp Interaction mode gives you a log of Lisp expressions and the result of their evaluation.

Lisp Mode

Lisp mode is used for editing and running code written in Lisp dialects other than Emacs-Lisp. Emacs uses Lisp mode automatically for files whose names end with a **.l** or **.lisp** suffix. You can also select Lisp mode by:

• Issuing the **M-x lisp-mode** command, or

• Visiting a file that contains a file mode specification in the first nonblank line:

```
;;; -*-lisp-*-
```

There is one command for evaluating Lisp expressions in this mode: **C-M-x**. This command passes the expression surrounding or following the cursor to an inferior Lisp process.

Before using **C-M-x**, you must start an inferior Lisp process with the **M-x run-lisp** command. To start the inferior Lisp process, Emacs looks for an interpreter program named **lisp** in the directories specified by the variable *exec-path*. This variable is set initially from your PATH environment variable, but may be set to a different value in your **.emacs** start-up file. If your system does not have an interpreter program named **lisp**, or if the program is not in the directory specified by *exec-path*, Emacs displays a message saying that it could not find **lisp**.

Once the inferior Lisp process is started, Emacs creates an Inferior Lisp mode window named ***lisp***; any text you type is sent to the inferior Lisp process and the output of the process is inserted back into the buffer. Thus, you get similar capability to that provided by Lisp Interaction mode, but with an external Lisp. Once you've started the inferior Lisp process, you can switch back to Lisp mode buffer (for example, with **C-x b**) and use the **C-M-x** command.

Note that you need only create one inferior Lisp process for all Lisp buffers. All Lisp mode buffers can use the same inferior Lisp process.

Once the inferior Lisp process is started and you are back in the Lisp mode buffer, you can pass Lisp expressions to the inferior process for evaluation with the **C-M-x** command. Conceptually, **C-M-x** sends the expression preceding the cursor to the inferior process for evaluation in the inferior Lisp process's environment. Emacs sends the expression to the process by:

1. Saving the expression into a temporary file, and

2. Sending a (load *filename*) command to the inferior process, where *filename* is the name of the file temporary file.

By default, Emacs uses a load command of the form

```
(load "%s")
```

where **"%s"** represents a string that Emacs replaces with the name of the temporary file. For most Lisp dialects, this load command is sufficient to ensure proper evaluation with the **C-M-x** command.

Inferior Lisp Mode

As mentioned above, Inferior Lisp mode is enabled with **M-x run-lisp**. Any expressions you type are sent to the inferior Lisp interpreter for evaluation, and the result of the evaluation is inserted back into the ***lisp*** buffer. Just type an expression and press **RET** to have it evaluated by the Lisp subprocess.

Customizing Indentation (Advanced Usage)

Lisp mode indentation should be sufficient for most users. However, some users may wish to customize the default indentation style. How Lisp mode indents the pieces of an expression depends on what function the expression calls.

Indentation for Defuns

In expressions that start with **def**, the second line always indents, by default, 2 columns beyond the opening parenthesis—for example:

```
column 0
↓
(defvar sgml-mode-syntax-table nil
  "Syntax table for sgml-mode buffers.")          ← Indented 2 columns

(defun sgml-tab ()
  "Indent to next tab stop."                       ← Indented 2 columns
  (interactive)
  (indent-to (* (1+ (/ (current-indentation) sgml-indent))
    sgml-indent)))
    ↑
    column 2
```

This indentation is controlled by *lisp-body-indentation*. For example, setting *lisp-body-indentation* to 4 gives the following indentation on the same expressions:

```
column 0
↓
(defvar sgml-mode-syntax-table nil
    "Syntax table for sgml-mode buffers.")          ← Indented 4 columns

(defun sgml-tab ()
    "Indent to next tab stop."                       ← Indented 4 columns
    (interactive)
    (indent-to (* (1+ (/ (current-indentation) sgml-indent))
      sgml-indent)))
      ↑
      column 4
```

General Indentation Rules

When an expression has two or more arguments and breaks over multiple lines, Emacs uses the following rules for indentation:

- If the first argument is on the same line as the function, then the second argument is indented at the same level as the first argument. For example:

```
        indentation of first argument
        ↓
(if sgml-short-form
    (sgml-show-short-form s))
    ↑
    second argument is indented at same level
```

- If the first argument is on the next line, it is indented under the function name at a level appropriate for the function. For example:

```
(if
        sgml-uppercase          ← Second line indented at predetermined level for if
        (upcase s))                function (4 columns)
```

Note that this level of indentation can differ for various functions. Compare the indentation of the **if** function with the indentation produced for the **cond** function in the same situation:

```
(cond
  ((equal tight "1") "")    ← Second line indented 1 column for cond function
  ((equal tight "") "")
  ((equal tight "t") " tight")
  (t (sgml-get-tight)))
```

- All following lines are indented at the same level as the previous line having the same nesting level. So, for example, all the condition clauses of the preceding **cond** expression are indented at the same level as the second line. This is also why **defuns** have indentation that looks like this:

```
(defun sgml-rsect ()
  "<rsect>"
  (interactive)
  (insert (sgml-key "<rsect>"))
  (backward-char)
  (insert (sgml-get-id))
  (end-of-line)
  (insert (read-string "rsect title: "))
  (sgml-newline))
```

Since all the nested expressions in **sgml-rsect** have the same nesting level as the second line, they are all indented at the same level, too.

Overriding Default Indentation

The general indentation rules above apply as long as *lisp-indent-offset* is `nil`, its default value. If you change this variable to a number, then the second line of an expression is indented *lisp-indent-offset* columns from the opening parenthesis of the expression. For example, if you set *lisp-indent-offset* to 2, Emacs produces the following indentation:

```
column 0
↓
(if sgml-short-form
  (sgml-show-short-form s))
  ↑
  column 2
```

Compare this with the default indentation produced using the general rules described above:

```
column 0
↓
(if sgml-short-form
    (sgml-show-short-form s))
    ↑
    Column is the same as the first argument on previous line.
```

Customizing Commenting (Advanced Usage)

Like Emacs indentation capabilities, the behavior of commenting is controlled through variables, summarized in Table 8.7. (For details on making changes to these variables apply to each Emacs session, refer to Chapter 13, "Customizing the Emacs Environment.") Following Table 8.7 are more detailed descriptions of how to customize commenting with these variables.

Table 8.7. Lisp Modes Commenting Variables

Variable	Default Value and Purpose
comment-column	Default: **32** Column at which new comments are displayed or existing comments are aligned.

Table 8.7. Lisp Modes Commenting Variables

Variable	Default Value and Purpose
comment-start	Default: `"; "` String used to start a comment created by the **M-;** or **C-M-j** command.
comment-end	Default: `""` String to use to end a comment. Setting this variable to a value other than `""` is not very useful because Lisp comments are terminated by a newline.

comment-start-skip	Default: `";+ *"`
	
	 Regular expression Emacs uses when searching for the start of a comment. The default value says to look for one or more semicolons, followed by zero or more spaces. Thus, the following all match the default value of *comment-start-skip*:
	
	 `;;; start-of-line comments`
	 `;; comments aligned with code`
	 `; end-of-line comment`

Changing the Comment Column

The *comment-column* variable defines the column in which to begin comments created by **M-;**. You would normally set this variable with one of these commands:

- **C-x ;** (set *comment-column* to current cursor column),

- **C-u** *n* **C-x ;** (set *comment-column* to *n*),

- **C-u C-x ;** (set *comment-column* to same as comment on previous line).

Each Lisp mode buffer has a local copy of *comment-column*. However, you can make the variable **global**, forcing it to apply to all Lisp buffers. To do this, use the command **M-ESC (setq-default comment-column n)**, where *n* is the new comment column to use in all buffers.

Changing Comment Delimiters

The *comment-start* variables defines the string to use as the start of a comment created by **M-;**. Its default value is usually sufficient. However, you might want to modify it in some cases. For instance, Suppose you are revising source code for a new release, and you want to mark all comments that were added for the new release. You could do this by setting *comment-start* to include release information:

```
M-x set-variable RET
Set variable: comment-start RET
Set comment-start to value: "; v1.21: " RET        ← Quotes are required.
```

Then, if you issued the **M-;** command, it would create a comment that looked like this:

```
; v1.21: █
         ↑
```
The cursor is here, waiting for you to type the comment text.

Changing the Comment Search Pattern

The *comment-start-skip* variable contains a regular expression that Lisp mode uses to find the start of a comment. This variable should be set such that Emacs can find the start of comments as defined by *comment-start*. It should *never* match the null string, **" "**. For most users, the default comment regular expression search string is sufficient. You would probably only change this variable if you used a dialect of Lisp that had different comment syntax.

Summary

Table 8.8 summarizes the important points to remember in this chapter.

Table 8.8. Chapter 8 Summary

Topic	Summary
Selecting a Lisp Mode	Emacs Lisp Mode (for developing Emacs-Lisp defuns/programs): <ul><li>Name your source file with a `.el` extension, or</li><li>Invoke with the `M-x emacs-lisp-mode` command, or</li><li>Make sure the first nonblank line of source file is a comment that includes the string `-*-emacs-lisp-*-`</li></ul> Lisp Interaction Mode (evaluate Emacs-Lisp defuns interactively): <ul><li>Invoke with the `M-x lisp-interaction-mode` command</li></ul> Lisp Mode (develop Lisp defuns/programs in other dialects): <ul><li>Name your source file with a `.l` or `.lisp` extension, or</li><li>Invoke with the `M-x lisp-mode` command, or</li><li>Make sure the first nonblank line of source file is a comment that includes the string `-*-lisp-*-`</li></ul> Inferior Lisp Mode (evaluate other Lisp dialect defuns interactively): <ul><li>Invoke with the `M-x run-lisp` command</li></ul>
Assumptions about Lisp modes	<ul><li>Emacs assumes a `(` in column zero is start of a defun. Escape any `(` in column zero which do not comply with this rule with a backslash `\`.</li></ul>

Table 8.8, con't.

Topic	Summary
Evaluating Lisp expressions	Emacs-Lisp Mode: • Evaluate expression preceding cursor: `C-x C-e` • Evaluate expression surrounding the cursor: `C-M-x` • Evaluate all expressions in current region: `M-x eval-region` • Evaluate all expressions in current buffer: `M-x eval-current-buffer` Lisp Interaction Mode: • Evaluate expression preceding the cursor: `C-j` Lisp Mode: • Evaluate expression preceding the cursor: `C-M-x` Inferior Lisp Mode • Type expression.
Motion commands (all modes)	• Move to start of current or previous defun: `C-M-a` • Move to end of current or next defun: `C-M-e` • Move forward over current or next sexp: `C-M-f` • Move backward over current or previous sexp: `C-M-b` • Move over next list: `C-M-n` • Move backward over previous list: `C-M-p` • Move to next higher list in nested list: `C-M-u` • Move to next lower list in nested list: `C-M-d`
Region commands	• Put region around defun containing cursor: `C-M-h` • Put a mark after the next sexp: `C-M-@`
Transpose command	Transpose sexps around cursor: `C-M-t`
Kill command	Kill the next sexp: `C-M-k`
Symbol completion	Complete Emacs-Lisp symbol being typed: `M-TAB` (or `ESC-TAB`)

Table 8.8, con't.

Topic	Summary
Indentation	Commands: • Indent current line: **TAB** • Finish current line and open next line indented: **C−j** • Re-indent all lines in current region: **C−M−** • Re-indent the contents of a list: **C−M−q** • Shift the contents of a list rigidly: **C−u** **TAB** Default Indentation Rules: • If first argument is on same line as function, arguments on subsequent lines are indented at same level as first argument. • If first argument is on line following function, arguments are indented at level appropriate for function. • All following lines are indented at same level as previous lines having the same nesting level. Style Variables: • Distance to indent body of defun from opening parenthesis: *list-body-indentation* • Distance to indent body of expression from opening parenthesis: *list-indent-offset*
Comments	Commands: • Append a comment to current line at *comment-column*: **M−;** • Set *comment-column* to current cursor column: **C−x ;** • Set *comment-column* to *n* : **C−u** *n* **C−x ;** • Set *comment-column* same as previous comment: **C−u C−x ;** • Delete comment on current line: **C−u − C−x ;** • Finish current comment line and start a new comment: **C−M−j** Style Variables: • Column where comments are created/aligned: *comment-column* • String to use as start of comment (**"; "**): *comment-start* • String to use as end of comment (**""**): *comment-end* • Regular expression used when searching for start of a comment (**";+ *"**): *comment-start-skip*

Part 3
Additional Emacs Features

This part of the book describes features of the Emacs environment that supplement its editing and programming capabilities. In addition to the text and source code editing modes already discussed, Emacs provides several specialized modes and utilities for performing common computing tasks, including:

- a utility for sending and receiving electronic mail,

- an online help facility,

- a mode for performing common file management tasks, such as copying, deleting, etc.,

- a mode to help you manage your Emacs buffers,

- a spelling checker,

- a mode for running a UNIX shell in an Emacs window,

- a feature that automatically saves your files at specified intervals

- specialized editing modes for TeX, Troff, and pictures.

Each of the chapters in this part of the book are independent and require only that you understand the basic text editing commands described in Chapters 1 and 2. Reading these chapters is optional, but we highly recommend at least a perusal of Chapter 9, which describes the online help facility, and Chapter 11, which contains some useful file and buffer management techniques. Otherwise, read these chapters according to your needs and interests.

The following chapters are included in Part 3:

- Chapter 9: Getting Online Help

- Chapter 10: Using Emacs for Electronic Mail

- Chapter 11: Managing Files and Buffers

- Chapter 12: Miscellaneous Emacs Features

9
Getting Online Help

This chapter describes how to use Emacs' online help facility. It covers the following information:

- Running help commands
- Getting online instructions for using the help facility
- Getting command information

Emacs provides online help in the following areas:

- **Help on help**—how to use the help facility
- **Emacs commands**—details about what a specific command does and what function the command binds to (more on command-to-function bindings later)
- **Variables**—documentation and current value
- **Mode specifics**—information about commands and variables that are uniquely defined for a particular mode
- **Syntax tables**—how Emacs classifies various characters
- **Lossage**—a record of the last 100 keystrokes you typed
- **Tutorial**—a "hands-on" tutorial you can use to acquaint yourself with basic Emacs commands
- **News**—a summary of changes made to Emacs, with latest revisions shown first
- **Info**—a browser for the "info" documentation tree
- **Copyright, ordering, etc.**—copyright, disclaimers, how to order Emacs from the Free Software Foundation, and restrictions on copying Emacs

In addition, Emacs provides a powerful **apropos** capability for searching for commands that contain a particular string.

Running Help Commands

The usual way to access the help facility is to run `C-h` followed by a letter designating the kind of help information you want. For example, `C-h k` displays documentation for a command key sequence. Table 9.1 shows which `C-h` command to use to get the various types of help summarized above.

Unfortunately, the `C-h` command does not access the help facility on all systems, because `C-h` is sometimes defined to perform the function of the `DEL` key. On such systems, the help command is bound to some other key. For example, on our system, `C-8` accesses the help facility; on others the `DEL` (Backspace) key accesses help while `C-h` performs the function of `DEL`. If `C-h` does not access help on your system,

- ask your system administrator which key to use, or

- if you understand `.emacs` start-up files, look there to see which key help is bound to. See Chapter 13 for more information on the `.emacs` file.

See "Finding Your Online Help and DEL Keys" in Chapter 1 for more information.

Emacs also provides a set of `M-x` commands to access specific types of help. For example, `M-x describe-key` displays the same information provided by `C-h k`. In Table 9.1, both the short form (`C-h`) and long form (`M-x`) commands are shown. If your `C-h` key is the same as your `DEL` key and you don't know the alternate help key, you can use the long form to access help.

Table 9.1. Accessing the Different Types of Help

Help Type	Commands and Comments
Help	Short form: `C-h C-h` or `C-h ?` Long form: `M-x help-for-help` Displays a one-line summary of help keys. Can also provide a summary of the types of help available.
Variables	Short form: `C-h v` Long form: `M-x describe-variable` Displays the value of a variable. For details on why you would use this command, see Chapter 13, "Customizing the Emacs Environment."

Table 9.1, con't.

Help Type	Commands and Comments
Mode specific	Short form: `C-h m` Long form: `M-x describe-mode` Displays help information unique to the current mode (for example, commands and variables that are available only in the mode).
Commands	Short form: `C-h k` Long form: `M-x describe-key` Displays documentation for a command key sequence. Also shows the command key binding. A **binding** is a mapping between a key sequence and an Emacs function. (See the section, "Getting Command Information" for details.)
	Short form: `C-h c` Long form: `M-x describe-key-briefly` Displays the binding for a command key sequence.
	Short form: `C-h w` Long form: `M-x where-is` Shows what key is bound to a function.
	Short form: `C-h b` Long form: `M-x describe-bindings` Shows *all* command key bindings in this mode.
	Short form: `C-h a` Long form: `M-x command-apropos` Runs **apropos**, a feature that displays all commands that "match" a search string. For example, you could find all commands that deal with "lines." This is one of the most powerful help features available in Emacs.

Table 9.1, con't.

Help Type	Commands and Comments
Syntax tables	Short form: `C-h s` Long form: `M-x describe-syntax` Displays syntax table information. For details on how you would use this command, see Chapter 13, "Customizing the Emacs Environment."
Lossage	Short form: `C-h l` (letter l) Long form: `M-x view-lossage` Displays the last 100 characters typed. If you got unexpected results from a command, you might use this command to see if you made a typing mistake.
Tutorial	Short form: `C-h t` Long form: `M-x help-with-tutorial` If the online tutorial is installed, this command creates a buffer named **TUTORIAL** in Fundamental mode. You can learn basic Emacs editing commands by following the directions in the tutorial.
Info	Short form: `C-h i` Long form: `M-x info` Runs the info explorer program, which browses the Info documentation tree. The *GNU Emacs Manual* is stored in the Info documentation tree and can be read using this command. The command creates a window in Info Narrow mode, which has special commands for viewing the documentation tree. For a tutorial on using the info explorer, type **h** after running the info explorer program.
Copyright	Short form: `C-h C-c` Long form: `M-x describe-copying` Display information and restrictions related to copying GNU Emacs.

Table 9.1, con't.

Help Type	Commands and Comments
Distribution	Short form: `C-h C-d` Long form: `M-x describe-distribution` Display information about how to order Emacs from the Free Software Foundation.
Warranty	Short form: `C-h C-w` Long form: `M-x describe-no-warranty` Display the information and disclaimers related to not getting any warranty for the Emacs product.
News	Short form: `C-h n` Long form: `M-x view-emacs-news` Display the contents of the NEWS file in a buffer named NEWS in Text mode. This file contains a history of changes made to Emacs, with most recent changes first. For example, you may see the X11 windows are now supported under System V.

Most help commands show help text in a buffer in another window. For example, if you run `C-x k` to get information on a command key sequence, Emacs splits the current window in half horizontally (if it wasn't already split), and displays the help text in the other window. The window containing help information is usually a buffer named `*Help*`, but not always (as in the case of the Info viewer). Because help commands use a separate window, the following commands are particularly useful when viewing help text:

- `C-x o` to switch the cursor to the other (`*Help*`) window

- In most `*Help*` windows, you can use the regular cursor motion commands to move about the buffer (if it is too large to fit in the window)

- `C-x 1` to hide all windows other than the current window

- `C-M-v` to scroll the other window

Getting Instructions for Using Help

If you run **C-h ?** or **C-h C-h**, Emacs displays the following in the echo area:

```
A B C F I K L M N S T V W C-c C-d C-w. Type C-H again for more help:
```

This serves as a memory jogger, displaying the key letters you can type after **C-h** to get help. At this point, you could type one of the key letters to access the help, or you could type **C-h** again to display a more detailed listing of help types. For example, pressing **C-h** again on our system displayed this information in another window:

```
You have typed C-H, the help character. Type a Help option:

A   command-apropos. Give a substring, and see a list of commands
                (functions interactively callable) that contain
                that substring. See also the apropos command.
B   describe-bindings. Display table of all key bindings.
C   describe-key-briefly. Type a command key sequence;
                it prints the function name that sequence runs.
F   describe-function. Type a function name and get documentation of
                it.
I   info. The info documentation reader.
K   describe-key. Type a command key sequence;
                it displays the full documentation.
                ...
```

You could now type one of the letters to get the type of help information desired.

To summarize, you can type any of the following commands to display help information:

```
C-h key
C-h ? key
C-h ? C-h key
M-x function-name
```

Getting Command Information

Before learning how to get help information on Emacs commands, you should know a little about how Emacs executes commands. All commands, except those starting with **M-x**, are actually shorthand notations for longer command names, known as **functions**. In Emacs terminology, the command **binds to** the function. For example, the command **C-n** is bound to the **next-line** function; when you press **C-n**, Emacs runs an "internal" function named **next-line**, which performs the action.

This is important because the help commands often deal with the function name and not the command key sequence. This is also *very* important if you do certain customizations, such as changing command key bindings (as described in Chapter 13).

As an interesting side note, when you run a **M-x** command, you actually run the function by name. For example, you could run **M-x next-line** instead of **C-n**, although there wouldn't be much sense in this. Functions that are not bound to any command key sequence must be run using **M-x**; for example, the **goto-line** function is not bound to any command key, so it must be run as **M-x goto-line**.

Displaying a Command Key Binding

To see what function a command is bound to, use **C-h c**, which prompts with:

```
Describe key briefly:
```

Pressing **C-p** displays the message:

```
C-p runs the command previous-line
```

An interesting thing happens if you type a regular text character in response to the above prompt. For example, if you typed **f**, Emacs displays this:

```
f runs the command self-insert-command
```

This means that when you press the letter **f**, Emacs actually runs a function called **self-insert-command**, which inserts the typed letter into the buffer. This is true for any visible text character.

Typing a Meta command also produces interesting results. If you typed **M-e** in response to the prompt, Emacs displays:

```
ESC e runs the command forward-sentence
```

If you use a dedicated Meta key on your system, you may have forgotten that you can use **ESC** to run Meta commands. That is, **ESC-e** is the same as **M-e**. Help commands often display the Meta key as **ESC**.

Displaying Command Documentation

To get detailed information about a command (including binding), use **C-h k**, which displays in a ***Help*** window information about a command. **C-h k** prompts in the echo area with:

```
Describe a key:
```

Typing **C-n** in response to this prompt displayed the following information on our system:

```
next-line:
Move cursor vertically down ARG lines.
If there is no character in the target line exactly under the current
column, the cursor is positioned after the character in that line
which spans this column, or at the end of the line if it is not long
enough. If there is no line in the buffer after this one, a newline
character is inserted to create a line and the cursor moves to that
line.

The command C-x C-n can be used to create
a semipermanent goal column to which this command always moves.
Then it does not try to move vertically.

If you are thinking of using this in a Lisp program, consider
using 'forward-line' instead. It is usually easier to use
and more reliable (no dependence on goal column, etc.).
```

The first line (**next-line:** in the example above) is the name of the function bound to the command key. This is followed by several lines of descriptive text about how to use the command. The term **ARG** appears quite frequently in the help text. In this context, it means that you can specify a numeric argument to the command.

Displaying a Function Binding

The **C-h w** command shows what command key, if any, is bound to function. It prompts in the echo area with:

```
Where is command: _
```

If you type **what-line RET** to this prompt, Emacs responds with:

```
what-line is not on any keys
```

If you type **previous-line RET**, Emacs responds with:

```
previous-line is on C-p
```

You might use this command if you use the long form of a command (**M-x** *function-name*) and would like to find out if there is a shorter command key sequence.

Showing All Command Key Bindings

If you want to see all the command key bindings in the current mode, use **C-h b**.
For example, in Text mode on our system, this information was displayed in a
Help buffer in another window:

```
Local Bindings:
key               binding
---               -------

LFD               eval-print-last-sexp
TAB               lisp-indent-line
DEL               backward-delete-char-untabify
ESC               Prefix Command

ESC C-x           eval-defun
ESC C-q           indent-sexp

Global Bindings:

C-@               set-mark-command
C-a               beginning-of-line
C-b               backward-char
C-c               mode-specific-command-prefix
C-d               delete-char
        . . .
```

You might use this command just to peruse all the key bindings to see what's
available. Or you might use it to see what command keys aren't yet bound to any
function, making them available to be bound to other functions (as described in
Chapter 13, "Customizing the Emacs Environment").

Searching for Commands (Apropos)

When you want to know which command performs a specific editing operation, use
the **C-h a** (**Apropos**) command. This command prompts for a search string (which
can be a regular expression):

```
Command apropos (regexp): _
```

After you type a string and press **RET**, Emacs searches through all function names,
finds those that contain the string, and displays documentation for these functions in
another window.

You can use Apropos most effectively when you understand the conventions for naming Emacs commands and think through the type of search you want to make. For example, Emacs functions that deal with columns usually contain the word `column`. If you type `column RET` in response to the Apropos prompt, Emacs displays the following information:

```
increment-numbers-in-column
  Function: Add INCR to each of the numbers in the column closest to
    the point.
indent-to-column
  Function: indent-to(col &optional minimum)
set-comment-column            C-x ;
  Function: Set the comment column based on point.
set-fill-column               C-x f
  Function: Set fill-column to current column, or to argument if
    given.
set-goal-column               C-x C-n
  Function: Set the current horizontal position as a goal for C-n and
    C-p.
sort-columns
  Function: Sort lines in region alphabetically by a certain range
    of columns.
sum-column
  Function: Return the sum of the integers in the rectangle delimited
```

By experimenting with ways to specify Apropos strings, you can soon use Apropos to quickly hunt down commands. Try experimenting with the following strings, noting that they pertain to important constructs in Emacs:

```
char        fill        mark        register
buffer      indent      mode        sentence
delete      insert      page        sexp
defun       kill        paragraph   word
dir         line        region      yank
file        list
```

Summary

Table 9.2 summarizes the important points from this chapter.

Table 9.2. Chapter 9 Summary

Topic	Summary
Help Types	• Help: `C-h C-h` or `C-h ?` or `M-x help-for-help` • Variables: `C-h v` or `M-x describe-variable` • Mode: `C-h m` or `M-x describe-mode` • Key command sequence: `C-h k` or `M-x describe-key` • Key binding: `C-h c` or `M-x describe-key-briefly` • Function bound to which key: `C-h w` or `M-x where-is` • All key bindings: `C-h b` or `M-x describe-bindings` • Apropos (find commands): `C-h a` or `M-x command-apropos` • Syntax tables: `C-h s` or `M-x describe-syntax` • Last 100 characters typed: `C-h l` or `M-x view-lossage` • Tutorial: `C-h t` or `M-x help-with-tutorial` • Info documentation tree: `C-h i` or `M-x info` • License: `C-h C-c` or `M-x describe-copying` • Ordering: `C-h C-d` or `M-x describe-distribution` • No warranty: `C-h C-w` or `M-x describe-no-warranty` • News: `C-h n` or `M-x view-emacs-news`
Useful commands while viewing help	• Switch cursor to another window: `C-x o` • Hide all windows except current window: `C-x 1` • Scroll other window: `C-M-v` • All usual motion commands

10
Using Emacs for Electronic Mail

It is not always easy or convenient to exit Emacs and use a UNIX facility such as **mail**, **mailx**, or **elm** to process electronic mail. You can escape from Emacs to a UNIX shell and execute UNIX commands, but you cannot easily handle electronic mail this way.

This section explains how to use the Emacs electronic mail facility, RMAIL. The main topics covered are:

- The relationship between the RMAIL facility and other UNIX mail facilities

- Reading mail messages

- Exiting from the RMAIL buffer

- Moving around your mail messages

- Saving messages to files

- Removing messages

- Getting new mail

- Using a mail summary to scan messages

- Composing and sending messages

- Using multiple mailbox files

- Using mode line status messages (labels)

- Reading digest messages

- Associating UNIX mailbox files with RMAIL mailbox files (advanced usage)

The RMAIL Facility and Other UNIX Mail Facilities

In UNIX, you have a "mailbox" file to hold your electronic mail messages. For example, **/usr/mail/janed** or **/usr/spool/mail/janed** might be the mailbox file for a user named Jane Doe.

Emacs' mail facility, RMAIL, uses a mailbox file named **RMAIL** in your home directory. When you begin an RMAIL session, the messages in your UNIX mailbox (if any) are copied to your **RMAIL** file. The UNIX mailbox file is then deleted to conserve disk space.

Because Emacs mailbox files are incompatible with the mailbox files used by other UNIX mail facilities, we recommend using either Emacs or your favorite UNIX mail facility to process your mail—but not both. Using RMAIL with other UNIX mail facilities can become very confusing, because your messages can become split between two different mailbox files.

If you're not sure whether you'd like to use RMAIL as your mail handler but would like to try it for a while, we recommend starting out with an empty UNIX mailbox. Use your current mail program to read, save, and delete all messages in your mailbox—then start using RMAIL. Because RMAIL copies all messages from, and then deletes, your UNIX mailbox, you must commit to using RMAIL at least until all existing messages have been processed. If you have many outstanding messages, this could take quite some time.

Reading Mail Messages

When a new mail message arrives in your mailbox, the mode line for your current buffer will display the word **Mail**. For example, you might see:

```
--%%-Emacs: misc 1:26 pm 0.05 Mail (Text)-Top-
```

To read your mail, start the Emacs mail facility, RMAIL, by typing **M-x rmail**. If this is the first time you have used Emacs to process your mail, Emacs creates the mailbox file **RMAIL** in your home directory. All messages in your current UNIX mail file are copied into the **RMAIL** file; your UNIX mailbox file is then deleted.

Mail messages are displayed in a read-only buffer, also named **RMAIL**. If you have no mail messages, Emacs displays a message something like that shown in Figure 10.1. Otherwise, Emacs displays your first new (unread) message.

The **RMAIL** buffer displays one message at a time. A message is divided into a header and a message body, as shown in Figure 10.2. The **header** contains information about the sender, time and date the message was sent, and so on, but be aware that the order and format of the header fields vary widely among UNIX mailers. The **message body** contains the text of the message.

The message displayed in your **RMAIL** buffer is called the **current message**. The number of the current message is displayed in the mode line, as indicated in Figure 10.2.

```
BABYL OPTIONS:
Version: 5
Labels:
Note:    This is the header of an rmail file.
Note:    If you are seeing it in rmail,
Note:     it means the file has no messages in it.




-----Emacs: RMAIL   11:45 am  0.12   (RMAIL Narrow)-------- All----------
(No new mail has arrived)
```

Figure 10.1. Message Displayed When No Mail in Mailbox File

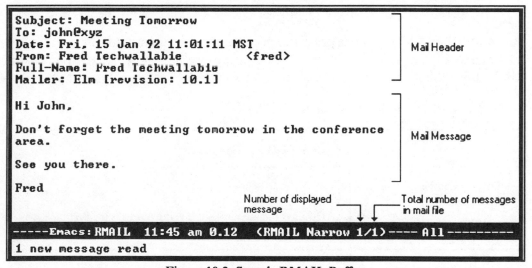

```
Subject: Meeting Tomorrow
To: john@xyz
Date: Fri, 15 Jan 92 11:01:11 MST          Mail Header
From: Fred Techwallabie        <fred>
Full-Name: Fred Techwallabie
Mailer: Elm [revision: 10.1]

Hi John,

Don't forget the meeting tomorrow in the conference    Mail Message
area.

See you there.

Fred
                              Number of displayed          Total number of messages
                              message                      in mail file
-----Emacs: RMAIL   11:45 am  0.12   (RMAIL Narrow 1/1)---- All----------
1 new message read
```

Figure 10.2. Sample RMAIL Buffer

Exiting from the RMAIL Buffer

You can keep your **RMAIL** buffer for the duration of your Emacs session, switching back to it as needed. When you exit Emacs, you'll be asked whether you want to save **RMAIL** (provided it has been modified—for example, by marking messages for deletion). If you type **y**, modifications to **RMAIL** will be saved. This means that all messages marked for deletion will still be marked for deletion when you next read your mail, but they will not be actually removed from your **RMAIL** mailbox until you expunge them (see "Removing Messages" later in this chapter).

In most cases, the best way to exit RMAIL is to type **q** while the **RMAIL** buffer is selected. This expunges all messages marked for deletion, saves the remaining messages back to your **RMAIL** mailbox file, then removes the **RMAIL** buffer.

Still another—but less graceful—method of exiting is using **C-x k** to kill the **RMAIL** buffer. This removes the **RMAIL** buffer, but does not expunge deleted messages or save the **RMAIL** file.

Moving Around Your Mail Messages

You can use the normal commands to move within the current message: **C-n**, **C-p**, **C-v**, **M-v**. **SPC** is also provided as a short cut for **C-v** (next page), and **DEL** for **M-v** (previous page). The command **.** (period) moves you to the top of the current message.

In addition, RMAIL mode provides special motion commands for moving among mail messages, described in Table 10.1. (You can precede the **n**, **p**, **M-n** and **M-p** commands with a numeric repeat count; you do not need to type **C-u** first.)

Table 10.1. RMAIL Motion Commands

Operation	Command and Comments
Display another message	*n*j Displays the *n*th message. Typing **j** selects the first message. Typing **4j** displays the 4th message.
Display next undeleted message	n Moves to the next undeleted message, skipping deleted ones.

Table 10.1, con't.

Operation	Command and Comments
Display previous undeleted message	**P** Moves to the previous undeleted message, skipping deleted ones.
Display next message	**M-n** Moves to the next message, even if marked for deletion.
Display previous message	**M-p** Moves to the previous message, even if marked for deletion.
Display last message	**>** Move to the last message.
Display message matching a regexp	**M-s** Move to the next message matching a regexp. At the prompt, type the regexp and press **RET**. If you simply press **RET**, Emacs uses your last regexp. Preceding the command with minus sign (– **M-x**) searches backward for a previous message that matches the regexp.

Saving Messages to Files

RMAIL provides several ways to save messages, either back into the **RMAIL** file, or into other files. Table 10.2 summarizes these commands.

Table 10.2. RMAIL Commands for Saving Messages

Operation	Command and Comments
Expunge deleted messages and save all others in mailbox	**s** Expunges deleted messages, and writes remaining messages to the **RMAIL** file.

Table 10.2, con't.

Operation	Command and Comments
Save all messages in mailbox	`C-x C-s` Same as **s**, but does not expunge deleted messages.
Save current message to a file (RMAIL format)	`o` Appends a copy of the current message to a file in RMAIL format. At the prompt, type the file name and press **RET**.
Save current message to a file (UNIX mail format)	`C-o` Like **o**, but saves the message using UNIX mail format. Use this for messages you want to read with other UNIX mail utilities; RMAIL can read them, too.

Messages saved to files with either **o** or **C-o** are labeled as **filed** messages. Emacs indicates a message has been filed in the mode line of each message, as in:

```
--- Emacs: RMAIL  5:49pm 0.05  (RMAIL Narrow 5/5,filed)--- 5%---
                                                  ↑
                            indicates message has been saved
```

Saving Messages in RMAIL vs. UNIX Mail Format

When you save a message with **o**, it is saved in a file using RMAIL format. RMAIL format includes the "no mail" header which is displayed when the mailbox is empty (see Figure 10.1) and other internal RMAIL headers and messages. This format is best used when appending messages to alternate mailbox files that will be later read by the RMAIL facility (see the section, "Using Multiple Mailbox Files," later in this chapter).

Saving a message with **C-o**, writes the message to the file in UNIX mail format, which includes only the standard mail headers plus the message text. This format can be read by other UNIX mail facilities such as **elm**, **mail**, and **mailx**. Because it contains less header information, use this format to archive your messages—that is, use it when you simply want to save them as text files and don't intend to read them with RMAIL again. You can also use it to append a message to your UNIX mailbox file, so that it will be read the next time you use a UNIX mail facility.

Removing Messages

Removing messages is a two-step process:

1. Mark each message for deletion, then

2. Expunge (remove) all messages marked for deletion.

Table 10.3 lists Emacs commands for marking and unmarking messages for deletion, and expunging marked messages.

Table 10.3. RMAIL Commands for Deleting Messages

Operation	Command and Comments
Mark current message for deletion and move to next message	**d** Marks the current message for deletion and moves to the next undeleted message. Labels message as `deleted`.
Mark current message for deletion and move to previous message	**C-d** Like **d** but moves to the previous undeleted message.
Unmark (undelete) a message currently marked for deletion	**u** If the current message is marked for deletion, remove its deletion mark; otherwise, undelete the nearest preceding message marked for deletion.
Expunge all messages marked for deletion	**x** or **e** Both commands remove all messages marked for deletion from the mailbox file, `RMAIL`.

If the current message is marked for deletion, the mode line displays the word `deleted`, as in:

```
--- Emacs: RMAIL  5:49pm 0.05  (RMAIL Narrow 5/5,deleted)---5%---
                                                     ↑
                          indicates message is marked for deletion
```

No messages are actually deleted until you expunge them with **x** or **e**, giving you the opportunity to change your mind and undelete messages with **u**. If the current message remains current after you type a **d** or **C-d** command, this tells you that all messages in the **RMAIL** file have been marked for deletion.

Getting New Mail

New mail messages that arrive during your RMAIL session are not automatically read into your **RMAIL** buffer. Thus, you may exit from RMAIL only to find that new messages have arrived since you started your RMAIL session; you must then restart RMAIL to read them.

To force RMAIL to read new messages, type **g** while in the **RMAIL** buffer. This retrieves all new messages from your UNIX mailbox file and appends them to the messages already in your **RMAIL** buffer.

Using a Mail Summary to Scan Messages

If your mailbox file contains many messages, you will probably want to create a mail summary buffer for scanning your messages. A mail summary buffer contains a list of lines, each providing a summary for one of the messages in the mailbox. Each line shows the message number, sender, labels, and subject. For example:

```
3   10-Dec        jane@axyz     { deleted}     Monthly Report
↑    ↑              ↑             ↑              ↑
msg date sent      sender        labels         subject
no.
```

Creating a Mail Summary Buffer

To create a summary buffer, select the **RMAIL** buffer you want to summarize, and type one of the commands listed in Table 10.4. Emacs splits the screen (if necessary) and creates the summary buffer in another window, allowing you to continue viewing the **RMAIL** buffer (see Figure 10.3). Emacs names the summary buffer by appending **-summary** to the mailbox name, as in **RMAIL-summary**. If visiting multiple mailboxes, you can create a separate summary buffer for each.

Table 10.4. Commands for Creating a Mail Summary Buffer

Operation	Command and Comments
Summarize all messages	h or C-M-h Create a summary buffer for the current **RMAIL** buffer, containing summaries of *all* messages in the mailbox.
Summarize messages with label	l or C-M-l Summarize only messages that have at least one of the specified labels. At the prompt, type your labels, separated by commas, and press **RET**. For example, you might want to summarize only those messages that you have saved (those with the `filed` label). For a list of labels, see "Using Mode Line Status Messages (Labels)."
Summarize messages with recipient	C-M-r Summarize only those messages that have at least one of the specified recipients. At the prompt, type the recipients (e.g., `jane@ace`), separated by commas, and press **RET**.

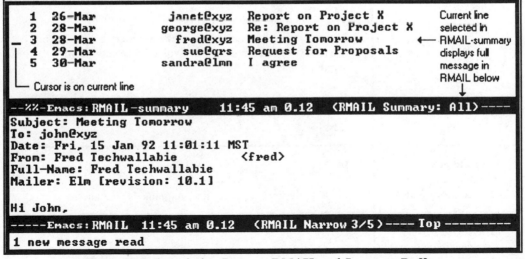

Figure 10.3. Association Between RMAIL and Summary Buffers

Reading Your Mail with a Summary Buffer

The summary buffer provides a convenient way to scan, view, and delete messages in the **RMAIL** buffer. As you move the cursor from one line to the next in the summary buffer, Emacs displays the corresponding complete message in the **RMAIL** buffer (see Figure 10.3). You can also delete and undelete messages in the **RMAIL** buffer by typing commands from the summary buffer.

Table 10.5 describes the commands for moving around and manipulating mail messages from the summary buffer.

Table 10.5. Mail Summary Buffer Commands

Operation	Command and Comments
Delete message	**d** Mark the current line's message for deletion and move to next line.
Undelete message	**u** If the current line's message is marked for deletion, remove its deletion mark; otherwise, undelete the nearest preceding message marked for deletion.
Select message	*n***j** Moves to the *n*th summary line in the summary buffer. Typing **j** selects the first summary line. Typing **4j** selects the 4th summary line. If you have only one window, the command creates a window for the associated **RMAIL** buffer and shows the associated message.
Move to next message (skip deleted messages)	**n** Move to the next summary line, skipping deleted lines.
Move to next message (including deleted messages)	**C-n** Like **n**, but moves to the next line, even if marked for deletion.

Table 10.5, con't.

Operation	Command and Comments
Move to previous message (skip deleted messages)	**p** Move to the previous summary line, skipping deleted lines.
Move to previous message (including deleted messages)	**C-p** Like **p**, but moves to the previous line, even if marked for deletion.
Exit RMAIL	**q** Deletes all messages marked for deletion, exits the RMAIL facility, and selects the buffer that was current when you invoked the facility. Compare this action with **x** (below).
Exit summary window	**x** Exits the summary window and selects the **RMAIL** buffer. The summary buffer still exists, but is no longer selected. This command does **not** delete messages that have been marked for deletion.
Scroll other window forward	**SPC** Scrolls the other window forward, typically the message in the **RMAIL** buffer.
Scroll other window backward	**DEL** Like **SPC**, but scrolls backward.

Composing and Sending Messages

You can send a mail message at any time during an Emacs session. To compose your mail message, you must first create a buffer named ***mail*** using one of the commands listed in Table 10.6. This buffer has a major mode named Mail that provides the usual text editing commands found in Text mode, plus commands for sending messages.

Table 10.6 lists commands for creating the ***mail*** buffer, and Table 10.7 lists commands for sending messages from it. Subsequent sections provide additional instructions for editing the header fields and body of your message.

Table 10.6. Commands for Creating the *mail* Buffer

Operation	Command* and Comments
Create (or switch to) ***mail*** buffer	**C-x m** or **M-x mail** Creates a new ***mail*** buffer with **To:** and **Subject:** headers, or switches to the current ***mail*** buffer, if one exists.
Create (or switch to) ***mail*** buffer in another window	**m** or **C-x 4 m** Like the commands above, but splits the screen and creates the ***mail*** buffer in the other window. The only difference between **C-x 4 m** and **m** is that **m** allows you to yank messages out of the **RMAIL** buffer using the **C-c y** command (described later in this section), and **C-x 4 m** does **not** allow you to do this. **m**, therefore, is usually the best command to use.
Compose a reply to current **RMAIL** message	**r** Creates (or switches to) the ***mail*** buffer for the purpose of replying to the current message in the **RMAIL** buffer. This commands presets the **To:**, **Subject:**, **CC:**, and **In-reply-to:** headers. You can edit these headers if desired. Labels the current message as **answered** on the mode line.
Forward the current **RMAIL** message	**f** Copies the current message in the **RMAIL** buffer to the ***mail*** buffer so you can send it to others. Simply fill in the recipients names and send it using **C-c C-c** or **C-c C-s** (see Table 10.7).
Continue composing the current message in ***mail*** buffer	**c** Switch to the ***mail*** buffer and continue editing the message there.

* These commands are executed from the **RMAIL** buffer

Table 10.7. Commands for Sending the Message in the *mail* Buffer

Operation	Command* and Comments
Send the message in the *mail* buffer and switch buffers	C-c C-c Sends the message to the recipients listed in the message headers (To:, CC:, BCC:, etc.), and selects another buffer.
Send message and remain in *mail* buffer	C-c C-s Send the message and leave *mail* selected, presumably so you can revise the message and resend it.

* These commands are executed from the ***mail*** buffer

Editing the Mail Message Header

When you create the ***mail*** buffer using one of the commands in Table 10.6, Emacs provides a mail message template containing essential header fields for you to fill in, as shown in Figure 10.4. The header fields in the template depend upon which command you used to create the ***mail*** buffer.

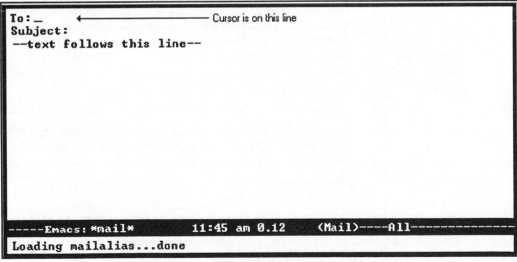

Figure 10.4. Emacs Mail Message Template

The information that appears in the header fields is created in one of two ways:

1. Emacs enters the information automatically. For example, the `Date:` and `From:` headers are automatically created and filled in after you send a mail message; they never appear in the `*mail*` buffer.

2. The sender enters information. For example, `To:` and `Subject:` headers are entered by the sender, using standard text-editing commands.

Table 10.8 describes some of the fields that commonly appear in a mail header.

Table 10.8. Mail Header Fields

Header	Meaning
`To:`	UNIX mail address(es) for the person(s) receiving the message.
`Subject:`	Subject of the message.
`CC:`	Carbon copy. UNIX mailing address(es) for person(s) receiving a copy of the message.
`BCC:`	Blind carbon copy. Like `CC:`, but the names are not listed in the header of the message that is sent.
`FCC:`	File carbon copy. Name of a file to which the message will be appended when sent. To automatically include an `FCC:` field with a default file name in every message you send, set the value of the variable *mail-archive-file-name* to the name of the file. All messages will then be archived automatically into the file.
`From:`	Sender's UNIX mail address.
`In-Reply-To:`	Contains a description of a message to which you are replying. RMAIL provides this field when you reply to a message with `r`.
`Reply-To:`	UNIX mail address of another person to whom your reply is sent. Same effect as `From:`.

All header fields that contain the UNIX mail addresses of people (or files) receiving the message (`To:`, `CC:`, `BCC:`, `FCC:`) can contain multiple recipients, separated by commas or spaces. If your home directory has a mail alias file (`.mailrc`), RMAIL scans it the first time you send a message during an RMAIL session, expanding aliases found in the `To:`, `CC:`, and `BCC:` fields.

If your list of recipients is long, you can continue the list onto subsequent lines, provided they start with one or more spaces. You may also include more than one of these fields in your header if you prefer. Thus, the following headers are equivalent:

Header One: Continuation Lines	Header Two: Multiple To: Fields

`To: john@xyz judy@xyz`
`    mike@xyz jeanne@xyz`
`    bill@xyz janie@xyz`
	`To: john@xyz judy@xyz`
	`To: mike@xyz jeanne@xyz`
	`To: bill@xyz janie@xyz`

It is not necessary to specify all headers in every message; include only those you need. If you type in headers yourself, make sure each header field starts at the beginning of a line and contains a field name followed by a colon. Or, consider using the commands in Table 10.9 to create and move to various header fields.

Table 10.9. Commands for Creating and Moving to Message Headers

Operation	Command and Comments
Create or move to `To:` header	`C-c C-f C-t` Move to the `To:` header. If none exists, create one.
Create or move to `Subject:` header	`C-c C-f C-s` Move to the `Subject:` header. If none exists, create one.
Create or move to `CC:` header	`C-c C-f C-c` Move to the `CC:` header. If none exists, create one.

Editing the Mail Header Separator (Don't!)

The information in the header is separated from the message by the following line:

```
--text follows this line--
```

This line is *not* sent with the message, but is used only to delineate the message body from the header lines. To change this line to another text string, set the value of the variable *mail-head-separator* to the desired string. **Do not** delete this line from a message you are composing, otherwise Emacs will issue the following complaint when you attempt to send the message:

```
Search failed: "^--text follows this line--^J"
```

If this happens, however, you can simply type the header separator below the last header field in your message and resend it.

Editing the Message Body

Use the following guidelines to edit the message body to your satisfaction:

• Again, be careful not to delete the header separator:

```
--text follows this line--
```

• Keep lines less than eighty characters long; you may want to turn on auto-fill-mode (see Chapter 3).

• Be aware that your system may limit the maximum size of a mail message.

• Don't include binary files in your mail message.

• You can kill text in other buffers and yank it into your mail message.

In general, use normal Text mode commands to compose your message. In addition, you can use the special Mail mode commands listed in Table 10.10 to edit your message.

Table 10.10. Commands for Composing Mail Messages

Operation	Command and Comments
Insert signature	`C-c C-w` Retrieve the file named `.signature` in your home directory and insert it at the end of your message. You can put whatever you want in this file. It usually contains identification information such as your name, company, and e-mail address, but may include more creative contents.

Table 10.10, con't.

Operation	Command and Comments
Insert **RMAIL** buffer message into your ***mail*** buffer message	`C-c C-y` Insert the current message from the **RMAIL** buffer at the current cursor position in the ***mail*** buffer. This command is active only when you initiate your mail message with one of these RMAIL commands used to respond to messages: **m, c, r,** or **f** (these commands were explained earlier in this chapter). The yanked message is indented four spaces. You can insert another message by selecting a new message in the RMAIL buffer, returning to the ***mail*** buffer, and typing `C-c C-y` again. A numeric argument (`C-u` *n* `C-c C-y`) indents the inserted message by *n* columns. If no number *n* is included, the message is not indented, and all headers are inserted (usually, most headers are not included with the message).
Fill message text	`C-c C-q` Fill the text of messages inserted with `C-c C-y`.

Sending Your Message

When finished editing, send your message by typing `C-c C-c` (send message and hide the ***mail*** buffer), or `C-c C-s` (send message and remain in the ***mail*** buffer). Emacs reports that your mail has been sent. Both commands for sending mail leave the ***mail*** buffer intact, although they do mark the buffer as unmodified after the message is sent. To clear the previous message from the buffer, type `C-x m` again.

Starting a New Message

After you send a message, Emacs retains the old message in the ***mail*** buffer so you can edit it and send it again if you wish. To clear the ***mail*** buffer and start a new message, type `C-x m` or `M-x mail` again; you may also do this to abandon your current message and start a new one. However, if you type the `C-x m` or `M-x mail` command without having sent the current message in the ***mail*** buffer, Emacs asks:

```
Unsent message being composed; erase it? (y or n)
```

Answering with **n** retains the current message and selects the ***mail*** buffer; answering with **y** also selects the ***mail*** buffer, but erases its old contents.

You can have only one ***mail*** buffer at a time, a fact that can lead to some curious behavior if your screen is split into two windows. Suppose you have one window that contains the ***mail*** buffer and another that contains a Text buffer. You type **C-x m** from the other buffer. Emacs replaces the Text buffer in the window with the ***mail*** buffer, and you now have two windows containing ***mail*** buffers, as in Figure 10.5.

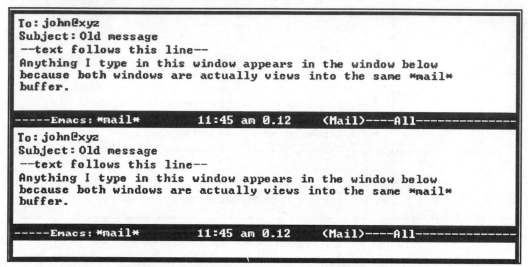

Figure 10.5. Two Views into the Same ***mail*** Buffer

You might think these are two different ***mail*** buffers, each capable of holding a different mail message, but they are actually two views of the same buffer. You quickly discover this when you begin typing in one buffer and the other buffer echoes what you type. To return the original Text buffer to the window, type **C-x b RET**.

Sending Replies to Messages

When replying to a message, you work in both mail buffers: first in **RMAIL**, which contains the message you are replying to, and then in ***mail***, in which you compose a reply. You may move between the two buffers with the usual window commands.

To send a reply to a message, follow these steps:

1. Display the message you want to reply to in the **RMAIL** buffer.

2. Use **r** (see Table 10.6) to switch to the ***mail*** buffer and compose your reply.

3. Send your message with **C-c C-c**.

Forwarding a Message to Others

Forwarding a message to other UNIX users is similar to replying to a message. You work in both mail buffers: first in **RMAIL**, which contains the message you want to forward, and then in ***mail***, in which you fill in the recipients' names and send your reply. You may move between the two buffers as needed with standard window commands.

To forward a message, follow these steps:

1. Display the message you want to forward in the **RMAIL** buffer.

2. Use the **f** command (see Table 10.6) to switch to the ***mail*** buffer so that you can compose your reply. The message is automatically copied into the ***mail*** buffer.

3. Fill in the recipients' names in the **To:**, **CC:**, and **BCC:** fields.

4. Send your message with **C-c C-c**.

Using Mode Line Status Messages (Labels)

The mode line for the **RMAIL** buffer includes status messages that describe the current message. These status messages—such as **filed**, **deleted**, and so on—are actually indicators of labels that RMAIL has assigned to a mail message. A **label** is simply a word that is attached to a message to indicate an action that has been taken.

Labels are listed after the message number indicator, as shown in Figure 10.6. Table 10.11 describes the meaning of the standard message labels.

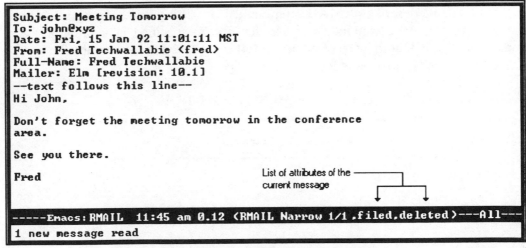

```
Subject: Meeting Tomorrow
To: john@xyz
Date: Fri, 15 Jan 92 11:01:11 MST
From: Fred Techwallabie <fred>
Full-Name: Fred Techwallabie
Mailer: Elm [revision: 10.1]
--text follows this line--
Hi John,

Don't forget the meeting tomorrow in the conference
area.

See you there.

Fred                          List of attributes of the
                              current message

-----Emacs: RMAIL  11:45 am 0.12 <RMAIL Narrow 1/1 .filed.deleted>---All---
1 new message read
```

Figure 10.6. Mode Line Status Messages

Table 10.11. RMAIL Mode Line Status Messages

Message	Meaning
deleted	Current message has been marked for deletion.
filed	Current message has been saved to a file.
answered	You have sent a reply to the current message.
forwarded	Current message was forwarded to you.
edited	You have edited the message within RMAIL (not normally done, since RMAIL is a read-only buffer).
unseen	Message has never been current. Since you only view current messages, you'll never see this.

Creating and Searching for Message Labels

In addition to the system-generated labels listed in Table 10.11 (called **attributes** in Emacs terminology), you can assign your own custom labels to messages, and search for messages that have a particular label. These features let you organize your messages into groups—say by topic, project, or sender—and selectively view messages having a particular label (see the l command in "Using a Mail Summary to Scan Messages" earlier in this chapter.

Table 10.12 describes RMAIL commands for setting and searching for mail message labels. All commands will use the label(s) specified in a previous label command as the default, even when no default is displayed in the prompt. To accept the default label(s), just press **RET** at the prompt.

Table 10.12. Commands for Manipulating Mail Message Labels

Operation	Command and Comments
Assign label	a Assigns a label to the current message. Type the label at the prompt and press **RET**. If space permits, the label appears in the mode line.

Table 10.12. con't.

Operation	Command and Comments
Remove label	**k** Removes a label from the current message. Type the label at the prompt and press **RET**.
Move to next labeled message	**C-M-n** Moves forward to the next message that has any of the specified labels. At the prompt, type all labels you want to search for, separated by commas, and press **RET**. A numeric argument specifies a repeat count, as in **C-u 5 C-M-n**.
Move to previous labeled message	**C-M-p** Like the **C-M-p** but moves backward to a previous message.

For example, you could use the **a** command to label each message in your mailbox, thereby imposing a classification scheme on an otherwise random set of messages. Then, to view all messages with a particular label, say **objectives**, you could simply type **C-M-n** repeatedly:

```
C-M-n
Move to next msg with labels: objectives RET    ←Go to 1st message with label
C-M-n
Move to next msg with labels: RET               ←Go to 2nd message (default)
C-M-n
Move to next msg with labels: RET               ←Go to 3rd message (default)
```

This technique is particularly useful for searching mailbox files containing archived messages, as described in the next section.

Using Multiple Mailbox Files

You can create multiple mailbox files to archive your mail messages after reading them. Rather than keep each message in a separate file (which would make them difficult to find), or in your primary **RMAIL** mailbox file (which would be cumbersome), you can create multiple mailbox files (in addition to your primary **RMAIL** file) to store messages in.

For example, when a message comes into your **RMAIL** mailbox file that you want to save for future reference, you can append it to another mailbox file. This way, your primary mailbox is used only for "active" messages, and does not become cluttered with old, archived mail. You can use the **o** command to append messages to a mailbox file, as described in the previous section, "Saving Messages to Files." When you want to read the messages you have saved, use the **i** command to visit the alternate mailbox file.

Caveat to the o Command

If you use **o** to append a message to a mailbox file that you are currently visiting in Emacs, be aware that the message is appended to the *buffer*, **not** to the *file*.

For example, suppose your current buffer is **RMAIL**, but you are also visiting another mailbox file named **misc.mail** in another buffer. When you uses **o** to append a message from **RMAIL** to **misc.mail**, the message is appended to the **misc.mail** buffer, **not** to the **misc.mail** file. The message will be saved to the **misc.mail** file only when you save the **misc.mail** buffer to its associated file.

Caveat to the C-o Command

Avoid using **C-o** to append a message to another mailbox file that you are visiting. **C-o** always appends the message to the disk file, even if you are currently visiting the file in a buffer. So, when you save the buffer to its file, the message appended to the file is lost.

For example, suppose, as before, you are visiting both the **RMAIL** and **misc.mail** mailbox files, and that you use **C-o** to append a message in **RMAIL** to **misc.mail**. Unlike **o** in the previous example, the message is appended to the **misc.mail** file, **not** to the **misc.mail** buffer. Now the contents of the **misc.mail** buffer and the **misc.mail** file are different, and when you attempt to save the **misc.mail** buffer to the **misc.mail** file, Emacs issues a simultaneous editing warning. If you proceed with the save, the buffer (which does not contain the appended message) overwrites the file (which does contain the message), and the message that was appended to the file is lost. For more information, see "Preventing Simultaneous Editing" in Chapter 4.

Reading Digest Messages

You may occasionally receive a single mail message that is actually a composite of several messages. Such messages are called **digest messages** and may be created under the following circumstances:

- On moderated mailing lists, in which all messages received for a person during a day or week are packaged together and mailed to the person as one message.

- When someone wants to send you all messages that have been exchanged on a particular issue. For example, someone may want to send you all messages that have been sent regarding a problem you need to solve. Rather than forwarding each message individually, the messages can be bundled together.

Emacs **does not** provide a facility for creating digest messages. However, it does provide a command for separating any digest messages you receive into their component messages for easier reading. To do this, type:

```
M-x undigestify-rmail-message
```

This command places the individual messages into your **RMAIL** buffer following the digest message, and then marks the digest message for deletion.

Associating UNIX Mailbox Files with RMAIL Mailbox Files (Advanced Usage)

Each **RMAIL** mailbox file can have a set of UNIX mailbox files associated with it. When you visit the **RMAIL** mailbox file, all UNIX mailbox files associated with the **RMAIL** mailbox are copied into it, and the UNIX mailbox files are then deleted.

We have discussed the simplest case, in which your UNIX mailbox file is automatically copied into your **RMAIL** file when starting RMAIL. When you use a mailbox file other than **RMAIL**, you must visit it in an **RMAIL** buffer and optionally associate a list of UNIX mailbox files with it. Table 10.13 has the commands.

Table 10.13. RMAIL Commands for Using Alternate Mailboxes

Operation	Command and Comments
Read alternate mailbox	i Runs RMAIL on an alternate mailbox file, prompting: **Run rmail on RMAIL file:** ~/ Press **RET** to use the **RMAIL** file, or type an alternate file and press **RET**. Other mail formats are converted as required to RMAIL format. You can also run **M-x rmail-input** from any buffer to achieve the same results.

Table 10.13, con't.

Operation	Command and Comments
Associate UNIX mailbox files with RMAIL mailbox	`M-x set-rmail-inbox-list` Lets you specify a list of UNIX mailbox files that will be automatically copied into the current RMAIL mailbox whenever you visit it or execute the **g** (get new mail) command. RMAIL prompts you to enter a list of mailboxes. Type a list of mailbox files, separated by commas, and press **RET**. RMAIL retains the list until you change it.
Merge mail	**g** Merges new mail that has arrived in all associated UNIX mailbox files. If you use a numeric argument (**C-u** *n* **g**), RMAIL prompts you to enter the name of a specific UNIX mailbox file to merge into the current RMAIL mailbox file.

Summary

Table 10.14 summarizes the main points in this chapter.

Table 10.14. Chapter 10 Summary

Topic	Summary
Starting and stopping RMAIL	• Start RMAIL with the RMAIL mailbox: **M-x rmail** • Save undeleted messages and exit RMAIL: **q**
Reading mail	• Read RMAIL mailbox: **M-x rmail** • Read alternate mailbox: **i** • Read in new mail received since starting RMAIL: **g**

Table 10.14, con't.

Topic	Summary
Moving through mail messages	• Display 1st message: **1j** • Display *n*th message: *n***j** • Display next message: **M-n** • Display next message (skip deleted messages): **n** • Display previous message: **M-p** • Display previous message (skip deleted messages): **p** • Display last message: **>** • Display message matching a regexp: **M-s**
Removing messages	• Mark message for deletion and go to next message: **d** • Mark message for deletion and go to previous message: **C-d** • Unmark message for deletion: **u** • Expunge (remove) all messages marked for deletion: **x** or **e**
Saving messages	• Expunge deleted messages and save all others in mailbox: **s** • Save all messages in mailbox: **C-x C-s** • Save current message to a file (RMAIL format): **o** • Save current message to a file (UNIX format): **C-o**

Table 10.14, con't.

Topic	Summary
Sending messages	Create/clear `*mail*` buffer: • Create `*mail*` buffer to compose message: `C-x m` or `M-x mail` • Clear `*mail*` buffer and start new message: `C-x m` • Create `*mail*` buffer in other window: `m` or `C-x 4 m` Send message in `*mail*` buffer: • Send message in `*mail*` buffer and switch buffers: `C-c C-c` • Send message in `*mail*` buffer and remain in `*mail*`: `C-c C-s` Compose message in `*mail*` buffer: • Create or move to `To:` header: `C-c C-f C-t` • Create or move to `Subject:` header: `C-c C-f C-s` • Create or move to `CC:` header: `C-c C-f C-c` • Insert signature at end of message: `C-c C-w` • Insert current message in mailbox buffer: `C-c C-y` • Fill text of inserted message: `C-c C-q`
Replying to and forwarding messages	• Reply to the current message: `r` • Forward current message: `f` • Continue editing current message in `*mail*` as response: `c` • Send a new message, enabling `C-c C-y`: `m`
Using alternate mailboxes	• Read alternate mailbox: `i` • Set UNIX mailbox files for RMAIL mailbox: `M-x set-rmail-inbox-list` • Merge new mail received in UNIX mailbox files: `g`

Table 10.14, con't.

Topic	Summary
Using mail summaries	Create summary buffer: • Create summary of all messages in mailbox: **h** or **C-M-h** • Create summary of messages with label: **l** or **C-M-l** • Create summary of messages with recipient: **r** or **C-M-r** Manipulate summary buffer: • Mark current summary line's message for deletion: **d** • Unmark current summary line's message for deletion: **u** • Move to *n*th message: *n***j** • Move to next message: **C-n** • Move to next message (skip deleted messages): **n** • Move to previous message: **C-p** • Move to previous message: (skip deleted messages): **p** • Exit RMAIL: **q** • Exit mail summary window: **x** • Scroll other (mailbox) window forward: **SPC** • Scroll other (mailbox) window backward: **DEL**
Using labels	• Assign a label to message: **a** • Remove a label from message: **k** • Move to next message that has label: **C-M-n** • Move to previous message that has label: **C-M-p**
Expanding digest messages	• Expand digest message into component messages: **M-x undigestify-rmail-message**

11
Managing Files and Buffers

This chapter describes Emacs features that allow you to manage your files and buffers more efficiently. The main topics discussed in this chapter are:

- Using the Dired facility to manage files
- Moving the cursor in a Dired buffer
- Managing multiple buffers with buffer menus

Using the Dired Facility to Manage Files

Emacs' Dired facility—also known as the "directory editor"—provides an easy, intuitive way to manage your files from within Emacs. Using Dired, you can navigate through your directory structure—deleting, renaming, and copying files along the way. In addition, you can visit or simply view a file's contents. You perform these operations in a special Dired mode window that is created when you run the **C-x d** or **M-x dired** command (or **C-x 4 d** to start Dired in another window). Emacs then prompts you for the name of an initial directory:

```
Dired (directory): ~/█
```

After you type a directory path and press **RET**, Emacs brings up a Dired window containing a long listing (the same as that produced by the **ls -l** UNIX command). For example, specifying **~/emacs** on our system produced a window like that shown in Figure 11.1.

```
█ total 5302
  drwxr-xr-x    5 michael  users       3072 Apr  4 20:18 .
  drwxr-xr-x   31 michael  users       3072 Mar 27 13:09 ..
  -rw-r--r--    1 michael  users        385 Feb 19 22:42 Abbrevs
  -rw-r--r--    1 michael  users        697 Feb 27 18:49 Apropos
  -rw-r--r--    1 michael  users       7540 Feb 27 18:50 Bindings
  -rwxr--r--    1 michael  users        193 Apr 15  1990 ChangeLog
  -rw-r--r--    1 michael  users        139 Feb 27 18:54 Cover
  drwxr-xr-x    2 michael  users         64 Apr  7 15:47 Examples
  -rw-r--r--    1 michael  users        348 Feb 27 18:58 Function
--%%-Dired: emacs              8:47pm 0.01 Mail    (Dired)----Top--------
Reading directory /user/michael/emacs/...done
```

Figure 11.1. File Listing in the Dired Buffer

Moving the Cursor in a Dired Buffer

In the initial Dired window, the cursor is in the upper-left corner. Within a Dired window, you can use all the usual cursor motion commands to move about the window, although they may not work exactly as you are accustomed. For example, the **C-p** and **C-n** commands are rebound in Dired mode to the functions **dired-previous-line** and **dired-next-line**, which move the cursor to the start of the previous or next file name. For example, running three **C-n** commands in the window shown in Figure 11.1 moved the cursor to the start of the third file name, as seen in Figure 11.2.

You can also use searching commands to look for a file in a very long listing. For example, doing an incremental search (**C-s**) for the file **outline** repositioned the cursor and scrolled the window as shown in Figure 11.3.

```
    total 5302
    drwxr-xr-x    5 michael  users       3072 Apr  4 20:18 .
    drwxr-xr-x   31 michael  users       3072 Mar 27 13:09 ..
    -rw-r--r--    1 michael  users        385 Feb 19 22:42 ▓bbrevs
    -rw-r--r--    1 michael  users        697 Feb 27 18:49 Apropos
    -rw-r--r--    1 michael  users       7540 Feb 27 18:50 Bindings
    -rwxr--r--    1 michael  users        193 Apr 15  1990 ChangeLog
    -rw-r--r--    1 michael  users        139 Feb 27 18:54 Cover
    drwxr-xr-x    2 michael  users         64 Apr  7 15:47 Examples
    -rw-r--r--    1 michael  users        348 Feb 27 18:58 Function
--%%-Dired: emacs          8:47pm 0.01 Mail  (Dired)----Top-------
Reading directory /user/michael/emacs/...done
```

Figure 11.2. Cursor Movement in the Dired Buffer

```
    -rw-rw-rw-    1 michael  users         23 Oct 13 11:33 lisprog.l
    -rw-r--r--    1 michael  users        942 Feb 24 02:12 macros
    -rw-rw-rw-    1 michael  users      77769 Feb 24 02:07 macros.pcl
    -rw-rw-rw-    1 michael  users       1781 Nov 15 19:04 mail.to.foo
    -rwxr--r--    1 michael  users        475 Aug  7  1990 newprog.p
    -rw-r--r--    1 michael  users      10490 Dec 11 22:32 outline█
    -rw-r--r--    1 michael  users      10979 Dec 11 22:32 outline.pag
    -rw-r--r--    1 michael  users        456 Dec 11 22:33 outline.toc
    -rw-rw-rw-    1 michael  users       2024 Oct 16 19:59 pascal.mode
    -rwxr-xr-x    1 michael  users      75666 Aug 22  1990 prog
--%%-Dired: emacs          8:47pm 0.01 Mail  (Dired)----57%-------
I-search: outline
```

Figure 11.3. Results of an Incremental Search

Cursor movement commands that are unique to Dired are summarized in Table 11.1.

Table 11.1. Special Dired Cursor Movement Commands

Operation	Commands and Description
Move down one line	C-n or n or SPC Moves the cursor down one line, keeping the cursor in the file name column of the directory listing.
Move up one line	C-p or p Like above, but moves the cursor up one line.

Running Dired File Management Commands

In Dired mode, you cannot type text in the Dired buffer. Instead, the usual character keys are bound to various file management functions, summarized in Table 11.2. Dired lets you perform many common file operations directly from the buffer, including copying a file, renaming a file, changing a file's access permissions, and visiting a file.

These commands apply to the file on the current cursor line. For instance, in the screen shown in Figure 11.3, any of the following commands would work on the `outline` file.

Table 11.2. Dired File Management Commands

Operation	Command and Description
Copy file	`c` Makes a copy of the file. Prompts for the name of the copy, filling in part of the path name for you. For example, if you run `c` on the file `foo` in the directory `bar`, Emacs prompts with: `Copy to: ~/bar/`█ To make a copy in the same directory, type the file name and press **RET**. To make the copy in a different directory, simply edit the file name with **DEL**. If you make a copy in the same directory, Emacs updates the Dired buffer to reflect the change.
Rename file	`r` Renames the current file. Like the `c` command, it prompts for the new file name, supplying part of the path name for you. For example, if you rename `report` in the directory `misc`, Emacs prompts with: `Rename report to: ~/misc/`█ You type the new name and press **RET**. Again, Emacs updates the Dired window to reflect the change, if necessary.

Table 11.2, con't.

Operation	Command and Description
Mark file for deletion	**d** Marks the current file for deletion. To guard against accidental deletions, this command does not actually delete the file. Instead, you must delete marked files with the **x** command, described below. To unmark a file, use the **u** command or DEL, also described below. Files marked for deletion have a D placed on first column of the line. In addition to the **d** command, Dired has several useful commands for marking files for deletion, summarized in Table 11.3.
Unmark a file and move down	**u** Unmarks the current file for deletion and moves the cursor to the next line. Works on lines that have a D in the first column.
Unmark a file and move up	DEL Like the **u** command, but moves the cursor to the previous line.
Delete marked files	**x** Deletes all files that have been marked for deletion.
Re-read directory	**g** Rereads the directory and updates the buffer display.
Visit file or directory	**e** or **f** When used on a line containing a file name, visits the file (like the C-x C-f command. When used on a line containing a directory name, it runs Dired again on the directory. In other words, you get another Dired buffer that operates on the directory.

Table 11.2, con't.

Operation	Command and Description
Visit file or directory in other window	**o** Like the **f** command, but opens another window for a visited file (in the case of a file) or another Dired window (in the case of a directory).
View file	**v** When used on a file, runs the **M-x view-file** command, which visits the file using a read-only buffer with special file-viewing commands. For example, **SPC** moves forward a screen, while **DEL** moves backward a screen. When used on a directory, invokes Dired (just like the **f** command).
Compress file	**C** Compresses the current file. For more information, see *compress(1)* in your UNIX reference.
Uncompress file	**U** Uncompresses the current file. For more information, see *uncompress(1)* in your UNIX reference.
Byte-compile file	**B** Byte-compiles the current file.
Change file's permissions	**M** Changes the access permissions of the current file. For more information, see *chmod(1)* in your UNIX reference.
Change file's group ownership	**G** Changes the group ownership of the current file, provided permissions allow you to do so.

Table 11.2, con't.

Operation	Command and Description
Change file's user ownership	O Changes the user ownership of the current file, provided permissions allow you to do so.
Display brief help on Dired	? Displays a brief listing of common Dired commands in the minibuffer.
Display complete help on Dired	h Opens another window (if necessary) and displays an extensive help message about Dired commands and usage.

Marking Files for Deletion

In addition to the **d** command, Dired mode has several commands for marking files for deletion, summarized in Table 11.3. These commands are useful in deleting the numerous recovery and backup files that Emacs can generate.

Table 11.3. Commands to Mark Backup and Recovery Files for Deletion

To Delete...	Command and Comments
Recovery files	# Marks all recovery files for deletion—files whose names start and end with #. (For details on recovery files, see the section "Recovering Files after System Crashes" in Chapter 12.)
All backup files	~ Marks all backup files for deletion—files whose names end with a tilde (~).

Table 11.3, con't.

To Delete...	Command and Comments
Excess backup files	. (period) Marks all numeric backup files for deletion—files whose names end in tilde and a number—except for the oldest and newest.

Managing Multiple Buffers with Buffer-Menus

Emacs' Buffer-Menu facility lets you manipulate buffers in a buffer that contains a "menu" of existing buffers. This is useful when you work with several buffers at once, allowing you to save them or delete ther. as a group instead of individually.

As with the Dired facility, you can use cursor positioning commands to move the cursor among buffers in the menu, and run special buffer-menu commands that act on the current buffer. To invoke the Buffer-Menu facility, run **M-x buffer-menu**, which displays a buffer menu in a buffer named ***Buffer List*** that uses a special Buffer Menu mode. If necessary, Emacs creates a new window for the buffer. Figure 11.4 shows an example buffer menu window.

```
MR Buffer           Size   Mode         File
-- ------           ----   ----         ----
.*  chap13.txt      36875  Text         /user/michael/emacs/chap13.txt
 *  *Buffer List*   0      Buffer Menu
    foo.c           166    C            /user/michael/emacs/foo.c
*%  emacs           5283   Dired
*%  michael         4323   Dired
 *  *scratch*       0      Lisp Interaction
 *  *Help*          12     Text
--%%-Emacs: *Buffer List* 9:05pm 0.05 Mail (Buffer Menu)---All---
Commands: d,s,x; 1,2,m,u,q; delete; ~; ? for help.
```

Figure 11.4. Sample Buffer Menu

Notice that the buffer menu contains the same information as is displayed by the **C-x C-b** command: the buffer's status, name, size, mode, and associated file (if any). In fact, the buffer created by **C-x C-b** is a buffer menu. If you select this buffer, you can use the buffer menu commands described here.

As a quick memory refresher, the first column contains status information, denoted by the following characters:

- **.** (period) Indicates the buffer is the currently selected buffer.
- ***** Indicates the buffer has been modified since it was last saved.
- **%** Indicates the buffer is a read-only buffer.

Notice, also, that the cursor sits on the first line containing buffer information. This is the buffer to which buffer menu commands would apply. For example, if you pressed **s** in the above example, Emacs would mark the buffer to be saved by placing an **S** in place of the asterisk; a subsequent **x** command would cause the buffer's contents to be saved to the specified file, and the **S** would be replaced by a space, indicating that the buffer has not been modified since it was last saved.

Table 11.4 summarizes the commands you can run in Buffer Menu mode. These commands can be grouped into two categories: commands that delete and/or save buffers, and commands that select which buffers are displayed.

Table 11.4. Buffer-Menu Commands

Operation	Command and Description
Commands That Save and/or Delete Buffers	
Mark for saving	**s** Marks the current buffer to be saved by a later **x** command. If the buffer has been modified, its * status is replaced by **S** until the **x** command is run, at which point its status changes to unmodified since last save. Before running **x**, you can undo the save mark with the **u** or DEL command.
Mark for deleting	**d** or **k** and **C-d** These commands mark the buffer to be deleted by a later **x** command. The **d** and **k** commands move to the next line after marking for deletion; the **C-d** command moves to the previous line after marking. Buffers marked for deletion have a **D** in the first column. The buffers are not actually deleted until you issue the **x** command. Before then, you can use **u** or DEL to unmark the deletion.
Carry out saves and deletions	**x** Saves all buffers marked with **S**, then deletes all buffers marked with **D**. If a buffer marked with **D** has been modified (has a * in the status column), Emacs prompts for verification before deleting the buffer. If a buffer is marked for *both* saving and deleting, it is saved first, then deleted.

Table 11.4, con't.

Operation	Command and Description
Commands That Save and/or Delete Buffers, con't.	
Undo save and delete marks	**u** and **DEL** These commands undo S and D marks for the current buffer. The **u** command moves to the next line after undoing the marks, while **DEL** moves to the previous line.
Make unmodified	**~** Sets a buffer's status to unmodified. If the buffer currently has an asterisk in the status column, it is removed. If you delete an unmodified buffer, Emacs does not prompt for verification.
Commands That Select Buffers for Display	
Select buffer in 1 window	**1** Immediately selects the current buffer for display in a single window. All other windows are hidden.
Select buffer in place of ***Buffer List***	**f** Immediately selects the current buffer and displays it in place of the ***Buffer List*** window.
Select buffer other window	**o** Immediately selects the current buffer and displays it in another window, keeping the ***Buffer List*** window visible.
Flag buffer for display	**m** Marks the current buffer to be displayed by a later **2** or **q** command. Buffers marked for display have a greater-than sign (>) in the first column.

Table 11.4, con't.

Operation	Command and Description
Commands That Select Buffers for Display, con't.	
Display this and previous buffer	**2** Selects the current buffer, and displays it along with the buffer that occupied the current window before `*Buffer List*`. In other words, this command creates two windows: One contains the current buffer; the other contains the buffer that was displayed in the window before `*Buffer List*` was selected.
Display this and all marked buffers	**q** Selects the current buffer, and creates a window for it and any other buffers that were marked with **m**. This is a convenient way to set up multiple windows for multiple buffers. Once you've created multiple windows, you can switch back and forth between them using the `C-x o` (other buffer) or `C-x b` (select buffer) commands.

Summary

Table 11.5 summarizes the main points in this chapter.

Table 11.5. Chapter 11 Summary

Topic	Summary
Starting Dired	• Start Dired: `C-x d` or `M-x dired` • Start Dired in another window: `C-x 4 d`
Get help on Dired	• Display brief help on Dired: **?** • Display complete help on Dired: **h**
Moving the cursor	• Move to next file: `C-n` or n or `SPC` • Move to previous file: `C-p` or **p**

Table 11.5, con't.

Topic	Summary
Search for file	• Incremental search for file: C–s
Copy and rename files	• Copy current file: c • Rename current file: r
Delete files	• Mark current file for deletion: d • Mark all recovery files for deletion: # • Mark all backup files for deletion: ~ • Mark excess backup files for deletion: . • Unmark current file and move down: u • Unmark current file and move up: DEL • Delete files marked for deletion: x
Visit/view files	• Re-read current directory: g • Visit current file or directory: e or f • Visit current file or directory in other window: o • View current file: v
Compress files	• Compress current file: C • Uncompress current file: U
Change file permissions/owner	• Change current file's permissions: M • Change current file's group ownership: G • Change current file's user ownership: O
Compile file	• Byte-compile current file: B

Table 11.5, con't.

Topic	Summary
Starting the Buffer-Menu facility	• Start Buffer-Menu facility: `M-x buffer-menu`
Save and delete buffers	• Mark current buffer for saving: `s` • Mark current buffer for deleting and move down: `d` or `k` • Mark current buffer for deleting and move up: `C-d` • Save and delete marked buffers: `x` • Undo save/delete marks for current buffer and move down: `u` • Undo save/delete marks for current buffer and move up: `DEL`
Set buffer status to unmodified	• Set current buffer's status to unmodified: `~`
Select buffer	• Select current buffer in one window: `1` • Select current buffer in place of *Buffer List*: `f` • Select current buffer in other window: `o` • Flag current buffer for later display: `m` • Display current buffer and previous buffer: `2` • Display current buffer and all buffers flagged with `m`: `q`

12
Miscellaneous Emacs Features

This chapter describes Emacs features that don't fall neatly into the other categories described in this book. The main topics discussed here are:

- Checking your spelling
- Rerunning commands from the command history
- Recovering files after system crashes
- Using UNIX commands in Emacs
- Running a UNIX shell in an Emacs buffer
- Nroff major mode
- TeX modes: LaTeX and Plain TeX
- Picture mode
- Doctor mode

Checking Your Spelling

If you are an experienced UNIX user, you may be familiar with the `spell` command, which checks the spelling of words in a file. Spell-checking—using the `spell` spelling checker—is built in to Emacs itself, so you don't have to exit Emacs to check spelling. Not only does Emacs check the spelling of words, it allows you to query-replace all occurrences of a misspelled word. Emacs has commands to check the spelling of individual words, all the words in a region, or all the words in the entire buffer. Table 12.1 summarizes these commands; more detailed discussions of these commands follow the table.

Table 12.1. Spell-Checking Commands

Operation	Command and Comments
Check word's spelling	`M-$` Checks the spelling of the word containing the cursor. If the cursor is between words, `M-$` checks the spelling of the word preceding the cursor. If the word is spelled correctly, Emacs displays a message such as `"correct..."` in the echo area. If the word is misspelled, Emacs prompts for its replacement and query-replaces all occurrences of the incorrectly spelled word.
Check buffer's spelling	`M-x spell-buffer` Checks the spelling of all words in the buffer. For each misspelled word, Emacs prompts you for a replacement; then does a query-replace for all occurrences of the misspelled word (just like the `M-$` command).
Check region's spelling	`M-x spell-region` Acts just like the `M-x spell-buffer` command, but only checks words in the current region.

Checking a Word (M-$)

To check the spelling of a single word, position the cursor on or immediately after the word you want to check; then run `M-$`. For instance, if you place the cursor in either of the locations shown below (or anywhere in between), Emacs checks the spelling of the word "misspell."

```
Did I misspell█any words in this sentence?
Did I █isspell any words in this sentence?
```

If you were to run **M-$** in this example, Emacs would display the following message:

```
Checking spelling of misspell...
```

Since the word is spelled correctly, Emacs displays "**correct...**" in the echo area. More interesting behavior occurs with misspelled words, such as "wierd" in the following example:

```
Wierd█is a very wierd word.
I can never spell wierd correctly.
```

In this case, Emacs displays the message:

```
'wierd' not recognized; edit a replacement: wierd
```

At this point, you can edit a replacement for "wierd" in the echo area. The most useful commands for doing this are:

C-b	To move the cursor back within the replacement word
C-f	To move the cursor forward
C-a	To move to the start of the word
C-e	To move to the end of the word
C-d	To delete the character under the cursor
DEL	To back up over and delete characters. (Note: because many Emacs implementations swap the **DEL** and **C-h** keys, **DEL** may not back up over and delete characters.)

Once you have edited the replacement ("weird" in the above example), type **RET** to accept the edited version. Emacs then query-replaces all occurrences by prompting with:

```
Query replacing \bwierd\b with weird:
```

To replace an occurrence, type **SPC**; to skip an occurrence, type **DEL**. In fact, you can specify any of the usual query-replace command characters (summarized in Chapter 3, "More Efficient Editing"). For instance, you could type **!** to replace all remaining occurrences *without prompting for verification.*

Notice also that the query-replacement preserves the letter case of the word being replaced. Thus, in the above example, "Wierd" is replaced with "Weird", and "wierd" is replaced with "weird."

Checking the Words in a Buffer (M-x spell-buffer)

To check the spelling of all words in the current buffer, use **M-x spell-buffer**. For each misspelled word in the buffer, Emacs displays the same prompt as the **M-$** command, namely:

```
word not recognized; edit a replacement: word
```

After you edit a replacement, Emacs query-replaces all occurrences, just like the **M-$** command. Occasionally, Emacs may mistakenly identify a word as misspelled. This occurs typically with proper nouns (city and person names), acronyms, and jargon. When this happens, you can avoid changing the word by simply not editing a replacement. If the replacement text is the same as the "misspelled" word, Emacs will not query-replace it. For example, if you spell-checked a buffer containing the name "Schoonover," Emacs prompts with:

```
'schoonover' not recognized; edit a replacement: schoonover
```

To avoid the replacement, press **RET**.

Checking the Words in a Region (M-x spell-region)

M-x spell-region works exactly the same as **M-x spell-buffer**, except that it only checks the spelling and query-replaces words in the current region. Words outside the region are not affected.

Rerunning Commands from the Command History

Emacs' Electric History mode provides a menu of commands you have used during your editing session and lets you select and rerun them. Only commands that require you to type arguments in the minibuffer (such as **M-x** commands) are saved in the Electric History.

To create a buffer containing the command menu, run the **M-x electric-command-history** command. Emacs opens another window containing a list of commands you've used, as shown in Figure 12.1. Table 12.2 lists commands you can use to move through and manipulate the command list.

To rerun a command, move the cursor to the desired command and press **SPC**. Emacs displays the command in the minibuffer; to redo it, simply press **RET**.

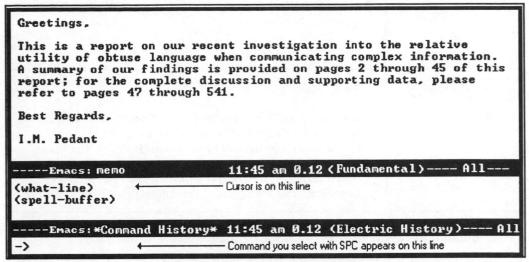

Figure 12.1. Electric History Buffer

Table 12.2. Electric History Commands

Operation	Command and Comments
Move to next line	**RET** Moves the cursor to the next command in the history menu.
Move to previous line	**DEL** Moves the cursor to the previous command in the history menu.
Rerun (redo) the current command	**SPC** or **!** Selects the current command and displays it in the minibuffer, preceded by the prompt: **Redo:** *command* To rerun the command, press **RET**, or press **C-g** to cancel. Commands are always rerun in the original buffer in which they were first run.

Table 12.2, con't.

Operation	Command and Comments
Quit	q or C-c C-c or C-] Quit electric history and restore original windows.
List commands	? Displays a list of commands available in Electric History mode. Note that the `*Help*` buffer created to display these commands may be replaced by the Electric History buffer when you try to move the cursor. To view the `*Help*` buffer again, press q to quit the Electric History buffer. The `*Help*` buffer then reappears, allowing you to scroll through the commands.

The command history listing is controlled by the following variables:

- *list-command-history-max*, which sets the maximum number of commands that will be "remembered" by the command history.

- *command-history*, which holds the commands that have been run recently.

- *list-command-history-filter*, which determines which commands in *command-history* should be excluded from the history listing.

For details on these variables, execute the **M-x describe-variable** command and see "Using Variables to Change Emacs' Behavior" in Chapter 13).

Recovering Files After System Crashes

Although it is unlikely, Emacs may abort during an editing session. Some reasons why this would occur are:

- The UNIX system crashes.

- You are using Emacs from a modem connection and the phone line "goes down."

- The Emacs process gets terminated with the UNIX **kill** command.

- You use Emacs on a remote system (e.g., via the **remsh** command) and for whatever reason, you lose the network connection.

In some editors, you would lose all your editing changes, unless you happened to save your work just before the crash. Emacs protects your work by automatically saving the most recent buffer contents after every 300 keystrokes.

The most recent text is *not* saved to the visited file. Instead, it is placed in a special **auto-save** file, whose name is the same as the visited file except that it starts and ends with **#**. For example, if you edit a file named **/user/tom/foo.c**, Emacs saves the most recent buffer to the auto-save file **/user/tom/#foo.c#**.

To recover from a crash, using the most recent text placed in the auto-save file, use the **M-x recover-file** command. You would typically use this command after restarting Emacs after the crash. This command prompts you for the name of the file to recover with:

```
Recover file: ~/█
```

For example, if a crash occurred while you were editing **~/foo.c**, you would respond with **foo.c RET**. After you specify a file, Emacs asks for verification before proceeding:

```
Recover auto save file /user/tom/#foo.c#? (yes or no) █
```

You must type a full **yes** or **no** to the prompt. To help you determine if you really want to proceed with the recovery operation, Emacs displays a long directory listing for the visited file and the recovery file in a window named ***Directory***. For instance, using the above example, you might see something like this in the ***Directory*** window:

```
-rw-rw-rw  1 tom  users  3264 Apr 6 11:21 /user/tom/#foo.c#
-rw-rw-rw  1 tom  users  2964 Apr 6 10:01 /user/tom/foo.c
```

From this, we can see that the visited file was last saved at 10:01am and contained 2,964 characters. And the auto-saved file was last saved at 11:21am (an hour and twenty minutes later) and it contains 3,264 characters (300 more than the visited file).

If you type **yes** to the prompt above, Emacs loads the recovery file (as if it were the visited file) and disables auto-saving. That is, Emacs will no longer automatically save to the recover file unless you explicitly re-enable auto-saving the with **M-x auto-save-mode** command. It is usually a good idea to run **C-x C-s** after **M-x recover-file** in order to save the recovered files contents back into the visited file.

Incidentally, if you rename a buffer—for example, by running the **C-x w** command—Emacs changes the name of the auto-save file accordingly. For example, if you are editing a buffer whose visited file is **/users/jeanne/recipes**, and you write the buffer with **C-x w recipes.old**, all subsequent auto-saves go to the file **/users/jeanne/#recipes.old#**.

There are, of course, many variations on the way Emacs auto-saves files. For details on how to tailor the process to your needs, read the remainder of this section.

Controlling How Often Auto-Saves Occur

By default, Emacs performs an auto-save every 300 keystrokes. You can change this number by setting the *auto-save-interval* variable. Also, Emacs auto-saves only those buffers that have enabled auto-saving and that have changed since the last auto-save. (Note that, by default, Emacs enables auto-saving for any buffers that were created by visiting a file.) You can force Emacs to auto-save before 300 keystrokes by running the **M-x do-auto-save** command.

Enabling and Disabling Auto-Saving

By default, auto-saving is enabled for all buffers of visited files, but disabled for buffers that don't have a corresponding visited file. For example, if you visit file **foo** with **C-x f**, Emacs enables auto-saving for the buffer; however, Emacs does not enable auto-saving for an RMAIL or Help mode buffer. If you prefer to disable auto-saving for all buffers as the default behavior, set the variable *auto-save-default* to **nil** (see Chapter 13).

To explicitly set a buffer's auto-save status, use the **M-x auto-save-mode** command, which toggles auto-saving for the current buffer. For example, to turn off auto-saving in a buffer for a visited file, run **M-x auto-save-mode**. As another example, suppose you want to extensively edit a ***Help*** buffer (for use in some other file); you could use **M-x auto-save-mode** to enable auto-saving for the buffer.

Auto-Saving to the Visited File

Why doesn't Emacs auto-save to the visited file? Because Emacs assumes that you want to keep the visited file as an "original" copy, which you could revert back to with **M-x revert-buffer**. If, instead, you prefer the auto-save to occur to the visited file, set the variable *auto-save-visited-file-name* to **t** (or any non-**nil** value).

Also by default, Emacs deletes the auto-save file whenever you save the visited file. To keep the auto-save file around, set the variable *delete-auto-save-files* to **nil**.

Where Are Unvisited Buffers Auto-Saved?

When auto-saving a buffer that does not have an associated file, Emacs auto-saves to a file whose name is constructed by adding **#%** to the start of the buffer name and **#** to the end. For example, when auto-saving a ***Help*** buffer, Emacs auto-saves to **#%*Help*#**.

Using UNIX Commands in Emacs

Table 12.3 summarizes commands that allow you to run UNIX commands in an Emacs buffer. The Emacs variable *shell-file-name* determines what UNIX shell Emacs uses when running UNIX commands in a subshell. Emacs determines an appropriate value for *shell-file-name* by looking at your SHELL environment variable, which may be set in your `.profile` or `.login` start-up file). Another important point to note is that you can use **C-g** to terminate a subprocess spawned by either **M-!** or **M-|**.

Table 12.3. Running UNIX Commands from Emacs

Operation	Command and Comments
Run UNIX command	**M-!** or **C-u M-!** **M-!** prompts for the name of a UNIX command that you want to run: `Shell command:` █ You type the name and press **RET**, and Emacs runs the command and displays its output in a buffer named `*Shell Command Output*`. Alternatively, if you run **M-!** with a numeric argument (for example, **C-u M-!** or **M-1 M !**), Emacs inserts the UNIX command's output into the current buffer. The cursor is left at the start of the text and mark is placed at the end of the text.
Run UNIX command on text in region	**M-|** or **C-u M-|** **M-|** prompts for the name of UNIX command, and pipes the contents of the current region to the command. Like the **M-!** command, it displays the UNIX command's output in a buffer named `*Shell Command Output*`, unless you specify a numeric argument, in which case it replaces the current region with the output of the UNIX command. In the latter case, Emacs leaves the cursor at the start of the text and mark at the end. (Users familiar with the **vi** editor may recognize this as the **!** command, which passes text to a UNIX filter.)

Table 12.3, con't.

Operation	Command and Comments
Run UNIX shell in window	`M-x shell` Spawns a subshell whose standard input, standard output, and standard error are passed through a buffer named `*shell*`. You can run UNIX commands interactively in such a buffer. That is, you type commands to a shell prompt in the buffer, press RET, and the output of the commands is inserted back into the buffer. For details on using a `*shell*` buffer, see "Running a UNIX Shell in an Emacs Buffer," later in this chapter.

Examples of Using M-! and M-|

The simplest form of these commands is **M-!** without an argument, which simply displays the output of a UNIX command in a buffer named `*Shell Command Output*`. It does *not* pass any text from Emacs to the UNIX command. Typically, you would use **M-!** to run a command that simply displays some information about some facet of your UNIX system. For example, suppose you want to use the `finger` command to get information about your system administrator; you would run **M-!** `finger root` **RET**, which would display information similar to that shown in Figure 12.2.

```
Login name: root                          In real life: Foobar Jones
Directory: /                              Shell: /bin/sh
Last login Sat Apr  6 22:04 on pty/tty0
No plan.




--**-Emacs: *Shell Command Output* 7:59pm 0.01 Mail (Text)-All---
```

Figure 12.2. Unix finger Command Output

In some situations, you need to insert the output of a UNIX command into the current buffer. Although you could do this by killing the text in the `*Shell Command Output*` buffer and yanking it into the current buffer, it is much more convenient to simply specify an argument to the **M-!** command. For example, suppose you need to insert a calendar into the buffer shown in Figure 12.3.

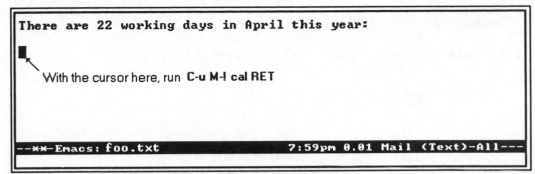

Figure 12.3. Sample Buffer Needing a Calendar

With the cursor located as shown, you could run **C-u M-! cal RET** to insert the output of the UNIX **cal** command, as shown in Figure 12.4.

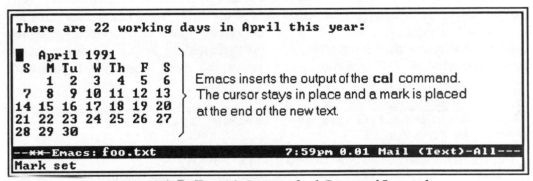

Figure 12.4. Buffer with Output of cal Command Inserted

Often it is useful to pass a region of text as input to a UNIX command. One instance where this is extremely useful is when you are developing shell scripts. Using the **M- |** command, you can pass regions of your shell script to a shell for execution, and view the output in another window. For example, suppose you place a region around the fragment of code shown in Figure 12.5, which you hope will rename all the files in the current directory to lower case.

```
   Set mark here with C-SPC or C-@
[]
echo "Renaming all files to lowercase letters:"
for f in *
do
   toFile=`echo $f | tr '[A-Z]' '[a-z]'`
   echo mv $f $toFile
done
█
      Move cursor here to define the region
--**-Emacs: script.sh      9:17pm 0.00 Mail   (Text)----All-----
```

Figure 12.5. Sample Region of Code

Notice that the code in Figure 12.5 doesn't actually rename the files. Instead, it uses the UNIX **echo** command so that problem areas (such as renaming a file on to itself) can be identified and corrective action can be taken. To see what the series of **mv** commands generated by this code would be, run **M-| sh RET**, which passes the lines to the Bourne shell for evaluation. Shortly thereafter, Emacs shows the output in another window. For example, on our system, the screen looked like Figure 12.6.

```
echo "Renaming all files to lowercase letters:"
for f in *
do
   toFile=`echo $f | tr '[A-Z]' '[a-z]'`
   echo mv $f $toFile
done                           -
--**-Emacs: script.sh      9:17pm 0.00 Mail   (Text)----All-----
Renaming all files to lowercase letters:
mv #foo.tag# #foo.tag#
mv Abbrevs abbrevs
mv Apropos apropos
mv ChangeLog changelog
mv chap13.txt chap13.txt
--**-Emacs: *Shell Command Output* 9:17pm 0.00 (Text)--All---
Shell command on region: sh RET
```

Figure 12.6. Output of Sample Code

By examining the output in the ***Shell Command Output*** buffer, we determine that the appropriate **mv** commands would be generated. Now it is merely a matter of taking the **mv** commands out of the **echo** command.

As a final example, you may occasionally want to replace the text in a region with the output of a UNIX filter that takes the region text as input. For example, suppose you have a large number of lines, some of which may be duplicates. One way to eliminate duplicate lines is to run the UNIX **sort** command with the **-m** (merge) option. To use this command to merge lines in Emacs, create a region around the lines, then run **C-u M-|** **sort -m RET**.

Running a UNIX Shell in an Emacs Buffer

As mentioned previously, the **M-x shell** command runs a shell in an Emacs buffer named ***shell***. You can then run commands and see their output in the buffer, just as if you were running the commands in a shell outside Emacs. This buffer works fine for most commands that simply display output, but not so well for commands that do cursor positioning or custom terminal I/O. For example, the UNIX **clear** command does not work in a shell buffer.

To ensure that the ***shell*** buffer's directory is the same as the UNIX shell's current working directory, Emacs monitors any **cd, pushd,** and **popd** commands and updates the ***shell*** buffer's directory accordingly.

Note to users who alias cd: If you use different aliases for **cd, pushd,** or **popd,** Emacs will not recognize your aliases by default. However, you can make Emacs recognize your aliases by changing the values of the variables *shell-cd-regexp, shell-pushd-regexp,* and *shell-popd-regexp* variables. Each variable contains a regular expression that identifies the command that performs the respective directory operation. Thus, if you use an alias of **chd** instead of the **cd** command to change directories, you could set *shell-cd-regexp* to **"chd"** to make Emacs recognize your alias instead of **cd.**

Note to Emacs-Lisp programmers: If Emacs encounters an error when trying to change a directory for the ***shell*** buffer, it calls the function whose name is stored in the *shell-set-directory-error-hook* variable, *if* the variable is not **nil.** The function is called with no arguments.

Shell Initialization

When you start a shell with the **M-x shell** command, Emacs goes through the following initialization procedures:

1. Emacs first determines what shell to use from the variable *explicit-shell-file-name,* if it is set and non-**nil.**

2. If that variable is not set or is **nil,** Emacs uses the value of the ESHELL environment variable as the start-up shell.

3. If ESHELL does not exist or is not set, Emacs uses the SHELL environment variable, which contains the name of your default login shell. Typically, Emacs uses the SHELL variable because most users don't set *explicit-shell-file-name* or ESHELL.

Note: If the path name specified in any of the above variables is relative, Emacs searches for the shell in the directories specified by the *exec-path* variable.

4. At this point, if Emacs still cannot determine which shell to use, it uses **/bin/sh** as a default.

5. At this point, Emacs starts the specified shell. Once the shell is started, Emacs passes its text from the file **.emacs_***shellName*, where *shellName* is the base name of the shell. This file is used to provide additional start-up commands to a shell for **shell-mode**. This file is optional, but if it exists, its commands are sent to the shell, after which input is accepted from the user. For example, if the start-up shell was **/bin/ksh**, Emacs passes the shell input from the file named **.emacs_ksh** before accepting user commands.

Shell Mode Commands

A ***shell*** buffer actually uses a special Shell mode, which supports the commands shown in Table 12.4. In addition to these commands, the usual Fundamental mode commands work. For example, **DEL** backspaces over the previous character. Because some Fundamental mode commands are important to the shell (for example, **C-d** sends end-of-file to the shell), Shell mode provides special **C-c** prefix commands that accomplish the same tasks. For example, **C-c C-d** sends end-of-file to the shell, whereas **C-d** alone would simply delete the character under the cursor.

Table 12.4. Shell Mode Commands

Operation	Command and Comments
Editing the Command Line	
Send line as input	**RET** All text from the shell prompt (defined by the variable *shell-prompt-pattern*) to the end of the line is sent as standard input to the shell.
Kill line	**C-c C-u** Kills all input text since the last **RET** command. This has a similar effect to the kill-line character in a real shell.

Table 12.4, con't.

Operation	Command and Comments
	Editing the Command Line, con't.
Kill previous word	`C-c C-w` Kill the word preceding the cursor. This is similar to the Fundamental mode command **M-DEL**.
Retype previous input	`C-c C-y` Copies the text you typed before the last **RET**. This allows you to rerun the previous command you typed at the shell prompt (like `C-p` or **k** in the Korn shell).
	Controlling Jobs
Send EOF	`C-c C-d` Sends an end-of-file character as input to the shell or the currently running process in the shell. If only a shell is running, this typically has the effect of terminating the shell.
Send Control-C interrupt	`C-c C-c` Sends the interrupt signal to the shell or currently running process. Similar in effect to typing `C-c` in a real shell.
Stop the shell or process	`C-c C-z` Sends the suspend signal to the shell or currently running process. Like the `C-z` command in a real shell.
Send quit interrupt	`C-c C-\` Sends the quit signal to the shell or currently running process.

Table 12.4, con't.

Operation	Command and Comments
	Manipulating Shell Output
Delete last output	`C-c C-o` Kills the last output that was inserted into the `*shell*` buffer, and inserts the message "`*** output flushed ***`" in its place. The killed text can be yanked back into the same or another buffer.
Scroll last output to top	`C-c C-r` Scrolls the window so that the first line of the last batch of output is placed at the top line of the window.

Nroff Major Mode

Emacs provides a special Nroff major mode (enabled by the `M-x nroff-mode` command) for editing `nroff` files. In this mode, you get all the Text mode commands, as well as the commands shown in Table 12.5. A nice feature about this mode is that the filling commands affect only the lines between `nroff` commands. In addition, the `C-x [` and `C-x ]` commands (backward and forward a page), move you to the previous or next line containing an `nroff` `.bp` command. Perhaps the nicest and most powerful feature is the Electric Nroff minor mode, which, if enabled by typing `M-x electric-nroff-mode` in an `nroff-mode` buffer, automatically inserts the closing `nroff` code for any opening `nroff` code that you type. For example, if you type `.fn` to start a footnote, Emacs inserts `.ef` (end footnote) on the following line.

Table 12.5. Nroff Mode Commands

Operation	Command and Comments
Previous text line	`M-p` Moves the cursor to the previous line that does not contain an `nroff` command.

Table 12.5, con't.

Operation	Command and Comments
Next text line	**M-n** Moves the cursor to the next line that does not contain an **nroff** command.
Total text lines	**M-?** Displays the total number of lines that do not contain **nroff** commands.

TeX Modes: LaTeX and Plain TeX

TeX is a typesetting language developed by Donald Knuth. There is also a set of TeX macros, called LaTeX, that many people use. Emacs provides major modes for editing both types of TeX files—Plain TeX mode and LaTeX mode. To invoke a TeX mode, use the **M-x tex-mode** command; Emacs will try to determine which TeX mode to use, based on the contents of the buffer. If the buffer is empty or if Emacs cannot determine which mode to use, it uses Plain TeX mode. You can also explicitly specify which mode to use by running either **M-x plain-tex-mode** or **M-x latex-mode**.

Configuring Emacs to Use TeX Modes

Before running TeX jobs and using the Emacs TeX printing commands, you will probably need to change a few Emacs variables. For details on making these changes apply to all future Emacs editing sessions, see the section in Chapter 13 on "Setting a Variable in Your .emacs File."

Before using the TeX modes, make sure your TeX and LaTeX programs are named **tex** and **latex**, respectively. The Emacs TeX modes assume your program files are named this way.

Next, you should set the TeX configuration variables listed in Table 12.6 to match your particular system configuration.

Table 12.6. TeX Mode Configuration Variables

Variable	Description
TeX-directory	Default value: `"/tmp/"` Set the value of this variable to the directory where temporary files generated by TeX jobs will be placed. The commands that create these temporary files are `C-c`, `C-r`, and `C-c  C-b` (discussed in the next section).
TeX-dvi-print-command	Default value: `"lpr -d"` Set the value of this variable to the command string used to print a `.dvi` file. This string is used by the `C-c  C-p` command.
TeX-show-queue-command	Default value: `"lpq"` Set the value of this variable to the command string used to show the print queue your job is on. This string is used by the `C-c  C-q` command, after you have sent a file to the printer with the `C-c  C-p` command.

TeX Mode Commands

Plain TeX and LaTeX modes are very similar. They differ mainly in the way they recognize TeX commands and macros. For example, in LaTeX mode, you have an additional command (`C-c  C-f`) that inserts a closing **\end** to balance an opening **\begin**.

Table 12.7 summarizes commands available in the TeX modes. Two classes of commands are provided:

- Commands that insert text, such as quote characters, paragraph breaks, and braces

- Commands that process TeX-coded text and print the output

We assume that you are already familiar with TeX, so we don't discuss the TeX/LaTeX commands themselves.

Table 12.7. TeX Mode Commands

Operation	Command and Comments
Commands to Insert Text	
Insert appropriate quote character(s)	**"** When Emacs sees the double quote, it inserts either a double quote (**"**), two single quotes (**' '**), or two back quotes (**` `**), whichever is appropriate for the context.
Check balanced characters and create new paragraph	**LFD** Check to make sure all braces and dollar signs are balanced in the current paragraph; then place a paragraph break in the buffer.
Insert balanced braces	**M-{** Insert a pair of balanced braces and set the cursor so that any text you type appears between the braces.
Move past unmatched **{**	**M-}** Move the cursor past the next unmatched opening brace. Useful in finding unbalanced braces.
Insert **\end** for LaTeX block	**C-c C-f** Inserts a closing, matching **\end** for an opening **\begin** in a LaTeX block.
Commands to Process TeX and Print	
Pass region to TeX	**C-c C-r** Run the TeX command on the current region.
Pass buffer to TeX	**C-c C-b** Run the TeX command on the buffer's contents.

Table 12.7, con't.

Operation	Command and Comments
Commands to Process TeX and Print, con't.	
Center TeX output	**C–c C–l** The previous two commands create a window containing TeX command messages. The **C–c C–l** command re-centers this output in the window. If errors occur during TeX processing, you can respond to the TeX prompts in this window as well.
Print TeX output	**C–c C–p** Print the output file generated by **C–c C–r** or **C–c C–b**.
Show Print queue	**C–c C–q** Show all the TeX print jobs currently underway.

When using a TeX printing command, Emacs creates a special "TeX shell." If TeX errors are encountered that require you to interact with the process, you can switch to this shell and issue standard UNIX commands.

Picture Mode

Picture mode lets you draw pictures with ASCII characters. For example, using Picture mode, you can easily create pictures such as that shown in Figure 12.7.

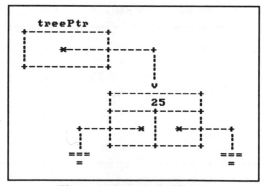

Figure 12.7. Sample Picture

Granted, you could just create such ASCII pictures in Text or Fundamental mode, but Picture mode has useful commands to make it easier to create them. Here are some of the characteristics of Picture mode:

- To enter Picture mode, use **M-x picture-mode**. This command keeps track of what mode you were in when you entered Picture mode. To exit Picture mode and return to the mode you were using before Picture mode, run **C-c C-c**.

- Picture mode always uses Overwrite minor mode—that is, any characters you type replace any characters already in the buffer at the current location.

- There are no line endings, per se, in Picture mode. You can think of the text you edit in Picture mode as appearing the lower-right quadrant of an X/Y axis that stretches to infinity. This model of text editing is known as the **quarter-plane model**.

- All the usual Fundamental mode commands work in Picture mode, but may work somewhat differently, based on the quarter-plane model. Some of the important are:

  - **C-f** moves the cursor forward *always on the same line*. If the cursor moves past the last visible character, Emacs automatically inserts blanks at the "end" of the line.

  - **C-p** moves the cursor to the same column on the previous line, even if that column extends past the "end" of the previous line. Congruent behavior occurs for the **C-n** command.

  - Since there really aren't line endings in this mode, **C-e** moves the cursor immediately after the last nonblank character on the line.

  - **C-d** replaces the current character with a blank, while the **DEL** command replaces the previous character with a blank.

  - **C-k** erases all remaining visible characters on the line.

  - **TAB** moves the cursor to the next tab stop. (Tab stops are defined with **C-c TAB**, as usual.) **C-u TAB** also moves to the next tab stop, but erases text up to the next tab stop as well.

  - The rectangle commands **C-c C-k** and **C-c C-w** commands only erase a rectangle; they do not actually kill the rectangle unless you specify a numeric argument (for example, **C-u C-c C-k**).

  - The rectangle commands **C-c C-y** and **C-c C-x**, which yank a rectangle back into the buffer, *overwrite* the rectangle into the buffer.

Aligning the Cursor with "Interesting" Characters

Often it is desirable to line up the cursor with a particular character on the previous line; the **M-TAB** command can help you do this. For example, suppose you are drawing a box and have finished drawing the "top:"

```
    +--------------+
```

If you move the cursor to the next line and run **M-TAB**, the cursor moves to the column under the plus sign! This is because, by default, Emacs considers the plus, as well as several other characters, to be **interesting characters**. Interesting characters are characters that generally signify alignment boundaries in ASCII drawings. These characters are defined by the variable *picture-tab-chars*. The default value for this variable is **"!-~"**; that is, the set of all printable characters.

If you run **M-TAB** with an argument (**C-u M-TAB**), Emacs moves the cursor to the next interesting character on the current line.

Drawing Lines

As you type text in Picture mode, the cursor normally advances to the right. This default behavior allows you to draw a horizontal line by pressing the – or _ key several times in succession. But what if you wanted to draw line in another direction? For instance, what if you wanted to create a vertical line using | characters? Or an angled line using \ characters? Using the commands in Table 12.8, you can change the direction the cursor moves after inserting a character, allowing you to draw lines in directions other than horizontal and to the right. For instance, if you run **C-c .**, the cursor moves to the same column in the next line after you type a character. Thus, you could create a vertical line by typing | several times. You can then change direction using another command in Table 12.8.

After using these commands, you will want to return to the normal left-to-right method of entering characters by typing **C-c >**.

Table 12.8. Line-Drawing Direction Commands

After Inserting Character, Move...	Command
To the right one character (move "East"). This is the default direction when you first enter Picture mode.	**C-c >**
To the left one character (move "West").	**C-c <**

Table 12.8. Line-Drawing Direction Commands

After Inserting Character, Move...	Command
Up one line in the same column (move "North").	c–c ^
Down one line in the same column (move "South").	c–c .
Up one line and right one column (move "Northeast").	c–c '
Down one line and right one column (move "Southeast").	c–c \
Up one line and left one column (move "Northwest").	c–c `
Down one line and left one column (move "Southwest").	c–c /

As an example of using the above commands, suppose you want to draw an octagon (stop-sign shape) using _, |, /, and \ characters—for example:

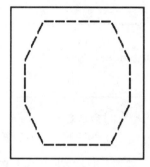

You might start by creating the left vertical side first, using the commands as shown below:

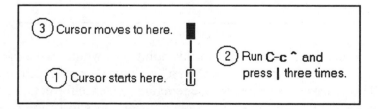

Next, you could create the upper-left side with these commands:

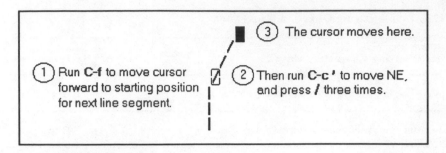

You can now create the top with these commands:

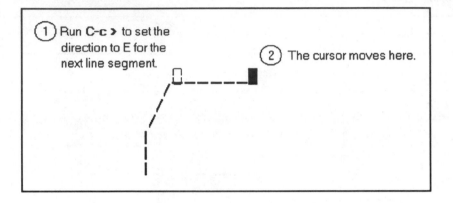

Now head down the upper-right side:

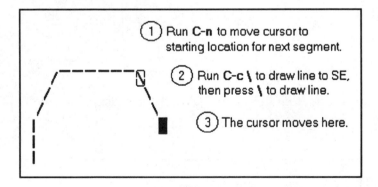

You get the picture (so to speak). From this point, you would make the lower-right edge by changing the direction to "Southwest" with the **C-c /** command and use **/** characters. The process is repeated for the remaining sides of the octagon. You might try doing this on your own to get the "feel" of using these direction commands for drawing lines. When finished, return to normal character entry by typing **C-c >**.

Doctor Mode

Last, and somewhere close to least, Emacs provides Doctor mode, an amusing (or irritating) mode (depending on your sense of humor) that prompts you with questions, as if you were being analyzed by an extremely bad psychotherapist. If you're having a lousy day, run **M-x doctor** to get some help (at least as valuable as what you paid for it). When you want to finish the session, press **RET** twice without typing anything in between.

Summary

Table 12.9 summarizes the main points from this chapter.

Table 12.9. Chapter 12 Summary

Topic	Summary
Checking your spelling	• Check word: **M-$** • Check buffer: **M-x spell-buffer** • Check region: **M-x spell-region** • Replace next occurrence of misspelling: **SPC** • Skip next occurrence of misspelling: **DEL**
Using Electric Command History	Commands: • Run Electric Command History: **M-x electric-command-history** • Move to next line: **RET** • Move to previous line: **DEL** • Rerun current command: **SPC** or **!** • Quit: **q** or **C-c C-c** or **C-]** • List all commands: **?** Variables: • Maximum number of commands: *list-command-history-max* • List of executed commands: *command-history* • Commands to exclude from history: *list-command-history-filter*

Table 12.9, con't.

Topic	Summary
Recovering files after system crashes and controlling auto-saving	Commands: • Recover auto-save file: **M-x recover-file** • Resave recovered file back into original file: **C-x C-s** • Force auto-save: **M-x do-auto-save** Variables: • Number of keystrokes before auto-save: *auto-save-interval* • Auto-save to visited file: *auto-save-visited-file-name* • Retain auto-save file after saving visited file: *delete-auto-save-files* (set to **nil**)
Using UNIX commands	Commands: • Run UNIX command: **M-!** • Run UNIX command and insert output into buffer: **C-u M-!** • Run UNIX command on text in region: **M-|** • Run UNIX command and replace region with output: **C-u M-|** • Run UNIX shell in window: **M-x shell** Shell Mode Commands: • Send line as input: **RET** • Kill line: **C-c C-u** • Kill previous word: **C-c C-w** • Re-type previous input: **C-c C-y** • Send EOF: **C-c C-d** • Send Control-C interrupt: **C-c C-c** • Stop the shell or process: **C-c C-z** • Send quit interrupt: **C-c C-** • Delete last output: **C-c C-o** • Scroll last output to top: **C-c C-r** Variables: • Shell used by Emacs: *shell-file-name*

Table 12.9, con't.

Topic	Summary
Nroff Major mode	• Enable Nroff major mode: `M-x nroff-mode` • Move to previous .bp command: `C-x [` • Move to next .bp command: `C-x ]` • Move to previous text line: `M-p` • Move to next text line: `M-n` • Display total number of text lines: `M-?` • Insert closing codes: `M-x electric-nroff-mode`
TeX and LaTeX modes	Commands: • Enable TeX mode and determine correct TeX mode: `M-x tex-mode` • Enable Plain TeX mode: `M-x plain-tex-mode` • Enable LaTeX mode: `M-x latex-mode` • Insert quote characters: `"` • Check balanced characters and create new paragraph: `LFD` • Insert balanced braces: `M-{` • Move past unmatched {: `M-}` • Insert \end for LaTeX block: `C-c C-f` • Pass region to TeX: `C-c C-r` • Pass buffer to TeX: `C-c C-b` • Center TeX output: `C-c C-l` • Print TeX output: `C-c C-p` • Show print queue: `C-c C-q` Variables: • Directory used for temporary files: *TeX-directory* • Command to print .dvi files: *TeX-dvi-print-command* • Command to show print queue: *TeX-show-queue-command*

Table 12.9, con't.

Topic	Summary
Picture mode	• Enable Picture Mode: `M-x picture-mode` • Exit Picture Mode: `C-c C-c` • Move cursor forward (always on same line): `C-f` • Move cursor to same column on previous line: `C-p` • Move cursor to same column on next line: `C-n` • Replace current character with blank: `C-d` • Replace previous character with blank: `DEL` • Erase all visible characters on line: `C-k` • Move to next tab stop: `TAB` • Move to next tab stop and erase: `C-u TAB` • Erase rectangle: `C-c C-k` and `C-c C-w` • Kill rectangle: `C-u C-c C-k` and `C-u C-c C-w` • Overwrite rectangle into buffer: `C-c C-y` and `C-c C-x` • Align with interesting characters: `M-TAB` • Align with interesting characters on this line: `C-u M-TAB` • Draw horizontal line: – or _ • Draw vertical line: | After inserting character, move: • East: `C-c >` • West: `C-c <` • North: `C-c ^` • South: `C-c .` • Northeast: `C-c '` • Southeast: `C-c \` • Northwest: `C-c ` ` •   Southwest: `C-c /` Variables: • List of interesting characters: *picture-tab-chars*
Doctor mode	• Run Doctor mode: `M-x doctor` • Escape from Doctor mode: press `RET` twice

Part 4
Customizing and Administering Emacs

This part of the book describes techniques for customizing the Emacs environment to suit your personal preferences, as well as tips for installing and maintaining Emacs. Some of the topics discussed here are considered advanced usage and may be of interest only to programmers and UNIX system administrators. Others, such as using variables to customize Emacs, will interest anyone who wants to change Emacs' default behavior. We recommend skimming the topics in Chapters 13 and 14 to find any topics that may interest you.

The following chapters are included in Part 4:

- Chapter 13: Customizing the Emacs Environment

- Chapter 14: Administering Emacs

13
Customizing the Emacs Environment

One of Emacs' most powerful features is its customizability. You can change virtually any existing functionality to suit your preferences and needs. Here the topics covered in this chapter:

- Using an `.emacs` start-up file

- Using variables to change Emacs' behavior

- Changing command key bindings

- Forcing confirmation for a function

- More about variables (advanced usage)

- More about key bindings (advanced usage)

- Examples of `.emacs` customizations

Using a .emacs Start-Up File

To customize Emacs' behavior, you can use special customization commands that prompt for customization parameters, or you can make calls to Emacs-Lisp functions in a `.emacs` start-up file in your home directory. Changes made via commands stay in effect for the current editing session only. To make changes permanent, use a `.emacs` file. Customizations included in this file are executed whenever you start Emacs.

Two common `.emacs` file customizations are setting variables and setting or changing key bindings, both of which are discussed in this chapter. Advanced users may also want to create new Emacs-Lisp functions and place them in the `.emacs` file as well. See Appendix B for a brief discussion of writing Emacs-Lisp functions.

The person who administers your Emacs system may have already created a `.emacs` file for you. If this is the case, you can peruse the file to see what customizations may have already been installed on your system.

Examples of modifying your `.emacs` file appear throughout this chapter. The last section, "Examples of .emacs Customizations," may prove especially helpful.

Using Variables to Change Emacs' Behavior

The behavior of various Emacs commands can be changed by modifying the value of Emacs **variables**. A variable is a symbol name that has an associated value. Typically, a variable has a numeric value, a string value, or is `nil`. Figure 13.1 shows three Emacs variables—*fill-column*, *initial-major-mode*, and *fill-prefix*—which have a numeric value, a string value, and a `nil` value, respectively.

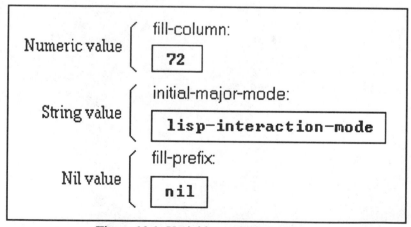

Figure 13.1. Variables and Their Values

Nil and T Values

When a variable has a `nil` value, its corresponding capability is **disabled.** For example, the *fill-prefix* is disabled by default, but when you assign it a value with the `C-x .` command (as described in "Filling Text" in Chapter 3), Emacs uses that value as the fill prefix for filled lines of text.

Any value other than `nil` is called a "non-`nil`" value. For variables whose effect is either enabled or disabled, a non-`nil` value will enable the feature, while a `nil` value disables it. Often a feature is enabled by setting a variable to `t` (shorthand for "true").

String Values

When specifying a string value for an Emacs variable, enclose it in double quotes. In addition, the following special characters can be included within strings:

`\n`	Newline
`\t`	Tab
`\e`	Escape
`\b`	Backspace
`\f`	Formfeed
`\"`	To embed a double quote
`\\`	To insert a backslash
`\ooo`	Insert the character whose octal code is *ooo*
`\C-`	Indicates a Control key (e.g., `\C-x` for Control-x)
`\M-`	Indicates a Meta key (e.g., `\M-w` for Meta-w)
`\M-\C-`	Indicates a Control-Meta key (e.g., `\M-\C-\` for Control-Meta-\)

Displaying a Variable's Value

All variables are assigned a default value when you start an Emacs session. To examine a variable's value, use `C-h v` or `M-x describe-variable`. Emacs prompts for the variable whose value you want to view and displays its value and a description of what it does in a help window. Type `C-x 1` to remove the help window.

For example, to examine the value of *fill-column*:

```
C-h v                                      ← Invoke the command.
Describe variable: fill-column RET         ← Type the variable name.
```

Emacs then displays information similar to the following text in another window:

```
fill-column's value is 70

Documentation:
fill-column
*Column beyond which automatic line-wrapping should happen.
Automatically becomes local when set in any fashion.
```

Interactively Setting a Variable

To set a variable's value interactively, use the **M-x set-variable** command, which prompts for the name of the variable. When specifying a string value to this prompt, be sure to enclose it in double quotes (as described above). When specifying **nil** or **t** or a numeric value, do *not* use quotes!

The **M-x set-variable** command changes the value of a variable for this session only. To make such changes permanent, you must set variables in your **.emacs** file (as described in the next subsection).

For example, to set the value of *fill-prefix* using **M-x set-variable** instead of the **C-x .** command:

```
M-x set variable RET              ← Invoke the command.
Set variable: fill-prefix RET     ← Type the variable name.
Set fill-prefix to value: ":-)" RET   ← Type the value, including the
                                          surrounding quotes.
```

Emacs often provides commands that set variables more efficiently. For example, the **C-x f** command sets the variable *fill-column* to the current cursor column, and the **C-x .** command sets the *fill-prefix* variable to the string preceding the cursor. But in many cases, the only way to set variables is with **M-x set-variable**.

Setting a Variable in Your .emacs File

To make a variable change permanent—that is, to make it take effect whenever you start up Emacs—you must set the variable in your **.emacs** start-up file. Values defined this way override the system defaults. To do this, use the Emacs-Lisp **setq** function. For instance, the following expression sets *comment-column* to 65:

```
(setq comment-column 65)
```

The enclosing parentheses are required. The **setq** function appears first, followed by the variable name, followed by the value. Any number of tabs or spaces can appear between the different pieces of the **setq** call; you could use this feature to align variable names and values in your **.emacs** file.

Once you've placed call to `setq` in your `.emacs` file, you must restart Emacs for the change to actually take effect. Alternatively, you could save the file and run `M-x load-file RET .emacs RET`, to evaluate the code without leaving Emacs.

Some Useful Variables

Table 13.1 lists some commonly modified variables that affect Emacs commands.

Table 13.1. Variables to Modify Behavior

Behavior	Variable and Comments
Case sensitivity during search and replace operations	*case-fold-search* Default: `t` By default, Emacs search and replace operations are not sensitive to letter case—`foo` is equal to `Foo` is equal to `FOO`. To make search operations case-sensitive, set this variable to `nil`.
	case-replace Default: `t` Controls how Emacs does letter case conversion during search-and-replace operations. If `t`, Emacs keeps letter case the same in a replacement string if the replacement string is lowercase; otherwise, Emacs gives the replaced string the same case as the replacement string. If this variable is `nil`, Emacs matches the letter case of the search string exactly and does not attempt to keep the letter case of any replaced strings.
Initial mode Emacs starts up in	*initial-major-mode* Default: `lisp-interaction-mode` Defines the mode of the `*scratch*` buffer. For example, to change the initial mode to Text mode, set this variable to `text-mode`.

Table 13.1, con't.

Behavior	Variable and Comments
Setting a major mode based on file name suffix	*auto-mode-alist* Default: See value displayed by `C-h v` on your system. This variable contains a list of file name suffixes and the corresponding mode that Emacs should use when loading a file with that suffix. For an example on using this variable, see the section "Examples of .emacs Customizations" later in this chapter.
Video attributes of mode line	*mode-line-inverse-video* Default: `t` If `nil`, the mode line is displayed in normal video (light characters on a dark background); otherwise, it is displayed in inverse video.
Video attributes of all lines	*inverse-video* Default: `nil` If a non-nil value (`t`) is used, Emacs attempts to invert the video attributes of all lines on the screen.
Visible bell	*visible-bell* Default: `nil` If non-nil, Emacs attempts to make the screen blink when it would otherwise ring the bell.
Meta key enabled	*meta-flag* Default: depends on the *termcap* entry for your terminal. If `nil`, the Meta key is disabled (you have to use `ESC` as the Meta key). Otherwise, Meta is enabled.
Line overlap for screen scrolling	*next-screen-context-lines* Default: `2` Controls the number of lines from the bottom (top) of a window that are kept when a window is scrolled down (up).

Table 13.1, con't.

Behavior	Variable and Comments
Cursor behavior at end-of-line	*track-eol* Default: `nil` If the cursor is at the end of a line and this variable is not `nil`, then `C-p` and `C-n` commands keep the cursor at the end of the line. Otherwise, Emacs moves the cursor to the closest vertical column.
Truncate continued lines	*truncate-lines* Default: `nil` If `nil`, lines wider than the window continue onto the next line and a backslash (\) is placed at the right margin to indicate continued lines. If a non-`nil` value is used, Emacs places a dollar sign ($) at the right-most column of each line that extends past right window margin, and the rest of the line is not displayed.
Delay before displaying keystrokes in echo area	*echo-keystrokes* Default: `1` Specifies the number of seconds Emacs waits before displaying an incomplete command keystroke in the echo area. If it is 0, Emacs does not echo keystrokes at all.
Display of control characters	*ctl-arrow* Default: `t` Normally, control characters are displayed with ^ followed by the corresponding character. For example, Control-L is shown as `^L`. To make Emacs display control characters as octal escape sequences (e.g., \014 instead of `^L`), set this variable to `nil`.
Fill column	*fill-column* Default: `70` Used with text filling commands. Filled text does not extend past this column. You can also set this with the `C-x f` command.

Table 13.1, con't.

Behavior	Variable and Comments
Incremental search special keys	*search-delete-char* Default: DEL Key to use to backspace in an incremental search string. The default value may cause problems if the backspace key is not DEL.
	search-exit-char Default: ESC Key to terminate incremental search.
	search-quote-char Default: C-q Command to use to insert control characters in a search string.
	search-reverse-char Default: C-r Command to use to continue search backward.
	search-yank-line-char Default: C-y Command to yank rest of line from buffer into search string.
	search-yank-word-char Default: C-w Command to yank next word from buffer into search string.
Regular expression to match end of sentence	*sentence-end* Default: use C-h v to determine. Contains a regular expression defining the pattern to match as the end of a sentence. (For details on regular expressions, see the section "Searching and Replacing Regexps" in Chapter 4, "Advanced Editing.")

Table 13.1, con't.

Behavior	Variable and Comments
Use spaces instead of tabs for indentation	*indent-tabs-mode* Default: **t** By default, tab characters are used in indentation. To allow only spaces in indentation, set this variable to nil.
Enable/disable Auto-Saving	*auto-save-default* Default: **t** When set to **nil**, turns off auto-saving; when **t**, turns on auto-saving (see Chapter 4).
Enable/disable Abbrev mode	*abbrev-mode* Default: **nil** When set to **nil**, turns off Abbrev mode; when **t**, turns on Abbrev mode (see Chapter 3).
Kill ring size	*kill-ring-max* Default: **30** Sets the number of blocks in the kill ring (see Chapter 3).

Changing Command Key Bindings

A **key binding** is a link between a command key sequence and an Emacs function. For example, the **C-n** key binds to the **next-line** function, the **C-x C-s** key sequence binds to the **save-buffer** function, and **C-x 4 b** binds to the function **switch-to-buffer-other-window**. Figure 13.2 illustrates this idea.

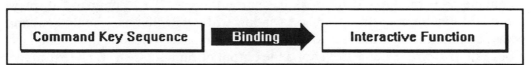

Figure 13.2. Command Key Binding

The function that a key sequence binds to is an **interactive function**, which means that the function can be executed via a command key sequence or **M-x**. (See Appendix B for details on interactive functions.) For example, as mentioned above, **C-n** binds to the **next-line** function. Since **next-line** is interactive, you could execute it using **M-x next-line** instead, although this isn't as convenient.

Some interactive functions are not bound to any key and, therefore, can only be executed with the **M-x** prefix. The **what-line** function is an example of such a function: Normally, you can execute this only with **M-x what-line**. Such functions are prime candidates for being bound to unused or unneeded command keys. For example, it might be useful to bind **goto-line** to a command key for quicker access.

Finding Free or Unneeded Key Bindings

Before setting a command key binding, you must know what command key sequence you can use. For example, you probably wouldn't want to bind a function to the **C-p** (previous line) command. Instead, you would want to use a command key sequence that is either unused by any functions, or that is bound to a function that you don't require. There are two commands you can use to determine what a particular command key sequence is bound to: **C-h k** and **C-h b**.

Viewing Individual Bindings The **C-h k** command prompts for a command key sequence and shows the function to which the key sequence is bound. If the key sequence is unbound, Emacs displays the message *key_sequence* **is undefined** in the echo area. This means that the key sequence is a good candidate for binding to a function. For instance, suppose you want to bind the command key sequence **C-x ?** to the **what-line** function, but only if **C-x ?** is not already in use. You could use **C-h k** as follows:

```
C-h k                          ← Invoke the command.
Describe key briefly: C-x ?    ← Type the key sequence C-x ?.
C-x ? is undefined             ← Emacs displays this in the minibuffer; the key
                                 sequence is not already in use.
```

Viewing All Key Bindings An alternative, and in some ways more convenient, method of viewing key bindings is to use the **C-h b** command, which displays all command key bindings defined in the current mode. This command displays command key bindings in a ***Help*** window with two columns: The first column shows command keys; the second shows the functions to which the command keys bind. For example, Figure 13.3 shows the output of running **C-h b** in Text mode. You could then scan this output, searching for command key sequences that aren't bound to any function.

```
Local Bindings:
key         binding
---         -------


ESC             Prefix Command
TAB             tab-to-tab-stop

ESC S           center-paragraph
ESC s           center-line


Global Bindings:

C-@             set-mark-command
C-a             beginning-of-line
C-b             backward-char
C-c             mode-specific-command-prefix
C-d             delete-char
C-e             end-of-line
C-f             forward-char
   .
   .
   .
```

Figure 13.3. Using C-h b to View Key Bindings

Local bindings are key bindings defined specifically for the current buffer. **Global bindings** are key bindings that apply to *all* buffers. For example, the above listing shows that **C-a** binds to the **beginning-of-line** function.

Local bindings provide a way for a mode to override global bindings: Whenever a local binding exists, it overrides the corresponding global binding. For example, the global binding for **TAB** is **indent-for-tab-command**. This is the binding used in Fundamental mode. However, other modes have a local binding for **TAB**, which overrides the global binding:

- Text mode sets the local binding to **tab-to-tab-stop**.

- C mode sets the local binding to **c-indent-command**.

- Lisp modes set the local binding to **lisp-indent-line**.

Notice also that the **C-h b** command groups command key bindings by command key prefix—that is, by the key that introduces a multiple-key sequence. The different groupings are:

1. **Single-character commands**—for example, C-p, TAB, C-a.

2. **Mode-specific commands**—commands that are unique to a specific mode. These commands begin with the C-c prefix. Examples of these commands are C-c C-n (next statement) in FORTRAN mode, C-c C-f (forward to same level) in Outline mode, and C-c > (move right after insertion) in Picture mode.

3. **Help commands**—commands that invoke various help functions. These commands begin with C-h. Examples of these commands are C-h v (describe variable), C-h f (describe function), and C-h b (list command key bindings).

4. **Control-X commands**—commands that begin with the C-x prefix. These commands are usually not mode-specific. Examples are C-x C-s (save buffer), C-x b (switch to buffer), and C-x f (set fill-column).

5. **Meta commands**—commands that begin with the ESC (M-) prefix. These commands are usually not mode-specific. Examples are M-$ (check spelling of word), M-w (move forward a word), and M-! (run shell command).

6. **Control-X-4 commands**—commands that begin with the C-x 4 prefix. These commands are usually not mode-specific. Examples are C-x 4 C-f (find file in another window), C-x 4 . (find a tag in another window), and C-x 4 d (run Dired in another window).

Setting Bindings Interactively

Table 13.2 summarizes the commands you can use to interactively change key bindings. Keep in mind that these commands apply only to the current editing session. To make permanent changes, you must modify your .emacs file, as described later in this section.

Table 13.2. Commands for Setting Key Bindings Interactively

Operation	Command and Comments
Set global key binding	`M-x global-set-key` Prompts for a command key sequence you want to rebind. Then prompts for the name of the function you want to bind it to. The change is made to global bindings, and applies to all modes, except modes that have a local binding for the key.

Table 13.2, con't.

Operation	Command and Comments
Set local key binding	`M-x local-set-key` Same as `M-x global-set-key`, but defines it as a local binding. The change applies to all buffers that use the mode in which the command was invoked.

For example, you may find it cumbersome to type `M-x compile` every time you compile a program. To bind the command key sequence `C-x C` to this command in *all* modes, use `M-x global-set-key` as follows:

```
M-x global-set-key              ← Invoke the command.
Set key globally: C-x C         ← Type C-x C.
Set key C-x C to command: compile   ← Type compile.
```

Now, for the duration of this Emacs session, when you type `C-x C`, Emacs invokes the `compile` function. As another example, suppose you want to bind `C-x ?` to the `what-line` function, but only in the current mode. You would do it this way:

```
M-x local-set-key               ← Invoke the command.
Set key locally: C-x ?          ← Type C-x ?.
Set key C-x C to command: what-line   ← Type what-line.
```

If you run this command in Text mode, `C-x ?` is bound to `what-line` in every buffer that uses Text mode. However, this binding will not be visible to other buffers.

Setting Bindings in Your .emacs File

Several Emacs-Lisp functions deal with setting command key bindings. However, one—the `global-set-key` function—is sufficient for most users. (Yes, this is the same function that Emacs executes when you run `M-x global-set-key`.) This function takes two arguments: a string defining the key sequence, and the name of the function the key sequence binds to. For example, to bind the `C-x @` key sequence to the `goto-line` function, include this line in your `.emacs` file:

```
(global-set-key "\C-x@" 'goto-line)
```

The function name must be preceded by a single quote; this tells Emacs that the parameter is a symbol name.

The command key sequence is a string enclosed in double quotes. Shown below are the ways to represent the different types of prefix keys in this string:

\C-	Single-character control keys (e.g., "\C-a" for C-a)
\M-	Meta keys (e.g., "\M-z" for M-z, and "\M-\C-x" for C-M-x)
\C-x	Key sequences that start with C-x (e.g., "\C-x?" for C-x ?)
\C-x4	Key sequences that start with C-x 4 (e.g., "\C-x4$" for C-x 4 $)
\C-c	Key sequences that start with C-c (e.g., "\C-cC" for C-c C)
\C-h	Help keys (e.g., "\C-h!" for C-h !)

As another example, the following line would bind **compile** function (normally run by **M-x compile**) to the **C-c C** command:

```
(global-set-key "\C-cC" 'compile)
```

Forcing Confirmation for a Function

In some cases (mostly for novice users), you may want Emacs to ask for confirmation before executing a particular function. For example, the **kill-abbrevs** function undefines all defined abbreviations, but it kills them without asking your approval.

To force Emacs to ask for confirmation before executing a function, use **M-x disable-command**. It prompts you for the name of the function for which you want confirmation. Then it modifies your **.emacs** start-up file, adding Emacs-Lisp code that will force confirmation for the command whenever you enter Emacs again. The following forces confirmation for the **kill-all-abbrevs** command:

```
M-x disable-command
Disable command: kill-all-abbrevs          ← Type kill-all-abbrevs.
Wrote /users/caroline/.emacs               ← Emacs updates your .emacs file.
```

The function call that Emacs places in your **.emacs** file looks like this:

```
(put 'kill-all-abbrevs 'disabled t)
```

Now if you run **M-x kill-all-abbrevs**, Emacs displays the following information in another window:

```
You have invoked the disabled command kill-all-abbrevs:
Undefine all defined abbrevs.

You can now type Space to try the command just this once,  but
leave it disabled, Y to try it and enable it (no questions if you
use it again), N to do nothing (command remains disabled).
```

And Emacs prompts in the minibuffer with:

```
Type y, n, or space: █
```

If the last parameter is a string, Emacs displays that string as part of the confirmation message. For example,

```
(put 'kill-all-abbrevs 'disabled "No restoring killed abbrevs!\n")
```

causes Emacs to display the message:

```
You have invoked the disabled command kill-all-abbrevs:
No restoring killed abbrevs!
Undefine all defined abbrevs.

You can now type
Space to try the command just this once, but leave it disabled,
Y to try it and enable it (no questions if you use it again),
N to do nothing (command remains disabled).
```

More About Variables (Advanced Usage)

This section describes some advanced Emacs features that deal with variables:

- Global (default) and local variables
- Making a variable local to a buffer
- Examining a variable's default value
- Using local variable lists for specific files
- Viewing and editing lists of options

Global (Default) and Local Variables

A variable can have a global value, local value, or both. A **global** value is "visible" to all buffers that reference the variable. A **local** value is "visible" only in a buffer in which it is defined and takes precedence over the global value. For example, the variable *fill-column* has a global value and local value. When Emacs creates a new buffer, it assigns a local value to *fill-column*, taken from the global value. Thereafter, if you modify the *fill-column* variable, the local value is used and the global value ignored. In this way, a global value can be said to be the default value.

Relatively few variables have local values; some of the important ones are: *abbrev-mode*, *case-fold-search*, *comment-column*, *ctl-arrow*, *fill-column*, *fill-prefix*, *indent-tabs-mode, left-margin, mode-line-format, overwrite-mode, selective-display-ellipses, selective-display, tab-width*, and *truncate-lines*.

Making a Variable Local to a Buffer

Table 13.3 summarizes the commands for creating and killing local variables.

Table 13.3. Commands for Making Variables Local

Operation	Command and Comments
Make variable local	`M-x make-local-variable` Emacs prompts for the name of a variable that you want to have a local value in the current buffer. Thereafter, when you change the variable's value, only the local copy is changed, and only in the current buffer.
Kill local variable	`M-x kill-local-variable` Emacs prompts for the name of a variable that has a local value. Thereafter, the variable no longer has a local value, and the global value is used instead.
Make variable local if set	`M-x make-variable-buffer-local` Emacs prompts for the name of a variable that you want to become local when you set its value. That is, Emacs postpones making the variable local until its value is set.

Note: Changing major modes kills all local variables. Therefore, if you switch back to a mode that had local variables, they will no longer be in effect.

Setting and Examining a Variable's Default Value

If a variable has both a local and global value, then setting its value with **M-x set-variable** sets only the local value. In such cases, you may still want to set the variable's global (default) value. To do this, evaluate the following Emacs-Lisp expression

```
(setq-default name value)
```

For example, every buffer has a local copy of *fill-column*. To set the default value to 79, you could use the **M–ESC** command to evaluate the following expression:

```
(setq-default fill-column 79)
```

To view a variable's default value, you can evaluate with **M–ESC**:

```
(default-value 'name)
```

For example, to view the default value of *case-fold-search*, evaluate with **M–ESC**:

```
(default-value 'case-fold-search)
```

On our system, the default is **t**, meaning the letter case is not significant when searching for strings.

Using Local Variable Lists for Specific Files

Occasionally you may have a file for which you always use a unique set of option values. In such a case, you can either set the options explicitly every time you use the file, which could become quite tedious. Or you can include a **variable list** at the end of the file, which Emacs reads and evaluates when visiting the file. The general form of a variable list is:

[*prefix*] `Local Variables:` [*suffix*]	← Marks the start of the variable list
[*prefix*] *mode*: *name* [*suffix*]	← Optional line specifying the mode.
[*prefix*] *name*: *value* [*suffix*]	← Optional lines specifying variable.
[*prefix*] *name*: *value* [*suffix*]	names and values.
[*prefix*] *eval*: *expression* [*suffix*]	← Optional lines specifying
[*prefix*] *eval*: *expression* [*suffix*]	Emacs-Lisp expressions to evaluate.
[*prefix*] `End:` [*suffix*]	

This may look intimidating, but is actually quite simple. To mark the start of the list, the first line contains the string `Local Variables:`; to mark the end of the list, the last line contains the string `End:`. In between these lines, you can place *name:value* pairs (in any order). For example, the following *name:value* pair sets the *case-fold-search* variable to **nil**:

```
case-fold-search:nil
```

The [*prefix*] and [*suffix*] mean that each line can have an optional prefix string, suffix string, or both. This allows you to include these lines within comment delimiters that are appropriate for the mode you've chosen. For example, to include the variable list inside of C-style comments (**/* */**):

```
/* Local Variables: */
/* case-fold-search:nil */
/* End: */
```

The prefix and suffix must be the same on each line. In addition to name:value pairs, you can have these lines:

- **mode:***name*

    where *name* is the name of the mode to use for the file. If present, the mode specification should appear before other lines in the variable list. The following mode declaration tells Emacs to use Emacs-Lisp mode:

    ```
    mode:emacs-lisp
    ```

    Incidentally, this line has the same effect as the following mode specification line at the start of the file:

    ```
    ;;; -*-emacs-lisp-*-
    ```

- **eval:***expression*

    where *expression* is an Emacs-Lisp expression to evaluate on visiting the file. For example, the following line would set the *fill-column* to 75:

    ```
    eval:(setq fill-column 75)
    ```

Note: In order for Emacs to read and evaluate a variable list, it must start within 3,000 characters of the end of the file. In addition, if the file contains page breaks (**^L** characters), the variable list must fall after the last page break.

Table 13.4 shows some example variable lists and what they do.

Table 13.4. Example Variable Lists

Variable List	Description
`Local Variables:` `End:`	An empty variable list with no prefix or suffix. There is no good reason for doing this other than to show it can be done.

Table 13.4, con't.

Variable List	Description

`## Local Variables:`
`## mode:text`
`## End:`
	A list that sets the buffer's mode to Text mode. The list also uses a prefix ("`## `").

`/* Local Variables: */`
`/* mode:c */`
`/* fill-column:79 */`
`/* eval:(setq comment-column 50) */`
`/* End: */`
	A list that sets the mode to C, the *fill-column* to 79, and evaluates an expression to set the *comment-column* to 50. The prefix and suffix are the C comment delimiters.

Viewing and Editing Lists of Options

Certain Emacs variables are known as **options**—specifically, variables that are defined by the **defvar** function, and whose documentation string starts with an asterisk. For example, the following call to **defvar** creates an option variable named *my-foo* with value **nil** and option string **"*Oh my goodness!"**:

```
(defvar my-foo nil "*Oh my goodness!")
```

For details on **defvar**, see Appendix B, "Emacs-Lisp Programming."

Sometimes you may want to view or change several options at once. In such cases, using the above commands one at a time for each option could get tedious. Emacs provides commands for viewing and changing multiple options in a special buffer named ***List Options***. Table 13.5 summarizes the commands for bringing up a ***List Options*** buffer.

Table 13.5. Creating the *List Options* Buffer

Operation	Command and Comments
Create `*List Options*` buffer	`M-x list-options` Creates a window for the `*List Options*` buffer, but does not select the window.

Table 13.5, con't.

Operation	Command and Comments
Create and select `*List Options*` buffer	`M-x edit-options` Same as `M-x list-options`, except that it selects the `*List Options*` buffer immediately.

Figure 13.4 shows what the `*List Options*` buffer might look like when you run one of the above commands. Each option's value and documentation string is displayed. In this example, two options are shown:

- *display-time-and-date* has a value of `nil`. The documentation string indicates that the variable controls the display of the day and date in the mode line. Setting the variable to a non-`nil` value, such as `t`, will cause the day and date to be displayed.

- *display-time-echo-area* also is `nil`. If this variable is set to a non-`nil` value, Emacs displays the date and time in the echo area (minibuffer) instead of the mode line.

```
;;
;; display-time-day-and-date:
      nil
*Non-nil means M-x display-time should display day and date as well
as time.
;;
;; display-time-echo-area:
      nil
*Non-nil means display time in the echo area instead of the mode line.
Note that using the minibuffer clears the time display until the next
time the clock updates.




----- Emacs: *List Options*     7:08pm 0.03 Mail    (Options)----46%-----
```

Figure 13.4. The *List Options* Buffer

Options mode provides special commands for scrolling through the options list and changing option values, summarized in Table 13.6.

Table 13.6. Options Mode Commands

Operation	Command and Comments
Move to next	**n** Move to the next option in the list.
Move to previous	**p** Move to the previous option in the list.
Toggle value	**x** If the option's value is **t**, change it to **nil**. If the option's value is **nil**, change it to **t**. Use this only with variables that have a **t** or **nil** value.
Set to **t**	**1** Set the option's value to **t**.
Set to **nil**	**0** Set the option's value to **nil**.
Edit value	**s** Edit the option's value. Use this command with variables that have string or numeric values.

More About Key Bindings (Advanced Usage)

This section provides additional details on setting key bindings with Emacs-Lisp.

Key bindings are implemented using Emacs-Lisp objects called **keymaps**. The highest level keymap is the **global-map**, which is a vector of length 128. Each entry in the vector is the name of a function to which the corresponding key is bound. That is, when you press a key, its ASCII value (in the range 0 to 127) acts as an index into global-map to the function to execute when that key is pressed.

This is true even for non-control characters, such as **1**, **a**, and **<**. Such printable ASCII characters bind to the function **self-insert-command**, which simply inserts the character into the buffer. The following line, displayed by the **C-h b** command, shows that all characters between the space and the tilde, inclusive, call this function:

```
Global Bindings:
   .
   .
   .
SPC .. ~            self-insert-command
```

Characters that do *not* bind to any function (for example, **C-z**, **C-**, and **C-^**) are bound to the symbol **nil**. If you type such characters, Emacs beeps, indicating that they are not bound to a function. Such characters do not show up in the global key map displayed by the **C-h b** command. Similarly, some keys may be bound to the function **undefined**, which has the same effect as being bound to **nil**, except that they *do* appear when you run **C-h b**.

You can view the value of *global-map* with **C-h v** (describe variable). Shown below is the partial output of this command on our system. It shows that key code 0 (**C-@**) binds to the **set-mark-command** function, key code 1 (**C-a**) binds to **beginning-of-line**, key code 2 (**C-b**) binds to **backward-char**, etc., up to key code 127 (**DEL**), which binds to **delete-backward-char**. (A **key code** is the numeric code that is sent to Emacs when you press a key.)

```
                          Key Code 0        Key Code 1       Key Code 2
                       ┌──────────────┐  ┌──────────────┐ ┌──────────────┐  ...
global-map's value is [set-mark-command beginning-of-line backward-char
mode-specific-command-prefix delete-char end-of-line forward-char
keyboard-quit help-command indent-for-tab-command newline-and-indent
kill-line recenter newline next-line open-line previous-line quoted-insert
isearch-backward isearch-forward transpose-chars universal-argument scroll-up
kill-region Control-X-prefix yank nil ESC-prefix nil abort-recursive-edit nil
undo self-insert-command self-insert-command
   .
   .
   .
delete-backward-char]
└──────────────────┘
       Key Code 127
```

How Emacs Handles Prefix Keys

A **prefix key** is a key that leads in to a multiple-key command sequence. For instance, in the **C-x C-s** command, **C-x** is a prefix key. **C-x**, **C-h** (for help commands), **ESC** (for **M-** commands), and **C-c** (custom mode commands) are prefix keys. In addition, **4** is a prefix key when it follows **C-x** (for example, **C-x 4 f**).

In **global-map**, prefix keys bind to a special kind of function, whose definition is actually another keymap. When you press a prefix key, Emacs waits for you to press a key defined in the prefix keymap. If the second key you press is not defined (**nil**) in the prefix keymap, Emacs beeps. Table 13.7 defines the prefix keymaps that are directly accessible through **global-map**.

Table 13.7. Prefix Keymaps

Prefix Key	Binds to Function	Expands to Prefix Key Map
C-x	Control-X-prefix	*ctl-x-map*
C-h	help-command	*help-map*
ESC	ESC-prefix	*esc-map*
C-c	mode-specific-command-prefix	*mode-specific-map*

An additional level of indexing is provided in *ctl-x-map*. The entry for the character **4** binds to *ctl-x-4-prefix*, which expands to *ctl-x-4-map*. This is how you get the **C-x 4** ... commands. Figure 13.5 summarizes how the prefix keys bind to prefix key maps.

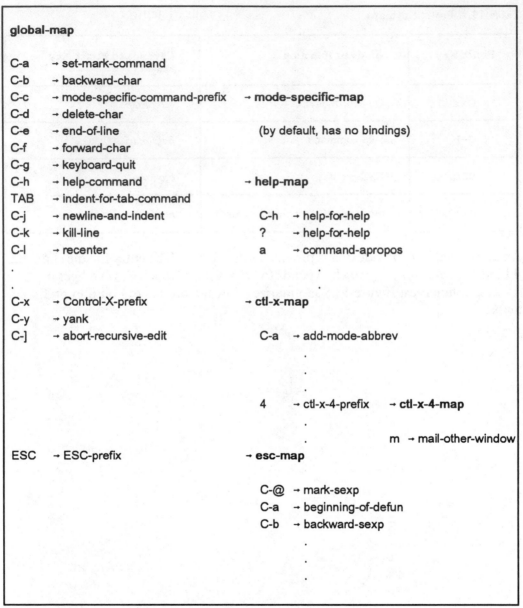

global-map

C-a	→ set-mark-command		
C-b	→ backward-char		
C-c	→ mode-specific-command-prefix	→ **mode-specific-map**	
C-d	→ delete-char		
C-e	→ end-of-line	(by default, has no bindings)	
C-f	→ forward-char		
C-g	→ keyboard-quit		
C-h	→ help-command	→ **help-map**	
TAB	→ indent-for-tab-command		
C-j	→ newline-and-indent	C-h → help-for-help	
C-k	→ kill-line	? → help-for-help	
C-l	→ recenter	a → command-apropos	

```
C-x     → Control-X-prefix          → ctl-x-map
C-y     → yank
C-]     → abort-recursive-edit       C-a   → add-mode-abbrev
                                          .
                                          .
                                          .
                                      4     → ctl-x-4-prefix    → ctl-x-4-map
                                          .
                                          .            m  → mail-other-window
ESC     → ESC-prefix                 → esc-map

                                      C-@   → mark-sexp
                                      C-a   → beginning-of-defun
                                      C-b   → backward-sexp
                                          .
                                          .
                                          .
```

Figure 13.5. How Prefix Keys Work

What Are Sparse Keymaps?

Like *global-map*, the keymaps *ctl-x-map*, *esc-map*, and *ctl-x-4* are implemented as vectors of length 128. However, the keymaps *help-map* and *mode-specific-map* are implemented as **sparse keymaps**. A sparse keymap is an Emacs-Lisp list whose **car** is the symbol **keymap** and whose **rest** is elements of the form **(char . binding)**.

Using **C-h v** to view the *help-map* variable on our system produced the output shown in Figure 13.6.

```
help-map's value is (keymap (118 . describe-variable)
  (119 . where-is) (116 . help-with-tutorial)
  (115 . describe-syntax) (110 . view-emacs-news)
  (14 . view-emacs-news) (109 . describe-mode)
  (108 . view-lossage)  (105 . info) (102 . describe-function)
  (100 . describe-function)  (107 . describe-key)
  (99 . describe-key-briefly) (98 . describe-bindings)
  (97 . command-apropos) (23 . describe-no-warranty)
  (4 . describe-distribution) (3 . describe-copying)
  (63 . help-for-help)  (8 . help-for-help))


Documentation:
Keymap for characters following the Help key.
```

Figure 13.6. Description of the help-map Variable

So, for instance, the key code 118 (**v**) binds to **describe-variable**; key code 119 (**w**) binds to **where-is**; and key code 116 (**t**) binds to **help-with-tutorial**.

Sparse keymaps are used for small keymaps; they save space. It is helpful to know the general format of sparse keymaps if you ever have to modify one. However, Emacs commands for changing key bindings hide the underlying implementation from the user; that is, you don't have to understand their syntax to change them.

Local Keymaps

Global keymaps are available to all modes. Occasionally, though, it is useful to define key bindings only for a particular mode. **Local keymaps** define local bindings. When you run the **M-x local-set-key** command, it modifies the local keymap.

Each major mode has a local keymap. In general, a local keymap's name is *modename*-map. For example, the local map for C mode is named *c-mode-map*, the local map for Text mode is *text-mode-map*, and the local map for Lisp modes is *lisp-mode-map*.

Key bindings in a local keymap override the global bindings. For example, *global-map* binds **TAB** to the function **indent-for-tab-command**. But this mapping is overridden in C mode because *c-mode-map* binds **TAB** to the function **c-indent-command**. Thus, if you press **TAB** in C mode, Emacs runs the local binding **c-indent-command**; the global binding is ignored.

Local keymaps are usually sparse keymaps. You can view local keymaps by running either **C-h b** (show bindings for current mode) or **C-h v** (describe the local keymap variable).

Prefix keys can also appear in local maps. Major modes use this feature to override the definitions of certain commands that start with **C-x**. However, prefix keys are treated differently than other single-character keys in the local map. If a prefix key is defined in both the global and local map, Emacs checks the next character typed against the corresponding global and local prefix keymaps. If the next character is defined in the local prefix keymap, its binding is used; otherwise, Emacs uses the global binding.

Using Emacs-Lisp to Set Bindings

Table 13.8 summarizes the Emacs-Lisp functions you can use to set key bindings. You could include these functions in your `.emacs` start-up file to make them apply to each editing session.

The command parameter to these functions is an Emacs-Lisp string representing the command key sequence binding.

Table 13.8. Emacs-Lisp Commands for Setting Key Bindings

Operation	Function Syntax and Comments
Set binding in global keymap	`(global-set-key` *command* `'` *function*`)` Binds the *command* key sequence to the specified *function*. `global-set-key` automatically sets the binding in the appropriate keymap, based on the prefix characters in the command string. For example, if *command* is `\C-z`, Emacs sets the binding in *global-map*; if *command* is `\C-xC`, Emacs sets the binding in *ctl-x-map*; and if *command* is `\M-\C-%`, Emacs sets it in *esc-map*.
Set binding in any map	`(define-key` *keymap* *command* `'` *symbol*`)` Similar to `global-set-key`, except that you specify which *keymap* to set the binding in.

Table 13.8, con't.

Operation	Function Syntax and Comments
Search and replace all bindings to a function	`(substitute-key-definition 'function1 'function2 keymap)` Searches for and replaces all bindings to *function1* with *function2* in the specified *keymap*.
Unset a global key binding	`(global-unset-key command)` Removes any global binding associated with the key sequence. This is useful when you want to rebind a key to be a prefix. Before you can do this, you must remove any special meaning the key currently has. In vector keymaps, it sets the entry to `nil`. In sparse keymaps, it removes the `(keycode . symbol)` pair from the keymap.

Shown below are some examples of using each function:

```
(global-set-key "\C-xC" 'compile)
```

> Binds the key sequence **C-x C** to the **compile** function. Eliminates having to type **M-x compile**.

```
(define-key text-mode-map "\C-c?" 'what-line)
```

> Binds the key sequence **C-c ?** to the **what-line** function, only in Text mode.

```
(define-key c-mode-map "\C-^" 'goto-line)
```

> Binds the key **C-^** to the **goto-line** function, only in C mode.

```
(substitute-key-definition 'fortran-next-statement
                           'next-line fortran-mode-map)
```

> Replaces all current bindings to **fortran-next-statement** with **next-line**, only in FORTRAN mode.

Examples of .emacs Customizations

This section lists example customizations that you can add to your start-up file. Some of the examples are Emacs-Lisp functions; see Appendix B for additional information.

```
(setq default-major-mode 'text-mode)
```

Makes Emacs use Text mode as the major mode for files whose names do not have a distinguishing suffix. Normally, Emacs would use Fundamental mode.

```
(setq-default fill-column 79)
```

Sets the default fill column to 79. The usual default value is 70.

```
(setq text-mode-hook 'turn-on-auto-fill)
```

Causes Emacs to turn on Auto Fill minor mode whenever Text mode is enabled. The variable *text-mode-hook* is expected to contain the name of an Emacs-Lisp function that is called whenever the specified mode is enabled. There are similar variables for other modes (for example, *c-mode-hook*, *lisp-mode-hook*, etc).

```
(global-set-key "\C-x?" 'what-line)
```

Binds **C-x** ? to the **what-line** function—same as using **M-x what-line**.

```
(global-set-key "\C-x_" 'goto-line)
```

Binds **C-x** _ to the **goto-line** function—same as using **M-x goto-line**.

```
(put 'kill-all-abbrevs 'disabled t)
```

Forces confirmation (yes or no) before executing **M-x kill-all-abbrevs**.

```
(defun goto-midpoint ()
  (interactive)
  (save-restriction
    (widen)
    (goto-char (/ (- (point-max)
                     (point-min))
                2))))
(global-set-key "\C-^" 'goto-midpoint)
```

Defines the Emacs-Lisp defun **goto-midpoint**, which moves the cursor to the middle line in the buffer (see the previous section on writing your own functions). It then binds the key **C-^** to this new function.

```
(defun goto-pct (pct)
  (interactive "NPercent location: ")
  (let ((pct-loc (cond ((< pct    0) 0)
                       ((> pct 100) 100)
                       (   t        pct))))
    (goto-char (/ (* pct-loc (point-max)) 100))))
```

Defines a function named goto-pct that moves the cursor to a percent location within a buffer. Invoked as **M-x goto-pct**, this function prompts for the percent location with **Percent location:** in the echo area.

```
(setq auto-mode-alist
      (cons '("\\.C\\'" . c-mode) auto-mode-alist))
```

Causes Emacs to use C mode for any file whose name ends in an uppercase "C."

```
(setq auto-mode-alist
      (cons '("\\.txt\\'" . text-mode) auto-mode-alist))
```

Tells Emacs to use Text mode by default for any file whose name ends in .txt.

```
(condition-case ()
   (read-abbrev-file nil t)
  (file-error nil))
(setq text-mode-hook
      (function
       (lambda () setq abbrev-mode t))))
```

One of the more advanced customizations, this one enables Abbrev minor mode for any Text mode buffer. You could enable Abbrev minor mode for any other mode using the same code, but substituting a different mode name for **text-mode**. For example, the following code enables Abbrev minor mode for C mode:

```
(condition-case ()
   (read-abbrev-file nil t)
  (file-error nil))
(setq c-mode-hook
      (function
       lambda () setq abbrev-mode t))))
```

Summary

Table 13.9 summarizes the main points of this chapter.

Table 13.9. Chapter 13 Summary

Topic	Summary
`.emacs` start-up file	Resides in your home directory. Contains Emacs-Lisp code that Emacs "installs" when you start up. Definitions in this file override system defaults. You may have a `.emacs` that is maintained by your Emacs administrator.
Display variable values	`C-h v` or `M-x describe-variable` to see variable's value and documentation.
Set variable interactively	`M-x set-variable RET` *variable-name* `RET` *value* `RET`

Variable values	• To enable some features: `t`
	• To disable some features: `nil`
	• String values:
	    • Enclose in double quotes.
	    • Special characters in strings:
	
	      `\n` Newline
	      `\t` Tab
	      `\b` Backspace
	      `\e` Escape
	      `\f` Formfeed
	      `\\` Backslash
	      `\`*ooo* Octal value *ooo*
	      `\C-` Control character
	      `\M-` Meta character

Setting a variable in `.emacs`	Use Emacs-Lisp `setq` function: `(setq` *var-name value*`)`
Setting command key bindings interactively	• Use `M-x global-set-key` to set for all buffers. • Use `M-x local-set-key` to set for this buffer.

Table 13.9, con't.

Topic	Summary
Setting bindings in `.emacs`	• Use `global-set-key` to set global binding. • Use `define-key` to set for specific keymap. • Use `global-unset-key` to turn off binding.
Forcing conformation for a function	Use `M-x disable-command.`

14
Administering Emacs

This chapter discusses miscellany that you may find useful in maintaining Emacs. This chapter is written primarily for the system administrator but may provide useful information for other users as well. The main topics discussed here are:

- Finding Emacs and identifying its parts
- Using News (or Notes) to get information
- Installing Emacs

Finding Emacs and Identifying Its Parts

Emacs may already exist on your system. The simplest way to determine if Emacs is already installed is to try to run it by typing **emacs** at the shell prompt:

```
$ emacs
```

If you get an error message such as "Command not found", or if Emacs simply does not start up, you may have any of the following situations:

- Emacs is not installed on your system.

- The executable program named **emacs** does not work. If this is true, you may have gotten a different message.

- Your PATH variable does not include the path name of the directory where Emacs resides in the system.

- Emacs exists on the system, but goes by another name. On systems we tested, Emacs had names such as **gnu-emacs, maclisp, gnuvo,** and **x11macs.** The Emacs command is not always named **emacs.**

Emacs Is Not a Supported Product

The Free Software Foundation (FSF) provides no support GNU Emacs. If you install the software for Emacs, you will see that the Free Software Foundation has a disclaimer (accessible through the **C-h w** command) that denies any support of the product.

Where Does Emacs Reside?

There is no standard location for Emacs. However, if Emacs exists on your system, you can find its location using the **whereis** command:

```
$ whereis emacs
```

If the command finds the file, you get a message such as:

```
emacs:   /usr/local/bin/emacs
```

If your system does not have this executable file by any name you tried, your system probably does not have the Emacs environment. You will need to install it (see "Installing Emacs" later in this chapter).

Finding the Other Emacs Files

In addition to the **emacs** executable, Emacs comes with myriad other files (documentation, tools, help files, Emacs-Lisp libraries, and so on). If Emacs is running, you can determine the location of Emacs files by viewing the variable *exec-directory*. For example, running the **C-h v exec-directory** command on our system displayed the following:

```
exec-directory's value is "/usr/local/emacs/etc/"

Documentation:
exec-directory
Directory that holds programs that come with GNU Emacs,
intended for Emacs to invoke.
```

The person who installed Emacs should know the actual locations of the files if you are unable to view the value of the *exec-directory* variable. Although there could be almost any path to the files, one thing is usually true about the location: The path name ends with **emacs**.

Under the **emacs** directory, you may find the following subdirectories:

doc	Contains files such as **emacs.emacs** (the default Emacs start-up file), **makeref**, and **texdoc.sed**.
etc	Contains executable files for maintaining and customizing the Emacs environment.
info	Contains information files related to Emacs.
lisp	Contains libraries of Emacs-Lisp code used by Emacs and by programs developed in Emacs-Lisp. Files in this directory are essential to the execution of Emacs.
lock	Contains lock files for preventing simultaneous editing. The directory is empty except when a user has modified a visited buffer. The lock files are controlled by the *ask-user-about-lock* function.
templates	Contains language-related templates to facilitate programming.

More on the Emacs etc Directory

Besides having the files mentioned above, the **etc** directory contains files that have potentially valuable information. Table 14.1 summarizes these files.

Table 14.1. Files in the etc Directory

File Name	Description
APPLE	The Apple new look report.
DISTRIB	Information about the availability of GNU Emacs. This may have information about version 19.
FAQ	Has answers for frequently asked question about GNU Emacs.
FTP	Explains how to get software that runs on Emacs via the UNIX UUCP or FTP facilities.
GNU	Contains the GNU manifesto. Every Emacs user should read this file for the philosophy of the Free Software Foundation.
INTERVIEW	The text from a discussion between Richard Stallman and the editors of *Byte* magazine concerning his views on UNIX-compatible software.
MACHINES	Lists the machines and systems on which GNU Emacs is supported.
MAILINGLISTS	Contains mailing lists for GNU projects.
OPTIONS	Describes in detail how command line options work.
SERVICE	Contains a GNU service directory.
SUN-SUPPORT	Contains tools for GNU Emacs.
DIFF	Differences between GNU Emacs and Twenex Emacs.
CCADIFF	Differences between GNU Emacs and Gosling Emacs.
COPYING	Contains the GNU Emacs General Public License.
TUTORIAL	Contains the text of the online tutorial used by C-h t.

Table 14.1, con't.

File Name	Description
NEWS	Is the GNU Emacs history of user-visible changes to Emacs.

Using News (or Notes) to Get Emacs Information

Your UNIX system may be able to use the News (or Notes) facility, which is widely used among the UNIX community as a forum for discussing all sorts of topics. If your system can access News, you can get abundant information about Emacs by visiting an Emacs news group.

From our system, we have access to the news groups named **comp.emacs**, **alt.emacs.gnews**, and **gnu.emacs**. The News facility provides commands for reading and processing the notes in a notestring. We suggest you investigate this on your own, knowing that reading News may provide a wealth of information about Emacs, especially information about installation, customizations, extensions, removing bugs, and getting maximum performance from your environment.

Installing Emacs

If your system does not have the Emacs files, or if you have the files but want to obtain newer versions, you have several alternatives for getting the software. In no order of importance, we suggest the following methods:

- Have another system administrator copy the files on to your system.

- If your system is on the Internet, use the FTP facility to obtain the software via the **anonymous** remote login. When we wrote this book, the host machine was named **rep.ai.mit.edu**. The file named

  ```
  /u2/emacs/GETTING.GNU.SOFTWARE
  ```

  had information about how to obtain the software. The later section, "Using Anonymous FTP to Get Files," contains information on using anonymous FTP.

- Write to the Free Software Foundation for information about getting Emacs:

  Free Software Foundation
  675 Massachusetts Avenue
  Cambridge MA 02139

Although you may see several indications that Emacs is free, you *will* be charged a distribution fee. In addition, you receive *only the source* for Emacs—you do *not* get binary executables. You must compile the source to create the executable **emacs** program. This process can vary greatly from platform to platform and is beyond the scope of this book. The files you receive from the FSF contain some information on how to compile the source. This underscores the desirability of getting the Emacs binary and files from someone else who already has it running on their system.

Getting Help on Installation

If you get the source files from FSF but are unable or unwilling to create the binary executables yourself, you can get help from various individuals or organizations outlined in the Emacs distribution file **etc/SERVICE**. You can obtain this file (and the other files stored in the Emacs **etc** directory) via anonymous FTP from **prep.ai.mit.edu**; the files are stored in the **/pub/gnu/etc** directory.

Using Anonymous FTP to Get Files

If you are unfamiliar with using anonymous FTP, this section will show you a sample session used to obtain a file from the **prep.ai.mit.edu** server. To log in anonymously to this system, specify the user name **anonymous** and use your mail address as the password. For example, suppose your login is **phred** on the system **headcheez**; shown below is the series of commands you would use to gain access to the GNU archive system. (The underlined text is what you type.)

```
$ ftp prep.ai.mit.edu
Connected to prep.ai.mit.edu
220 prep.ai.mit.edu FTP server (Version ...)
Name (prep.ai.mit.edu:phred): anonymous      ← Type username "anonymous".
331 Guest login ok, send ident as password
Password: phred@headcheez.com                 ← Specify your mail address.
230 Guest login ok, access restrictions apply.
Remote system type is UNIX.
Using binary mode to transfer files.
ftp>                                          ← You are logged in.
```

Once logged in, you can obtain the required files by using the **cd** command to change to the appropriate directory, then using the **get** command to retrieve the files to your system. When you are finished getting files, you can exit from **ftp** with the **bye** command. (As you change directories, you can use the **ls** command to see what files are in the current directory.) Shown below is the series of commands you could use to get the **etc/SERVICE** file onto your system:

```
ftp> cd pub/gnu/emacs                    ← Change directory.
250 CWD command successful.
ftp> get SYSTEM                          ← Get the file.
150 Opening BINARY mode data connection for SYSTEM (... bytes).
226 Transfer complete.
... bytes received in .. seconds (... Kbytes/s)
ftp> █
```

At this point, you could get more files from the system if you wanted. When you are finished obtaining the required files, you can exit from FTP with the **bye** command.

Installing Emacs from Tape

When you get the Emacs software on a tape, you generally have one of two methods for copying the files onto your UNIX system: Use the **tar** command, or use an update facility if your system has one.

Nearly all UNIX systems have the **tar** command, which is a tape file archiver. If you use **tar**, proceed as follows:

1. Become the superuser of your UNIX system (often called the root user). This gives you full access to the UNIX system.

2. Insert the tape in the tape drive and wait until it is ready to use. Typically, a "busy" indicator will go off or otherwise say you that the tape is ready to use.

3. Make a directory for holding the files you copy from the tape.

4. Change to the temporary directory by running the cd command.

5. Using the **tar command,** extract all the files from the tape that contains Emacs. Assuming the device file for your tape drive is named **rct**, the following command should work on most systems. To be safe, study how **tar** works on your UNIX system.

   ```
   $ tar -xvf /dev/rct *
   ```

   In effect, the command creates a file archive in the current directory, using the verbose mode so you can see the files being transferred.

6. When the file transfer completes, remove the tape from the tape drive. You can then move the files to other locations if necessary.

Summary

Table 14.2 summarizes the important points in this chapter.

Table 14.2. Chapter 14 Summary

Topic	Summary
Reasons why Emacs might not start on your system	• Emacs is not installed. • The `emacs` program does not work. • Your PATH environment variable does not include the directory containing `emacs`. • Emacs exists but goes by another name.
How to locate the `emacs` executable	• Use the UNIX `whereis emacs` command. • Use the UNIX `which emacs` command if more than one version is installed.
How to locate supporting Emacs files	Look at the value of the Emacs variable *exec-directory* using one of these commands: • `C-h v exec-directory RET` • `M-x describe-variable RET exec-directory RET`
Getting additional information on Emacs	If you have the UNIX News (or Notes) facility, you may be able to get information from other users about Emacs. The following News groups are devoted to Emacs coverage: `comp.emacs`, `alt.emacs.gnews`, `gnu.emacs`.

Obtaining Emacs software	• Via anonymous FTP from `prep.ai.mit.edu`
	• From the Free Software Foundation (you will be charged a fee):
	    Free Software Foundation
	    675 Massachusetts Avenue
	    Cambridge MA 02139

Appendix A
Editing in Pascal Mode

The standard GNU Emacs package that you get from the Free Software Foundation does *not* include a mode for editing Pascal programs. However, there are several Pascal modes available in the public domain. This appendix describes one of these Pascal modes, which was developed by Vincent Broman and is based on a similar mode for editing Modula-2 programs. We chose to discuss this mode because it was readily available on our system. This appendix describes how to obtain and use this mode. If it does not suit your needs, we encourage you to obtain any of the other Pascal modes available (as described in the section, "Obtaining a Pascal Mode"). The main topics covered in this appendix are:

- Obtaining a Pascal mode

- Enabling Pascal mode

- Assumptions about Pascal source

- Moving the cursor

- Indenting programs

- Commands that build Pascal constructs

- Creating a new program

- Commenting programs

- Working with sexps and lists (advanced usage)

- Customizing indentation

- Customizing commenting (advanced usage)

Obtaining a Pascal Mode

To use the Pascal mode described in this appendix, you must have the appropriate Emacs-Lisp files installed on your system. This mode, like all other Emacs modes, is defined in a file containing Emacs-Lisp code. We obtained this file using anonymous **ftp** to a system at Ohio State University that maintains an archive of "public domain" Emacs-Lisp code (libraries). As of the writing of this book, this system was named **tut.cis.ohio-state.edu**. You may know of other systems that contain Emacs-Lisp libraries, and could search for a Pascal mode there instead.

To log in anonymously to this system, we specified the username **anonymous** and used our mail address as the password. For example, suppose your login is **phred** on the system **headcheez**. Shown below is the series of commands you would use to gain access to the archive system. (The underlined text is what you type.)

```
$ ftp tut.cis.ohio-state.edu
Connected to tut.cis.ohio-state.edu.
220 tut.cis.ohio-state.edu FTP server (Version ...)
Name (tut.cis.ohio-state.edu:phred): anonymous   ←Username "anonymous".
331 Guest login ok, send ident as password
Password: phred@headcheez.com              ← Type your mail address.
230 Guest login ok, access restrictions apply.
Remote system type is UNIX.
Using binary mode to transfer files.
ftp> █                                       ← You are logged in.
```

Once logged in, you can obtain the required files by using the **cd** command to change to the appropriate directory, then using the **get** command to retrieve the files to your system. When you are finished getting files, you can exit from **ftp** with the **bye** command. (As you change directories, you can use the **ls** command to see what files are in the current directory.)

The locations of all Emacs-Lisp libraries in the archive are stored in a file **LCD-datafile.Z** in the directory **.../pub/gnu/emacs/elisp-archive**. To determine where Pascal mode files are located on the archive, you must read this file.

This file, like many of the files on the archive, is a compressed file (indicated by the **.Z** file name suffix). After retrieving the file to your system, you can uncompress it using the UNIX **uncompress** command. Shown below is the series of commands for retrieving the file **LDC-archive.Z** to your system, uncompressing it, and viewing it:

```
ftp> cd pub/gnu/emacs/elisp-archive            ← Change directory.
250 CWD command successful.
ftp> get LDC-datafile.Z                         ← Get the file.
150 Opening BINARY mode data connection for LCD-datafile.Z (n bytes).
226 Transfer complete.
```

```
33084 bytes received in 21 seconds (1.5 Kbytes/s)
ftp> ! uncompress LCD-datafile.Z          ← Use ! to run uncompress
ftp> ! more LCD-datafile                   ← Now view the file.
       .
       .
       .
ftp> █
```

Two Pascal modes stored on this system are of particular interest: the Pascal mode created by Glen Ditchfield of the University of Waterloo (`pas-mode.el`), and the Pascal mode created by Vincent Broman of the Navel Ocean Systems Center (`pascalmode.el`). Once you have determined the files' location, you can get and uncompress them, just like you did with the file `LCD-datafile.Z`.

The two modes have different philosophies of how a Pascal mode should work. Ditchfield's mode basically expands abbreviations of Pascal keywords as you type them, automatically creating the correct syntax and placing the cursor at the appropriate location. (For example, when you type `fun`, Emacs calls the function `pascal-function-hook`, defined in the Emacs-Lisp file, to create a function body with indentation.) Broman's mode, in contrast, has special `C-c` commands for creating various Pascal constructs; these commands prompt you for various information required to build each construct (for example, arguments for a procedure definition, or an expression for an `if` statement).

Both modes are more than adequate for creating and editing Pascal programs. Which mode you choose to use is purely a matter of personal preference. By discussing only Broman's Pascal mode, we do not intend to bias readers toward that mode; it just happened to be the mode we were familiar with. However, you may find Ditchfield's mode just as useful, or more so.

Once you have the files on your system, you should install them in the appropriate Emacs-Lisp directory (defined by the *load-path* variable). For example, on our system, the files are stored in `/usr/local/emacs/lisp/local`.

Enabling Pascal Mode

To make Pascal mode available to Emacs, you must first load the desired library using the `M-x load-library` command from Emacs. For example, if the file `/usr/local/emacs/lisp/local/pascalmode.elc` contains Broman's mode, you could load it with `M-x load-library RET pascalmode RET`.

On our system, once Pascal mode is loaded, Emacs automatically uses Pascal mode for file names ending with `.p` or `.pas`. If Emacs does not automatically use Pascal mode for such files, you can enable the mode with the `M-x pascal-mode` command, or put a mode-specification line as the first nonblank line in the file—that is, `{-*-pascal-*-}`.

Assumptions About Pascal Source

Pascal mode differs from some programming modes in that it has commands for building language constructs. For example, there are commands to build **procedure** and **function** statements, which prompt for parameters lists; there are commands that build **while** and **for** statements, which prompt for the test expression. Because these commands build the Pascal constructs in a particular programming style, it is best to use them consistently and to avoid other styles. Otherwise, some construct-building commands might not work as expected.

Moving the Cursor

A Pascal program is actually a single procedure that may contain nested procedures and functions. Because the program is a single procedure, the **C-M-a** and **C-M-e** (move to previous or next procedure) commands simply move to the start or end of the program, as do the Fundamental mode commands **C-M-<** and **C-M->**. To get around this limitation, Pascal mode provides additional motion commands for moving among nested procedures, functions, and begin-end blocks. These commands look at the indentation level of program lines, rather than procedure or function declarations. Table A.1 summarizes these commands.

Table A.1. Pascal Mode Motion Commands

Operation	Command and Comments
Move backward to lesser or same indent level	**C-c <** Moves backward to the line having the same or lesser indentation. Use this to move back to the start of a procedure or function definition. Once the cursor is at the start of a procedure or function definition, this command moves backward to the previous procedure or function definition at the same level.
Move forward to lesser or same indent level	**C-c >** Same as **C-c <** except that it moves forward in the file.

Table A.1, con't.

Operation	Command and Comments
Move backward to lesser indent level	**M-x pascal-backward-to-less-indent** Same as **C-c** < except when the cursor is on a procedure or function definition line. In this case, it moves to the next line with a lesser indentation level, instead of moving to the previous definition at the same level.
Move forward to lesser indent level	**M-x pascal-forward-to-less-indent** Same as **M-x pascal-backward-to-less-indent**, except that it moves forward in the file.

For example, suppose the cursor is on the line **fib := i** in the following code. If you issued three consecutive **C-c** < commands, the cursor would move first to the preceding **if** statement, then to the **begin**, and finally to the **function** declaration. If you then used **C-c** >, the cursor would move to the **function pow** line.

```
function fib (i : integer): integer;        ← 4. C-c < moves here.
{Compute fibonacci(i) recursively.}
    begin                                   ← 3. C-c < moves here.
        if ((i = 0) or (i = 1)) then        ← 2. C-c < moves here.
            fib := i                        ← 1. Cursor starts here.
        else
            fib := fib(i - 1) + fib(i - 2);
    end; {fib}

function pow (x : integer;                  ← 5. C-c > moves here.
              y : exponent): integer;
{Compute x to the y power recursively.}
    begin
        if (y = 0) then
            pow := 1
        else
            pow := x * pow( x, y - 1 );
    end; {pow}
```

Try experimenting with these commands to see how they work. You may also find it useful to bind these commands to function keys, if your system supports them.

Indenting Programs

The usual programming mode indentation commands C-j and C-M-\ do *not* work in Pascal mode, and the **TAB** command works differently. Pascal mode uses an altogether different model of indentation: In general, each line is indented at the same level as the previous line. Automatic indentation is performed by commands that build Pascal constructs, described in the next section. Nevertheless, there are still some commands that perform indentation, summarized in Table A.2.

Table A.2. Pascal Mode Indentation Commands

Operation	Command and Comments
Indent current line	**TAB** Indent by the amount of the indent level. By default the indent level is 4 columns. Each time you use **TAB**, it indents another 4 columns.
Unindent line	C-c **TAB** Acts like a backward **TAB**. It undoes the last **TAB** command.

Commands That Build Pascal Constructs

Pascal mode provides a number of commands that automatically build various Pascal constructs, indented consistently, and commented appropriately. By using these commands, you help enforce consistency to an aesthetically pleasing and readable Pascal programming style that is shared by all users who use the commands. In addition, the commands help reduce typographical errors, such as forgetting closing **end** statements in a **begin-end** pair.

Most control constructs and declarations of Pascal can be inserted by typing C-c followed by a character mnemonic for the construct. If the construct needs any parameters, Emacs prompts for them in the minibuffer. For example, if you run C-c i, Emacs inserts an **if** on the current line and prompts you for a **condition** to test for in the **if** statement, as shown in Figure A.1.

After you type the condition, Emacs places it between **if** and **then** keywords, and opens up the next line, indented properly for the statement part of the **if** statement (Figure A.2).

```
          •
          •
          •
     if   •
          •
          •
          •
```
```
-----Emacs: prog.p      10:05am 0.02 Mail   <Pascal>---- Bottom --------
expression: <Tree <> NIL>                    ← Type this expression
```

Figure A.1. Creating an if Statement

```
          •
          •
          •
     if <Tree <> NIL then
     _  ←──────────────────── The cursor is here, waiting for you to type
          •
          •
          •
```
```
-----Emacs: prog.p      10:05am 0.02 Mail   <Pascal>---- Bottom --------
     expression: <Tree <> NIL>               ← Type this expression
```

Figure A.2. Completed if Condition

At this point, you could type a statement or invoke another **C-c** structure command. For example, if you run **C-c b** at this point, Emacs inserts a **begin-end** pair and prompts you for a comment about the block, as shown in Figure A.3.

After you type the comment, Emacs puts the comment in the braces following the **end** statement and puts the cursor in the **begin-end** block, waiting for you to type another command, as shown in Figure A.4.

Generally, you should invoke the commands right after typing **RET**; that is, the functions expect to be invoked on a new line. Exceptions to this rule are commands that create array, record, procedure body, and function body, which should be invoked at the end of the current line.

```
             .
             .
             .

    if <Tree <> NIL> then
       begin

       end; <>    ◄──────── The comment is inserted here
             .

             .

             .




-----Emacs: prog.p     10:05am 0.02 Mail   <Pascal>---- Bottom --------
comment about block: Initialize the tree.  ◄── Type the comment
```

Figure A.3. Adding a Comment

```
             .
             .
             .

    if <Tree <> NIL> then
       begin
       ─    ◄──────────────── The cursor is here, waiting for your next command
       end; <Initialize the tree.>
             .

             .

             .


-----Emacs: prog.p     10:05am 0.02 Mail   <Pascal>---- Bottom --------
```

Figure A.4. Completed Comment

Creating a New Program

To start a new program, execute the **C-c P** command, which creates a **program** statement and prompts you for the program's parameter list (for example, **input, output**). It also creates the main program's **begin-end** block and creates an empty comment under the program statement. When finished, **C-c P** puts the cursor immediately under program statement, waiting for you to type a command. Figure A.5 shows how the program looks after executing **C-c P** and specifying a program name of **newprog** and a program parameter list of **input, output**.

```
program newprog (input, output);
()

begin           ◄─────────────────── The cursor is here. You could enter const or type, etc.

end. (Program)




-----Emacs: newprog.p  10:05am 0.02 Mail  (Pascal)---- All ------------
```

Figure A.5. Starting a New Program

At this point, you might want to enter **const**, **type**, or **var** declarations. Again, Pascal mode provides commands for doing this: **C-c C-c** for **const**, **C-c C-t** for **type**, and **C-c C-v** for **var**.

Terminating a Pascal Construct Command

At any point during the execution of a Pascal construct command, you can terminate it with **C-g**, just like any other command. Any text generated by the command up to that point will still remain in the source file.

Entering Optional Parameters

Some commands prompt you for optional parameters. For example, the **C-c C-p** command generates a procedure statement, including the formal parameter list. Emacs prompts you for the parameter definitions, each of which it places in the procedure's formal parameter list. Since a procedure could conceivably have *no* parameters, each parameter is considered optional. For example, compare the following two procedure definitions created with **C-c C-p**:

```
procedure ProcNone;                    ← Has no parameters.

procedure ProcThree( arg1 : integer;   ← Has three parameters.
                     var arg2 : real;
                     arg3 : boolean );
```

Emacs indicates optional parameters by enclosing the parameter's prompt in square brackets `[ ]`. For example, the `C-c C-p` command displays the following prompts in the minibuffer for each optional parameter:

```
[argument and type]:          ← Type the first optional argument.
[next argument and type]:      ← Type the second argument.
[next argument and type]:      ← Type the third argument.
            .
            .
            .
```

You do *not* have to type semicolons after each parameter; Emacs does it for you. When you are finished entering optional parameters, type **RET** without entering parameter information. Emacs closes out the procedure definition for you.

Undoing Pascal Construct Commands

As with most other Emacs commands, you can undo the effect of Pascal construct commands with `C-x u`. This command will undo all of the text added by each construct command. For example, if you use `C-c P` to create the program statement and program body, `C-x u` will remove everything created by that command—the **program** statement, comment block, and **begin-end** block.

Changing Keyword Case

By default, the constructs created in Pascal mode are in lowercase letters. You can toggle between uppercase and lowercase letters with the `C-c K` command (uppercase K). It is **not** retroactive. That is, `C-c K` will not change the case of keywords already typed; it only affects subsequent keywords.

Displaying the Current Procedure or Function's Name

At any time, you can see the name of the procedure (or function) in which the cursor resides by running the `C-c =` command. This command looks backward for the first procedure or function declaration it can find. It displays the procedure name in the minibuffer. This can help you find your location in a large piece of code.

Summary of Pascal Construct Commands

Table A.3 lists all Pascal construct commands, sorted by the keyword(s) they affect. As with other Emacs commands, the best way to understand these is to experiment with them.

Table A.3. Commands That Build Pascal Constructs

Keyword	Command and Comments
()	C-c (Inserts a pair of balanced parentheses. This is the same as M- (.
[]	C-c [Inserts a pair of balanced brackets.
array	C-c C-a Creates an array declaration. Prompts for the array indexes and array type.
begin-end	C-c b Creates a begin-end block, usually for use in an if-then, if-then-else, or while statement. Prompts for a comment to put at the end of the block.
case	C-c c Creates a case statement with a closing end statement. Prompts for the case selector expression.
const	C-c C-c Creates a const statement.
else	C-c e Adds an else clause to an if statement. Also, if you inadvertently leave a semicolon at the end of the previous line, this command removes it.

Table A.3, con't.

Keyword	Command and Comments
`else if`	`C-c C-e` Adds an `else` clause and starts another `if` statement after it. Prompts for the condition to test.
`external`	`C-c C-x` Adds an `external` statement to a procedure or function definition.
`for`	`C-c f` Creates a `for` statement. Prompts for the loop index variable to use and the range (e.g., `1 to 10`).
`function`	`C-c C-f` Creates a function specification. Optionally prompts for the function's name, parameters, and function type. Terminate optional parameters with **RET**.
`function`	`C-c p` After creating a function specification, use this command to create the main body of the function. Invoke this command at the end of the line containing the function specification statement.
`if`	`C-c i` Creates an `if` statement. Prompts for the condition to test. Appends `then` after the condition.
`include`	`C-c I` Creates an **INCLUDE** directive and prompts for the name of the include file. The include directive has the form `%include` *filename;*

Table A.3, con't.

Keyword	Command and Comments
procedure	C-c C-p Creates a procedure specification. Prompts for the procedure's name and any optional parameters. Terminate optional parameters with RET.
procedure	C-c p After creating the procedure specification, use this command to add a begin-end body to the procedure. Invoke this command at the end of the line containing the specification.
program	C-c P Creates a program statement and the begin-end block for the main program. Prompts for the program's name and header list (e.g., input, output). Use this command to start a program.
record	C-c C-r Creates a record statement with a closing end. You must enter the record fields in the buffer; Emacs does not prompt for them. Invoke this command on the same line in which the record is to be declared.
repeat	C-c r Creates a repeat-until statement. Prompts for the exit condition.
type	C-c C-t Creates a type statement.
var	C-c C-v Creates a var statement.
while	C-c w Creates a while statement. Prompts for the entry condition.

Table A.3, con't.

Keyword	Command and Comments
`with`	`C-c C-w` Creates a `with` statement. Prompts for the record on which to use `with`.

Commenting Programs

As described in the previous section, Pascal mode in many cases prompts for comments to be included with a construct. Thus, commenting is largely automatic when you use construct commands.

You can also explicitly add comments with the usual **M-;** command, available in all programming modes. In addition, Pascal mode has the two unique commenting commands, shown in Table A.4.

Table A.4. Pascal Mode Commenting Commands

Operation	Command and Comments
Add or align comment	`C-c {` Adds a new comment or aligns the comment on the current line. Same as the **M-;** command.
Add header comment	`C-c h` Adds a header comment containing the program's title, date of modification, and author.

C-c h is especially useful for adding introductory comments to a program. It does **not** interfere with SCCS and RCS identification strings. It prompts you for the program's title and creates a comment block containing the title, date of last modification, and the author's name. For example, we created the header comment shown in Figure A.6 on Saturday, April 28, at 10:34 in the morning.

If a Pascal program contains a header comment, Emacs automatically updates the program's date of modification whenever you load the file.

```
{
        Title:      List Program
        Last Mod:   Sat Apr 28 10:34:21 1990
        Author:     Michael Schoonover
                    <michael@headcheez>

}
```

Figure 4.6. Header Comment

Working with Sexps and Lists (Advanced Usage)

Emacs' Pascal mode provides commands for moving within and among balanced expressions containing parentheses () and brackets [ ]—that is, expressions (sexps) and lists. To use these commands effectively, you must know what expressions and lists are.

What Are Sexps and Lists in Pascal Mode?

A list in Pascal is any balanced grouping of parentheses or brackets. Thus, the following are all valid lists:

- Parenthetical Expressions:

    ```
    (idx < max)
    (left + text_width[i]*font_width)
    ```

- Parameter Lists:

    ```
    (x : integer;
     y : exponent)
    ```

- Array Dimension Declarators:

    ```
    [1..100]
    [1..MaxX, 1..MaxY, 1..MaxZ]
    ```

- Array Subscripts:

    ```
    [x,y,z]
    ```

Pascal comments, whether of the form **{ comment }** or **(* comment *)**, are *not* lists.

An expression (or **sexp** as it is called in Lisp terminology) is a symbol, number, or list. Thus, the following are all valid sexps:

- Each of these symbols:

  ```
  fib
  integer
  'Here are the arguments:'
  ^first
  foo
  ```

- Each of these numbers:

  ```
  -100
  3.14159
  ```

- This list:

  ```
  (x : integer;
   y : exponent)
  ```

- This list:

  ```
  (left + text_width[i]*font_width)
  ```

- This list:

  ```
  [ xcoord, ycoord, zcoord ]
  ```

Notice that an sexp can actually contain other sexps, which in turn can contain more sexps. For example, the sexp **(left + text_width[i]*font_width)** contains these sexps:

```
left          A symbol
text_width    A symbol
[i]           A list
font_width    A symbol
```

And the embedded list **[i]** contains the sexp **i**.

The fact that lists and sexps can contain nested lists and sexps is important because it affects the way the list and sexp motion commands work. What constitutes a list or sexp depends on where the cursor is located.

List and Sexp Motion Commands

Table A.5 summarizes the most useful commands for navigating in and among sexps and lists in Pascal mode. The best way to learn how to use these commands is to experiment.

Table A.5. Pascal Mode List and Sexp Motion Commands

Operation	Command and Comments
Forward over sexp	`C-M-f` Move forward over the current or next sexp, where sexp is defined to be any symbol, number, string constant, or list.
Backward over sexp	`C-M-b` Move backward over the current or previous sexp.
Forward over list	`C-M-n` Move forward over next list.
Backward over list	`C-M-p` Move backward over the previous list.
Up a list	`C-M-u` Move backward into the next higher list in a nested list.
Down a list	`C-M-d` Move forward into the next lower list in a nested list.

Marking Sexps

In addition to the Fundamental and Text mode marking commands, Pascal mode provides the command `C-M-@` for marking sexps. As an example of using `C-M-@`, Figure A.7 shows how a region is placed around the argument list for the **pow** function. If you executed `C-w` (kill region) at this point, it would delete the argument list.

```
Cursor is here
      function pow (x : integer;          Mark is placed here
                    y : exponent)): integer;
      {Compute x to the y power recursively.}
          begin
              if (y - 0) then
                  pow := 1
              else
                  pow := x * pow( x, y - 1 );
          end; {pow}
```

Figure A.7. Region Defined Around Argument List of
Function pow

Killing Sexps

The **C-M-k** command kills forward to end of the current or next sexp. It is equivalent to running **C-M-@** to mark the end of the next sexp; then executing **C-w** to kill the marked region. For example, if the cursor is positioned as shown below:

```
              Cursor is positioned here
              ↓
  function pow (x : foo;
                y : bar): integer;
```

Then the **C-M-k** command would delete the argument declaration list for **pow**:

```
              Cursor is here after the arguments are killed
              ↓
  function pow : integer;
```

Transposing Sexps

The **C-M-t** command transposes sexps around the current cursor position. For example, in the following **if** statement, **max** and **num** are in the incorrect order in the expression:

```
          Cursor is here
          ↓
  if (max > num) then
      max := num;
```

Using the **C-M-t** command, you can switch **max** and **num** around the **>** operator. When the command is done, the cursor is placed after the expression following the **>**:

```
            Cursor is here
                  ↓
if (num > max) then
    max := num;
```

Different behavior can be obtained by specifying negative or positive arguments to this command. Experiment to see how this works.

Customizing Indentation

The default indentation for each level of nesting in a Pascal program is 4. To change this default, use the **C-c S** command, which prompts for the number of columns to indent in the future.

Customizing Commenting (Advanced Usage)

The variables that can be used to modify comments in C can also be used to change the way commenting works in Pascal mode. Table A.6 summarizes these variables. (Setting variables and making such changes "permanent" is described in Chapter 13, "Customizing the Emacs Environment.")

Table A.6. Pascal Mode Commenting Variables

Variable	Default Value and Purpose
comment-column	Default: 32 Column at which new comments are displayed or existing comments are aligned.
comment-start	Default: **" { "** String to use to start a comment.
comment-end	Default: **" } "** String to use to end a comment.

Table A.6, con't.

Variable	Default Value and Purpose
comment-start-skip	Default: `"{[ \t]*\\\|(\\*[ \t]*"` Regular expression for Emacs to use when searching for the start of a comment. The default value matches either `(* *)` or `{ }` style comments.

comment-multi-line	Default: `nil`
	
	Affects how Emacs handles multi-line comments.
	
	Multi-line comments are produced either with the `C-M-j` command, or by typing past the *fill-column* when auto-fill mode is enabled.
	
	The default value `nil` produces multi-line comments of the form:
	
	`{ The first line of a }`
	`{ multi-line comment. }`
	
	A non-`nil` value (say `t`) produces multi-line comments of the form:
	
	`{ The first line of a`
	`  multi-line comment. }`

Changing the Comment Column

The *comment-column* variable determines which column the next comment starts in. You would normally set this variable with either the `C-x ;`, `C-u` *n* `C-x ;`, or `C-u C-x ;` command. For example, to make *comment-column* match the column used in comments on previous lines, you would use `C-u C-x ;`.

Each Pascal mode buffer has a local copy of *comment-column*. However, you can make the variable **global**, forcing it to apply to all Pascal buffers. To do this, use the command `M-ESC (setq-default comment-column` *n*`)`, where *n* is the new comment-column to use in all buffers.

Changing Comment Delimiters

The *comment-start* and *comment-end* variables control the appearance of delimiters around comment text. Their default values produce a comment of the form:

```
{comment text that you type}
↑                            ↑
comment-start                comment-end
```

To get **(* *)** style comments, set *comment-start* to **" (* "** and *comment-end* to
" *) ".

Another possible use of *comment-start* and *comment-end* is to include additional information with comments. For example, suppose you are revising source code for a new release and want to mark all comments that were added for the new release. You could do this by setting *comment-start* to include release information:

```
M-x set-variable RET
Set variable: comment-start RET
Set comment-start to value: "{v1.21: " RET      ← The quotes are required.
```

Then, if you issued the **M-;** command, it would create a comment that looked like this:

```
for i := 0 to 10 do              {v 1.21: }
                                           ↑
                                  The cursor is here, waiting for
                                  you to type comment text.
```

Changing the Comment Search Pattern

The comment search pattern is a regular expression that Pascal mode uses to find the start of a comment. Clearly, this variable should be set such that Emacs can find the start of comments as defined by comment-start. It should *never* match the null string, "". Its default value is **"{ [\t]*\\| (* [\t]*"**, which matches the start of a comment plus everything up to its body. It matches either of these comment styles:

```
(*  *) or {}
```

For most users, this comment string is sufficient. You should only change this variable if you use a dialect of Pascal that has different comment syntax.

Handling Multi-Line Comments

The *comment-multi-line* variable controls how **C–M–j** or auto-filling acts within a comment. Its default value is **nil**, causing the comment on the current line to be terminated with the value of *comment-end*, and a new comment started on the next line. For example, it produces multi-line comments of this style:

```
{This is the first line of the comment.}
{And this is the second line.}
```

If it is not **nil**, then the comment on the current line is **not** terminated, and the comment is continued on the next line—for example:

```
{This is the first line of the comment.
 And this is the second line.}
```

There is no clear advantage to either style. It's a matter of personal taste.

Summary

Table A.7 summarizes the important points to remember from this appendix.

Table A.7. Appendix A Summary

Topic	Summary
Selecting Pascal Mode	• First, be sure that you have a Pascal mode. If the mode described in this chapter is present, you can then: • Name your source file with a `.p` or `.pas` extension, or • Invoke Pascal mode with the **M–x pascal–mode** command, or • Make sure the first nonblank line of your source file is a comment that includes the string `–*–pascal–*–`
Assumptions about Pascal mode	Pascal mode includes commands to build Pascal constructs. Try not to alter the style used by these commands, or they may not work as expected.

Table A.7, con't.

Topic	Summary
Motion commands	• Move to start of program: `C-M-a` • Move to end of program: `C-M-e` • Move backward to line having same or lesser indent: `C-c <` • Move forward to line having same or lesser indent level: `C-c >` • Move backward to line having lesser indent: `M-x pascal-backward-to-less-indent` • Move forward to line having lesser indent: `M-x pascal-forward-to-less-indent` • Move forward over sexp: `C-M-f` • Move backward over sexp: `C-M-b` • Move over next list: `C-M-n` • Move backward over list: `C-M-p` • Move to next-higher list in nested list: `C-M-u` • Move to next-lower list in nested list: `C-M-d`
Region commands	• Put region around entire program: `C-M-h` • Put a mark after the next sexp: `C-M-@`
Transpose command	Transpose sexps around cursor: `C-M-t`
Kill command	Kill forward to end of current or next sexp: `C-M-k`
Indentation commands	• Indent by current indent level: `TAB` • Undo last `TAB` command: `C-c TAB` • The usual programming mode indentation commands `C-j` and `C-M-\` do not work in Pascal mode. • Change default indent for each level of nesting to n: `C-u n C-c S`

Table A.7, con't.

Topic	Summary
Pascal construct commands	• Terminate construct command: `C-g` • Undo construct command: `C-x u` • Change keyword case: `C-c K` • Display current procedure or function name: `C-c =` • Stop entering optional parameters: press **RET** without entering a value. • Insert pair of balanced parentheses: `C-c (` • Insert pair of balanced brackets: `C-c [` • Create `array` declaration: `C-c C-a` • Create `begin-end` block: `C-c b` • Create `case` statement: `C-c c` • Create `const` statement: `C-c C-c` • Add `else` clause to `if` statement: `C-c e` • Adds `else` clause and starts another `if` statement: `C-c C-e` • Adds `external` statement to procedure or function definition: `C-c C-x` • Create a `for` statement: `C-c f` • Create a function specification: `C-c C-f` (terminate optional parameters with **RET**) • Create main body of function: `C-c p` • Create `if` statement: `C-c i` • Create `INCLUDE` directive: `C-c I` • Create procedure specification: `C-c p` • Create `program` statement and `begin-end` block: `C-c P` • Create `record` statement: `C-c C-r` • Create `repeat-until` statement: `C-c r` • Create `type` statement: `C-c C-t` • Create `var` statement: `C-c C-v` • Create `while` statement: `C-c w` • Create `with` statement: `C-c C-w`

Table A.7, con't.

Topic	Summary
Comments	Commands: • Create new comment on line containing no comment: **M-;** • Align existing comment on current line: **M-;** • Add new or align existing comment (same as **M-;**): **C-c {** • Add header comment: **C-c h** • Set *comment-column* to current cursor column: **C-x ;** • Set *comment-column* to *n*: **C-u** *n* **C-x ;** • Set *comment-column* same as previous comment: **C-u C-x ;** • Delete comment on current line or all in region: **C-u - C-x ;** • Insert new comment on next line or align next comment: **C-M-j** Style Variables: • Column where comments are created/aligned: *comment-column* • String to use as start of comment (**" { "**): *comment-start* • String to use as end of comment (**" } "**): *comment-end* • Regular expression used when searching for start of a comment (**" { [\t] * \\ | (\\ * [\t] * "**): *comment-start-skip* • Affects handling of multi-line comments: *comment-multi-line*

Appendix B
Emacs-Lisp Programming

This appendix provides an overview of programming in Emacs-Lisp. A detailed reference and tutorial on Emacs-Lisp goes far beyond the scope of this book. For an excellent, comprehensive reference and guide on Emacs-Lisp programming, refer to the Free Software Foundation's *Emacs Lisp Reference Manual*. In lieu of obtaining that manual, advanced users may be able to get a start on Emacs-Lisp programming from the information contained in this appendix. The topics covered in this appendix are:

- An overview of Emacs-Lisp programming
- Getting documentation on Emacs-Lisp defuns and variables
- Lisp symbol completion
- Loading Emacs-Lisp libraries
- Compiling Emacs-Lisp code
- Debugging Emacs-Lisp code (advanced usage)
- Converting Mocklisp to Emacs-Lisp (for Mocklisp users)

This appendix does *not* discuss how to edit Emacs-Lisp code. For details on that subject, refer to Chapter 8, "Editing in Lisp Modes."

An Overview of Emacs-Lisp Programming

If you are familiar with Lisp programming (for example, Common Lisp), it should be fairly easy to pick up Emacs-Lisp. However, be aware that Emacs-Lisp is a unique dialect of Lisp and you will have some learning to do. For example, the following comparison with Common Lisp is found in the FAQ (Frequently Asked Questions) file provided with Emacs:

> GNU Emacs Lisp is case-sensitive, uses dynamic scoping, doesn't have packages, doesn't have multiple return values, doesn't have reader macros, etc.

If you are unfamiliar with Lisp programming, there are several excellent books on the subject, such as David Touretzky's *Common Lisp: A Gentle Introduction to Symbolic Computation* and Guy Steele's *Common Lisp: The Language*.

The remainder of this section provides an overview of Emacs-Lisp programming that should be useful to readers with programming experience. For detailed information on Emacs-Lisp programming, refer to the Free Software Foundation's *Emacs Lisp Reference Manual*.

Calling Functions

At the heart of Emacs-Lisp programming are **functions** (or **defuns** as they are often called in Lisp terminology). This section describes, for novice users, how to call functions in Emacs-Lisp. Readers familiar with Lisp can skip this section.

In most programming languages, calls to functions take the form of the function name, followed by a comma-separated parameter list enclosed in parentheses:

function_name ([*param1* [, *param2*]...])

In contrast, Emacs-Lisp syntax requires the function name to appear as the first element inside the parentheses, followed by optional parameters separated by spaces instead of commas:

(*function_name* [*param1* [*param2*]...])

For example, suppose you have a C function named `substring` that takes three arguments—a string, a starting position, and an ending position—and returns a substring. In C, a call to this function would look like this:

```
substring ("ABCDEFG", 3, 4);
```

In Emacs-Lisp, a call to a similar function would look like this:

```
(substring "ABCDEFG" 3 4)
```

Emacs-Lisp Data Types

The primary data types you will work with in Emacs-Lisp are `nil`, `t`, symbols, integers, and strings (described in Table B.1).

Table B.1. Emacs-Lisp Data Types

Data Type	Description
`nil`	Used to represent a boolean "false" value. Do *not* quote this value. Often times you set an Emacs variable to `nil` to disable a feature.
`t`	Used to represent a boolean "true" value. Do *not* quote this value. Often used to enable an Emacs feature through a variable.
Symbols	Symbols are the names of function or variables. They usually consist of letters and hyphens. For example, *comment-column* is the symbol name for the variable that keeps track of the comment column. Do *not* quote symbol names.
Integers	Decimal numbers, which can have an optional preceding minus sign. Emacs uses 24-bit precision representation for integers.
Characters	A single character is represented by a question mark followed by the character—for example, `?z` is the character "z."
Strings	Character string constants must appear in double quotes. Shown below are special character escapes that can appear in strings:

`\n`	Newline
`\t`	Tab
`\f`	Formfeed
`\"`	Embedded double quote
`\b`	Backspace
`\e`	Escape
`\`*ooo*	Character whose octal code is *ooo*
`\C-`	Control character (e.g., `\C-a` for Ctrl-a)
`\M-`	Meta character (e.g., `\M-a` for Meta-a)
`\M-\C-`	Control-meta character (e.g., `\M-\C-a` for Ctrl-Meta-a)

A Useful Set of Emacs-Lisp Functions

Emacs-Lisp has a rich set of functions for doing various tasks associated with text editing—for example, moving the cursor, keeping track of point, searching for a text string, deleting text, and so on. Many of these functions are actually executed when you run Emacs commands. For example, when you run the **C-p** command, Emacs calls the function **previous-line**. Or when you run **M-x what-line**, Emacs calls the **what-line** function to display the current line number.

As described in Chapter 9, you can get online information about command key bindings with the **C-h k** command and you can get information about an Emacs-Lisp function with **C-h f**. If you are adventurous, you may be able to find out most of what you need about Emacs-Lisp functions from these help commands alone. Nevertheless, you probably won't be able to discover everything you need to know. For example, how do you determine the location of point and mark? Or how do you search for a string? And, most importantly, what is the correct way to use various functions? The best answers to such questions can be found in the Free Software Foundation's *Emacs Lisp Reference Manual*. Nevertheless, we have put together a list of Emacs-Lisp functions that you may find useful to at least get a start writing Emacs-Lisp functions (see Table B.2).

Table B.2. Some Useful Emacs-Lisp Functions

To do this...	Use this function...
Getting buffer information	
Get current indentation level	**(current-indentation)** Returns the indentation of the current line—that is, the column of the first non-whitespace character on the line.
Get the location of point	**(point)** Returns the location of point in the current buffer.
Get the location of mark	**(mark)** Returns the location of mark in the current buffer.

Table B.2, con't.

To do this...	Use this function...
Getting buffer information, con't.	
Get location of beginning of editable region	`(point-min)` Returns the location of the first editable character in the current buffer. Normally, this is just one (1). However, if narrowing is in effect (via **M-x narrow-to-region** or **M-x narrow-to-page**), `(point-min)` returns the location of the first character in the region.
Get location of end of editable region	`(point-max)` Like `(point-min)` but returns the location of the last editable character.
Moving the cursor	
Forward one or more characters	`(forward-char n)` *n* is the number of characters to move over; if *n* is not specified, moves forward one character. Advances point as well.
Backward one or more characters	`(backward-char n)` Like `(forward-char)` but moves backward.
Next line	`(forward-line n)` Move to the start of the line that is *n* lines past the current line. If no *n* is specified, moves forward 1 line.
Previous line	`(backward-line n)` Like `forward-line` but moves to the previous line.
Start of line	`(beginning-of-line n)` Move point to the start of the current line. If *n* is specified, the function first moves forward *n - 1* lines.

Table B.2, con't.

To do this...	Use this function...
Moving the cursor, con't.	
End of line	`(end-of-line n)` Like `(beginning-of-line)` but moves point to the end of the line.

Move to specified character	`(goto-char n)`
	
	Move to character location *n* in the current buffer. For example, to go to the first line in the buffer, use:
	
	`(goto-char (point-min))`

Move to specified line number	`(goto-line n)` Moves the cursor to the start of line *n*.
Inserting text	

Insert string into buffer	`(insert str)`
	
	Inserts the string represented by *str* into the buffer at the location of point. For example, to insert the string "**END**" at the end of the buffer, use:
	
	`(goto-char (point-max))`
	`(insert "**END**")`
	
	You can include these special characters in the string:
	
	`\t` Insert a tab
	`\n` Insert a newline
	`\\` Insert a backslash

Insert a newline	`(newline n)` Inserts a newline into the buffer at point. If *n* is specified, insert *n* newlines.

Table B.2, con't.

To do this...	Use this function...
	Searching for text
Search forward for string	(search-forward *str bound noerror count*) Searches forward for string *str*. If *str* is found, Emacs places the cursor at the end of the string and returns **t**. The arguments *bound, noerror,* and *count* are optional. The *bound* parameter is a buffer location, at which Emacs terminates the search. The *noerror* parameter, if set to **t**, says to not return an error if *str* is not found. The *count* parameter determines how many occurrences to search for. For example, to search forward to the end of the buffer for the string "foobar": (search-forward "foobar") Search the next 1000 characters for "xyz": (search-forward "xyz" (+ (point) 1000)) Search for the 3rd occurrence of "pdq": (search-forward "pdq" (point-max) t 3)
Search backward for string	(search-backward *str bound noerror count*) Like (search-forward) but look backward instead.
	Working with the minibuffer (echo area)
Display message in echo area	(message *str*) Displays the string *str* in the echo area.
Suspend execution	(sit-for *n*) Wait for *n* seconds before continuing. This is preempted if user types any key.

Table B.2, con't.

To do this...	Use this function...
	Working with the minibuffer (echo area), con't.
Beep or flash screen	`(ding `*arg*`)` Beep the bell or flash the screen, whichever is supported on the terminal. If no *arg* is given, this also terminates any keyboard macro currently being defined.

Read a string in the minibuffer	`(read-string `*prompt initvalue*`)`
	
	Reads a string in the echo area, prompting with the value of the *prompt* parameter. If *initvalue* is given, Emacs uses it as an initial value. For example,
	
	`(setq inp (read-string "ans> " "yes"))`
	
	This code displays this prompt:
	
	`ans> yes`█
	
	If you press RET, Emacs assigns "yes" to the variable `inp`. You could also backspace over the "yes" string and enter another value.

Read character in minibuffer	`(read-char)` Reads a single character from the minibuffer *without echoing it*. Returns a number representing the character's value.
	Working with text
Concatenate string	`(concat `*s1 s2...*`)` Returns a string that is the concatenation of the string arguments. There can be more than two arguments.
Get substring	`(substring `*string from_pos* `[`*to_pos*`])` Returns a substring of *string* starting at *from_pos* and ending at *to_pos*. If *to_pos* is omitted, returns the substring starting at *from_pos* and continuing to the end of *string*.

Table B.2, con't.

To do this...	Use this function...
	Working with text, con't.

Get string from buffer	`(buffer-string` *from_pos to_pos*`)`
	
	Returns a string from the current buffer starting at *from_pos* and ending at *to_pos*. For example, to return the first one-tenth of the buffer:
	
	`(buffer-string 1 (/ (point-max) 10))`

Change to uppercase or lowercase	`(upcase` *s*`)`
	`(downcase` *s*`)`
	
	Returns the result of converting *s* to uppercase (or lowercase).

	Functions and variables

Define a function	`(defun` *name* `(`*args*`)`
	  `"`*documentation string*`"`
	  function body
	`)`
	
	Defines function that is referenced by *name* and has zero or more arguments. The *documentation string*, if present, is displayed by the help command **C-h f**. The *function body* contains Emacs-Lisp statements that are executed when you call the function name.

Define a variable	`(defvar` *varname value* `"`*documentation string*`"`) Defines a variable named *varname* and initial value *value*. If present, the *documentation string* will be displayed by the **C-h v** command. If the documentation string starts with an asterisk, the variable will be displayed by the **M-x edit-options** command.
Set a variable	`(setq` *variable value*`)` Set *variable* to *value*.

Table B.2, con't.

To do this...	Use this function...
	Functions and variables, con't.
Make function executable as Emacs command	`(interactive)` Makes the function in which it appears available to you as an Emacs user, either by the **M-x** command or by being bound to a command key. Also provides a mechanism through which commands can set their parameters from the minibuffer. This is discussed in detail later in the section "Interactive vs. Non-Interactive Functions."
	Basic math

Addition	`(+ `*list_of_values*`)`
	
	Returns the result of adding the *list_of_values*. For example, the following call returns the sum of 1, 2, 3, 4, and 5:
	
	`(+ 1 2 3 4 5)`

Subtraction	`(- `*list_of_values*`)`
	
	Returns the result of applying the subtraction operator on successive elements of the *list_of_values*. Typically, you would just have two values and it would subtract the second from the first. For example, the following call returns the number of characters between point and the end of the buffer:
	
	`(- (point-max) (point))`

Multiplication	`(* `*list_of_values*`)`
	
	Returns the product of the *list_of_values*. For example, the following call returns the product of 12,345,679 and 9:
	
	`(* 12345679 9)`

Table B.2, con't.

To do this...	Use this function...
	Basic math, con't.
Division	(/ *list_of_values*) Returns the result of applying the division operator to successive elements of *list_of_values*. For example, to get the character location that is one tenth from the start of the buffer: `(/ (point-max) 10)`
	Condition testing
Integer equal	(= *n1 n2*) Returns t if integers *n1* and *n2* are equal; `nil` otherwise.
Integer greater than and less than	(> *n1 n2*) (< *n1 n2*) Returns t if integer *n1* is greater than (less than) *n2;* `nil` otherwise.
Strings equal	(`string=` *str1 str2*) Returns t if strings *str1* and *str2* are the same; `nil` otherwise.
Objects equal	(eq *obj1 obj2*) Returns t if *obj1* and *obj2* are the same Lisp object; `nil` otherwise.
Equal structure and contents	(`equal` *obj1 obj2*) Returns t if the Lisp objects *obj1* and *obj2* have the same type, structure, and contents; otherwise, returns `nil`. Thus, you could use this function to compare strings, numbers, lists, and symbols. In essence, this is a general purpose equality testing function.

Table B.2, con't.

To do this...	Use this function...
	Condition testing, con't.

Logical not	`(not obj)`
	
	Return t if *obj* evaluates to nil. For example, to test if **str-var1** does not equal "FINISHED":
	
	`(not (string= str-var1 "FINISHED"))`

	Control flow

Compound statement	`(progn statement_list)`
	
	Runs all the function calls in *statement_list*; and returns the value returned by the last call in *statement_list*. For example, the following code swaps two variables and returns the value of the second variable:
	
	`(progn`
	`        (setq tmp-var var1)`
	`        (setq var1 var2)`
	`        (setq var2 tmp-var))`

If-then-else statement	`(if cond then_clause [else_clause])`
	
	If *cond* evaluates to t, then execute the *then_clause;* otherwise, execute the *else_clause* if it is present. For example, the following code assigns the variable **tmpvar** to **maxvar** if it is larger than **maxvar**:
	
	`(if (> tmpvar maxvar) (setq maxvar tmpvar))`
	
	And the following call converts a string to uppercase or lowercase, or leaves it alone, depending on the value of **str-case**:
	
	`(if (string= str-case "upper")`
	`    (setq newstr (upcase oldstr))`
	`    (if (string= str-case "lower")`
	`            (setq newstr (downcase oldstr))`
	`    )`
	`)`

Table B.2, con't.

To do this...	Use this function...
	Control flow, con't.

While statement	`(while` *cond stmt*`)`
	
	 While *cond* is not `nil`, execute *stmt*. For example, the following code prints the value of a variable in the echo area until the value is zero, decrementing it each time through the loop:
	
	 ```(while (not (= idx 0)```
	``` (progn```
	``` (message "idx = %d" idx)```
	``` (setq idx (- idx 1))```
	```)```
	```)```

Developing Your Function

When developing your Emacs-Lisp function, use Emacs-Lisp mode. There are several good reasons for using this mode:

- You can use Emacs-Lisp libraries.

- You can install your functions into Emacs as you are developing them.

- You can use the Emacs-Lisp debugger.

The rest of this section assumes you are using Emacs-Lisp mode to develop your functions.

Interactive vs. Non-Interactive Functions

There are two types of Emacs-Lisp functions: **interactive** and **non-interactive**. Interactive functions can be run as editing commands; non-interactive functions cannot. All Emacs editing commands are bound to interactive functions. Interactive functions may call non-interactive functions, and vice versa.

An example of an interactive function is **previous-line**, which moves the cursor to the previous line in the file. An example of a non-interactive function is **second**, which returns the second element in an Emacs-Lisp list. You can invoke the **previous-line** function via **C-p** command, but there is no editing command to invoke **second**, nor would it really make sense in the context of editing commands.

Although non-interactive functions cannot be run as editing commands, you can still evaluate them. For example, you could use **M–ESC** to evaluate the expression `(second '(one two three))` in the minibuffer. Emacs displays the result `two` in the minibuffer.

Declaring Interactive Functions

To make an Emacs-Lisp function interactive, include a call to the `interactive` function, which tells Emacs that the function can be called interactively. The general form of an interactive Emacs-Lisp function is:

```
(defun functionName (args)       ← Function name and argument definition.
  "documentation"                ← Optional documentation string.
  (interactive "template")       ← Call to interactive.
  functionBody)                  ← The actual code called in the function. May
                                   include calls to other interactive functions or
                                   non-interactive functions.
```

The interactive Function

The `interactive` function tells Emacs how to parse arguments to the Emacs-Lisp function. In its simplest form, `interactive` has no arguments, meaning that Emacs-Lisp does not pass any arguments to the function. For example, the following custom function goes to the middle character in a buffer; it does not require any arguments.

```
(defun goto-midpoint ()            ; there are no arguments
  "Move cursor to the middle character in buffer."
  (interactive)                    ; interactive, but no args
  (save-restriction                ; save any buffer restrictions
    (widen)                        ; widen to entire buffer
    (goto-char (/ (- (point-max)   ; midpoint = (max - min)/2
                     (point-min))
                  2)))))           ; prior restrictions restored
```

This use of `interactive` is fine for functions that do not require arguments. Usually, though, an interactive function requires arguments. In these cases, the call to `interactive` includes a string that defines how to pass arguments to the function. For example, the definition of the `goto-line` function (found in the Emacs-Lisp library `simple.el`), looks like this:

```
(defun goto-line (arg)
  "Goto line ARG, counting from line 1 at beginning of buffer."
  (interactive "NGoto line: ")
  (save-restriction
    (widen)
    (goto-char 1)
    (forward-line (1- arg))))
```

Notice that **goto-line** has one argument, **arg**. The call to **interactive** has the argument (**"NGoto line: "**). In general, the argument to **interactive** is a string, containing a code letter, followed by a prompt. In the example above, the code letter **N** tells Emacs that the function expects a numeric argument, and that if the user doesn't specify it with a numeric prefix, then prompt with **Goto line:** .

Thus, if you execute the **goto-line** function with a numeric prefix, as in the command **C-u 10 M-x goto-line RET**, Emacs passes the numeric argument (10) to the **goto-line** function. If you do not include a numeric prefix, as in the command **M-x goto-line**, Emacs prompts for it with **Goto line:** in the minibuffer.

Not all Emacs-Lisp functions prompt you for arguments, however. For example, the **next-line** function simply advances the number of lines you specify. Its call to **interactive** looks like this,

```
(interactive "p")
```

meaning that Emacs should convert the prefix argument, if any, to a number and pass it to the function. Thus, **C-u - 10 C-n** causes Emacs to pass -10 to **next-line**.

Specifying Read-Only Interactive Commands

There are some commands you would not want to perform in a read-only buffer; for example, you would want to disable any commands that add or delete text. To do this, specify an asterisk (*) before the code letter. For example, the call to **interactive** in the **kill-word** function looks like this:

```
(interactive "*p")
```

If you're in a read-only buffer and try to run a function whose **interactive** string starts with *, Emacs displays an error message:

```
Buffer is read-only: <# buffer bufferName>
```

Prompting for Multiple Interactive Arguments

The examples shown thus far have all been for single arguments. Occasionally, however, you may need to prompt for multiple arguments. To specify multiple prompts, start each additional prompt on a new line without terminating the string. For example, suppose you create a function that swaps two lines in a file, given their line numbers. The call to `interactive` might look like this:

```
    (interactive "nFirst line to swap:
nSecond line to swap: ")
↑
column 0
```

Passing Emacs-Lisp Expressions as Arguments

Finally, the least common type of argument specified to `interactive` is an Emacs-Lisp expression. In this case, Emacs evaluates the expression and passes it as the argument(s) to the function. In the following example, the expression `(list (/ (point-max) 2))` is evaluated and passed as the parameter `mid-char`:

```
(defun goto-midpoint (mid-char)
   (interactive (list (/ (point-max) 2)))
   (goto-char mid-char))
```

The expression used should normally evaluate to a list. Thus, a list of parameters can be passed to the function.

Code Letters to the interactive Function

Table B.3 summarizes the different code letters that can be passed in the `interactive` function string to get different types of input arguments.

Table B.3. Code Letters to the interactive Function String

To Read This	Letter and Description

Function name	**a**
	
	Reads the name of an Emacs-Lisp function and performs Lisp symbol completion. For example, the following function reads a function name and displays the function's name in the minibuffer.
	
	``lisp
	(defun read-func (func-name)
	    (interactive "aFunction name: ")
	    (eval-expression 'func-name))
	``
	
	If Emacs cannot find a symbol to match the one entered at the prompt, it displays [no match] after the symbol name.

Name of existing buffer	**b**
	
	Reads the name of an existing Emacs buffer and performs symbol completion. For example, the following function reads a buffer name and inserts it into the buffer:
	
	``lisp
	(defun read-buf (buf-name)
	    (interactive "bBuffer name: ")
	    (insert buf-name))
	``
	
	If you attempt to enter a buffer name that does not exist, Emacs displays the message [no match] and waits for you to type an existing name.

Name of buffer	**B** Same as **b**, but Emacs does not force you to enter the name of an existing buffer. This is useful for functions that can work on either new or existing buffers.

Table B.3, con't.

To Read This	Letter and Description

Character	c
	
	Reads a single character. Returns a value as soon as the user presses the key. The following function prompts for a single-character Y or N and inserts a corresponding **yes** or **no** string into the current buffer:
	
	<pre>(defun read-y-or-n (char-val)
	  (interactive "cYes or No? ")
	  (let ((letter (downcase char-val)))
	    (cond ((equal letter ?y) (insert "yes"))
	          ((equal letter ?n) (insert "no"))
	          (t (insert "no")))))</pre>

Cursor location	d
	
	Returns the value of the current cursor location as a byte location from the start of the buffer. You would not use this letter with a prompt. The following function moves the cursor to the midpoint between the start of the file and the current cursor location:
	
	<pre>(defun half-back (cursor-loc)
	    (interactive "d")
	    (goto-char (/ cursor-loc 2)))</pre>

Directory name	D
	
	Reads a directory name and performs file name completion (like the **C-x i** command). It uses the current working directory as a default value. The following function reads a path name and stores it into the variable **work-dir**:
	
	<pre>(defun get-work-dir (dir-name)
	    (interactive "DWork directory: ")
	    (setq work-dir dir-name))</pre>

Existing file name	f Essentially the same as **D**, but reads a file name instead. If the user enters a file name that does not exist, Emacs displays **[no match]** in the minibuffer and waits for the user to enter a valid name of an existing file.

Table B.3, con't.

To Read This	Letter and Description
File name	**F** Same as **f**, but does not force the user to enter the name of an existing file. The user can enter the name of a nonexistent file. The **C-x C-f** command uses this code letter to get the name of a file to edit; they file may or may not exist.

Key sequences	**k**
	
	Reads a key sequence without performing its command key binding. The following example prompts for a key sequence and inserts the key sequence into the current buffer:
	
	```(defun insert-key-sequence (keys) (interactive "kKey sequence: ") (insert keys))```
	
	If you installed this function (with **C-x C-e**) and run it (with **M-x insert-key-sequence**), you would see this prompt:
	
	```Key sequence:```
	
	If you then typed the command key sequence **C-x C-4 m**, the characters would appear after the prompt until the sequence was complete. At that point, Emacs passes the key sequence to the function, which then inserts it into the current buffer.

Location of mark	**m** Returns the value of the current mark, as set by the **C-SPC** command. As with the **d** code letter, you would not specify a prompt. The following function moves the cursor to the mark: ```(defun goto-mark (mark-loc) (interactive "m") (goto-char mark-loc))```

Table B.3, con't.

To Read This	Letter and Description

Number	**n**
	
	Reads a number in the minibuffer. If the user specifies a numeric prefix (C-u n), it is **not** passed to the function. Therefore, this code letter should only be used in functions where passing a numeric argument from the prefix would not necessarily make sense. The following function sets the variable chap-no:
	
	```\n(defun set-chap-no (n)\n (interactive "nChapter number: ")\n (setq chap-no n))\n```
	
	Another situation where this would make sense is when a function requires multiple numeric arguments. For example, the following call to **interactive** sets up prompts for three numeric arguments:
	
	```\n (interactive "nStarting line:\nnEnding line:\nnSearch for number: ")\n```

Prefix or number	**N** If the function is called with a numeric prefix (C-u n), then pass it as an argument; otherwise, prompt for a numeric argument. For example, the following function goes to a location expressed as a percent of the file size: ```\n(defun goto-pct (pct)\n (interactive "NPercent location: ")\n (let ((pct-loc (cond ((< pct 0) 0)\n ((> pct 100) 100)\n (t pct))))\n (goto-char\n (/ (* pct-loc (point-max)) 100))))\n``` If you invoked this as C-u 5 M-x goto-pct RET, the function would goto the character corresponding to five percent of the file. Alternatively, if you execute it as M-x goto-pct RET, Emacs prompts you for the location with **Percent location:** in the minibuffer.

Table B.3, con't.

To Read This	Letter and Description
Prefix number	**P** Like **N**, but passes **only** a numeric prefix. It does not prompt for the value. For example, in the previous function, if the `interactive` call looked like this `(interactive "p")` Emacs would only accept a numeric prefix (**C-u** *n*) and would not prompt for the value. If a prefix is given, it is returned as a list; otherwise, `nil` is returned.
Raw prefix argument	**p** Accepts a prefix argument without doing any conversion or checking. Will not prompt for the argument.

Bounds of the current region	**r**
	
	Returns the current cursor location and the location of mark as two parameters; the smaller of the two is passed as the first parameter. A prompt is not useful with this code letter. The following function puts "escape" tags around a region:
	
	``
	(defun escape-it (beg end)
	    "Put <esc> <\\esc> around a region."
	    (interactive "r")
	    (goto-char end)
	    (insert "<\\esc>")
	    (goto-char beg)
	    (insert "<esc>")
	(goto-char (point)))
	``

String	**s**
	
	Reads any string of characters, terminated by the **RET** key. The following function prompts for a name, converts it to uppercase, and inserts it into the current buffer:
	
	``
	(defun get-name (name-str)
	    (interactive "sYour name: ")
	    (insert (upcase name-str)))
	``

Table B.3, con't.

To Read This	Letter and Description
Symbol name	**s** Reads an Emacs-Lisp symbol name, terminated by the **RET** key.
Variable name	**v** Reads a variable name. Will do symbol completion.
Lisp expression	**x** Reads an Emacs-Lisp expression, but does not evaluate it; the expression is passed as an argument to the function.

Evaluated lisp expression	**X**
	
	Reads and evaluates an Emacs-Lisp expression and passes the resulting value to the function. The following function prompts for an expression and goes to the line that the expression evaluates to:
	
	`(defun goto-expr (expr-val)`
	`    (interactive "XLine number expr: ")`
	`    (goto-line expr-val))`
	
	For example, if you respond to the prompt as shown below, the cursor moves to the eleventh line in the file:
	
	`Line number expr: `<u>`(+ (point-min) 10)`</u>` RET`

Getting Documentation on Emacs-Lisp Defuns and Variables

The **C-h f** (or **M-x describe-function**) command displays documentation for an Emacs-Lisp defun, while **C-h v** (or **M-x describe-variable**) displays documentation for an Emacs-Lisp variable. These commands are part of Emacs' online help facility. They prompt you for the name of the defun or variable to describe. For example, if you type **C-h f if RET**, Emacs displays the following in a ***Help*** buffer in another window:

```
if:
if(args)
(if C T E...) if C yields non-NIL do T, else do E...
Returns the value of T or the value of the last of the E's.
There may be no E's; then if C yields NIL, the value is NIL.
```

If you do not provide a function or variable name, Emacs uses a default name, taken from nearby Lisp code. In the case of a defun, Emacs uses the name of the defun used in the innermost list containing the cursor. In the case of a variable, Emacs uses the symbol name under or immediately preceding the cursor.

For example, if the cursor is positioned over the ' in the following sexp,

```
(second (rest '(1 2 3)))
```

Then the **C-h f** command will prompt you for a function name as:

```
Describe function (default rest): █
```

Emacs chose **rest** as the default defun because it is the defun called in the innermost list **(rest '(1 2 3))** around the cursor. If you press **RET**, Emacs displays the following ***Help*** buffer in another window:

```
rest:
Synonym for `cdr'
```

Similarly for variables, if the cursor is positioned between *fill-column* and *comment-column* in the following line of code:

```
(- fill-column█comment-column)
```

Then, Emacs assumes you want information on *fill-column* since it immediately precedes the cursor.

```
Describe variable (default fill-column): █
```

If you press **ET**, Emacs creates a ***Help*** buffer containing the following message:

```
fill-column's value is 70

Documentation:
fill-column
*Column beyond which automatic line-wrapping should happen.
```

Lisp Symbol Completion

As with file name completion, Emacs can complete Lisp symbols for you automatically via the **M-TAB** command. Lisp symbol completion works in all modes, not just Lisp modes. However, it works *only* for symbols that have been defined (by executing Emacs-Lisp code). It will not work for symbols that are in a buffer that have not yet been evaluated.

If you type **M-TAB** at the end of a partially completed symbol name, Emacs attempts to complete the symbol name. For example, if you type **M-TAB** with the cursor positioned immediately after the **sec** in the following code, Emacs expands **sec** to **second**:

Before: (sec█
                                       ↑
                                     cursor

After **M-TAB**:   (second █
                                          ↑
                          Emacs completes symbol **second**; cursor is here.

If an open parenthesis precedes the symbol name, as in the above example, Emacs searches only for defuns that match the symbol, because such a construct is assumed to be a function call.

If more than one completion for a Lisp symbol is possible, Emacs creates a window containing all possible completions. For example, if you used **M-TAB** on the partial symbol **(eq**, Emacs creates a ***Help*** buffer in another window, with the following message:

```
Possible completions are:
eq                               equal
eql
```

This means that Emacs knows about three symbols that start with **eq**, and you must select which one you want.

If Emacs cannot complete a symbol, it displays this message in the minibuffer:

```
Can't find completion for symbol_name
```

Emacs also looks for user-defined symbols. For example, if you evaluated the **pow** defun in Emacs-Lisp or Lisp Interaction mode, Emacs could complete it for you. (Evaluating defuns interactively is described in the section "Evaluating Lisp Code" below.) However, Emacs cannot complete user-defined symbols that are passed to an external Lisp interpreter (that is, symbols defined in Lisp or Inferior Lisp modes).

Evaluating Lisp Code

This section is just a quick memory jogger for commands you can use to evaluate Emacs-Lisp code in the minibuffer or in Emacs-Lisp or Lisp Interaction mode.

Evaluating Code in the Minibuffer

To evaluate Emacs-Lisp code in the minibuffer, use the **M-ESC** (or **ESC-ESC**) command. It prompts you for the expression to evaluate in the minibuffer:

```
Eval: █    ← You type the Emacs-Lisp expression to evaluate
```

It then displays the result of the evaluation in the minibuffer. For example, if you typed the expression **(+ 1 1)** to the **Eval:** prompt, as:

```
Eval: (+ 1 1) RET
```

Emacs displays the result **2** in the minibuffer.

Emacs-Lisp Mode

Emacs-Lisp mode provides commands for evaluating a single defun, all the code within a region, or an entire buffer. Any expressions evaluated in this mode are "installed" into Emacs for the duration of the Emacs session. For instance, if you evaluate a defun named **foo**, it can be called by other Emacs-Lisp functions or can be executed from the minibuffer using **M-ESC** (or **ESC-ESC**).

Table B.4 summarizes the various commands for evaluating Lisp code.

Table B.4. Summary of Emacs-Lisp Mode's Evaluation Commands

Operation	Command and Comments
Evaluate preceding expression	`C-x C-e` Evaluates the Emacs-Lisp expression preceding the cursor and displays the result in the minibuffer.

Table B.4, con't.

Operation	Command and Comments
Evaluate expression	`C-M-x` This command is essentially the same as `C-x C-e`, except that it evaluates the expression that *contains* the cursor or that immediately follows the cursor.
Evaluate code in region	`M-x eval-region` Evaluates all the Emacs-Lisp code in the current region.
Evaluate all code in buffer	`M-x eval-current-buffer` Evaluates all Emacs-Lisp code in the buffer. This command is useful for installing all changes from an Emacs-Lisp buffer into Emacs for the duration of the session.

As an example of how `C-x C-e` evaluation works, suppose you've written the following and positioned the cursor as shown:

```
(defun foo (x) (concat "foo" x))█
```

If you type `C-x C-e`, the message **foo** is displayed in the minibuffer. Now, if you type **M-ESC** (or **ESC-ESC**) to evaluate an expression in the minibuffer, and type:

```
Eval: (foo "bar") RET
```

The message **foobar** is displayed in the minibuffer, indicating that Emacs evaluated the defun **foo** that you defined above.

When given a numeric argument, the `C-M-x` and `C-x C-e` commands insert the resulting value of the evaluation into the buffer at the location of the cursor.

Lisp Interaction Mode

Lisp Interaction mode is identical to Emacs-Lisp mode, except that it has an additional command, `C-j` (or **LFD**). The `C-j` command evaluates the Lisp expression preceding the cursor and inserts the resulting value into the buffer. This is why the mode is called Lisp Interaction mode: it shows the interaction between you and the Lisp interpreter in the same buffer.

Shown below is the output resulting in a Lisp Interaction buffer. Underscored lines were typed in; all others Emacs inserted.

```
(+ 1 2 3) C-j
6
(defun foo (x) (concat "foo" x)) C-j
foo
(foo "bar") C-j
"foobar"
```

Thus, Lisp Interaction mode gives you a "log" of Lisp expressions and the result of their evaluation.

Loading Emacs-Lisp Libraries

Emacs supports a **library** of Emacs-Lisp source files that you can use in developing Emacs-Lisp programs. Many of these libraries are automatically loaded when you start Emacs; some you must load explicitly.

Locating the Libraries on Your System

Where Emacs-Lisp libraries are located depends on what system Emacs runs on. For example, on the system we used, the libraries are located under the directories **/usr/local/emacs/lisp** and **/usr/local/emacs/lisp/local,** but may be located elsewhere on other systems.

The *load-path* variable defines the path names that Emacs searches for libraries. This variable should automatically be set to the correct value when Emacs starts up, so there should be no need to change it. However, you might still want to look at its value to determine where the libraries are stored on your system. For example, you could use **M-x describe-variable** to display the value of *load-path:*

```
M-x describe-variable RET
Describe variable: load-path RET
```

In response to this command, Emacs creates a ***Help*** buffer in another window. On our system, this buffer displayed the following message:

```
load-path's value is ("/usr/local/emacs/lisp/local"
                      "/usr/local/emacs/lisp" nil)

Documentation:
load-path
```

```
*List of directories to search for files to load.
Each element is a string (directory name) or nil (default directory).
Initialized based on EMACSLOADPATH environment variable, if any,
```

Once you know the location of the libraries, you can examine them by loading them into a read-only buffer. The Emacs-Lisp source code for each Emacs mode is defined in these files, as are various library packages, such as **float.el**, which defines defuns for doing floating-point math in Emacs-Lisp, or **yow.el**, which defines code to display zippyisms.

You can also set *load-path* in your **.emacs** start-up file to include directories containing your own custom libraries. That way, the **M-x load-library** command will find your custom libraries, as well as the standard libraries.

.el vs. .elc Libraries

As you look through the Emacs-Lisp library directories, notice that often there are two versions of a file: one whose name ends in **.el** and another ending in **.elc**. Files ending with **.el** are Emacs-Lisp source files and can be edited in Emacs-Lisp mode. The **.elc** version of a file is created by **byte-compiling** the file into smaller, faster-running code that cannot be edited (byte-compiling is discussed later in "Compiling Emacs-Lisp Code").

Loading and Running an Emacs-Lisp File

To load and run a file containing Emacs-Lisp code, without visiting the file in a buffer, use the **M-x load-file** command. It prompts in the minibuffer for the path name of a file to load and execute:

```
M-x load-file RET                                  ← Run the command.
Load file: ~/emacs/mycode.el RET                   ← Enter the file's name.
Loading /users/caroline/emacs/mycode.el...         ← Emacs loads the file.
```

M-x load-file will load either **.el** or **.elc** files. It does not create a buffer for loaded files—it merely reads and executes them. Any code contained in the files becomes part of the Emacs environment until you leave Emacs. For example, if the file contained defuns, you could execute them using **M-ESC** (or **ESC-ESC**).

You could put this command in your **.emacs** start-up file to load any special Emacs-Lisp functions you have defined. For example, if you defined some functions to use when developing Emacs-Lisp programs and then stored them in a file named **~/mydefuns.el**, you could put the following line in your local **.emacs** start-up file to have them loaded automatically whenever you start Emacs:

```
(load-file "~/mydefuns.el")
```

Note that the file will load and run faster if it has been byte-compiled (as described later). Adding such customizations to your `.emacs` start-up file is described in Chapter 13, "Customizing the Emacs Environment."

Loading and Running an Emacs-Lisp Library

The `M-x load-library` command loads and executes a file of Emacs-Lisp code from the library directories. It prompts you for the name of the library. You do *not* have to supply the `.el` or `.elc` suffix. By default, Emacs searches for a library whose name ends with `.elc`. If one does not exist, it searches for the library name ending with `.el`. Finally, if that file does not exist, it searches for the specified name. For example, you could load the `float` library as shown below:

```
M-x load-library RET          ← Run the command.
Load library: float RET       ← You type float to the prompt.
Loading float...done          ← Emacs displays this message.
```

If the `.elc` version of the library (`float.elc`) exists in the *load-path* directories, Emacs loads it rather than the `.el` version. If only the `.el` version exists (`float.el`), then Emacs loads it. You can override the default library selection by specifying the desired suffix:

```
M-x load-library RET          ← Run the command.
Load library: float.el RET    ← Tell Emacs to load the .el version.
Loading float.el...done       ← Emacs loads the .el version, not .elc.
```

Once a library is loaded, its defuns and variables become available to Emacs-Lisp, just as with the `M-x load-file` command.

As with `load-file`, you may want to place `load-library` commands in your `.emacs` start-up file to load standard libraries that are not ordinarily loaded when Emacs starts up.

Compiling Emacs-Lisp Code

Emacs has commands for compiling either a single Emacs-Lisp (`.el`) file, or *all* the `.el` files in a particular directory. Compiling is useful because it makes Emacs-Lisp code load and run faster than uncompiled source. Compiling basically converts the Emacs-Lisp source to a "tokenized" form that can be processed more quickly; it doesn't convert it to machine code.

Byte-Compiling a Single File

Use the **M-x byte-compile-file** command to compile your own **.el** Emacs-Lisp files into **.elc** files. This command prompts for the name of the file to compile. If you do not supply a file name—that is, if you just hit **RET**—Emacs assumes you want to byte-compile the file being visited in the current buffer. Emacs shows you the status of the byte-compile in the minibuffer.

For example, to byte-compile Emacs-Lisp code in a file named **mystuff.el** in your home directory, run **M-x byte-compile-file**, as shown below:

```
M-x byte-compile-file RET            ← Run the command.
Byte compile file: ~/▌ RET            ← Do not type ~/; just press RET to
                                        use current buffer as the default.
```

Emacs then displays the following messages in the minibuffer:

```
Compiling /users/caroline/mystuff.el ...   ← Emacs displays this message
                                             during the compilation.
Wrote /users/caroline/mystuff.elc          ← When the compilation is
                                             finished, Emacs displays this
                                             message.
```

At this point, you now have a file named **mystuff.elc** that you can load with **M-x load-file RET mystuff.elc RET**.

If any errors occur during a compilation, Emacs displays an error message in the minibuffer and the compilation is aborted.

Byte-Compiling All the Files in a Directory

The **M-x byte-recompile-directory** command prompts you for the path name of a directory containing **.el** files, and recompiles the **.el** that have a corresponding **.elc** file and that have changed since the file was last byte-compiled. As such, it acts as a **make** facility. If an empty argument is passed to this command (as in **C-u M-x byte-recompile-directory**), Emacs asks whether you want to also recompile **.el** files that have no corresponding **.elc** file. You must respond with **y** or **n**.

In addition, before doing a compilation, Emacs will ask you whether you want to save buffers that have changed since the last compilation. This ensures that any changes you make will be in the files before they are byte-compiled.

Compiling from the UNIX Command Line

You can also compile .el from the UNIX command line (outside of Emacs) by running Emacs in batch mode. The syntax of the Emacs command when used to compile .el files is:

```
emacs -batch -f batch-byte-compile filename...
```

where *filename* is the name of one or more files that you want to compile. For example, to compile the files named **mydefuns.el** and **custom.el** in the current directory, you would type the following command to the UNIX prompt:

```
emacs -batch -f batch-byte-compile mydefuns.el custom.el
```

Debugging Emacs-Lisp Code (Advanced Usage)

Emacs provides a debugger for Emacs-Lisp code. Normally, the debugger is disabled. There are three debugging levels that you can enable, described in Table B.5.

Table B.5. Enabling Debugging Levels

Debugging Level	How to Enable	Description
Go to debugger when Lisp error occurs	Set *debug-on-error* variable to non-**nil**	Use this mode to trap run-time Emacs-Lisp errors. An example of such an error occurs when you press C-b when the cursor is at the start of a buffer. Pressing C-g to terminate a command does not generate an Emacs-Lisp error.
Go to debugger when C-g is pressed	Set *debug-on-quit* variable to non-**nil**	Use this mode to trap C-g. This is especially useful in debugging infinite loops. It has no effect on errors.
Go to debugger when a defun is entered	Run **M-x** debug-on-entry	Use this mode when you want to use the debugger whenever a particular defun executes. This command prompts you for the name of the defun you want to debug; type it and press **RET**.

Canceling Debug-on-Entry

There are two ways to turn off debug-on-entry for a particular defun:

1. Use the **M-x cancel-debug-on-entry** command, which prompts for the name of the defun.

2. Modify and reevaluate the defun. That is, making changes to a defun turns off debugging for the defun.

Setting Breakpoints

To enable the debugger at a specific location within some Emacs-Lisp code (that is, to set a **breakpoint**), insert the Emacs-Lisp expression **(debug)** in the source; then install the changes with **C-M-x** (evaluate the defun surrounding the cursor).

For example, suppose you have written the following defun, **sgml-block**, region:

```
(defun sgml-block (beg end)
   (interactive "r")
   (goto-char end)
   (sgml-newline)
   (goto-char beg)
   (sgml-newline))
```

To invoke the debugger just after the expression **(goto-char end)** is evaluated, insert **(debug)** after that line; then evaluate the defun by running **C-M-x**:

```
(defun sgml-block (beg end)
   (interactive "r")
   (goto-char end)
   (debug)                        ← Add this line to the defun
   (sgml-newline)
   (goto-char beg)
   (sgml-newline))
```

Using Debug Mode Commands

When the debugger is invoked, it brings up a buffer in another window named ***Backtrace***. The ***Backtrace*** window displays code being executed in the debugger. The first line in this buffer is a message describing why the debugger was invoked. The rest of the buffer contains calls to Emacs-Lisp defuns, including the parameters that were passed to them.

The ***Backtrace*** buffer is read-only and uses a special Debugger mode. In this mode, letters are defined as debugger commands; you cannot type text into the buffer.

However, you do have the usual editing commands available (for example, you could use C-x o to switch between windows, or C-x C-f to visit a file).

Always exit the debugger using an appropriate command in the *Backtrace* window. The reason is that the debugger is actually a recursive editing level, and improperly exiting a recursive editing level can confuse Emacs. Recursive editing levels are denoted by square brackets around the mode name [(Debugger)]. A **recursive editing level** is basically an Emacs function that is called from within an Emacs function. Thus, the debugger is called from within other Emacs commands.

Certain debugger commands operate on a **stack frame,** which is a snapshot of the calling stack when a defun was called. You can set or unset a flag that tells the debugger to stop on exit from a frame. The **current stack frame** is the frame whose line contains the cursor; you can change the current stack frame by using the C-p and C-n commands to move "up" and "down" among the displayed stack frames.

Table B.6 summarizes the Debug mode commands, which are used mainly to step through the Emacs-Lisp code an expression at a time.

Table B.6. Emacs-Lisp Debugger Commands

Operation	Command and Description
Continue	c Exit the debugger and continue execution as if the debugger was not entered.
Single-step	d Continue execution, but reenter the debugger the next time a defun is called. This is useful for evaluating the sub-expressions within an expression, one at a time, to see what values they return.
Set uplevel breakpoint	b Set up to reenter the debugger when the current stack frame is exited. Frames that invoke the debugger are marked with an asterisk. By default, the debugger enables this feature for defuns that are flagged by the M-x debug-on-entry command.
Clear uplevel breakpoint	u Says not to enter the debugger on exiting from the current frame. Undoes a b command.

Table B.6, con't.

Operation	Command and Description
Evaluate	**e** Read and evaluate a Lisp expression in the minibuffer and displays its value in the minibuffer.
Quit	**q** Quit the program being debugged. This is useful when you have enabled *debug-on-quit* and really *do* want to quit the program when you press **C-g**.
Set return value	**r** Returns a value from the debugger. This is used to insert your own values on return from a call frame (as set up by the **b** command).

An Example Debug Session

Suppose you've written the following defun, which is supposed to compute **x** to the **y** power, where **y** is a nonnegative integer.

```
(defun pow (x y)
  (if (equal y 0)
      1
    (if (equal y 1)
        y
      (* x (pow x (- y 1)))))))
```

You install the function in Emacs-Lisp mode using the **C-M-x** command. To see if it works, you run **M-ESC** to evaluate an expression using the defun:

```
M-ESC                    ← To evaluate an expression in the minibuffer.
Eval: (pow 2 3) RET      ← See what 2 to the 3rd power is.
4                        ← It should be 8.
```

You decide to use the debugger to find the problem. Since the defun is not generating an error, it does not make sense to use *debug-on-error*. Nor does it make sense to *debug-on-quit*. The logical choice in this case is to use **M-x debug-on-entry**.

```
M-x debug-on-entry RET              ← Invoke the command.
Debug on entry (to function): pow RET   ← Type the name of the defun.
```

Now when you evaluate the expression using **M-ESC**, Emacs brings up a
Backtrace window that looks something like this:

```
Entering:
* pow(2 3)
  eval((pow 2 3))
  byte-code(" ... " [values expression t nil eval prin1] 4)
  eval-expression((pow 2 3))
  call-interactively(eval-expression)
```

Basically, this means that the debugger was entered and that **pow** was called with the
arguments 2 and 3, respectively. If you press **c** while in the ***Backtrace*** window, the
debugger exits and the defun continues. However, since pow is recursive, it enters the
debugger again when **pow** calls itself in the last case. This changes the ***Backtrace***
window to look like this:

```
* pow(2 2)                          ← Invoking pow invokes debug.
  (* ...computing arguments...)     ← (* x (pow x (- y 1))).
  (if ...)                          ← (if (equal y 1)... No.
  (if ...)                          ← (if (equal y 0)... No.
* pow(2 3)
  eval((pow 2 3))
  byte-code(" ... " [values expression t nil eval prin1] 4)
    eval-expression((pow 2 3))
    call-interactively(eval-expression)
```

There are now two frames displayed, one for each invocation of **pow**. Each frame is
preceded by an asterisk (*), indicating that the debugger will be reentered when the frame
is exited—that is, when this particular invocation of **pow** comes back with a value. Thus,
you will be able to see the values returned by **pow** during the recursion.

If you press **c** again, the same thing happens because **y** is still greater than 1. The
Backtrace window now looks like this:

```
Entering:
* pow(2 1)                          ← Invoking pow invokes debug again.
  (* ...computing arguments...)     ← (* x (pow x (- y 1))).
  (if ...)                          ← (if (equal y 1)... No.
  (if ...)                          ← (if (equal y 0)... No.
* pow(2 2)
  (* ...computing arguments...)
  (if ...)
  (if ...)
```

```
* pow(2 3)
  eval((pow 2 3))
  byte-code(" ... " [values expression t nil eval prin1] 4)
  eval-expression((pow 2 3))
  call-interactively(eval-expression)
```

Now, when you press **c**, you get a different result, because **y** finally equals 1—the value in the base of the recursion. Thus **pow** does not invoke itself again. Now the ***Backtrace*** window looks like this:

```
Return value: 1                          ← Return value of (pow 2 1), from the
  pow(2 1)                                 statement (if (equal y 1)
  (* ...computing arguments...)                            y
  (if ...)
  (if ...)
* pow(2 2)
  (* ...computing arguments...)
  (if ...)
  (if ...)
* pow(2 3)
  eval((pow 2 3))
  byte-code(" ... " [values expression t nil eval prin1] 4)
  eval-expression((pow 2 3))
  call-interactively(eval-expression)
```

Something is suspicious: 2 to the power of 1 does not equal 1. It should be the value of **x**. This is your clue to look at the code for the base case of **(if (equal y 1)**.... And, in fact, the code does contain an error. It should return **x**, not **y**!

So the bug is found, but let's continue anyway. If you press **c** again, the ***Backtrace*** buffer looks like this:

```
Return value: 2
  pow(2 2)
  (* ...computing arguments...)
  (if ...)
  (if ...)
* pow(2 3)
eval((pow 2 3))
byte-code(" ... " [values expression t nil eval prin1] 4)
eval-expression((pow 2 3))
call-interactively(eval-expression)
```

Notice that the stack frame for the call to **(pow 2 1)** disappeared. Also notice that the stack frame for **(pow 2 2)** is no longer preceded by *****, indicating the stack frame is finished computing and has returned the value 2. That is, **(pow 2 2)** is equal to 2, which is wrong. The error in the base case is propagating back through the recursion.

If you press **c** again, the window looks like this:

```
Return value: 4
  pow(2 3)
  eval((pow 2 3))
  byte-code(" ... " [values expression t nil eval prin1] 4)
  eval-expression((pow 2 3))
  call-interactively(eval-expression)
```

This shows that the return value of **(pow 2 3)** is 4. Now if you press **c** one last time, the ***Backtrace*** window disappears altogether and the function result is placed in the minibuffer, as it would have been if you hadn't entered the debugger to begin with.

An Example Using d to Step through Subexpressions

In contrast to the **c** command, which exits the debugger altogether until the next invocation of the function, the **d** command stays in the debugger, evaluating the next subexpression in the current expression. For example, suppose you debug the **pow** defun again, but instead of issuing the **c** command, you use **d** the first time into the debugger. The ***Backtrace*** window would look like this:

```
Beginning evaluation of function call form:
* (if ...computing arguments...)          ← d command creates a new frame.
* pow(2 3)                                 ← This is the stack frame on entry.
  eval((pow 2 3))
  byte-code(" ... " [values expression t nil eval prin1] 4)
  eval-expression((pow 2 3))
  call-interactively(eval-expression)
```

The **d** command caused the debugger to execute the next subexpression in the defun **pow**, which happens to be the first **if** statement. If you press **d** again, the buffer looks like this:

```
Beginning evaluation of function call form:
* (equal ...computing arguments...)       ← Now equal is evaluated.
* (if ...)
* pow(2 3)
  eval((pow 2 3))
  byte-code(" ... " [values expression t nil eval prin1] 4)
  eval-expression((pow 2 3))
  call-interactively(eval-expression)
```

Now the **(equal ...)** predicate is being evaluated as an argument to the **(if ...)** predicate. Pressing **d** again causes the debugger to evaluate the arguments to the **equal** predicate and return a **t** or **nil** value, in this case **nil**.

```
Return value: nil                          ← 3 does not equal 0; return nil.
  equal(3 0)                               ← Compare 3 to 0.
* (if ...)
* pow(2 3)
  eval((pow 2 3))
  byte-code(" ... " [values expression t nil eval prin1] 4)
  eval-expression((pow 2 3))
  call-interactively(eval-expression)
```

Pressing **d** again brings the debugger to the stack frame for the **if** predicate. You can continue execution this way, single-stepping through all the subexpressions in the call to **pow**.

Remember that the debugger will stop on exit from a stack frame if the frame is marked by an asterisk. The **d** command automatically inserts these marks for each subexpression's stack frame. To remove these marks, use the **u** command, which undoes the mark for the current stack frame. (Remember that you can change the current stack frame by moving the cursor up or down in the ***Backtrace*** window.) When the mark is removed, the debugger does not stop on completion of the stack frame, and goes on to the next higher expression.

Converting Mocklisp to Emacs-Lisp (for Mocklisp Users)

To convert a buffer containing Mocklisp code into Emacs-Lisp, use the **M-x convert-mocklisp-buffer** command. The code will change in the buffer. You can then save the code into an Emacs-Lisp file whose name ends with **.el**; the original Mocklisp file is not affected.

You can evaluate and execute the resulting **.el** file, but because of some quirks in Mocklisp's implementation of true and false values, the converted code cannot be byte-compiled into an **.elc** file.

Summary

Table B.7 summarizes the important points to remember from this appendix.

Table B.7. Appendix B Summary

Topic	Summary
Evaluating Emacs-Lisp expressions	Emacs-Lisp Mode: • Evaluate expression preceding cursor: `C-x C-e` • Evaluate expression surrounding the cursor: `C-M-x` • Evaluate all expressions in current region: `M-x eval-region` • Evaluate all expressions in current buffer: `M-x eval-current-buffer` Lisp Interaction Mode: • All of the commands of Emacs-Lisp mode and... • Evaluate expression preceding the cursor: `C-j`
Symbol completion	Complete Emacs-Lisp symbol being typed: `M-TAB` (or `ESC-TAB`)
Display Emacs-Lisp documentation	• Display documentation for an Emacs-Lisp function: `C-h f` • Display documentation for an Emacs-Lisp variable: `C-h v`
Emacs-Lisp libraries	• Library directories are specified by the *load-path* variable. • Library files ending in `.el` contain Emacs-Lisp source. • Library files ending in `.elc` contain byte-compiled code. • Load and execute an Emacs-Lisp library file: `M-x load-library`
Load and execute Emacs-Lisp file	Load and execute an Emacs-Lisp file: `M-x load-file` (Remains installed for duration of editing session. You must explicitly specify an `.el` or `.elc` suffix with the file name.)

Table B.7, con't.

Topic	Summary
Compiling	• Compile current buffer or `.el` file you specify, creating a `.elc` byte-compiled file: `M-x byte-compile-file` • Byte-compile all `.el` files in a directory that have changed since the compile: `M-x byte-recompile-directory` • Compile from the UNIX command line: `emacs -batch -f batch-byte-compile` *file1 file2...*
Debugging	Enable Debugger: • On encountering an Emacs-Lisp error: set *debug-on-error* to `non-nil` • On pressing the `C-g` key: set *debug-on-quit* to `non-nil` • On entry to a particular defun: `M-x debug-on-entry` Cancel Debugger: • Cancels debug-on-entry for a defun: `M-x cancel-debug-on-entry` • Changing a defun also cancels debug-on-entry for the defun Set Breakpoint: • Put the defun `(debug)` in the code at desired location. Debugger commands enabled in `*Backtrace*` buffer: • Exit debugger and continue execution: `c` • Continue execution, but reenter debugger next time defun is called: `d` • Set flag to reenter debugger when current stack frame is exited: `b` • Undo a `b` command: `u` • Evaluate Lisp expression in the minibuffer: `e` • Quit program being debugged: `q` • Return a value from debugger: `r`
Convert Mocklisp code	Convert Mocklisp code into Emacs-Lisp: `M-x convert-mocklisp-buffer`

Appendix C
Switching from vi to Emacs

This appendix is provided for those who currently use **vi** as their main editor and who would like to switch to using Emacs. It provides a mapping between **vi** commands and the corresponding Emacs commands to accomplish the same editing task. Commands are grouped by functional categories:

- The **vi** emulation mode in Emacs
- Starting the editor
- Saving text and exiting
- Line number information commands
- Inserting text
- Undoing commands
- Repeating commands
- Rerunning previous commands
- Moving the cursor
- Deleting text
- Using marks
- Searching for text
- Search and replace text
- Indenting text
- Copying and moving blocks of text
- Changing (overwriting) text
- Scrolling text
- Using shell commands

- Using macros
- Using abbreviations
- Miscellaneous commands

Because of the different design philosophies of the two editors, there is not always a one-to-one mapping between commands. For instance, the **ESC** command in **vi** puts you in command mode, but there is no such mode in Emacs, nor is there the need for one since you can intermingle commands and text insertion without switching between modes. In cases where there is not a one-to-one mapping, we try to show Emacs commands that most closely match the functionality provided by the **vi** commands.

The vi Emulation Mode in Emacs

If you prefer, you can set Emacs to accept **vi** editing commands by running **M-x vip-mode**, which runs a **vi** emulator. In this mode, you press **ESC** to enter **vi** command mode, just as you do in **vi**. To return from **vi** command mode to Emacs, type **C-z**.

For complete information on this mode, use **M-x view-file** to view the file **emacs/lisp/vip.el** and read the information at the top of the file. We suggest using this mode only when you absolutely have to—for example, when you're in a hurry to get something typed and it would be easier to just use familiar **vi** commands.

Starting the Editor

Table C.1. vi Command Line Options

vi Command	Description	Emacs Equivalent
vi *file*	Start up editor and edit *file*.	**emacs** *file*
vi -r *file*	Recover *file*, which was saved during an editor or system "crash."	Run **M-x recover-file RET** *file* **RET** after starting Emacs.
vi +*n file*	Edit *file* and place cursor on line *n*.	**emacs +***n file*

Table C.1, con't.

vi Command	Description	Emacs Equivalent
`vi +` *file*	Edit *file*, placing cursor on last line.	There is no command line option to do this in Emacs; you must run `M->` after starting Emacs.
`vi` *files...*	Edit multiple *files*. With `vi`, use `:n` to move to the next file; with Emacs, use `C-x b` to switch to another buffer.	`emacs` *files...*
`vi +/`*s file*	Edit *file*, moving the cursor to the first line containing pattern *s*.	There is no command line option to do this in Emacs; you must run `C-s` or `C-M-s` to search for the pattern *s* after starting Emacs.

Saving Text and Exiting

Table C.2. vi Saving and Exiting Commands

vi Command	Description	Emacs Equivalent

`ZZ`
`:wq`
`:x`
	Save files and exit.	`C-x C-c`, which prompts you for verification before saving each modified buffer, then exits Emacs.

`:w` *file*	Save *file*. If *file* is omitted, save current file.	`C-x C-s` saves current buffer; `C-x s` saves all buffers; `C-x C-w` writes the buffer to a new file name.

Table C.2, con't.

vi Command	Description	Emacs Equivalent
`:w!` *file*	Write *file*, even if it is write-protected. If *file* is not specified, save current file.	1. Load the file into Emacs. 2. Run `C-x C-q` to remove write protection from the file. 3. Edit the file and save using `C-x C-s`. When asked whether you really want to save, answer `yes`.
`:n,m w` *file*	Write lines *n* through *m* to *file*.	1. Define a region around the lines you want to save. (`M-x goto-line` moves the cursor to a specified line.) 2. Run `M-x write-region` and enter a file name.
`:n,m w>>`*file*	Append lines *n* through *m* to *file*.	1. Define a region around the lines you want to save. 2. Run `M-x append-to-file RET` *file* `RET`.
`:q`	Quit `vi`, saving changes since last write.	See discussion of `ZZ` above.
`:q!`	Quit `vi` without prompting for changed files.	`C-u C-x C-c`
`:e!`	Revert buffer back to its contents when it was last written.	`M-x revert-buffer`

Line Number Information Commands

Table C.3. vi Line Number Information Commands

vi Command	Description	Emacs Equivalent
`:.=`	Display current line's number.	`M-x what-line`

`:=`	Print number of lines in file.	`C-x h`
		`M-=`
		
		Note that this sequence causes side effect of moving the cursor to the beginning of the file.

`C-g`	Display file name, current line number, total lines, and percent of file location.	Emacs always displays a buffer's name and percent location in file. To get the line number and total lines, use the commands described above. In addition, `C-x =` displays the position (expressed in number of characters from beginning of file), and column of the cursor.

Inserting Text

Unlike **vi**, Emacs does not have a special text-insertion mode for entering text. Emacs always inserts printable characters into the buffer as you type them. Typed characters are inserted before the cursor; the cursor and any text following it move to the right as you type. Although the philosophy of **vi** and Emacs differs in this respect, we still try to show how to do a similar operation in Emacs.

Table C.4. vi Text-Insertion Commands

vi Command	Description	Emacs Equivalent
`C-v` *c*	Inserts nonprintable or control character (*c*) into the buffer.	`C-q` *c*

Table C.4, con't.

vi Command	Description	Emacs Equivalent
A	Append text to end of line.	Run C-e to go to the end of the line; then type the text.
a	Append text after cursor.	Run C-f to move cursor forward one character; then type the text.
I	Insert text before first nonblank character on line.	Run M-m to move to the first nonblank character; then type the text. To insert before the very first character on the line, run C-a and type the text.
i	Insert text before cursor.	Just type the text.
:r *file*	Insert text from *file* after the current line.	Move to the *beginning* of the next line; then run C-x i RET *file* RET.

Undoing Commands

Table C.5. vi Mistake-Undoing Commands

vi Command	Description	Emacs Equivalent
u	Undo last editing command.	C-x u or C-_ Emacs can undo the effects of hundreds of commands by simply repeating the undo command, while vi can only undo the last command.
U	Return line to its original state.	No real equivalent, except running multiple undo commands until line returns to its original state.

Repeating Commands

To specify a repeat count to a **vi** command, you type a number before typing the command—for example, **20dd** runs the delete-line command 20 times. There are two ways to specify a numeric repeat count to Emacs commands:

1. Use the **C-u** *num* command. For example, to run the **M-d** (delete word) command 5 times, run **C-u 5 M-d**. Running **C-u** without a numeric value is the same as specifying 1 as the numeric value; for example, **C-u C-f** is the same as **C-u 1 C-f**.

2. Use the Meta key to specify numbers before running the command. For example, to run **C-n** 50 times (to move the cursor down 50 lines in the buffer), execute the **M-5 M-0 C-n** command.

Numeric arguments to Emacs commands are not always used as repeat counts. For example, the **M-q** command justifies paragraphs to ragged-right margins; when run with a numeric argument (**C-u M-q**), it right-justifies paragraphs to the fill column.

Rerunning Previous Commands

The **vi** dot (**.**) command reruns the last **vi** command. Emacs has no equivalent to the dot command, but you can use **C-x ESC** to rerun the last command *that was run in the minibuffer*. This includes any command that you invoke with **M-x** as well as any command that prompts you for information in the echo area.

When you run **C-x ESC**, Emacs displays the previous minibuffer command in the echo area. You can edit the command using basic editing commands such as **C-b**, **C-f**, **C-d**, **DEL**, etc. To run the command, press **RET**.

While **vi** keeps track of only the last command executed, Emacs keeps track of many commands in its command history. After running **C-x ESC** to enter the command history mechanism, you can run **M-p** and **M-n** to move to the previous and next commands.

Moving the Cursor

Table C.6. vi Cursor Motion Commands

vi Command	Description	Emacs Equivalent
k C-p	Move the cursor to the previous line.	C-p

Table C.6, con't.

vi Command	Description	Emacs Equivalent
j C-n	Move the cursor to the next line.	C-n
h DEL	Move the cursor back one character.	C-b
l SPC	Move the cursor forward one character.	C-f
b B	Move to start of previous word; B ignores punctuation. The Emacs equivalent does not ignore punctuation.	M-b
w W	Move to start of next word; W ignores punctuation. The Emacs equivalent does not ignore punctuation.	M-f
0 I	Move to first character on line.	C-a
^	Move to first nonblank character on line.	M-m
$	Move to end of line.	C-e
-	Move to first nonblank character of previous line.	1. C-p to go to previous line. 2. M-m to go to first nonblank character.
+	Move to first nonblank character of next line.	1. C-n to go to next line. 2. M-m to go to first nonblank character.

Table C.6, con't.

vi Command	Description	Emacs Equivalent
n|	Go to column n on the current line.	1. `C-a` to go to the start of line. 2. `C-u` n `C-f` to the correct column.
1G	Go to first line in buffer.	`M-<`
G	Go to last line in buffer.	`M->`
nG	Go to line n in buffer.	`C-u` n `M-x goto-line` or 1. `M-<` to go to first line. 2. `C-u` $n-1$ `C-n` to go down to the correct line.
H	Reposition cursor to first line on screen (window).	`C-u 0 M-r`
nH	Reposition cursor to line n from top of screen (window).	`C-u` n `M-r`
M	Reposition cursor to middle line on screen (window).	`M-r`
L	Reposition cursor to last line on screen (window).	`C-u -1 M-r`
nL	Reposition cursor to line n from the bottom of screen (window).	No equivalent
(	Go to start of sentence.	`M-a`

Table C.6, con't.

vi Command	Description	Emacs Equivalent
)	Go to end of sentence.	M-e
{	Go to start of paragraph.	M-[
}	Go to end of paragraph.	M-]
[[	Move to start of section, defined by a { in column zero. This is primarily useful when editing C programs, which use { } as delimiters of a function body.	C-M-a (Move to start of function; works appropriately in any programming mode.)
]]	Move to beginning of next section, defined by { in column zero.	C-M-e (Move to end of function.)

Deleting Text

Table C.7. vi Deletion Commands

vi Command	Description	Emacs Equivalent
J	Delete newline at end of line, joining this line with the next line.	1. C-e to go to the end of the line. 2. C-d to delete the newline.
x	Delete character overlayed by cursor.	C-d
X	Delete character before cursor.	DEL
xp	Transpose characters.	C-t
dw	Delete from cursor to end of word.	M-d

Table C.7, con't.

vi Command	Description	Emacs Equivalent
db	Delete from cursor to start of word.	M-DEL
d$ D	Delete from cursor to end of line.	C-k
d^	Delete from cursor to start of line.	C-u 0 C-k or M-0 C-k
dd	Delete current line.	1. C-a to go to start of line. 2. C-k to delete to end of line. 3. C-k to delete the remaining blank line.
*n*dd	Delete *n* lines, starting at current line.	1. C-a to go to start of line. 2. C-u *n* C-k to delete *n* lines.
d*cmd*	Delete from the cursor to the location moved to by the cursor motion command *cmd*. For example, d1G deletes from the cursor to the start of the file; d/foo deletes from the cursor to the start of the string "foo".	1. Run C-SPC or C-@ to set mark at the cursor position. 2. Run the cursor motion command, M-< or C-s foo for instance. 3. Run C-w to delete the region defined between mark and the current cursor location.

Using Marks

In **vi** terminology, setting a mark stores the location of the cursor into a register ("a" through "z"). You can then jump to a mark. This differs from Emacs terminology, in which you store the location of the cursor into *registers*. To Emacs, a mark is a cursor location that defines the start of a *region*, the other end of which is defined by the cursor. Nevertheless, Emacs marks can be used in a similar fashion to **vi** marks; for example, you can jump to previous mark locations (stored in the mark ring).

Table C.8. vi Mark Commands

vi Command	Description	Emacs Equivalent
m*reg*	Set **vi** mark and store its location in register *reg* (letter "a" through "z"). In Emacs, you save the cursor location in a register (any printable character: "a" through "z", numbers, punctuation); however, you do not place a mark at the cursor location.	C-x / *reg*
' *reg*	Jump to **vi** mark set with m*reg* command. In Emacs, jump to location stored with C-x / *reg* command.	C-x j *reg*
' ' ` `	Move cursor to location of last mark.	C-u C-SPC or C-u C-@

Searching for Text

There are three main differences between **vi** and Emacs search commands:

- Letter case is significant in **vi** search commands by default; it is not significant in Emacs. This can, however, be changed in Emacs.

- By default, **vi** search commands perform regular expression searches. Emacs has separate commands for simple text searches and regular expression searches.

- **vi** begins a search only after you enter a search string and press **RET**. In contrast, Emacs searches as you type the search string—an **incremental search**. Emacs also lets you perform a nonincremental, **vi**-style search (see Table C.9).

Once a search string is found, you can exit an incremental search, leaving the cursor at its current location, by pressing **ESC** or by running a cursor motion command (e.g., **M-b** to go to the start of the word). To terminate the search altogether and go back to where you issued the search command, press **C-g** .

Emacs regular expression special characters are a superset of **vi** regular expression characters.

Table C.9. vi Searching Commands

vi Command	Description	Emacs Equivalent
/*regexp* RET	Incrementally search forward for regular expression *regexp*.	C-M-s *regexp*
?*regexp* RET	Incrementally search backward for regular expression *regexp*.	C-M-s *regexp* C-r
/*string* RET	Incrementally search forward for *string*.	C-s *string*
?*string* RET	Incrementally search backward for *string*.	C-r *string*
/*string* RET	vi-style search (nonincremental) forward for *string*.	C-s ESC *string* RET
?*string* RET	vi-style search (nonincremental) backward for *string*.	C-r ESC *string* RET
F*c* f*c* T*c* t*c*	Search forward or backward to first occurrence of character *c* on current line.	C-s *c* or C-r *c*
n N	Repeat last / or ? command.	If you are in the midst of an incremental search, you can use C-s or C-r to search for the next or previous text that matches. If you have exited a search, but still want to repeat it, you must run a search command (C-s, C-r, or C-M-s); then run C-s or C-r to reuse the previous search string.

Table C.9, con't.

vi Command	Description	Emacs Equivalent
`:set nomagic` `:set magic`	The `:set nomagic` command tells **vi** to *not* interpret regular expression special (magic) characters other than ^ or $. The `:set magic` toggles this condition.	To search with magic characters disabled: `C-s` *string* **RET** or `C-r` *string* **RET** To search with magic characters enabled: `C-M-s` *regexp* **RET**
`:set ic`	Ignore case when searching in **vi**. This is the default in Emacs. To toggle case-sensitivity, use `M-x toggle-case-fold-search`.	Set the variable *case-fold-search* to `nil` with `M-x set-variable`.
`:set noic`	Case significance is the default behavior in **vi**, but must be set in Emacs with `M-x toggle-case-fold-search`.	Set the variable *case-fold-search* to `t`.

Search and Replace Text

The main **vi** command for search-and-replace operations is

  : *n, m* **s** / *str1* / *str2* / *opts*

which replaces *str1* with *str2* on lines *n* through *m*. (*str1* can be a regular expression). If line numbers are omitted, it searches and replaces only the next occurrence. By default, **vi** searches and replaces without confirmation, and only replaces one occurrence per line. You can override this default behavior with an *opts* string, which can have these values:

g   Replace *all* occurrences on the line, rather than just the first occurrence.

c   Ask for confirmation before replacing text.

p   To print changed lines; this is typically used when you did not specify confirmation with **c**.

Emacs search-and-replace commands differ from **vi** commands in these main respects:

- Emacs search-and-replace commands always start at the current cursor location; you cannot specify line ranges.

- There are separate commands for searching-and-replacing regular expressions and searching-and-replacing strings.

- Some commands for searching-and-replacing prompt for confirmation before replacing text. You can, however, override this behavior during a search-and-replace.

- There are separate commands for search-and-replace without confirmation.

- Search-and-replace operations are always global, as defined by the **g** option to the **vi** search-and-replace command.

- There is no Emacs function similar to that provided by the **p** option to the **vi** command; however, it is not really needed since Emacs search-and-replace commands typically prompt for verification before replacing text.

Table C.10 summarizes the Emacs search-and-replace commands that provide similar functionality to the **vi** search-and-replace command. For details on these commands, refer to the appropriate sections in Chapters 2 and 3.

Table C.10. vi Search-and-Replace Commands

Emacs Command	Description
M-% *str1* **RET** *str2* **RET**	Search for *str1* and replace with *str2*. Before replacing a string, Emacs prompts with: **Query replacing** *str1* **with** *str2*: Valid responses to this prompt are: **SPC** to replace the text and continue searching. **DEL** to skip this occurrence without replacing the text. **ESC** exit the query-replace. **!** to replace *all* subsequent matches *without verification*. **^** back up to previous match.

Table C.10, con't.

Emacs Command	Description
`M-x query-replace-regexp` `RET` *regexp* `RET` *str* `RET`	Search for regular expression *regexp* and replace with string *str*. Like `M-%`, this command prompts for verification before replacing text. Respond to this prompt as described above for `M-%`.
`M-x replace-string RET` *str1* `RET` *str2* `RET`	Search for all subsequent occurrences of *str1* and replace with *str2* without verification.
`M-x replace-regexp RET` *regexp* `RET` *str* `RET`	Search for all subsequent occurrences of *regexp* and replace with *str* without verification.

Indenting Text

Table C.11. vi Indentation Commands

vi Command	Description	Emacs Equivalent
`C-i` `TAB`	Insert a tab character into the buffer.	• `C-q TAB` inserts a tab character. • `TAB` indents to the next tab stop in Fundamental and Text modes. In programming modes, `TAB` indents the current line appropriately for the language.
`:set sw=`*n* *m*`>>`	Set shift width to *n*; then shift *m* lines rigidly right by the shift width.	1. Define a region around the lines you want to shift. 2. Run the command `C-u` *n* `C-x TAB`.

Table C.11, con't.

vi Command	Description	Emacs Equivalent
`:set sw=`*n* *m*`<<`	Set shift width to *n;* then shift *m* lines rigidly left by the shift width.	1. Define a region around the lines you want to shift. 2. Run the `C-x TAB` command with a negative shift width: `C-u -`*n* `C-x TAB`.
`:set ai`	Turn on auto-indentation; useful in programming modes.	Auto-indentation is automatically turned on whenever you edit a C, FORTRAN, Pascal, or Lisp program. Indentation is customized to each programming mode.

Copying and Moving Blocks of Text

One important difference between Emacs and **vi** is that they use different terminology with respect to copying and moving blocks of text. In particular, the term **yank** has almost exact opposite meanings in the two editors:

- To move a block of text in **vi**, you **delete** the text and **place** it in the appropriate location. In Emacs, you **kill** the text and **yank** it back.

- To copy a block of text in **vi**, you **yank** the text and **place** it in the appropriate location. In Emacs, you **copy** the text to the kill ring and **yank** it back.

Another important difference is that with **vi**, you delete or yank a certain number of lines from a starting cursor location. In Emacs, you kill or grab a region, defined between the cursor and mark (set with **C-SPC** or **C-@**). The Emacs method is more intuitive, allowing you to clearly define the text to move or copy; whereas with **vi**, you must count the number of lines you want to move or copy.

Table C.12. vi Block Copy and Move Commands

vi Command	Description	Emacs Equivalent
1. Run *n*yy to yank the lines you want to copy. 2. Move to the location where you want to copy the yanked text. 3. Run P to place the yanked text before the cursor; run p to place the text after the cursor.	Copy a block of text from one location to another.	1. Run C–SPC or C–@ to set the mark at the start of the text you want to move. 2. Move to the end of the text, defining the region of text to move. 3. Run M–w to grab the text in the region and place it into the kill ring. 4. Move to the location where you want to copy the text. 5. Run C–y to yank the text from the kill ring into the buffer.
Same as the procedure for copying a block of text (described above), except that you use a deletion command in the first step (for example, *n*dd).	Move a block of *n* lines of text to a new location.	Same as the procedure for copying text (described above), except that you run C–w in step 3 to kill the text.
"*(a-z)*yy	Yank *n* lines into a register (a through z).	1. Define the region of lines to copy. 2. Run C–x x *r*, where *r* is the register (any printable character).

Table C.12, con't.

vi Command	Description	Emacs Equivalent
*"(a-z)n*dd	Delete *n* lines into a register (**a** through **z**).	1. Define the region of lines to delete. 2. Run C-u C-x x *r*, where *r* is the register (any printable character).
*"(a-z)*p or *"(a-z)*P	Place the contents of register (**a** through **z**) into buffer. P places text before cursor; p places text after cursor.	C-x g *r* This command always places the register's contents before the cursor.
*"n*p	Place the *nth* text deletion back into the buffer.	C-u *n* C-y
*"1*pu.u...	Scroll through the deletion buffer until you find the desired killed text.	C-y M-y M-y...

Changing (Overwriting) Text

Table C.13. vi Change and Overwrite Commands

vi Command	Description	Emacs Equivalent
r*c*	Replace current character with character *c*.	C-d *c*
R *text* ESC	Overwrite following characters with *text*.	M-x overwrite-mode toggles between text overwrite and text insertion modes.

Table C.13, con't.

vi Command	Description	Emacs Equivalent
s *text* ESC	Replace current character with *text*.	C-d *text*
S *text* ESC or cc *text* ESC	Replace current line with *text*.	C-a C-k *text*
cw *text* ESC	Replace word with *text*.	M-d *text*
C *text* ESC	Replace from cursor to end of line with *text*.	C-k *text*
c *cursCmd text* ESC	Replace from cursor to location moved to by *cursCmd*. For example, c/foo changes from the current cursor location to the first text matching the pattern foo.	1. Run C-SPC to set the mark. 2. Run the cursor motion command. 3. Run C-w to kill the region. 4. Type the replacement text.

Scrolling Text

Table C.14. vi Scrolling Commands

vi Command	Description	Emacs Equivalent
C-l (letter l)	Redraw screen. The Emacs equivalent redraws all windows and centers the line containing point within the window (like the z. vi command).	C-l
C-b	Move screen back one page.	M-v

Table C.14, con't.

vi Command	Description	Emacs Equivalent
C-f	Move screen forward one page.	C-v
C-u	Move screen up half a page.	This happens automatically when you move the cursor past the bottom of the screen. The amount of the scroll can be modified through the *scroll-step* variable.
C-d	Move screen down half a page.	This happens automatically when you move the cursor past the top of the screen.
C-e	Move screen up one line.	C-u 1 C-v
C-y	Move screen down one line.	C-u 1 M-v
z RET	Reposition current line to top line on screen (window).	C-u 0 C-l
z .	Reposition current line to middle of screen.	C-l or C-u C-l (to reposition without redrawing screen)
z -	Reposition current line to bottom of screen.	C-u -1 C-l
*n*z RET	Make line *n* the top line on the screen.	1. Use C-u *n* M-r to go to line *n* on the screen. 2. Run C-u 0 C-l to make the line the top one on the screen.

Table C.14, con't.

vi Command	Description	Emacs Equivalent
*n*z .	Reposition line *n* to the middle of the screen.	1. Use C-u *n* M-r to go to line *n* on the screen. 2. Run C-u C-1 to make it the middle line.
*n*z –	Reposition line *n* to be the bottom line on the screen.	1. Use C-u *n* M-r to go to line *n* on the screen. 2. Run C-u –1 C-1 to make it the bottom line.

Using Shell Commands

Table C.15. vi Shell and Filter Commands

vi Command	Description	Emacs Equivalent
: ! *cmd*	Run shell command *cmd*.	M-! *cmd*
: r ! *cmd*	Run shell command *cmd* and insert its output into the buffer.	C-u M-! *cmd*
: ! !	Repeat last shell command.	Use C-x ESC to scroll through the command history to the last M-! command. You can also use M-x electric-command-history (see Chapter 12).
: w ! *cmd*	Run *cmd* using current buffer contents as standard input. The Emacs equivalent saves the output from *cmd* into another buffer, which is displayed in another window.	1. Use C-x h to set a region around the entire buffer contents. 2. Run M-| *cmd*, which runs the shell command *cmd* using the current region as standard input.

Table C.15, con't.

vi Command	Description	Emacs Equivalent
! *cursor_cmd cmd*	Grab the text from current cursor position to position moved to by *cursor_cmd;* pass this text through the external shell command *cmd;* then replace the current text with the output of *cmd*.	1. Define a region. 2. Run `C-u M-|` *cmd* to pass the text through *cmd* and replace the region with the output.
`{!}adjust RET`	This is just a special instance of the above command, which passes the current paragraph through the shell filter `adjust` to justify the text.	`M-q`
`{!}sort RET`	Sort all the lines in the current paragraph.	Define a region, then run `M-x sort-lines`.
`:sh`	Start an inferior (sub-) shell. The Emacs equivalent, `M-x shell`, creates the shell in another window; `C-z` suspends Emacs and "escapes" to a shell (see Chapter 1).	`M-x shell` or `C-z`
`:set sh=`*path*	Set path name to use for inferior shell.	Set the variable `shell-file-name` to *path*. Use `M-x set-variable` to set the variable's value.
`:f` *newname*	Rename the current file (buffer) to *newname*.	`M-x set-visited-file-name RET` *newname* `RET` `C-x C-w` can also be used, but it also writes the buffer to the file.

Using Macros

Table C.16. vi Macro Commands

vi Command	Description	Emacs Equivalent
`:map` *key cmds*	Assign *cmds* to *key*.	1. Run `C-x (` to signal the start of the command sequence. 2. Run the *cmds*. 3. Run `C-x )` to end the macro definition. You can then run the macro with `C-x e`. Optionally, you can name the macro with `M-x name-last-kbd-macro`, then run it by name with `M-x` *macro-name*.
`:map`	Display all currently defined macros.	None.
`:unmap` *key*	Undefine the macro assigned to *key*.	None.

Using Abbreviations

To use Emacs' abbreviation capabilities, you must enable Abbrev minor mode with **M-x abbrev-mode**. Use the same command to turn off Abbrev mode.

Table C.17. vi Abbreviation Commands

vi Command	Description	Emacs Equivalent

`:ab` *str expansion*	Whenever you type *str*, expand it to *expansion* text.	`C-x +`
		 `C-x C-a`
		 `C-x -`
		 `C-x C-h`
		
		 (See Chapter 3.)

Table C.17, con't.

vi Command	Description	Emacs Equivalent
`:ab`	Display all abbreviations.	`M-x list-abbrevs`
`:una` *str*	Turn off *str* abbreviation.	`M-x kill-abbrevs` kills all abbreviations. `M-x edit-abbrevs` allows you to edit abbreviations, including killing abbreviations.

Miscellaneous Commands

Table C.18. vi Miscellaneous Commands

vi Command	Description	Emacs Equivalent
`:set all`	Show all options (variables).	`M-x list-options`
`:set ro`	Change file (buffer) to read-only.	`C-x C-q` (toggles read-only status)
`:set ts=`*n*	Set tab stops to *n*.	`M-x edit-tab-stops`
`:set wm=`*n*	Set wrap margin. **vi** sets the wrap margin *n* columns from the right edge of the screen; Emacs sets the fill column to *n*.	`C-x f` sets the fill column to the current cursor column. `C-u` *n* `C-x f` sets the fill column to *n*.

Appendix D
Emacs Command Reference

This appendix serves as a reference for Emacs commands and associated variables. Commands are grouped by functional categories—for example, cursor motion commands, file manipulation commands, text deletion commands, etc. Some commands may appear in more than one category. Within each functional category, commands are described first, then variables. Included with each command definition is the name of the Emacs function that is executed when you run the specified command. If you need more detail than is given in the tables, refer to the page number referenced in the last column of the table. Obscure and extremely simple commands are listed here only, and have no additional page references.

Abbreviations

Table D.1. Abbreviation Commands

Task	Command (Function)	Page
Enable or disable Abbrev minor mode	`M-x abbrev-mode` `(abbrev-mode)`	75
Create global abbreviation for word before cursor	`C-x +` `(add-global-abbrev)`	76
Create global abbreviation for *n* words before cursor	`C-u n C-x +` `(add-global-abbrev)`	76
Create local (this mode only) abbreviation for word before cursor	`C-x C-a` `(add-mode-abbrev)`	76

Table D.1. Abbreviation Commands, con't.

Task	Command (Function)	Page
Create local (this mode only) abbreviation for *n* words before cursor	`C-u` *n* `C-x C-a` (`add-mode-abbrev`)	76
Assign expansion text to global abbreviation before cursor	`C-x -` (`inverse-add-global-abbrev`)	77
Assign expansion text to local (mode) abbreviation before cursor	`C-x C-h` (`inverse-add-mode-abbrev`)	77
Expand text before cursor to prior word that starts with same text	`M-/` (`dabbrev-expand`)	82
Separate prefix text from abbreviation to follow	`M-'` (`abbrev-prefix-mark`)	78
Expand abbreviation before cursor when not in Abbrev minor mode	`C-x '` (`expand-abbrev`)	78
Undo the abbreviation expansion just performed	`M-x unexpand-abbrev` (`unexpand-abbrev`)	79
Expand abbreviations found in current region	`M-x expand-region-abbrevs` (`expand-region-abbrevs`)	79
List all abbreviations	`M-x list-abbrevs` (`list-abbrevs`)	79, 81
Edit abbreviations	`M-x edit-abbrevs` (`edit-abbrevs`)	81

Table D.1. Abbreviation Commands, con't.

Task	Command (Function)	Page
Save editing abbreviations	`C-c C-c` `(edit-abbrevs-redefine)`	81
Kill all abbreviations	`M-x kill-all-abbrevs` `(kill-all-abbrevs)`	81
Write abbreviation definition code to a file	`M-x write-abbrev-file` `(write-abbrev-file)`	81
Read and set up abbreviations from a file	`M-x read-abbrev-file` `(read-abbrev-file)`	82
Define abbreviations by evaluating text in current buffer	`M-x define-abbrevs` `(define-abbrevs)`	82
Insert code for defining existing abbreviations into current buffer	`M-x insert-abbrevs` `(insert-abbrevs)`	82

Table D.2. Abbreviation Variables

Task	Variable	Page
When abbrev contains capital letter, capitalize corresponding word (default)	*abbrev-all-caps* = `nil`	—
When abbrev contains capital letter, make corresponding text all uppercase	*abbrev-all-caps* = `t`	—

Buffers

Table D.3. Buffer Commands

Task	Command (Function)	Page
Set buffer to specified *mode*	`M-x` *mode* (*mode*)	33
Load file into new buffer in current window and set buffer's mode	`C-x C-f` (`find-file`)	28
Load file into new buffer in *other* window and set buffer's mode	`C-x 4 C-f` (`find-file-other-window`)	127
Load file into existing buffer and set buffer's mode	`C-x C-v` (`find-alternate-file`)	127
Insert a file into current buffer at point	`M-x insert-file` (`insert-file`)	127
List all buffers	`C-x C-b` (`list-buffers`)	29, 125
List file buffers only	`C-u C-x C-b` (`list-buffers`)	53
Select buffer in current window	`C-x b` (`switch-to-buffer`)	30, 124
Select buffer in other window	`C-x 4 b` (`switch-to-buffer-other-window`)	125
Save buffer to file	`C-x C-s` (`save-buffer`)	29
Save selected buffers to their respective files	`C-x s` (`save-some-buffers`)	128

Table D.3. Buffer Commands, con't.

Task	Command (Function)	Page
Save all buffers without verification	`C-u C-x s` `(save-some-buffers)`	128
Write a buffer to a file, renaming the buffer as well	`C-x C-w` `(write-file)`	29
Rename a buffer without renaming its file	`M-x rename-buffer` `(rename-buffer)`	125
Toggle a buffer's read-only status	`C-x C-q` `(toggle-read-only)`	125
Kill a buffer	`C-x k` `(kill-buffer)`	31, 125
Kill selected buffers, prompting for verification for each one	`M-x kill-some-buffers` `(kill-some-buffers)`	125
Narrow (restrict) editing of buffer to currently defined region	`C-x n` `(narrow-to-region)`	70
Widen editing to entire buffer (undo effect of `C-x n`)	`C-x w` `(widen)`	70
View buffer and allow only cursor motion commands	`M-x view-buffer` `(view-buffer)`	125
Insert text from other buffer at point in current buffer	`M-x insert-buffer` `(insert-buffer)`	126
Copy current region to point in other buffer, leaving point at *end* of text	`C-x a` `(append-to-buffer)`	126
Copy current region to point in other buffer, leaving point at *start* of text	`M-x prepend-to-buffer` `(prepend-to-buffer)`	126

Table D.3. Buffer Commands, con't.

Task	Command (Function)	Page
Delete text in other buffer, then copy current region to the buffer	`M-x copy-to-buffer` `(copy-to-buffer)`	126
Append current region to end of file	`M-x append-to-file` `(append-to-file)`	—
Enable Buffer Menu mode for buffer operations (see Table D.5, "Buffer Menu")	`M-x buffer-menu` `(buffer-menu)`	326
Revert buffer—restore its contents from the associated disk file	`M-x revert-buffer` `(revert-buffer)`	135, 340
Print buffer contents with UNIX `lpr -p` command	`M-x print-buffer` `(print-buffer)`	94
Print buffer contents with UNIX `lpr` command	`M-x lpr-buffer` `(lpr-buffer)`	94

Table D.4. Buffer Variables

Task	Variable	Page
Set buffer to read-only status	*buffer-read-only* = `t`	—
Set buffer to read/write status	*buffer-read-only* = `nil`	—

Buffer-Menu

Table D.5. Buffer-Menu Commands

Task	Command (Function)	Page
Enable Buffer-Menu. Once it is enabled, you can use the commands listed below	`M-x buffer-menu` `(buffer-menu)`	326
Move cursor to next line in buffer menu list	`SPC` `(next-line)`	—
Mark a buffer so that it is displayed on exit from Buffer-Menu	`m` `(Buffer-menu-mark)`	328
Select buffer of current line and make windows for all marked buffers as well	`q` `(Buffer-menu-select)`	329
Select buffer of current line	`1` `(Buffer-menu-1-window)`	328
Select current buffer and make window for previous marked buffer	`2` `(Buffer-menu-2-window)`	329
Select current buffer and use the window of the Buffer-Menu to display it	`f` `(Buffer-menu-this-window)`	328
Select current buffer in another window, keeping Buffer-Menu intact	`o` `(Buffer-menu-other-window)`	328
Clear file modification status	`~` `(Buffer-menu-not-modified)`	328

Table D.5. Buffer-Menu Commands, con't.

Task	Command (Function)	Page
Mark buffer so that it will be deleted when you type **x**; move to next line	`d` or `k` `(Buffer-menu-delete)`	327

Mark buffer so that it will be deleted when you type **x**; move to previous line	`C-d`
	`(Buffer-menu-delete-`
	`backwards)`
		327

Mark buffer so that it will be saved when you type **x**	`s` `(Buffer-menu-save)`	327
Save and delete buffers marked by **C-d**, **d**, **k**, and **s** commands	`x` `(Buffer-menu-execute)`	327
Unmark the current buffer	`u` `(Buffer-menu-unmark)`	328

Move to previous line and unmark the buffer	`DEL`
	`(Buffer-menu-backup-`
	`unmark)`
		328

Case Conversion

Table D.6. Case Conversion Commands

Task	Command (Function)	Page
Convert word to lowercase	`M-l` `(downcase-word)`	68
Convert previous word to lowercase	`C-u - M-l or M-- M-l` `(downcase-word)`	—

Table D.6. Case Conversion Commands, con't.

Task	Command (Function)	Page
Convert word to uppercase	`M-u` `(upcase-word)`	68
Convert previous word to all uppercase	`C-u - M-u or M-- M-u` `(upcase-word)`	—
Capitalize word	`M-c` `(capitalize-word)`	68
Capitalize previous word	`C-u - M-c or M-- M-c` `(capitalize-word)`	—
Convert all letters in region to lowercase	`C-x C-l` `(downcase-region)`	68
Convert all letters in region to uppercase	`C-x C-u` `(upcase-region)`	68

C Mode

Table D.7. C Mode Commands

Task	Command (Function)	Page
	Functions	
Move cursor to beginning of function	`C-M-a` `(beginning-of-defun)`	193
Move cursor to end of function	`C-M-e` `(end-of-defun)`	193
Place region around function, leaving cursor at beginning of function	`C-M-h` `(mark-defun)`	193

Table D.7. C Mode Commands, con't.

Task	Command (Function)	Page
Indentation		
Indent current line according to indentation style	`TAB` `(c-indent-line)`	194
Finish current line and open next line with proper indentation	`LFD` or `C-j` `(newline-and-indent)`	194
Insert actual tab character at point	`C-q TAB` `(quoted-insert)`	200
Indent all lines in current region according to indentation style	`C-M-\` `(indent-region)`	194
Indent all lines within list according to indentation style	`C-M-q` `(indent-c-exp)`	186
Commenting		
Append new comment to current line	`M-;` `(indent-for-comment)`	201
Align existing comment to comment column	`M-;` `(indent-for-comment)`	201
Continue current comment onto next line, indented properly	`M-LFD` or `C-M-j` `(indent-new-comment-line)`	202
Move cursor to start of comment text	`M-;` `(indent-for-comment)`	201
Set comment column to current cursor column	`C-x ;` `(set-comment-column)`	201

Table D.7. C Mode Commands, con't.

Task	Command (Function)	Page
Commenting, con't.		
Set comment column to same column as previous comment; create new comment	`C-u C-x ;` `(set-comment-column)`	201
Kill comment on current liner	`C-u - C-x ;` `(kill-comment)`	201
Balancing Parentheses		
Insert pair of balanced parentheses	`M-(` `(insert-parentheses)`	172
Move over closing parenthesis and open indented line	`M-)` `(move-over-close-and-reindent)`	—
Expressions (Sexps) and Lists		
Move backward to beginning of previous expression (sexp)	`C-M-b` `(backward-sexp)`	204
Move forward to end of next expression (sexp)	`C-M-f` `(forward-sexp)`	204
Kill the next expressions (sexp)	`C-M-k` `(kill-sexp)`	207
Place mark after next expression (sexp)	`C-M-@` `(mark-sexp)`	205
Transpose (swap) expressions (sexps) around point	`C-M-t` `(transpose-sexps)`	206
Move backward over list	`C-M-p` `(backward-list)`	205

Table D.7. C Mode Commands, con't.

Task	Command (Function)	Page
Expressions (Sexps) and Lists, con't.		
Move forward over list	`C-M-n` `(forward-list)`	205
Move backward "up" out of list	`C-M-u` `(backward-up-list)`	205
Move forward "down" into list	`C-M-d` `(down-list)`	205
Indent all lines within list according to current indentation style	`C-M-q` `(indent-sexp)`	186

Table D.8. C Mode Variables

Task	Variable	Page
Indentation of function arguments	*c-argdecl-indent*	208, 212
Indentation of statements in a compound block	*c-indent-level*	208, 214
Indentation of case, default, and label statements	*c-label-offset*	208, 215
Indentation of continued statements	*c-continued-statement-offset*	209, 212
Indentation of closing brace indentation when opening brace starts on same line as introducing statement	*c-brace-imaginary-offset*	210, 215

Table D.8. C Mode Variables, con't.

Task	Variable	Page
Indentation of opening and closing brace of compound statement	*c-continued-brace-offset*	211, 215
Indentation of lines starting with an open brace	*c-brace-offset*	211, 217
Force newlines around opening braces	*c-auto-newline* = `t`	194
Insert actual tab when `TAB` is pressed if cursor is within a line	*c-tab-always-indent* = `nil`	200
Always indent current line, regardless of position of point on line	*c-tab-always-indent* = `t`	200
Disable display of matching parenthesis	*blank-matching-paren* = `nil`	171
Enable display of matching parenthesis (default)	*blink-matching-paren* = `t`	171
How many characters to search backward for a matching parenthesis	*blink-matching-paren-distance* (default = 4000)	171
Set comment column	*comment-column* = *n*	201, 221
Change regular expression that matches start of comment	*comment-start-skip*	221
Terminate comment on current line when `M-LFD` is used	*comment-multi-line* = `nil`	222
Do *not* terminate comment on current line when `M-LFD` is used	*comment-multi-line* = `t`	222

Compilation

Table D.9. Compilation Commands

Task	Command (Function)	Page
Compile using UNIX `make` facility	`M-x compile` `(compile)`	181
Kill the compilation	`M-x kill-compiler` `(kill-compiler)`	181
Visit the line containing the next compilation error	`C-x ` ` `(next-error)`	181
Visit the first compilation error	`C-u C-x ` ` `(next-error)`	183
Run UNIX `grep` command to find matching lines	`M-x grep` `(grep)`	—
Kill the UNIX `grep` command	`M-x kill-grep` `(kill-grep)`	—

Table D.10. Compilation Variables

Task	Variable	Page
Change the default compilation command	*compile-command = "cmd"*	181

Cursor Motion

Table D.11. Cursor Motion Commands

Task	Command (Function)	Page
Backward one character	`C-b` `(backward-char)`	33

Table D.11. Cursor Motion Commands, con't.

Task	Command (Function)	Page
Forward one character	C-f (forward-char)	33, 353
Beginning of line	C-a (beginning-of-line)	33
End of line	C-e (end-of-line)	33, 353
Beginning of buffer	M-< (beginning-of-buffer)	34
End of buffer	M-> (end-of-buffer)	34
Line number	M-x goto-line (goto-line)	35, 53
Previous line	C-p (previous-line)	33, 353
Next line	C-n (next-line)	33, 353
Set goal column for C-p and C-n commands to current cursor position	C-x C-n (set-goal-column)	102
Cancel goal column of C-x C-n	C-u C-x C-n (set-goal-column)	102
Backward word	M-b (backward-word)	55
Forward word	M-f (forward-word)	55

Table D.11. Cursor Motion Commands, con't.

Task	Command (Function)	Page
Backward sentence	`M-a` `(backward-sentence)`	56
Forward sentence	`M-e` `(forward-sentence)`	56
Backward paragraph	`M-[` `(backward-paragraph)`	57
Forward paragraph	`M-]` `(forward-paragraph)`	57
Backward page	`C-x [` `(backward-page)`	58
Forward page	`C-x ]` `(forward-page)`	58
Scroll forward one window, leaving cursor at top of window	`C-v` `(scroll-up)`	91
Scroll backward one window, leaving cursor at top of window	`M-v` `(scroll-down)`	91
Middle line in window	`M-r` `(move-to-window-line)`	—
Line *n* in window	`C-u` *n* `M-r` `(move-to-window-line)`	—
Character location	`M-x goto-char` `(goto-char)`	34

Table D.11. Cursor Motion Commands, con't.

Task	Command (Function)	Page

Backward to function beginning (in C and Lisp modes)
 	
(in FORTRAN mode)
	`C-M-a`
	
	`(beginning-of-defun)`
	
	`(beginning-of-fortran-`
	`subprogram)`
		167, 193, 229, 252

Forward to function end (in C and Lisp modes)
 	
(in FORTRAN mode)
	`C-M-e`
	`(end-of-defun)`
	
	`(end-of-fortran-`
	`subprogram)`
		167, 193, 229, 252

Backward balanced expression (sexp)	`C-M-b` `(backward-sexp)`	185, 204, 238, 255
Forward balanced expression (sexp)	`C-M-f` `(forward-sexp)`	185, 204, 237, 254
Backward over balanced parentheses (list)	`C-M-p` `(backward-list)`	186, 205, 238, 256
Forward over balanced parentheses (list)	`C-M-n` `(forward-list)`	186, 205, 238, 254
Backward "up" out of balanced parentheses (list)	`C-M-u` `(backward-up-list)`	186, 205, 238, 256
Forward "down" into parentheses (list)	`C-M-d` `(down-list)`	186, 205, 238, 255

Table D.12. Cursor Motion Variables

Task	Variable	Page
Keep cursor at end of line when moving from line to line with C–p, C–n	*track-eol* = `t` *goal-column* = `nil`	102, 369
Keep cursor close to current column when moving to new line with C–p, C–n	*track-eol* = `nil` *goal-column* = `nil`	102, 369
Keep cursor in column *n* when moving to a new line with C–p, C–n	*track-eol* = `nil` *goal-column* = *n*	102, 369

Debugger (Emacs-Lisp)

Table D.13. Debugger (Emacs-Lisp) Commands

Task	Command (Function)	Page

Enable debugger on entry to *defun* (see other methods under variables below)	`M-x debug-on-entry RET`
	defun `RET`
	`(debug-on-entry)`
		459

Set breakpoint in defun	Call `(debug)` at desired breakpoint location	460
Cancel debug-on-entry	`M-x cancel-debug-on-entry RET` *defun* `RET` `(cancel-debug-on-entry)`	460
Exit debugger and continue execution	`c` `(debugger-continue)`	461
Continue execution and reenter debugger next time defun is called (single-step)	`d` `(debugger-step-through)`	461

Table D.13. Debugger (Emacs-Lisp) Commands, con't.

Task	Command (Function)	Page
Set up-level breakpoint	b `(debugger-frame)`	461
Clear up-level breakpoint	u `(debugger-frame-clear)`	461
Evaluate Emacs-Lisp expression and display its value in minibuffer	e `(debugger-eval-expression)`	462
Quit the program being debugged	q `(top-level)`	462
Return value from debugger	r `(debugger-return-value)`	462

Table D.14. Debugger (Emacs-Lisp) Variables

Task	Variable	Page
Enter debugger when error occurs	*debug-on-error* = `t`	459
Don't enter debugger when error occurs (default)	*debug-on-error* = `nil`	459
Enter debugger when C-g pressed	*debug-on-quit* = `t`	459
Don't enter debugger when C-g pressed (default)	*debug-on-quit* = `nil`	459

Deletion and Killing

Table D.15. Deletion and Killing Commands

Task	Command (Function)	Page
Delete preceding character	`DEL` `(delete-backward-char)`	19, 35
Delete cursor's character (character following point)	`C-d` `(delete-char)`	36
Delete blank lines surrounding this line	`C-x C-o` `(delete-blank-lines)`	59

Delete white space around
cursor, leaving none
	`M-\`
	`(delete-horizontal-`
	`space)`
		—

Delete white space around cursor, leaving one space	`M-SPC` `(just-one-space)`	—
Delete indentation from the following line and join the line to the end of this line	`M-^` `(delete-indentation)`	66
Kill from cursor to end of line	`C-k` `(kill-line)`	36, 353
Kill from cursor to beginning of line	`C-u 0 C-k` `(kill-line)`	—
Kill current region	`C-w` `(kill-region)`	40
Kill word backward	`M-DEL` `(backward-kill-word)`	55
Kill word forward	`M-d` `(kill-word)`	55

Table D.15. Deletion and Killing Commands, con't.

Task	Command (Function)	Page
Kill to beginning of sentence	`C-x DEL` `(backward-kill-sentence)`	56
Kill to end of sentence	`M-k` `(kill-sentence)`	56
Kill expression (sexp)	`C-M-k` `(kill-sexp)`	185, 207, 239, 258
Kill text from cursor to next occurrence of character	`M-z c` `(zap-to-char)`	—

Dired

Table D.16. Dired Commands

Task	Command (Function)	Page
Invoke Dired	`C-x d` `(dired)`	320
Invoke Dired and display in another window	`C-x 4 d` `(dired-other-window)`	137
Move to previous file name in listing	`C-p or p` `(dired-previous-line)`	321
Move to next file name in listing	`C-n or n or SPC` `(dired-next-line)`	321
Revert Dired listing to original state	`g` `(revert-buffer)`	323

Table D.16. Dired Commands, con't.

Task	Command (Function)	Page
Move to previous line and remove flags set by other dired commands	DEL (dired-backup-unflag)	323
Flag file for deletion	d (dired-flag-file-deleted)	323
Remove deletion flag	u (dired-unflag)	323
Delete flagged files	x (dired-do-deletions)	323
Flag auto-save files for deletion	# (dired-flag-auto-save-files)	325
Flag backup files for deletion	~ (dired-flag-backup-files)	325
Flag all but oldest and newest numeric backup files for deletion	. (dired-clean-directory)	326
Load and evaluate an Emacs-Lisp file	l (dired-load-file)	—
Visit the file	f or e (dired-find-file)	323
Visit the file in another window	o (dired-find-file-other-window)	324
View the file's contents; do not allow editing	v (dired-view-file)	324

Table D.16. Dired Commands, con't.

Task	Command (Function)	Page
Copy the file	c (dired-copy-file)	322
Rename the file	r (dired-rename-file)	322
Print the file using UNIX lpr command	P (dired-lpr-file)	—
Print the file using UNIX lpr -p command	M-P (dired-print-file)	—
Compress the file	C (dired-compress)	324
Uncompress the file	U (dired-uncompress)	324
Change file's mode (rwx)	M (dired-chmod)	324
Change file's owner	O (dired-chown)	325
Change file's group	G (dired-chgrp)	324

Display Management

Table D.17. Display Management Commands

Task	Command (Function)	Page
Scroll selected window forward, bringing bottom 2 lines to the top	C-v (scroll-up)	91

Table D.17. Display Management Commands, con't.

Task	Command (Function)	Page
Scroll selected window forward *n* lines	`C-u` *n* `C-v` (scroll-up)	—
Scroll selected window backward, bringing top 2 lines to the bottom	`M-v` (scroll-down)	91
Scroll selected window backward *n* lines	`C-u` *n* `M-v` (scroll-down)	—
Redisplay all windows and scroll current window so cursor is centered vertically	`C-l` (recenter)	92
Bring line *n* to the center of the window	`C-u` *n* `C-l` (recenter)	92
Scroll window left one screen width, less 2 columns	`C-x <` (scroll-left)	91
Scroll window left by *n* columns	`C-u` *n* `C-x <` (scroll-left)	91
Scroll window right one screen width, less 2 columns	`C-x >` (scroll-right)	92
Scroll window right *n* columns	`C-u` *n* `C-x >` (scroll-right)	92
Show only those lines that are indented less than *n* columns	`C-u` *n* `C-x $` (set-selective-display)	172
Show all lines, regardless of indentation level	`C-x $` (set-selective-display)	172
Display date/time information in mode line	`M-x display-time` (display-time)	102

Table D.17. Display Management Commands, con't.

Task	Command (Function)	Page
Split window vertically into two new windows	`C-x 2` (`split-window-vertically`)	93
Split window horizontally into two new windows	`C-x 5` (`split-window-horizontally`)	93
Scroll other ("next") window	`C-M-v` (`scroll-other-window`)	138
Remove all windows except the selected window; does not affect buffers	`C-x 1` (`delete-other-windows`)	93
Remove the current window; does not affect its buffer	`C-x 0` (`kill-window`)	93
Increase height of selected window by one line	`C-x ^` (`enlarge-window`)	138
Increase height of selected window *n* lines	`C-u n C-x ^` (`enlarge-window`)	138
Increase the width of the selected window by one column	`C-x }` (`enlarge-window-horizontally`)	138
Increase width of selected window by *n* columns	`C-u n C-x }` (`enlarge-window-horizontally`)	138

Table D.18. Display Management Variables

Task	Variable	Page
Change the number of overlapped lines left by C-v and M-v to *n* (default = 2)	*next-screen-context-lines* = *n*	368
When cursor moves past top or bottom of screen, scroll *n* lines	*scroll-step* = *n*	—
When cursor moves past top or bottom of screen, recenter cursor line (default)	*scroll-step* = 0	—
Truncate displayed lines that are longer than window width for this buffer	*truncate-lines* = t	369
Don't truncate displayed lines longer than window width for this buffer (default)	*truncate-lines* = nil	369
Enable truncation in *all* windows	*truncate-partial-width-windows* = t	—
Let the *truncate-lines* variable determine truncation per buffer	*truncate-partial-width-windows* = nil	—
Use inverse video for mode line (default)	*mode-line-inverse-video* = t	368
Don't use inverse video for mode line	*mode-line-inverse-video* = nil	368
Invert video lines from their normal settings	*inverse-video* = t	368
Leave video settings as they normally are (default)	*inverse-video* = nil	368

Table D.18. Display Management Variables, con't.

Task	Variable	Page
Attempt to do visible bell rather than audible bell	*visible-bell* = `t`	368
Don't use visible bell; use audible bell (default)	*visible-bell* = `nil`	368
Terminal supports alternate video pages; don't redraw screen on reentry from suspended session	*no-redraw-on-reenter* = `t`	—
Uncertain if alternate video pages supported; redraw screen on reentry	*no-redraw-on-reenter* = `nil`	—
Do not display multi-character command keys in echo area	*echo-keystrokes* = `0`	369
Display multi-character command keys in echo area, but wait *n* seconds first	*echo-keystrokes* = *n*	369
Do not display control characters as octal codes (default)	*ctl-arrow* = `t`	369
Display control characters as octal codes	*ctl-arrow* = `nil`	369
Change number of columns between displayed tab stops (default = 8)	*tab-width* = *n*	—
Display ellipses at the end of lines followed by invisible text (default)	*selective-display-ellipses* = `t`	—

Table D.18. Display Management Variables, con't.

Task	Variable	Page
Do *not* display ellipses at the end of lines followed by invisible text	*selective-display-ellipses* = `nil`	—

Editor Emulation (EDT, vi, Gosling Emacs)

Table D.19. Editor Emulation Commands

Task	Command (Function)	Page
Emulate EDT editor	`M-x edt-emulation-on` `(edt-emulation-on)`	—
Turn of EDT emulation	`M-x edt-emulation-off` `(edt-emulation-off)`	—
Emulate Gosling Emacs	`M-x set-gosmacs-bindings` `(set-gosmacs-bindings)`	—
Turn off Gosling Emacs emulation	`M-x set-gnu-bindings` `(set-gnu-bindings)`	—
Emulate **vi**	`M-x vip-mode` `(vip-mode)`	470
Exit **vi** emulation	`C-z` `(vi-nil)`	470

Emacs-Lisp Programming

Table D.20. Emacs-Lisp Programming Commands

Task	Command (Function)	Page
Evaluating Emacs-Lisp Expressions		
Evaluate expression preceding cursor	`C-x C-e` `(eval-last-sexp)`	265, 453
Evaluate expression surrounding cursor	`C-M-x` `(eval-defun)`	265, 454
Evaluate all expressions in current region	`M-x eval-region` `(eval-region)`	265, 454
Evaluate all expressions in current buffer	`M-x eval-current-buffer` `(eval-current-buffer)`	265, 454
Evaluate expression preceding cursor and insert result into buffer (Lisp Interaction)	`LFD` or `C-j` `(eval-print-last-sexp)`	266, 454
Symbol Completion and Documentation		
Attempt to complete Emacs-Lisp symbol being typed	`M-TAB` or `ESC-TAB` `(lisp-complete-symbol)`	452
Display documentation for Emacs-Lisp defun	`C-h f` `(describe-function)`	450
Display documentation for Emacs-Lisp variable	`C-h v` `(describe-variable)`	280, 365, 450

Table D.20. Emacs-Lisp Programming Commands, con't.

Task	Command (Function)	Page
Emacs-Lisp Libraries and Files		
Load and execute an Emacs-Lisp library	`M-x load-library` `(load-library)`	457
Load and execute an Emacs-Lisp file	`M-x load-file` `(load-file)`	456
Byte-Compiling		
Byte-compile current buffer or specified file	`M-x byte-compile-file` `(byte-compile-file)`	458
Byte-compile all files that have changed since last compile	`M-x byte-recompile-directory` `(byte-recompile-directory)`	458
Compile from UNIX command line	`emacs -batch -f batch-byte-compile` *files*	104, 459
Disassemble byte-compiled code	`M-x disassemble` `(disassemble)`	—
Convert Mocklisp code to Emacs-Lisp code	`M-x convert-mocklisp-buffer` `(convert-mocklisp-buffer)`	466

Table D.21. Emacs-Lisp Programming Variables

Task	Variable	Page
Set directory path for Emacs-Lisp libraries	*load-path*	455

Exiting

Table D.22. Exiting Commands

Task	Command (Function)	Page
Suspend Emacs, temporarily returning to UNIX shell	`C-z` `(suspend-emacs)`	6
Kill Emacs and save buffers (with verification)	`C-x C-c` `(save-buffers-kill-emacs)`	6
Kill Emacs without saving buffers	`C-u C-x C-c` `(save-buffers-kill-emacs)`	6

Files

Table D.23. File Commands

Task	Command (Function)	Page
Visit file in current window	`C-x C-f` `(find-file)`	28
Visit file in other window	`C-x 4 C-f` `(find-file-other-window)`	127
Visit a file, replacing the one in the current buffer	`C-x C-v` `(find-alternate-file)`	127
Save current buffer to its file	`C-x C-s` `(save-buffer)`	29
Save all visited files, prompting first for verification	`C-x s` `(save-some-buffers)`	128

Table D.23. File Commands, con't.

Task	Command (Function)	Page
Write the current buffer to a file other than the visited file	`C-x C-w` `(write-file)`	29
Clear a buffer's modified status	`M-~` `(not-modified)`	124
Change a buffer's file name	`M-x set-visited-file-name` `(set-visited-file-name)`	125
Revert a buffer to the original file's contents	`M-x revert-buffer` `(revert-buffer)`	135, 340
Recover a file from its auto-saved contents	`M-x recover-file` `(recover-file)`	339
List a directory (short listing)	`C-x C-d` `(list-directory)`	94
List a directory (long listing)	`C-u C-x C-d` `(list-directory)`	94
Invoke the directory editor	`C-x d` `(dired)`	320
Invoke the directory editor in another window	`C-x 4 d` `(dired-other-window)`	137
View a file's contents without allowing modification	`M-x view-file` `(view-file)`	—
Inserting a file's contents into the buffer at point	`M-x insert-file` `(insert-file)`	127
Writing a region to a file	`M-x write-region` `(write-region)`	—

Table D.23. File Commands, con't.

Task	Command (Function)	Page
Delete a file	`M-x delete-file` `(delete-file)`	—
Rename a file	`M-x rename-file` `(rename-file)`	—
Copy a file	`M-x copy-file` `(copy-file)`	—
Symbolically link a file	`M-x make-symbolic-link` `(make-symbolic-link)`	—

Table D.24. File Variables

Task	Variable	Page
Make single backups	*version-control* = `never`	132
Make numbered backups for all files	*version-control* = `t`	131
Make numbered backups only for files that already have them	*version-control* = `nil`	132
Control number of old versions to keep when deleting numbered backup files	*kept-old-versions* = *n*	134
Control number of latest versions to keep when deleting numbered backup files	*kept-new-versions* = *n*	134

Table D.24. File Variables, con't.

Task	Variable	Page
Delete excess numbered backups without verification	*trim-versions-without-asking* = `t`	134
Delete excess numbered backups with verification	*trim-versions-without-asking* = `nil`	134
Make auto-saving occur to a different file than the visited file	*auto-save-visited-file-name* = `nil`	130
Make auto-saving occur to the visited file	*auto-save-visited-file-name* = `t`	130
Disable auto-saving for a buffer	*auto-save-default* = `nil`	130
Enable auto-saving for a buffer (the default)	*auto-save-default* = `t`	130

Filling

Table D.25. Filling Commands

Task	Command (Function)	Page
Cause Emacs to automatically fill text when you type past the fill margin	`M-x auto-fill-mode` `(auto-fill-mode)`	64
Set the fill column to current cursor column	`C-x f` `(set-fill-column)`	62

Table D.25. Filling Commands, con't.

Task	Command (Function)	Page
Fill the current paragraph	`M-q` `(fill-paragraph)`	62
Fill all paragraphs in the current region	`M-g` `(fill-region)`	62

Fill all the text in a region, making one paragraph, even if it contains blank lines	`M-x fill-region-as-`
	`paragraph`
	`(fill-region-as-`
	`paragraph)`
		—

Center the current line	`M-s` `(center-line)`	64
Set the fill prefix used by `M-q` command	`C-x .` `(set-fill-prefix)`	63
Disable the fill prefix	`C-a C-x .` `(set-fill-prefix)`	63

Table D.26. Filling Variables

Task	Variable	Page
Change fill column to specific number	*fill-column* = *n*	369

FORTRAN Mode

Table D.27. FORTRAN Mode Commands

Task	Command (Function)	Page
Functions and Statements		
Beginning of subprogram	`C-M-a` (beginning-of-fortran-subprogram)	229
End of subprogram	`C-M-e` (end-of-fortran-subprogram)	229
Place region around subprogram	`C-M-h` (mark-fortran-subprogram)	230
Move to previous FORTRAN statement	`C-c C-p` (fortran-previous-statement)	230
Move to next FORTRAN statement	`C-c C-n` (fortran-next-statement)	229
Indentation		
Indent current line according to indentation style	`TAB` (fortran-indent-line)	230
Finish current line and start a continuation line	`M-LFD` or `C-M-j` (indent-new-comment-line)	231
Indent all the lines in the current subprogram	`C-M-q` (fortran-indent-subprogram)	231

Table D.27. FORTRAN Mode Commands, con't.

Task	Command (Function)	Page
Commenting		
Insert new comment; align existing comment; move to start of comment text	`M-;` `(fortran-comment-indent)`	234
Set comment column for non-standard (!) comments	`C-x ;` `(set-comment-column)`	234, 242
Kill non-standard comment	`C-u - C-x ;` `(kill-comment)`	—
Insert comment prefix in front of all lines in region	`C-c ;` `(fortran-comment-region)`	234
Remove comment prefix from all lines in region	`C-u C-c ;` `(fortran-comment-region)`	234
Column Alignment		
Show a column "ruler" above current line	`C-c C-r` `(fortran-column-ruler)`	232
Split window at column 72	`C-c C-w` `(fortran-window-create)`	232
FORTRAN Keyword Abbreviations		
Enable FORTRAN keyword abbreviations	`M-x abbrev-mode` `(abbrev-mode)`	235

Table D.27. FORTRAN Mode Commands, con't.

Task	Command (Function)	Page
FORTRAN Keyword Abbreviations, con't.		
List all keyword abbreviations in another window	`;?` or `;` `C-h` `(fortran-abbrev-start)`	235

Table D.28. FORTRAN Mode Variables

Task	Variable	Page
Changing maximum indentation for FORTRAN labels (default is 1)	*fortran-line-number-indent* = `n`	—
Disable automatic indentation of labels	*fortran-electric-line-number* = `nil`	—
Enable automatic indentation of labels (default)	*fortran-electric-line-number* = `t`	—
Change continuation character from the default ($)	*fortran-continuation-character* = *char*	231, 240
Indentation of statements within **do** loop	*fortran-do-indent*	239, 240
Indentation of statements within **if**	*fortran-if-indent*	239, 241
Indentation for continuation lines	*fortran-continuation-indent*	240, 241
Indentation of first-level statements	*fortran-minimum-statement-indent*	239, 240
Allow non-standard (`!`) comments	*comment-start* = `"!"`	233, 243

Table D.28. FORTRAN Mode Variables, con't.

Task	Variable	Page
Align text of standard comments at *fortran-comment-line-column*	*fortran-comment-indent-style* = `fixed`	242
Align text of standard comments with code plus *fortran-comment-line-column*	*fortran-comment-indent-style* = `relative`	242
Do not attempt to align text of standard comments	*fortran-comment-indent-style* = `nil`	242
Change character used as indentation for standard comments	*fortran-comment-indent-char* = *char*	243
Change comment prefix inserted by `C-c ;`	*fortran-comment-region* = *"prefix"*	234, 243
Change the column ruler string	*fortran-comment-ruler* = *"string"*	243

Help

Table D.29. Help Commands

Task	Command (Function)	Page
List all command names containing a specified string	`C-h a` *string* `RET` (`command-apropos`)	281, 287
List all command key bindings for current mode	`C-h b` (`describe-bindings`)	281, 287, 372
Name the function to which a command key is bound	`C-h c` *key* (`describe-key-briefly`)	281, 285

Table D.29. Help Commands, con't.

Task	Command (Function)	Page
Show documentation for an Emacs command function	`C-h f` *function* `RET` (`describe-function`)	280, 450
Run the information browser to get online manual information about Emacs	`C-h i` (`info`)	282
Give extended information about the function to which a key is bound	`C-h k` *key* (`describe-key`)	281, 285, 372
Show the last 100 characters typed	`C-h l` (`view-lossage`)	282
Describe the current major mode	`C-h m` (`describe-mode`)	281
Show history of changes made to Emacs	`C-h n` (`view-emacs-news`)	283
Show syntax table entries for current mode	`C-h s` (`describe-syntax`)	282
Run the Emacs online tutorial	`C-h t` (`help-with-tutorial`)	21, 282
Display the value and information about an Emacs variable	`C-h v` *varname* `RET` (`describe-variable`)	280, 365, 450
Show which keys run a particular function	`C-h w` *function* `RET` (`where-is`)	281, 286

Indentation

Table D.30. Indentation Commands

Task	Command (Function)	Page

Indent this line appropriately for:
    Fundamental mode
    Text mode
    C mode
    FORTRAN mode
    Lisp modes
	`TAB`
	`(indent-for-tab-command)`
	`(tab-to-tab-stop)`
	`(c-indent-line)`
	`(fortran-indent-line)`
	`(lisp-indent-line)`
		65,
		169,
		194,
		230,
		258

Insert a tab character	`C-q TAB` `(quoted-insert)`	64
Finish this line and start a new line indented appropriately	`LFD` `(newline-and-indent)`	169, 194, 231, 258
Insert newline after cursor; do *not* indent new line	`C-o` `(open-line)`	59
Delete indentation from the next line and merge it with this line	`M-^` `(delete-indentation)`	66
Split the current line, indenting remainder of line to same level	`C-M-o` `(split-line)`	66
Move to first non-blank, non-tab character on line	`M-m` `(back-to-indentation)`	34
Indent all lines in region to column *n* in text editing modes	`C-u n C-M-\` `(indent-region)`	65
Reindent lines in a region, according to the programming mode indentation style	`C-M-\` `(indent-region)`	169, 194, 231, 259

Table D.30. Indentation Commands, con't.

Task	Command (Function)	Page
Indent all lines in a region rigidly *n* columns	`C-u` *n* `C-x TAB` (`indent-rigidly`)	66
Indent to the next tab stop	`M-i` (`tab-to-tab-stop`)	65
Change tab stops	`M-x edit-tab-stops` (`edit-tab-stops`)	67
Indent to level determined from the previous line	`M-x indent-relative` (`indent-relative`)	—
Convert all tabs in region to spaces, while preserving indentation	`M-x untabify` (`untabify`)	67
Convert spaces to tabs, where possible, while preserving indentation	`M-x tabify` (`tabify`)	67
Indent all the lines within a list: C mode Lisp modes	`C-M-q` (`indent-c-exp`) (`indent-sexp`)	259
Indent all lines in FORTRAN subprogram	`C-M-q` (`fortran-indent-subprogram`)	231
Indent a list so that its first line is indented appropriately	`C-u TAB` (see `TAB` above)	258

Key Bindings

Table D.31. Key Binding Commands

Task	Command (Function)	Page
Viewing existing key binding	`C-h k` `(describe-key)`	281, 285, 372
Viewing all key bindings for a mode	`C-h b` `(describe-bindings)`	281, 287, 372
Set global key binding	`M-x global-set-key` `(global-set-key)`	374, 388
Set key binding for mode	`M-x local-set-key` `(local-set-key)`	375
Force confirmation for a function	`M-x disable-command` `RET` *function* `RET`	376
Change global keymap	*global-map*	383
Change keymap used for particular mode	*mode*-map	385
Change keymap used for `C-x` commands	*ctl-x-map*	385
Change keymap used for `C-h` commands	*help-map*	385
Change keymap used for Meta commands	*esc-map*	385
Change keymap used for `C-x 4` commands	*ctl-x-4-map*	385
Change keymap used for `C-c` commands	*mode-specific-map*	385

Killing and Yanking (Moving and Copying)

Table D.32. Killing and Yanking Commands

Task	Command (Function)	Page
	Killing Text	
Kill region (between cursor and mark)	C-w (kill-region)	40
Save region to kill ring without actually deleting the text	M-w (copy-region-as-kill)	42
Kill to end of line	C-k (kill-line)	36, 353
Kill to start of line	C-u 0 C-k (kill-line)	—
Kill to end of word	M-d (kill-word)	55
Kill to start of word	M-DEL (backward-kill-word)	55
Kill to end of sentence	M-k (kill-sentence)	56
Kill to start of sentence	C-x DEL (backward-kill-sentence)	56
Kill sexp	C-M-k (kill-sexp)	185, 207, 239, 258
Kill from cursor to character *c*	M-z *c* (zap-to-char)	—
Cause subsequent kill commands to append to most recent kill block	C-M-w (append-next-kill)	—

Table D.32. Killing and Yanking Commands, con't.

Task	Command (Function)	Page
Yanking Killed Text		
Yank most recently killed text	`C-y` `(yank)`	40, 71
Yank previous block from kill ring, replacing text yanked by `C-y`	`M-y` `(yank-pop)`	73
Step through kill ring after `C-y`	`M-y` `(yank-pop)`	73
Yank block *n* from the kill ring, where 1 is the most recent block	`C-u` *n* `C-y` `(yank)`	71

Table D.33. Killing and Yanking Variables

Task	Variable	Page
Change number of blocks in kill ring to *n*	*kill-ring-max = n*	73, 371

Lisp Modes

Table D.34. Lisp Modes Commands

Task	Command (Function)	Page
Mode Selection		
Select Emacs-Lisp mode	`M-x emacs-lisp-mode` `(emacs-lisp-mode)`	250

Table D.34. Lisp Modes Commands, con't.

Task	Command (Function)	Page
Mode Selection, con't.		
Select Lisp Interaction mode	`M-x lisp-interaction-mode` `(lisp-interaction-mode)`	251
Lisp mode	`M-x lisp-mode` `(lisp-mode)`	251
Inferior lisp	`M-x run-lisp` `(run-lisp)`	251
Defuns		
Move cursor to start of defun	`C-M-a` `(beginning-of-defun)`	252
Move cursor to end of defun	`C-M-e` `(end-of-defun)`	252
Place region around defun, leaving cursor at start of defun	`C-M-h` `(mark-defun)`	257
Sexps and Lists		
Move cursor forward over sexp	`C-M-f` `(forward-sexp)`	255
Move cursor backward over sexp	`C-M-b` `(backward-sexp)`	255
Move cursor forward over list	`C-M-n` `(forward-list)`	256
Move cursor backward over list	`C-M-p` `(backward-list)`	256

Table D.34. Lisp Modes Commands, con't.

Task	Command (Function)	Page
Sexps and Lists, con't.		
Move cursor backward and "up" out of list	`C-M-u` `(backward-up-list)`	256
Move cursor forward and "down" into list	`C-M-d` `(down-list)`	256
Transpose (swap) sexps around point	`C-M-t` `(transpose-sexps)`	257
Kill forward to end of sexp	`C-M-k` `(kill-sexp)`	258
Place mark after sexp, leave cursor put	`C-M-@` `(mark-sexp)`	185
Indentation		
Indent the current line appropriately for the current indentation style	`TAB` `(lisp-indent-line)`	258
Finish current line and open next line with appropriate indentation	`LFD` or `C-j` `(newline-and-indent)`	258
Indent all lines within list appropriately	`C-M-q` `(indent-sexp)`	259
Indent a list rigidly so that its first line is indented appropriately	`C-u TAB` `(lisp-indent-line)`	259, 260
Indent all lines in the current region appropriately	`C-M-\` `(indent-region)`	259

Table D.34. Lisp Modes Commands, con't.

Task	Command (Function)	Page
Commenting		
Create new comment; align existing comment; move to start of comment text	`M-;` `(indent-for-comment)`	261
Continue a comment onto the next line	`M-LFD or C-M-j` `(indent-new-comment-line)`	262
Set the comment column to current cursor column	`C-x ;` `(set-comment-column)`	263
Set comment column to *n*	`C-u n C-x ;` `(set-comment-column)`	—
Set comment column to same as previous comment	`C-u C-x ;` `(set-comment-column)`	264
Kill comment on line	`C-u - C-x ;` `(kill-comment)`	263
Balancing Parentheses		
Place parentheses around following sexp	`M-(` `(insert-parentheses)`	172
Move over sexp and indent it	`M-)` `(move-over-close-and-reindent)`	—
Evaluating Lisp Code		
Evaluate Emacs-Lisp expression in minibuffer	`M-ESC or ESC-ESC` `(eval-expression)`	264
Evaluate preceding expression (Lisp Interaction and Emacs-Lisp)	`C-x C-e` `(eval-last-sexp)`	265, 453

Table D.34. Lisp Modes Commands, con't.

Task	Command (Function)	Page
Evaluating Lisp Code, con't.		
Evaluate surrounding expression (Emacs-Lisp and Lisp Interaction)	`C-M-x` `(eval-defun)`	265, 454
Send surrounding expression to inferior lisp process for evaluation (Lisp and Inferior Lisp)	`C-M-x` `(lisp-send-defun)`	265, 454
Evaluate code in current region (Emacs-Lisp and Lisp Interaction)	`M-x eval-region` `(eval-region)`	265, 454
Evaluate all code in buffer (Emacs-Lisp and Lisp Interaction)	`M-x eval-current-buffer` `(eval-current-buffer)`	265, 454
Evaluate previous expression and insert output in buffer (Lisp Interaction)	`LFD` or `C-j` `(eval-print-last-sexp)`	266, 454

Table D.35. Lisp Modes Variables

Task	Variable	Page
Indent the second line of expression by *lisp-indent-offset* columns more than first	*lisp-indent-offset* = *n*	270
Use default indentation	*lisp-indent-offset* = `nil`	270
Indent the second line of functions starting with `def` by an additional *n* columns	*lisp-body-indentation* = *n*	268

Table D.35. Lisp Modes Variables, con't.

Task	Variable	Page
Change comment column	*comment-column* = *n*	270
Change string used to begin comment	*comment-start* = *"string"*	271
Change string appended to end of comment	*comment-end* = *"string"*	271
Change regular expression (*regexp*) matching start of comment start	*comment-start-skip* = *"regexp"*	271, 272
Begin continued comments with *comment-start* string	*comment-multi-line* = `nil` (`default`)	—
Do *not* create new comment delimiter for continued comments	*comment-multi-line* = `t`	—

Location and Date/Time

Table D.36. Location and Date/Time Commands

Task	Command (Function)	Page
Print ASCII code, position in buffer, and column of character covered by cursor	`C-x =` (`what-cursor-position`)	60
Display line number of line containing cursor	`M-x what-line` (`what-line`)	60
Display number of lines in region	`M-=` (`count-lines-region`)	60

Table D.36. Location and Date/Time Commands, con't.

Task	Command (Function)	Page
Display page number of page containing cursor	`M-x what-page` `(what-page)`	60
Display date and time in mode line	`M-x display-time` `(display-time)`	102
Getting online help	See Table D.29, "Help."	—

Macros

Table D.37. Macro Commands

Task	Command (Function)	Page
Start defining a keyboard macro (subsequent keystrokes are part of macro definition)	`C-x (` `(start-kbd-macro)`	84
End keyboard macro definition begun with the `C-x )` command	`C-x )` `(end-kbd-macro)`	84
Run the macro just defined	`C-x e` `(call-last-kbd-macro)`	84
Name the last keyboard macro defined (allowing it to be saved and used later)	`M-x name-last-kbd-macro` `(name-last-kbd-macro)`	85
Run the macro with the name *macroname*	`M-x` *macroname*	85

Table D.37. Macro Commands, con't.

Task	Command (Function)	Page
Run the last macro and add more keystrokes to its definition	`C-u C-x (` `(start-kbd-macro)`	—
Ask for confirmation at this point during macro execution	`C-x q` `(kbd-macro-query)`	87
Insert Emacs-Lisp code for macro into buffer	`M-x insert-kbd-macro` `(insert-kbd-macro)`	86

Mail

Table D.38. Mail Commands

Task	Command	Page
Starting and Stopping RMAIL		
Start RMAIL with the **RMAIL** mailbox	`M-x rmail`	292
Save undeleted messages and exit RMAIL	`q`	301
Reading Mail		
Read **RMAIL** mailbox	`M-x rmail`	292
Read alternate mailbox	`i`	312, 313
Read in new mail received since starting RMAIL	`g`	314

Table D.38. Mail Commands, con't.

Task	Command	Page
Moving Among Mail Messages		
Display first message	1j	294
Display *n*th message	*n*j	294
Display last message	>	295
Display next message	M-n	295
Display next message, skipping deleted messages, if any	n	300
Display previous message	M-p	295
Display previous message, skipping deleted messages, if any	p	301
Display message matching a regexp	M-s	295
Removing Messages		
Mark message for deletion and move to next message	d	297
Mark message for deletion and move to previous message	C-d	297
Unmark deletion flag set by d or C-d command	u	297
Expunge (remove) all messages marked for deletion	x or e	297

Table D.38. Mail Commands, con't.

Task	Command	Page
Saving Messages		
Expunge deleted messages and save all others in mailbox	`s`	295
Save all messages in mailbox	`C-x C-s`	296
Save current message to a file (RMAIL format)	`o`	296
Save current message to a file (UNIX format)	`C-o`	296
Composing and Sending Messages		
Create `*mail*` buffer to compose message	`C-x m` or `M-x mail`	302
Clear `*mail*` buffer to start new message	`C-x m`	302
Clear `*mail*` buffer in other window	`m` or `C-x 4 m`	302
Send message from `*mail*` buffer and switch buffers	`C-c C-c`	303
Send message from `*mail*` buffer and remain in `*mail*`	`C-c C-s`	303
Create or move to `To:` header	`C-c C-f C-t`	305
Create or move to `Subject:` header	`C-c C-f C-s`	305
Create or move to `CC:` header	`C-c C-f C-c`	305

Table D.38. Mail Commands, con't.

Task	Command	Page
Composing and Sending Messages, con't.		
Append text from `.signature` file to end of message	`C-c C-w`	306
Insert current message into mailbox buffer	`C-c C-y`	307
Fill paragraphs of inserted message	`C-c C-q`	307
Replying to and Forwarding Messages		
Reply to the current message	`r`	302
Forward the current message	`f`	302
Continue editing current message in `*mail*` as response	`c`	302
Send a new message, enabling `C-c C-y`	`m` or `C-x 4 m`	302
Using Alternate Mailboxes		
Read alternate mailbox	`i`	312, 313
Set UNIX mailbox files for RMAIL mailbox	`M-x set-rmail-inbox-list`	314
Merge new mail received in UNIX mailbox files	`g`	314

Table D.38. Mail Commands, con't.

Task	Command	Page
Using Mail Summaries		
Create summary of all messages in mailbox	h or C-M-h	299
Create summary of messages with label	l or C-M-l	299
Create summary of messages with recipient	r or C-M-r	299
Mark current line's message for deletion	d	300
Unmark current line's message for deletion	u	300
Move to *n*th message	*n*j	300
Move to next message	C-n	300
Move to next message, skipping deleted messages, if any	n	300
Move to previous message	C-p	301
Move to previous message, skipping deleted messages, if any	p	301
Exit RMAIL	q	301
Exit mail summary window	x	301
Scroll other (mailbox) window forward	SPC	301

Table D.38. Mail Commands, con't.

Task	Command	Page
Using Mail Summaries, con't.		
Scroll other (mailbox) window backward	DEL	301
Using Labels		
Assign a label to a message	a	310
Remove a label from a message	k	311
Move to the next message that has label	C-M-n	311
Move to previous message that has label	C-M-p	311
Digest Messages		
Expand digest message into component messages	M-x undigestify-rmail-message	313

Minibuffer Editing

Table D.39. Minibuffer Editing Commands

Task	Command (Function)	Page
Miscellaneous		
Increase height of minibuffer	C-x ^ (enlarge-window)	138
Scroll other window from minibuffer	C-M-v (scroll-other-window)	138

Table D.39. Minibuffer Editing Commands, con't.

Task	Command (Function)	Page
Command History		
Re-execute previous command executed in minibuffer	`C-x ESC` `(repeat-complex-command)`	140

While in minibuffer, move to previous command executed from minibuffer	`M-p`
	 `(previous-complex-`
	 `command)`
		140

While in minibuffer, move to next command executed from minibuffer	`M-n` `(next-complex-command)`	140

Display listing of commands executed in minibuffer	`M-x list-command-`
	 `history`
	 `(list-command-history)`
		140

Response Completion for M-x Commands and File Names		

Attempt to complete response and execute command	`RET`
	 `(minibuffer-complete-`
	 `and-exit)`
		141

Attempt to complete current word	`SPC`
	 `(minibuffer-complete-`
	 `word)`
		141

Attempt to complete response, but don't execute command	`TAB` `(minibuffer-complete)`	141

Display list of alternatives for response	`?`
	 `(minibuffer-completion-`
	 `help)`
		338

Table D.40. Minibuffer Editing Variables

Task	Variable	Page
Do not display multiple-character command keys in echo area	*echo-keystrokes* = `0`	369
Echo multiple-character command keys in echo area, but wait *n* seconds first	*echo-keystrokes* = *n*	369
Disable display of alternatives	*completion-auto-help* = `nil`	142
Enable display of alternatives (default)	*completion-auto-help* = `t`	142
Ignore some file name extensions	*completion-ignored-extensions* = *extlist*	142
Show all files, regardless of extensions	*completion-ignored-extensions* = `nil`	142

Modes

Table D.41. Mode Commands

Task	Command (Function)	Page
Select a new mode	`M-x` *modename*-`mode` (use `C-h a mode RET` for a list of modes available)	33

Table D.42. Mode Variables

Task	Variable	Page
Select a mode based on file name suffix when visiting a file	*auto-mode-alist* = *file name/mode pairs list*	368

Table D.42. Mode Variables, con't.

Task	Variable	Page
Select the initial mode Emacs starts up in (must set in `.emacs` file)	*initial-major-mode = mode*	367

Nroff Mode

Table D.43. Nroff Mode Commands

Task	Command (Function)	Page
Enable Nroff mode	`M-x nroff-mode` `(nroff-mode)`	348
Move to next text (non-command) line	`M-n` `(forward-text-line)`	349
Move to previous text (non-command) line	`M-p` `(backward-text-line)`	348
Display number of text (non-command) lines in region	`M-?`	349
Automatically insert closing nroff command when opening command typed	`M-x electric-nroff-mode` `(electric-nroff-mode)`	348

Numeric Prefix

Table D.44. Numeric Prefix Commands

Task	Command (Function)	Page
Type positive numeric prefix with Control-U	`C-u` *digit1 digit2...*	52

Table D.44. Numeric Prefix Commands, con't.

Task	Command (Function)	Page
Type negative numeric prefix with Control-U	`C-u - `*digit1 digit2...*	52
Type positive numeric prefix with Meta key	`M-` *digit1 digit2...*	53
Type negative numeric prefix with Meta key	`M--` *digit1 digit2...*	53

Outline Editing

Table D.45. Outline Editing Commands

Task	Command (Function)	Page
Moving Among Headings		
Enable outline mode	`M-x outline-mode` `(outline-mode)`	118

Move to next visible heading	`C-c C-n`
	`(outline-next-visible-`
	`heading)`
		120

Move to previous visible heading	`C-c C-p`
	`(outline-previous-`
	`visible-heading)`
		120

Move to next visible heading at same level as current heading	`C-c C-f`
	`(outline-forward-same-`
	`level)`
		120

Move to previous visible heading at same level as current heading	`C-c C-b`
	`(outline-backward-same-`
	`level)`
		120

Table D.45. Outline Editing Commands, con't.

Task	Command (Function)	Page
Moving Among Headings, con't.		
Move up and backward to the next "higher" visible heading	`C-c C-u` `(outline-up-heading)`	120
Collapsing and Expanding		
Hide all body lines under headings	`M-x hide-body` `(hide-body)`	122
Show all body lines (undo `M-x hide-body`)	`M-x show-all` `(show-all)`	122
Hide all lines under this heading (collapse the heading)	`C-c C-h` `(hide-subtree)`	122
Show all lines under this heading (expand the heading completely)	`C-c C-s` `(show-subtree)`	122
Hide body of current heading and its subheadings	`M-x hide-leaves` `(hide-leaves)`	122
Show all subheadings of this heading	`M-x show-branches` `(show-branches)`	122
Show next level (immediate) subheadings only	`C-c C-i` `(show-children)`	122
Hide this heading's body	`M-x hide-entry` `(hide-entry)`	122
Show this heading's body	`M-x show-entry` `(show-entry)`	122

Table D.46. Outline Editing Variables

Task	Variable	Page
Turn off display of ellipses for invisible lines	*selective-display-ellipses* = `nil`	—
Change regular expression (*regexp*) that matches the start of a heading line	*outline-regexp* = `"regexp"`	123

Pages

Table D.47. Page Commands

Task	Command (Function)	Page
Show current page number	`M-x what-page` `(what-page)`	60
Show lines in current page and line number of page	`C-x l` `(count-lines-page)`	58
Move to previous page break	`C-x [` `(backward-page)`	58
Move to next page break	`C-x ]` `(forward-page)`	58
Place a region around this page	`C-x C-p` `(mark-page)`	58

Table D.48. Page Variables

Task	Variable	Page
Change *regexp* that matches page break	*page-delimiter* = `"regexp"`	—

Table D.48. Page Variables, con't.

Task	Variable	Page
Use default regexp to match page break	*page-delimiter* = `"^\f"`	—

Paragraphs

Table D.49. Paragraph Commands

Task	Command (Function)	Page
Move backward to paragraph beginning	`M-[` `(backward-paragraph)`	57
Move forward to paragraph end	`M-]` `(forward-paragraph)`	57
Place region around current paragraph, leaving cursor at beginning	`M-h` `(mark-paragraph)`	57
Sort paragraphs in region	`M-x sort-paragraphs` `(sort-paragraphs)`	148

Table D.50. Paragraph Variables

Task	Variable	Page
Set *regexp* to match paragraph separator	*paragraph-separate* = `"regexp"`	144, 148
Set *regexp* to match paragraph start	*paragraph-start* = `"regexp"`	—

Picture Mode

Table D.51. Picture Mode Commands

Task	Command (Function)	Page
Enable Picture mode	`M-x picture-mode` (picture-mode)	353
Exit Picture mode and return to previous mode	`C-c C-c` (picture-mode-exit)	353
Move cursor forward one column	`C-f` (picture-forward-column)	353
Move cursor backward one column	`C-b` (picture-backward-column)	353
Move cursor to same column, previous line	`C-p` (picture-move-up)	353
Move cursor to same column, next line	`C-n` (picture-move-down)	353
Replace current character with blank	`C-d` (picture-clear-column)	353
Replace previous character with blank	`DEL` (picture-backward-clear-column)	353
Erase all remaining visible characters on line	`C-k` (picture-clear-line)	353
Move to next tab stop	`TAB` (picture-tab)	353
Move to next tab stop and erase	`C-u TAB` (picture-tab)	353

Table D.51. Picture Mode Commands, con't.

Task	Command (Function)	Page

Erase rectangle	`C-c C-k`
	`(picture-clear-`
	`rectangle)`
		353

Erase rectangle; shift any following text to the left	`C-u C-c C-k`
	`(picture-clear-`
	`rectangle)`
		353

Erase rectangle, placing it in register	`C-c C-w`
	`(picture-clear-`
	`rectangle-to-register)`
		353

Erase rectangle, placing it in register; shift any following text to the left	`C-u C-c C-w`
	`(picture-clear-`
	`rectangle-to-register)`
		353

Overwrite existing text with rectangle saved by `C-c C-k`	`C-c C-y` `(picture-yank-rectangle)`	353

Overwrite existing text with rectangle saved to register by `C-c C-w`	`C-c C-x`
	`(picture-yank-`
	`rectangle-from-`
	`register)`
		353

Align cursor with "interesting" characters above	`M-TAB` or `ESC-TAB` `(picture-tab-search)`	354
Selecting a Direction for Cursor to Move After Text Insertion		
Right (East)	`C-c >` `(picture-movement-right)`	354
Left (West)	`C-c <` `(picture-movement-left)`	354
Up (North)	`C-c ^` `(picture-movement-up)`	355

Table D.51. Picture Mode Commands, con't.

Task	Command (Function)	Page
Selecting a Direction for Cursor to Move After Text Insertion, con't.		
Down (South)	`C-c .` (`picture-movement-down`)	355
Up and right (Northeast)	`C-c '` (`picture-movement-ne`)	355
Up and left (Northwest)	`` C-c ` `` (`picture-movement-nw`)	355
Down and right (Southeast)	`C-c \` (`picture-movement-se`)	355
Down and left (Southwest)	`C-c /` (`picture-movement-sw`)	355

Table D.52. Picture Mode Variables

Task	Variable	Page
Change which characters Picture mode considers "interesting"	*picture-tab-chars*	354

Printing

Table D.53. Printing Commands

Task	Command (Function)	Page
Print buffer contents using UNIX command `lpr -p`	`M-x print-buffer` (`print-buffer`)	94

Table D.53. Printing Commands, con't.

Task	Command (Function)	Page
Print buffer contents using lpr command (no headings)	`M-x lpr-buffer` `(lpr-buffer)`	94
Print region with page headings using UNIX command `lpr -p`	`M-x print-region` `(print-region)`	94
Print region without page headings using UNIX command `lpr`	`M-x lpr-region` `(lpr-region)`	94

Table D.54. Printing Variables

Task	Variable	Page
Specify additional command line options to `lpr` command	*lpr-switches* = *"string"*	—

Rectangles

Table D.55. Rectangle Commands

Task	Command (Function)	Page
Clear region (replace all characters with spaces)	`M-x clear-rectangle` `(clear-rectangle)`	149
Delete a rectangle without saving it; shift following text in to fill the space	`M-x delete-rectangle` `(delete-rectangle)`	149
Kill a rectangle, saving in temporary storage; shift following text to fill space	`M-x kill-rectangle` `(kill-rectangle)`	150

Table D.55. Rectangle Commands, con't.

Task	Command (Function)	Page
Yank the rectangle previously killed with `M-x kill-rectangle`	`M-x yank-rectangle` `(yank-rectangle)`	150
Shift rectangle to the right, filling the vacated space with blanks	`M-x open-rectangle` `(open-rectangle)`	150
Copy rectangle into register r; don't erase the rectangle	`C-x r r` `(copy-region-to-rectangle)`	152
Kill rectangle into register r; shift any following text to fill the vacated area	`C-u C-x r r` `(copy-region-to-rectangle)`	152
Insert rectangle stored by `C-x r` command; existing text shifted right	`C-x g r` `(insert-register)`	152

Regions

Table D.56. Region Commands

Task	Command (Function)	Page
Set mark at point; you then define region by moving cursor	`C-SPC or C-@` `(set-mark-command)`	38
Show bounds of region by exchanging point with mark	`C-x C-x` `(exchange-point-and-mark)`	39
Place mark after word	`M-@` `(mark-word)`	55

Table D.56. Region Commands, con't.

Task	Command (Function)	Page
Create region of paragraph, with mark at end	`M-h` `(mark-paragraph)`	57
Create region of page, with mark at end of page	`C-x C-p` `(mark-page)`	58
Place region around current buffer	`C-x h` `(mark-whole-buffer)`	—
Place region around function	`C-M-h` `(depends on mode)`	167, 193, 230, 257
Place region between cursor and end of next sexp	`C-M-@` `(mark-sexp)`	185, 205, 238, 257
Kill current region, placing it in kill ring	`C-w` `(kill-region)`	40
Copy current region to kill ring	`M-w` `(copy-region-as-kill)`	42
Copy current region into register *r*	`C-x x` *r* `(copy-to-register)`	151
Copy region to end of a buffer	`C-x a` `(append-to-buffer)`	126
Copy region to start of a buffer	`M-x prepend-to-buffer` `(prepend-to-buffer)`	126
Copy region to end of a file	`M-x append-to-file` `(append-to-file)`	—
Convert all characters in region to uppercase	`C-x C-u` `(upcase-region)`	68
Convert all characters in region to lowercase	`C-x C-l` `(downcase-region)`	68

Table D.56. Region Commands, con't.

Task	Command (Function)	Page
Evaluate Emacs-Lisp code in region	`M-x eval-region` `(eval-region)`	265, 454
Fill the paragraphs in region	`M-g` `(fill-region)`	62
Fill the text in a region, making one paragraph	`M-x fill-region-as-` `paragraph` `(fill-region-as-` `paragraph)`	—
Print text in region using UNIX command `lpr`	`M-x lpr-region` `(lpr-region)`	94
Print text in region using UNIX command `lpr -p`	`M-x print-region` `(print-region)`	94
Indent all lines in region to column _n_ (text editing modes)	`C-u` _n_ `C-M-\` `(indent-region)`	65
Indent all lines in region to first tab stop (text editing modes)	`C-M-\` `(indent-region)`	—
Indent all lines in region rigidly _n_ columns	`C-u` _n_ `C-x TAB` `(indent-rigidly)`	66
Sorting lines in a region	See Table D.68, "Sorting"	—
Restrict editing to the current region (narrowing)	`C-x n` `(narrow-to-region)`	70
Allow editing of entire buffer (undo narrowing)	`C-x w` `(widen)`	70
Passing regions through shell commands	See Table D.66, "Shells"	—

Table D.56. Region Commands, con't.

Task	Command (Function)	Page
Move to previous mark in mark ring	`C-u C-SPC` or `C-u C-@` `(set-mark-command)`	71

Table D.57. Region Variables

Task	Variable	Page
Change the size of the mark ring to n	*mark-ring-max = n*	71

Registers

Table D.58. Register Commands

Task	Command (Function)	Page
Save point in register r	`C-x / r` `(point-to-register)`	150
Move to location stored in register r	`C-x j r` `(register-to-point)`	151
Copy region to register r	`C-x x r` `(copy-to-register)`	151
Kill region to register r	`C-u C-x x r` `(copy-to-register)`	151
Insert register r contents at point	`C-x g r` `(insert-register)`	151
Copy rectangle to register r	`C-x r r` `(copy-region-to-rectangle)`	152

Table D.58. Register Commands, con't.

Task	Command (Function)	Page

Kill rectangle to register *r*	`C-u C-x r r`
	`(copy-region-to-`
	`rectangle)`
		152

Insert at point the rectangle stored in register *r*	`C-x g` *r* `(insert-register)`	152
Display register's type (location, region, rectangle) and contents	`M-x view-register RET` *r* `(view-register)`	—

Searching

Table D.59. Searching Commands

Task	Command (Function)	Page
Incremental Search		
Incrementally search forward for *string*	`C-s` *string* `(isearch-forward)`	43
Incrementally search backward for *string*	`C-r` *string* `(isearch-backward)`	43
Incrementally search forward for *regexp*	`C-M-s` *regexp* `(isearch-forward-regexp)`	107

Incrementally search backward for *regexp*	`M-x isearch-backward-`
	`regexp RET` *regexp* `RET`
	`(isearch-backward-`
	`regexp)`
		107

While incremental search in effect, find next forward occurrence	`C-s`	45, 107

Table D.59. Searching Commands, con't.

Task	Command (Function)	Page
Incremental Search, con't.		
While incremental search in effect, find next previous occurrence	`C-r`	45, 107
Stop incremental search, leaving cursor at current location	`ESC`	44, 46
Stop incremental search, moving cursor to different location	Run cursor motion command (e.g., `C-a`)	44
Abort incremental search, leaving cursor at starting position	`C-g` (`keyboard-quit`)	44
Nonincremental Search		
Search for next occurrence of *string*	`C-s ESC` *string* `RET` (`search-forward`)	69
Search for previous occurrence of *string*	`C-r ESC` *string* `RET` (`search-backward`)	69
Search for next occurrence of one or more *words*, ignoring punctuation in text	`C-s ESC C-w` *words* `RET` (`word-search-forward`)	70
Search for prior occurrence of one or more *words*, ignoring punctuation in text	`C-r ESC C-w` *words* `RET` (`word-search-backward`)	70
Search forward for *regexp*	`C-M-s ESC` *regexp* `RET` (`re-search-forward`)	107
Search backward for *regexp*	`M-x re-search-backward` (`re-search-backward`)	107

Table D.60. Searching Variables

Task	Variable	Page
Letter Case Significance (Per Buffer)		
Make letter case significant (match case exactly)	*case-fold-search* = `nil`	117, 367
Ignore letter case during search (default)	*case-fold-search* = `t`	117, 367
Characters That Affect Incremental Search		
Change character that stops incremental search (default = `ESC`)	*search-exit-char* = *char*	—
Change character that does backspace in incremental search string (default = `ESC`)	*search-delete-char* = *char*	—
Change character that quotes special characters in incremental search string (default = `C-q`)	*search-quote-char* = *char*	—
Change character to repeat incremental search forward (default = `C-s`)	*search-repeat-char* = *char*	—
Change character to repeat incremental search backward (default = `C-r`)	*search-reverse-char* = *char*	—
Change character that yanks line from buffer into search string (default = `C-y`)	*search-yank-line-char* = *char*	—

Table D.60. Searching Variables, con't.

Task	Variable	Page
Characters That Affect Incremental Search, con't.		
Change character that yanks word from buffer into search string (default = C-w)	*search-yank-word-char = char*	—
Incremental Search on Slow Terminals		
Change baud rate at which slow-terminal search occurs to *n* (default = 1200)	*search-slow-speed = n*	—
Change number of lines used in slow-terminal search to *n* (default = 1)	*search-slow-window-lines = n*	—

Searching and Replacing

Table D.61. Search-and-Replace Commands

Task	Command (Function)	Page
Search-and-Replace with Verification (Query-Replace)		
Query-replace *string* with *replacement*	`M-%` *string* `RET` *replacement* `RET` (`query-replace`)	46
Query-replace *word* with *newword*	`C-u M-%` *word* `RET` *newword* `RET` (`query-replace`)	—
Query-replace *regexp* with *replacement*	`M-x query-replace-regexp RET` *regexp* `RET` *replacement* `RET` (`query-replace-regexp`)	117

Table D.61. Search-and-Replace Commands, con't.

Task	Command (Function)	Page
Commands You Can Use During Query-Replace		
Allow the replacement to occur	`SPC`	46
Do not replace; move to next occurrence	`DEL` or `,` (comma)	46
Terminate query-replace	`ESC` or `.` (period)	46
Make all subsequent replacements without confirmation	`!`	46
Go back to previous location where match was found	`^`	46
Display help for query-replace options	`C-h`	—
Enter recursive editing level to edit text, not mere replacement	`C-r`	—
Delete the occurrence, then enter recursive editing level like `C-r`	`C-w`	—
Exit from recursive editing level, returning to query-replace	`C-M-c`	—
Redisplay the screen	`C-l`	—

Table D.61. Search-and-Replace Commands, con't.

Task	Command (Function)	Page
Unconditional Search-and-Replace (Caution!)		
Search for all occurrences of *string* and replace it with *newstring*	`M-x replace-string RET` *string* `RET` *newstring* `RET` `(replace-string)`	70
Search for all occurrences of regular expression *regexp* and replace it with *newstring*	`M-x replace-regexp RET` *regexp* `RET` *newstring* `RET` `(replace-regexp)`	116
Move cursor to last occurrence of replaced *string* or *regexp*	`C-u SPC` or `C-u C-@` `(set-mark-command)`	71
Additional Search-and-Edit Commands		
Find all lines containing a *regexp* and display them in `*Occur*` buffer	`M-x occur RET` *regexp* `RET` `(occur)`	—
From an occur buffer, move to a line containing a match	`C-c C-c` `(occur-mode-goto-occurrence)`	—
Show how many matches of *regexp* follow point	`M-x count-matches RET` *regexp* `RET` `(count-matches)`	—
Delete lines following point that don't match a *regexp*	`M-x delete-non-matching-lines RET` *regexp* `RET` `(delete-non-matching-lines)`	—
Delete lines following point that contain a match of a *regexp*	`M-x delete-matching-lines RET` *regexp* `RET` `(delete-matching-lines)`	—

Table D.62. Search-and-Replace Variables

Task	Variable	Page
Do case conversion when replacing (default)	*case-replace* = `t`	367
Don't convert case when replacing	*case-replace* = `nil`	367
Case not significant when looking for the search string; conversion of replacement string depends on *case-replace*	*case-fold-search* = `t`	117, 367
Case significant when looking for search string; do *not* convert replacement string	*case-fold-search* = `nil`	117, 367

Sentences

Table D.63. Sentence Commands

Task	Command (Function)	Page
Move to beginning of sentence	`M-a` (`backward-sentence`)	56
Move to end of sentence	`M-e` (`forward-sentence`)	56
Kill text from cursor to end of sentence	`M-k` (`kill-sentence`)	56
Kill text from cursor to start of sentence	`C-x DEL` (`backward-kill-sentence`)	56

Table D.64. Sentence Variables

Task	Variable	Page
Change *regexp* matching end of sentence; default: `"[.?!][]\"')]*\\($\\ |\t\\\| \\)[ \t\n]*"`	*sentence-end* = `"regexp"`	56, 370

Sexps and Lists (Balanced Expressions)

Table D.65. Sexp and List (Balanced Expression) Commands

Task	Command (Function)	Page
Sexp Commands		
Move cursor forward over sexp	`C-M-f` `(forward-sexp)`	185, 204, 237, 254
Move cursor backward over sexp	`C-M-b` `(backward-sexp)`	185, 204, 238, 255
Kill from cursor to end of sexp	`C-M-k` `(kill-sexp)`	185, 207, 239, 258
Transpose sexps around point	`C-M-t` `(transpose-sexp)`	185, 206, 257
Place mark after the following sexp, leaving cursor put	`C-M-@` `(mark-sexp)`	185, 205
List Commands		
Move backward to next highest level in list in which cursor resides	`C-M-u` `(up-list)`	186, 205, 256
Move forward to next nested level of list in which cursor resides	`C-M-d` `(down-list)`	186, 205, 256

Table D.65. Sexp and List (Balanced Expression) Commands, con't.

Task	Command (Function)	Page
List Commands, con't.		
Move to end of this or next list	`C-M-n` `(forward-list)`	186, 205, 256
Move to beginning of this or previous list	`C-M-p` `(backward-list)`	186, 205, 256
Indent all lines within current list	`C-M-q` `(indent-sexp)`	186, 259
Rigidly shift a list so that its first line is properly indented	`C-u TAB` `(depends on mode)`	186, 259

Shells

Table D.66. Shell Commands

Task	Command (Function)	Page
Shell Filter Commands		
Run shell command and display output in `*Shell Command Output*` window	`M-!` *cmd* `RET` `(shell-command)`	341
Run shell command and insert its output into current buffer at point	`C-u M-!` *cmd* `RET` `(shell-command)`	341
Pass current region as standard input to shell command; display output in `*Shell Command Output*` window	`M-|` *cmd* `RET` `(shell-command-on-region)`	341

Table D.66. Shell Commands, con't.

Task	Command (Function)	Page
Shell Filter Commands, con't.		
Pass current region as standard input to shell command; replace region with resulting output	`C-u M-|` *cmd* `RET` (`shell-command-on-region`)	341
Running a Subshell in a Buffer Window (Shell Mode)		
Spawn a subshell sending standard input and output through buffer named `*shell*`	`M-x shell` (`shell`)	345
Send the text preceding the cursor as input to the shell (like typing a UNIX command and pressing **RET**)	`RET` (`shell-send-input`)	346
Send end-of-file to shell	`C-c C-d` (`shell-send-eof`)	347
Kill current input line to shell	`C-c C-u` (`shell-kill-input`)	346
Kill word preceding cursor	`C-c C-w` (`backward-kill-word`)	347
Send Control-C (abort) interrupt to shell or executing process	`C-c C-c` (`interrupt-shell-job`)	347
Send Control-Z (suspend) interrupt to shell or executing process	`C-c C-z` (`stop-shell-subjob`)	347
Send quit signal to shell or executing process	`C-c C-\` (`quit-shell-subjob`)	347

Table D.66. Shell Commands, con't.

Task	Command (Function)	Page
Running a Subshell in a Buffer Window (Shell Mode), con't.		
Remove the last output to the *shell* buffer	C-c C-o (kill-output-from-shell)	348
Display last shell output at top of window	C-c C-r (show-output-from-shell)	348
Repeat the last shell command input	C-c C-y (copy-last-shell-input)	347

Table D.67. Shell Variables

Task	Variable	Page
Specify shell to use (initialized from your SHELL environment variable)	*shell-file-name = shellpath*	341
Specify the shell to use when **M-x shell** is invoked (set from ESHELL or SHELL environment variable)	*explicit-shell-file-name = shellpath*	345
Tell Emacs your alias (if any) for UNIX **cd** command	*shell-cd-regexp = "cdregexp"*	345
Tell Emacs your alias (if any) for UNIX **pushd** command	*shell-pushd-regexp = "pushdregexp"*	345
Tell Emacs your alias (if any) for UNIX **popd** command	*shell-popd-regexp = "popdregexp"*	345
Tell Emacs what function to call if it looses its mind from a **cd**, **pushd**, or **popd** command	*shell-set-directory-error-hook = defun*	345

Sorting

Table D.68. Sorting Commands

Task	Command (Function)	Page
Sort all lines in region; compare entire lines	`M-x sort-lines` `(sort-lines)`	143, 144
Sort all lines in descending order; compare entire lines	`C-u M-x sort-lines` `(sort-lines)`	143, 145
Sort all lines in region; compare field n	`C-u` n `M-x sort-fields` `(sort-fields)`	143, 145
Sort all lines in region in descending order; compare field n	`C-u` $-n$ `M-x sort-fields` `(sort-fields)`	143
Sort all lines in region; compare numeric field n	`C-u` n `M-x sort-numeric-fields` `(sort-numeric-fields)`	143, 146
Sort all lines in region in descending order; compare field n	`C-u` $-n$ `M-x sort-numeric-fields` `(sort-numeric-fields)`	143, 146
Sort all lines in region; compare columns	`M-x sort-columns` `(sort-columns)`	144, 147
Sort all lines in region in descending order; compare columns	`C-u M-x sort-columns` `(sort-columns)`	144
Sort paragraphs in region; compare entire paragraphs	`M-x sort-paragraphs` `(sort-paragraphs)`	144, 148
Sort paragraphs in region in descending order; compare entire paragraphs	`C-u M-x sort-paragraphs` `(sort-paragraphs)`	144

Table D.68. Sorting Commands, con't.

Task	Command (Function)	Page
Sort pages in region; compare entire pages, excluding leading blank lines	`M-x sort-pages` `(sort-pages)`	144
Sort pages in descending order	`C-u M-x sort-pages` `(sort-pages)`	144

Spell-Checking

Table D.69. Spell-Checking Commands

Task	Command (Function)	Page
Using the Emacs Spelling Checker		
Check spelling of word	`M-$` `(spell-word)`	334
Check spelling of user-specified *string*	`M-x spell-string RET` *string* `RET` `(spell-string)`	—
Check spelling of all words in region	`M-x spell-region` `(spell-region)`	334, 336
Check spelling of all words in buffer	`M-x spell-buffer` `(spell-buffer)`	334, 336
Using ispell (Interactive, Friendly Spell-Checker)		
Check spelling of word using `ispell`	`M-x ispell-word` `(ispell-word)`	—
Check spelling of all words in region using `ispell`	`M-x ispell-region` `(ispell-region)`	—

Table D.69. Spell-Checking Commands, con't.

Task	Command (Function)	Page
Using ispell (Interactive, Friendly Spell-Checker), con't.		
Check spelling of all words in buffer using `ispell`	`M-x ispell-buffer` `(ispell-buffer)`	—

Tags

Table D.70. Tag Commands

Task	Command (Function)	Page
Generate a tag table (**TAGS** file)	UNIX/Emacs command: `etags` *files...*	175
Select a **TAGS** file	`M-x visit-tags-table` `(visit-tags-table)`	176
Find *tag*	`M-.` *tag* `RET` `(find-tag)`	176
Find *tag* and display it in other window	`C-x 4 .` *tag* `RET` `(find-tag-other-window)`	177
Find next occurrence of last search *tag*	`C-u M-.` `(find-tag)`	177
Find a regular expression in files specified by **TAGS** file	`M-x tags-search` `(tags-search)`	177
Query-replace a regular expression in files specified by **TAGS** file	`M-x tags-query-replace` `(tags-query-replace)`	178
Repeat last search command involving **TAGS** file	`M-,` (Meta-comma) `(tags-loop-continue)`	178

Table D.70. Tag Commands, con't.

Task	Command (Function)	Page
List all tags within a file	`M-x list-tags` `(list-tags)`	178
Search for tags matching regular expression	`M-x tags-apropos` `(tags-apropos)`	179
Visit first file specified in tag table	`C-u M-x next-file` `(next-file)`	178
Visit next file as specified in tag table	`M-x next-file` `(next-file)`	178

Table D.71. Tag Variables

Task	Variable	Page
Set name of TAGS table file	*tags-file-name* = *"path"*	176

TeX Mode

Table D.72. TeX Mode Commands

Task	Command (Function)	Page
Enabling a Mode		
Enable TeX mode	`M-x plain-tex-mode` `(plain-tex-mode)`	349
Enable LaTeX mode	`M-x latex-mode` `(latex-mode)`	349

Table D.72. TeX Mode Commands, con't.

Task	Command (Function)	Page
Text Insertion Commands		
Insert appropriate quote character(s)	`"` `(TeX-insert-quote)`	351

Check balanced characters and create new paragraph	`LFD`
	 `(TeX-terminate-`
	 `paragraph)`
		351

Check balanced characters in buffer and update mark ring	`M-x validate-TeX-buffer` `(validate-TeX-buffer)`	351
Insert balanced braces	`M-{` `(TeX-insert-braces)`	351
Move past unmatched }	`M-}` `(up-list)`	351
Insert \end for LaTeX block	`C-c C-f` `(TeX-close-LaTeX-block)`	351
Processing and Printing Commands		
Pass region to TeX	`C-c C-r` `(TeX-region)`	351
Pass buffer to TeX	`C-c C-b` `(TeX-buffer)`	351

Center TeX output in *TeX-shell* buffer window	`C-c C-l`
	 `(TeX-recenter-output-`
	 `buffer)`
		352

Kill TeX job	`C-c C-k` `(TeX-kill-job)`	—
Print TeX log	`C-c C-p` `(TeX-print)`	352

Table D.72. TeX Mode Commands, con't.

Task	Command (Function)	Page
Processing and Printing Commands, con't.		
Show TeX print queue	`C-c C-q` `(TeX-show-printer-queue)`	352

Table D.73. TeX Mode Variables

Task	Variable	Page
Tell Emacs which default TeX mode to use (default = plain-TeX-mode)	*TeX-default-mode = mode*	—
Tell Emacs where TeX temporary files are placed (default = `"/tmp/"`)	*TeX-directory =* `"path"`	350
Tell Emacs what command to use to print dvi files (default = `"lpr -d"`)	*TeX-dvi-print-command =* `"cmd"`	350
Tell Emacs what command to use to show print queue (default = `"lpq"`)	*TeX-show-queue-command =* `"cmd"`	350

Transposing

Table D.74. Transposing Commands

Task	Command (Function)	Page
Transpose characters around point	`C-t` `(transpose-chars)`	61

Table D.74. Transposing Commands, con't.

Task	Command (Function)	Page
Transpose words around point	`M-t` `(transpose-words)`	61
Transpose sexps around point	`C-M-t` `(transpose-sexps)`	185, 206, 257
Exchange this line with previous line, or vice versa if at first line	`C-x C-t` `(transpose-lines)`	61

Undo

Table D.75. Undo Commands

Task	Command (Function)	Page
Cancel command being typed or (in some cases) command in progress	`C-g` `(keyboard-quit)`	15
Undo the effects of the last command (when possible)	`C-x u` or `C-x _` `(undo)`	37
Cancel recursive editing and abort command	`C-]` `(abort-recursive-edit)`	—
Cancel all recursive editing levels	`M-x top-level` `(top-level)`	—

Variables

Table D.76. Variable Commands

Task	Command (Function)	Page
Show variable's documentation (if any) and value	`C-h v` *varname* `RET` `(describe-variable)`	280, 365, 450

Set variable's value	`M-x set-variable RET`
	varname `RET` *value* `RET`
	`(set-variable)`
		23,
		366

Make variable local to buffer	`M-x make-local-variable` `RET` *varname* `RET`	378
Kill local copy of variable	`M-x kill-local-variable` `RET` *varname* `RET`	378

Make variable local when its value is set	`M-x make-variable-`
	`buffer-local RET`
	varname `RET`
	`(make-variable-buffer-`
	`local)`
		378

Show all option variables in `*List Options*` buffer	`M-x list-options` `(list-options)`	381
Edit option variables in `*List Options*` buffer	`M-x edit-options` `(edit-options)`	382

Windows

Table D.77. Window Commands

Task	Command (Function)	Page
Scroll windows horizontally and vertically	See Table D.17, "Display Management"	—

Table D.77. Window Commands, con't.

Task	Command (Function)	Page
Split window vertically into two new windows	`C-x 2` `(split-window-vertically)`	93
Split window horizontally into two new windows	`C-x 5` `(split-window-horizontally)`	93
Select other ("next") window	`C-x o` `(other-window)`	93
Scroll other ("next") window	`C-M-v` `(scroll-other-window)`	138
Remove all windows except the selected window; does not affect buffers	`C-x 1` `(delete-other-windows)`	93
Remove the current window; does not affect its buffer	`C-x 0` `(kill-window)`	93
Increase height of selected window by one line	`C-x ^` `(enlarge-window)`	138
Increase height of selected window *n* lines	`C-u n C-x ^` `(enlarge-window)`	—
Increase the width of the selected window by one column	`C-x }` `(enlarge-window-horizontally)`	138
Increase width of selected window by *n* columns	`C-u n C-x }` `(enlarge-window-horizontally)`	—
Show where selected window's text does not match next window's text	`M-x compare-windows` `(compare-windows)`	—

Table D.77. Window Commands, con't.

Task	Command (Function)	Page
Select buffer in other window	C-x 4 b *buffer* RET (switch-to-buffer-other-window)	137
Visit file in other window	C-x 4 f *filename* RET (find-file-other-window)	137
Run Dired in other window	C-x 4 d *dir* RET (dired-other-window)	137
Compose mail message in other window	C-x 4 m (mail-other-window)	137
Find tag and display in other window	C-x 4 . (find-tag-other-window)	137

Words

Table D.78. Word Commands

Task	Command (Function)	Page
Move forward one word	M-f (forward-word)	55
Move backward one word	M-b (backward-word)	55
Kill (delete) to end of word	M-d (kill-word)	55
Kill (delete) to beginning of word	M-DEL (backward-kill-word)	55
Place mark at end of following word	M-@ (mark-word)	55

Table D.78. Word Commands, con't.

Task	Command (Function)	Page
Transpose words around point	`M-t` `(transpose-words)`	55
Search forward for words	`C-s ESC C-w` *words* `RET` `(word-search-forward)`	70
Search backward for words	`C-r ESC C-w` *words* `RET` `(word-search-backward)`	70

Index